THE
FATE OF
A NATION

William P. Cumming and Hugh F. Rankin

THE FATE OF A NATION

The American Revolution
through contemporary eyes

Phaidon

PHAIDON PRESS LIMITED
5 Cromwell Place, London SW7 2JL

~~Distributed in the United States of America by Praeger
Publishers Inc., 111 Fourth Avenue, New York, N.Y. 10003~~

First published 1975
All rights reserved by Phaidon Press Limited

ISBN 0 7148 1644 2
~~Library of Congress Catalog Card Number 74-29356~~

*Filmset in Great Britain by Keyspools Ltd, Golborne, Lancs.
Printed in Italy by Amilcare Pizzi SpA*

33538

Contents

Preface

THE PRIMARY PURPOSE of this book is to present the American Revolutionary struggle as it appeared to and was recorded by the participants, patriot and loyalist, American and British, French and German, and observers on both sides of the Atlantic. Much of the record is taken from the diaries, journals, letters, and reports written during the conflict and from the maps, drawings, portraits, and paintings made 'on the spot' by those who were witnesses or whose memory was still vivid. The contemporary selections in the text are tied together by running narrative, and the illustrations are accompanied by explanatory captions.

Although a serious attempt has been made to include what is authentically contemporary, that does not imply that the accounts are always accurate; some of the most powerful and influential publications were the partisan broadsheets, scurrilous cartoons and inflammatory drawings such as Paul Revere's 'Boston Massacre'. These are often more revealing of the spirit of the time than sober factual records. Some battle accounts also are not absolutely accurate, but they suggest that they are what the writer thought happened. Contemporary accounts have been quoted as written; however, because abbreviations are sometimes confusing, certain words have been completed to make easier reading.

Despite the emphasis of this book on the value of the contemporary record, it includes documents and illustrations which bear a date later than the years of the Revolution. The most frequent reason for this is that many writings and maps of the time were not published until years later, and are available only in their printed or engraved form. Other reasons, when not obvious, are explained in text or caption. The general policy of choice has been to exclude illustrations made later than 1800, however carefully prepared, romantically attractive, or concerned with events not portrayed by contemporaries.

The method of treatment chosen by the authors is to follow the course of military action and to introduce other aspects of the time as they specifically illumine an event or series of events. The captions for the maps and pictures are usually complementary to the text, and are often concerned with matters not military. *The Fate of a Nation* cannot and does not, however, attempt to be a complete history of the subject; many of its aspects, such as theories concerning the causes of the conflict or related developments beyond the continental bounds of the war, however important and significant, are omitted.

The inclusion of new manuscript records, maps and drawings, not hitherto published or unpublished since the eighteenth century, will be of great interest not only to the general reader but also to the specialist in the field. The authors have no particular new thesis concerning the origin or conduct of the war which they are proposing or defending, but they attempt to give as clear a record as possible of the history of the great events which they are describing.

Hugh F. Rankin has written the text and gathered the quoted selections. William P. Cumming has planned the work, located and chosen the illustrations, and written the commentaries on them.

Among those who deserve special acknowledgment is Mrs Elizabeth C. Cumming, who assisted in the research and contributed to the writing of the captions. Dr Helen Wallis and Mr Paul Hulton of the British Museum, Dr W. W. Ristow and his staff in the Library of Congress, Miss Jeannette Black of the John Carter Brown Library, Mr Harrington of the Brown Military Collection, and Mr Dupre of the New-York Historical Society have been especially helpful. Private owners of maps and pictures, especially the Duke of Northumberland, Dr Spencer Bernard of Nether Winchendon, and Mrs Gardner Richardson of Woodstock, Connecticut have kindly given permission to publish. Full acknowledgments are given in the List of Illustrations. Mr John Calmann, Miss Elisabeth Ingles, Miss Anne Dean and Miss Lavinia Keef of the Phaidon Press have aided generously in the preparation of the book, and Mr Elwyn Blacker is responsible for its design.

The authors also wish to thank the following publishers and libraries for permission to reprint material published or in their manuscript collections: the British Library for Additional Manuscripts 46840; Edinburgh University Library for selections from the Laing Manuscripts; Princeton University Library for the Diary of Dr John Boudinot; American Antiquarian Society for selections from the *Proceedings*, Vol. XL; Cambridge University Press for passages from the *Journal of Tho: Hughes*, edited by E. A. Benians; Harvard University Press for *The Diary of Frederick Mackenzie* and *The Taking of Ticonderoga* by Allen French; Houghton Mifflin Company for selections from Margaret Willard, *Letters on the American Revolution, 1774–1776*, and *Travels through the Interior Parts of North America* by Thomas Anburey; the Huntington Library and Art Gallery for passages from *The American Journal of Ambrose Serle, 1776–1778*, edited by Edward H. Tatum, Jr; Illinois State Historical Library for passages from *George Rogers Clark Papers, 1771–1781*, edited by James A. James; Institute of Early American History and Culture for selections from the *William and Mary Quarterly*; Massachusetts Historical Society for selections from the *Proceedings*, Vol. XL; University of Michigan Press for selections from *The Siege of Charleston*, edited by Bernhard A. Uhlendorf; New Hampshire Historical Society for selections from *The Papers and Letters of General John Sullivan*, edited by Otis G. Hammond; Pennsylvania Historical Society for numerous selections from *The Pennsylvania Magazine of History and Biography*; Princeton University Press for selections from *The Papers of Thomas Jefferson*, edited by Julian Boyd, and *The Autobiography of Benjamin Rush*, edited by George W. Corner; Yale University Press for passages from Janet Schaw, *The Journal of a Lady of Quality*, edited by Evangeline and Charles M. Andrews.

Chronological Table

1763	7 October	Proclamation of 1763
1764	5 April	Sugar Act
	19 April	Currency Act
1765	22 March	Stamp Act
	7–25 October	Stamp Act Congress
1766	18 March	Stamp Act repealed. Passage of Declaratory Act
1767	29 June	Townshend Acts passed
1770	5 March	Boston Massacre
	12 April	Townshend Acts repealed except tax on tea
1772	9 June	Gaspée Affair
1773	10 May	Tea Act
	16 December	Boston Tea Party
1774	31 March–20 May	Passage of Coercive or Intolerable Acts
	5 September–26 October	First Continental Congress
	17 September	Suffolk Resolves
1775	19 April	Lexington and Concord
	10 May	Second Continental Congress
	10 May	Capture of Ticonderoga
	15 June	Washington named Commander-in-Chief by Congress
	17 June	Bunker Hill
	28 August	Expedition against Canada
	9 December	Great Bridge
	31 December–1 January	Assault upon Quebec
1776	10 January	Thomas Paine's Common Sense
	27 February	Moore's Creek Bridge
	17 March	British evacuate Boston
	7 June	Richard Henry Lee's resolution for independence
	28 June	Charleston
	2 July	Independence resolution adopted by Congress
	4 July	Declaration of Independence adopted by Congress
	27 August	Battle of Long Island
	16 September	Harlem Heights
	11–13 October	Valcour Island
	28 October	White Plains
	16 November	Fort Washington
	8 December	British occupy Rhode Island
	19 December	Paine's American Crisis
	26 December	Trenton
1777	3 January	Princeton
	6 July	Ticonderoga falls to Burgoyne
	6 August	Oriskany
	16 August	Bennington
	11 September	Brandywine
	19 September	Freeman's Farm
	20 September	Paoli Massacre
	26 September	British occupy Philadelphia. Congress flees to Lancaster, Pennsylvania
	30 September	Congress moves to York, Pennsylvania
	4 October	Germantown
	7 October	Bemis Heights
	17 October	Burgoyne surrenders
	15 November	Congress adopts Articles of Confederation. Sent to states for ratification
	19 December	Washington goes into winter quarters at Valley Forge
1778	5 February	Franco-American treaties signed in Paris
	4 May	Congress ratifies French treaties
	18 June	Philadelphia evacuated by British
	28 June	Monmouth
	4 July	Wyoming Valley Massacre
	5 July	Kaskaskia falls to George Rogers Clark
	29 August	Newport
	11 November	Cherry Valley Massacre
	29 December	Savannah falls to the British
1779	25 February	Clark retakes Vincennes
	21 June	Spain declares war on Great Britain
	16 July	Stony Point
	August	Sullivan's Expedition
	19 August	Paulus Hook
	16 September–20 October	Siege of Savannah
	11–25 October	British evacuate Rhode Island
1780	29 February	League of Armed Neutrality proclaimed by Catherine of Russia
	12 May	Charleston falls to the British
	23 June	Springfield raid
	10 July	Rochambeau and French troops land in Newport
	16 August	Camden
	23 September	Capture of André
	7 October	King's Mountain
1781	1 January	Mutiny of the Pennsylvania Continentals
	17 January	Cowpens
	20 January	Mutiny of the New Jersey Continentals
	1 March	Congress ratifies Articles of Confederation
	15 March	Guilford Courthouse
	25 April	Hobkirk's Hill
	22 May–5 June	Augusta falls to the Americans
	19 June	Greene abandons siege of Ninety-Six
	6 July	Green Spring
	5–7 September	Battle of the Capes. De Grasse defeats British fleet
	8 September	Eutaw Springs
	28 September	Yorktown besieged
	19 October	Cornwallis surrenders
1782	11 July	Savannah evacuated by British
	14 December	Charleston evacuated by British
1783	15 March	Washington addresses officers at Newburgh

19 April	Congress proclaims end of war
24 June	Three hundred veterans demonstrate. Congress flees to Princeton
3 September	Definitive peace treaty (Treaty of Paris) signed by Great Britain and the United States
23 November	Congress disbands army
25 November	New York evacuated by the British
26 November	Congress moves to Annapolis
4 December	Washington's farewell to his officers, Fraunces' Tavern, New York
23 December	Washington resigns his commission

Bibliography

of works referred to in the captions. See also notes to the text.

ADAMS, CHARLES FRANCIS (ED.), *The Works of John Adams*, Boston, 1850–56, 10 vols.

ADAMS, JAMES T. (ED.), *Album of American History*, New York, Vol. I, 1944; Vol. II, 1945.

ADAMS, JOHN, AND ABIGAIL ADAMS, *Familiar Letters of John Adams and his Wife*, Boston 1876.

Album of American Battle Art 1755–1918. Washington, D.C., 1947.

ALDEN, JOHN R. *A History of the American Revolution*, New York, 1969.

ALLEN, GARDNER W., *A Naval History of the American Revolution*, Boston, 1913, 2 vols.

American Historical Record, Philadelphia, Vol. I (1872)–.

American Printmaking: the First 150 Years, New York, The Museum of Graphic Art, 1969.

ANBUREY, THOMAS, *Travels through the Interior Parts of America . . . By an Officer*, London, 1789. New edition, 2 vols.

BARNARD, EDWARD, *A New, Comprehensive, and Complete History of England*, London, 1783.

BASS, ROBERT D., *The Green Dragoon*, New York, 1957.

BENEZIT, E., *Dictionnaire des Peintres, Sculpteurs, Dessinateurs, et Graveurs*, Paris, 1960, 8 vols.

BERKELEY, EDMUND, AND DOROTHY S. BERKELEY, *Dr. John Mitchell: The Man who Made the Map of North America*, Chapel Hill, 1974.

BILODEAU, F. W., and others, *Art in South Carolina, 1670–1970*, Charston, S.C., 1970.

BLAIR, WALTER, THEODORE HORNBERGER, AND RANDALL STEWART, *The Literature of the United States*, Chicago, Ill., 1946.

Boston Gazette, The, Boston, No. I (1719)–.

BOWEN, CATHERINE DRINKER, *John Adams and the American Revolution*, Boston, 1950.

BRIGHAM, CLARENCE S., *Paul Revere's Engravings*, Worcester, Mass.: American Antiquarian Society, 1954.

BROWN, LLOYD A., *Early Maps of the Ohio Valley*, Pittsburgh, Pa., 1959.

BRUN, CHRISTIAN, *Guide to the Manuscript Maps in the William L. Clements Library*, Ann Arbor, Mich., 1959.

BUSH, ALFRED L., *The Life Portraits of Thomas Jefferson*, Charlottesville, Va., 1962.

CAMPBELL, PATRICK, *Travels in the Interior Inhabited Parts of North America, In the Years 1791 and 1792*, Edinburgh, 1793.

CAUGHEY, JOHN W., *Bernardo de Galvez in Louisiana, 1776–1783*, Berkeley, Cal., 1934.

CLINTON, SIR HENRY, *The American Rebellion: Sir Henry Clinton's Narrative of his Campaigns, 1775–1782*, WILLIAM B. WILLCOX, ed., New Haven, Conn., 1954.

COBBETT, WILLIAM, *The Parliamentary History of England*, London, 1806–20, 36 vols.

COLBERT, EDOUARD C. V., COMTE DE MAULEVRIER, *Voyage dans l'Intérieur des Etats-Unis et au Canada*, Gilbert Chinard, ed., Institut Français de Washington, Historical Documents, Cahier 8, Baltimore, 1935.

COLLOT, GEORGE, *Voyage dans l'Amérique Septentrionale*, Paris, [1801] 1826, 3 vols.

Columbian Magazine [later, *Universal Asylum*], Philadelphia, Vol. I (1786)–.

COMMAGER, HENRY STEELE AND RICHARD B. MORRIS (EDS.), *The Spirit of 'Seventy-Six*, Indianapolis and New York, 1958.

Connecticut Gazette, New London, Conn., I (1763)–.

COOK, FREDERICK (ED.), *Journals of the Military Expedition of Major General John Sullivan Against the Six Nations of Indians in 1779*, Auburn, N.Y., 1887.

CORNWALLIS, MAJOR-GENERAL CHARLES, EARL, *Correspondence of Cornwallis*, CHARLES ROSS (ED.), London, 1859, 3 vols.

CRARY, CATHERINE S. (ED.), *The Price of Loyalty: Tory Writings from the Revolutionary Era*, New York, 1973.

CUMMING, WILLIAM P., *British Maps of Colonial America*, Chicago, 1974.

CUMMING, WILLIAM P., *North Carolina in Maps*, Raleigh, N.C., 1966.

CUMMING, W. P. AND ELIZABETH C., 'The Treasure of Alnwick Castle', *American Heritage*, XX (1969), 22–23, 99–101.

DAVIDSON, CHALMERS G., *Piedmont Partisan*, Davidson, N.C., 1951.

DEVORSEY, LOUIS, JR., *The Indian Boundary Line in the Southern Colonies, 1763–1775*, Chapel Hill, N.C., 1966.

Dictionnaire Historique, Critique et Bibliographique, Paris, Menard et Desenne, 1821–23.

Dictionary of American Biography, New York, 1928–37, 20 vols.

Dictionary of National Biography, London, 1885–1901, 66 vols.

DIDEROT, DENIS AND JEAN L. D'ALEMBERT, *Recueil de Planches*,

DIDEROT—*continued*
 sur les Sciences, les Arts Libéraux, et les Arts Méchaniques, 11 vols., in: *L'Encyclopédie, ou Dictionnaire Raisonné*, Paris, 1762–72, vol. I (1763).
DRAPER, LYMAN C., *King's Mountain and Its Heroes*, Cincinnati, Ohio, 1881.
DUNCAN, HENRY, 'Journal of Captain Henry Duncan', Navy Records Society, *Naval Miscellany*, I (1902), 161.
Encyclopedia of World Art, New York, 1959–1968, 15 vols.
Encyclopedia; or, a Dictionary of Arts, Sciences, and Miscellaneous Literature, 18 vols., Philadelphia, [1790]–1798.
FADEN, WILLIAM, *North American Atlas*, London, 1777.
FANNING, CAPTAIN NATHANIEL, *Narrative of the Adventures of an American Naval Officer*, New York, 1806.
FORBES, ESTHER, *Paul Revere and the World He Lived In*, Boston, 1942.
FORCE, PETER (ED.), *American Archives: Fourth Series, Containing a Documentary History . . . March 7, 1774, to the Declaration of Independence*, Washington, D.C., 1837–46, 6 vols.
FORCE, PETER (ED.), *American Archives: Fifth Series . . . 1776–1783*, Washington, D.C., 1848–53, 3 vols.
FREDERIC, GEORGE S., AND EDWARD HAWKINS (EDS.), *Catalogue of Political and Personal Satires . . . in the British Museum*, Vol. IV, London, 1883.
Gentleman's Magazine, London, I (1731)–.
GEORGE, DOROTHY (ED.), *Catalogue of Political and Personal Satires . . . in the British Museum*, Vol. V, London, 1935.
GIBBES, R. W. (ED.), *Documentary History of the American Revolution . . . Chiefly in South Carolina . . . 1776–1782*, New York, 1853–57, 3 vols.
GIPSON, LAWRENCE H., *The Coming of the Revolution, 1763–1775*, New York, 1954.
GIPSON, LAWRENCE H., *Lewis Evans*, Philadelphia, 1939.
GIRDLESTONE, THOMAS, M. D., *Facts tending to prove that General Lee was never absent from this Country . . . during the Years 1767, 69, 70, 71, 72, and that he was the Author of Junius*, London, 1813.
GRAHAM, WILLIAM A., *General Joseph Graham and His Papers on North Carolina Revolutionary History*, Raleigh, N.C., 1904.
GREENE, GEORGE WASHINGTON, *The Life of Nathanael Greene*, Boston, 1890, 3 vols.
GRUBER, IRA D., *The Howe Brothers and the American Revolution*, New York, 1972.
GUEDALLA, PHILIP, *Fathers of the Revolution*, Garden City, N.Y., 1926.
HADDEN, JAMES M., *A Journal Kept in Canada and Upon Burgoyne's Campaign in 1776 and 1777*, Albany, N.Y., 1884.
HALSEY, RICHARD T. H., *The Boston Port Bill as Pictured by a Contemporary London Cartoonist*, New York, The Grolier Club, 1904.
HAMER, PHILIP M., 'John Stuart's Indian Policy during the Early Months of the American Revolution', *Mississippi Valley Historical Review*, XVII (1930–1), 351–66.
HARCOURT, WILLIAM, *The Harcourt Papers*, EDWARD W. HARCOURT (ED.), Oxford, 1880–1905, 12 vols.
HASTINGS, *Report on the Manuscripts of the Late Reginald Rawdon Hastings*, Great Britain Historical Manuscripts Commission, London, 1930–47, 4 vols.
HEISTER, LORENZ, *A General System of Surgery*, 8th edition, London, 1768, 2 vols.
HENDERSON, ARCHIBALD, 'Elizabeth Maxwell Steel: Patriot', *North Carolina Booklet*, Raleigh, N.C., XII (1912), 67–103.
HENRY, JOHN, *Account of Arnold's Campaign Against Quebec*, Albany, N.Y., 1877.
HIGGINBOTHAM, DON, *The War of American Independence; Military Attitudes, Policies, and Practice, 1763–1789*, New York, 1971.
HILLIARD D'AUBERTEUIL, MICHEL RENÉ, *Essais historiques et politiques sur les Anglo-Américains*, Bruxelles, 1782, 2 vols.
Historical Magazine, and Notes and Queries, Boston, I (1857)–.
HOWE, HENRY, *Historical Collections of Virginia*, Charleston, S.C., 1845.

HUBLEY, ADAM, *Journal, 1779–*, MS., 2 vols., Historical Society of Pennsylvania.
HUDSON, CHARLES, *History of the Town of Lexington, Middlesex County, from Its First Settlement to 1868*, Boston, 1913.
HULTON, ANN, *Letters of a Loyalist Lady . . . 1767–1776*, Cambridge, Mass., 1927.
HUTCHINSON, THOMAS (ED.), *Diary and Letters of Thomas Hutchinson . . .*, compiled by P. O. Hutchinson, Boston, 1884–6, 2 vols.
JEFFERSON, THOMAS, *Jefferson Himself: the Personal Narrative*, Bernard Mayo, ed., Boston, 1942.
JEFFERSON, THOMAS, *Writings*, PAUL L. FORD (ED.), New York, 1894.
The John Carter Brown Library, *Annual Report, 1955–56*, Providence, R.I., 1956.
KLINEFELTER, WALTER, *Lewis Evans and his Maps, Transactions of the American Philosophical Society*, N.S. LXI, pt. 7, Philadelphia, 1971.
LABAREE, BENJAMIN W., *The Boston Tea Party*, Oxford, 1964.
LAFAYETTE, MARQUIS DE, *Memoirs, Correspondence, and Manuscripts of General Lafayette*, published by his family, Vol. I, London and New York, 1837.
LITTLE, NINA F., 'Winthrop Chandler', *Art in America: an Illustrated Quarterly Magazine*, Brookline, Mass., 35, no. 2 (April 1947).
London Magazine, London, I (1732)–.
MACKENZIE, FREDERICK K., *Diary . . . 1775–1781*, Cambridge, Mass., 1932, 2 vols.
MCLEAN, J. R., *Flora MacDonald in America*, Lumberton, N.C., 1909.
MAGGS, JOHN, *Catalogue, No. 502*, Part VII, no. 5641, London, 1928.
MAHAN, ALFRED T., *The Major Operations of the Navies in the War of American Independence*, Boston, 1913.
Massachusetts Historical Society, Proceedings, Boston, I (1791)–.
Massachusetts Historical Society, Collections, Boston, I (1792)–.
MINISTÈRE DES AFFAIRES ETRANGERES, *Les Combattants Français de la Guerre Americaine, 1778–1783*, 58th Congress, 2nd session, Senate Doc. No. 77, Washington, D.C., 1905.
MORGAN, JOHN H., *Paintings by John Trumbull at Yale University*, New Haven, Conn., 1926.
MORISON, SAMUEL ELIOT, *John Paul Jones: A Sailor's Biography*, Boston, 1959.
MORISON, SAMUEL ELIOT, *The Maritime History of Massachusetts*, Boston, 1921.
MOULTRIE, WILLIAM, *Memoirs of the American Revolution*, New York, 1802, 2 vols.
MURRAY, JAMES, *An Impartial History of the Present War in America*, London, 1778–80, 3 vols.; Newcastle upon Tyne, 1778–80, 3 vols.
NELSON, CHARLES, *An Original, Compiled, and Corrected Account of Burgoyne's Campaign*, Albany, N.Y., 1844.
New York Magazine, New York, Vols. I–V (1790–5): N.S. I–II (1796–7).
Oxford Magazine; or, University Museum, London, I (1768)–.
Pennsylvania Archives, Second Series, Vol. I, 1880.
Pennsylvania Gazette, Philadelphia, No. 1 (1728)–.
Pennsylvania Magazine, Philadelphia, II (April 1776).
PICKERING, TIMOTHY, *An Easy Plan of Discipline for a Militia*, Salem, Mass., 1775.
Political Magazine, The, London, I (1780)–.
Political Register, and London Museum, London, I (1767)–.
PORTER, MRS. NANNIE FRANCISCO AND CATHERINE F. ALBERTSON, *The Romantic Record of Peter Francisco*, Staunton, Va., 1929.
RAMSEY, J. G. M., *The Annals of Tennessee*, Philadelphia, 1853.
RANKIN, HUGH F., *The American Revolution*, New York, 1964.
RANKIN, HUGH F., 'The Naval Flag of the American Revolution', *William and Mary Quarterly*, 3rd series, XI, no. 3 (1954), 339–53.
RANKIN, HUGH F., *The North Carolina Continentals*, Chapel Hill, N.C., 1971.

REED, JOHN F., *Valley Forge: Crucible of Victory*, Monmouth Beach, N.J., 1969.

REVERE, PAUL, 'Letter of Paul Revere to Dr. Jeremy Belknap' [1798], *Proceedings Massachusetts Historical Society*, XVI (1879), 372.

RIEDESEL, FREDERIKA CHARLOTTE, BARONESS VON, *Baroness von Riedesel and the American Revolution*, trans. and ed. by MARVIN L. BROWN, Chapel Hill, N.C., 1935.

ROBERTSON, ARCHIBALD, *Archibald Robertson Lieutenant-General His Diaries and Sketches in America 1762–1780*, HARRY MILLER LYDENBERG (ED.), New York, 1930.

Royal American Magazine, or Universal Repository of Instruction and Amusement, Boston, I–II (1774–5).

RUSH, BENJAMIN, *Letters of Benjamin Rush*, L. H. Butterfield, ed., Princeton, N.J., 1951.

RUTLEDGE, ANNE W., 'Charleston's First Artistic Couple', *Antiques* (August 1947), pp. 100–3.

SCHENCK, DAVID, *North Carolina: 1780–81*, Raleigh, N.C., 1889.

SENTER, ISAAC, 'The Journal of Isaac Senter, M.D., on a Secret Expedition against Quebec, 1775'. *The Magazine of History with Notes and Queries*, Extra No. 42, 1915.

SHERBURNE, JOHN H., *Life and Character of the Chevalier John Paul Jones*, Washington, D.C., 1825.

SIMCOE, JOHN G., LT. COL., *A Journal of the Operation of the Queen's Rangers from the End of . . . 1777 to the Conclusion of the Late American War*, Exeter, 1787, BM copy with MS. insertions.

SMITH, JOHN J., and JOHN F. WATSON, *American Historical and Literary Curiosities*, Philadelphia, 1847; 4th ed., New York, 1850.

SMITH, SAMUEL S., *The Battle of Monmouth*, Monmouth Beach, N.J., 1964.

SMITH, SAMUEL S., *The Battle of Princeton*, Monmouth Beach, N.J., 1967.

State Records of North Carolina, Walter Clark, ed., Goldsboro, N.C., Winston-Salem, N.C., etc., 1895–1914, 16 vols.

STEDMAN, CHARLES, *History of the Origin, Progress, and Termination of the American War*, London, 1794, 2 vols.

STEUBEN, FREDERICK WILLIAM, BARON VON, *Regulations for the Order and Discipline of the Troops of the United States*, Philadelphia, 1779.

STOCKING, ABNER, 'An Interesting Journal of the Expedition Against Quebec, 1775', *The Magazine of History with Notes and Queries*, Extra no. 75, 1921.

STOKES, I. N. PHELPS, and DANIEL C. HASKELL, *American Historical Prints: Early Views of American Cities . . .*, New York, 1933.

TARLETON, LT.-COL. BANASTRE, *A History of the Campaigns of 1780 and 1781, in the Southern Provinces of North America*, London, 1787.

THACHER, JAMES, M.D., *A Military Journal During the American Revolutionary War, from 1775–1783*, 2nd ed., Boston, 1827.

THOMSON, DON W., *Men and Meridians*, Vol. I, Ottawa, 1966.

TOWER, CHARLEMAGNE, JR., *The Marquis de LaFayette in the American Revolution*, Philadelphia, 1895, 2 vols.

TREVELYAN, GEORGE OTTO, *The American Revolution*, New York, 1899–1907, 4 vols.

TRUMBULL, JOHN, *Autobiography, Reminiscences and Letters of John Trumbull from 1756 to 1841*, New York, 1841.

TRUMBULL, JOHN, *M'Fingal: A Modern Epic Poem, in Four Cantos*, Embellished with Nine Copper Plates, Designed and engraved by E. Tisdale, New York, 1795.

TUTTLE, C. W., 'Earl Percy', *Captain Francis Campernowne*, Boston, 1889, pp. 241–267.

UHLENDORF, BERNARD A., ed. and trans., *The Siege of Charleston . . . The Von Jungkenn Papers in the William L. Clements Library*, Ann Arbor, Mich., 1938.

The Warren-Adams Letters, Collections of the Massachusetts Historical Society, LXXII(1917), LXXIII(1925), 2 vols.

WERTENBAKER, THOMAS J., *Father Knickerbocker Rebels: New York City During the Revolution*, New York, 1948.

WHARTON, FRANCIS (ED.), *The Revolutionary Diplomatic Correspondence of the United States*, Washington, D.C., 1889, 6 vols.

WINSOR, JUSTIN, *Narrative and Critical History of America*, Boston, 1887–9, 8 vols.

WOOD, WILLIAM, AND RALPH H. GABRIEL, *The Winning of Freedom, The Pageant of America*, Vol. 6, New Haven, Conn., 1927.

YOUNG, THOMAS, 'Memoir of Major Thomas Young', *The Orion*, III (1843), 87–88.

1. The Road to Lexington

1. The Indian Boundary Line of 1768

In 1763 the London government announced a Proclamation Line, limiting English settlements to the land east of the Allegheny Mountains, and reserving the regions beyond to the Indians, 'children of the great King'. It was based on ignorance of geography and of the actual extent of western settlements; the boundary line shown on this map was a modification which the Lords Commissioners for Trade and Plantations recommended to the King in 1768. Copies of the map were sent to the two Indian superintendents of the northern and southern departments in America with instructions to ratify and purchase the added territory from the Indians.

The new boundaries were not satisfactory to either the Indians or the colonists. Many colonists regarded the Proclamation Line as an infringement on their rights and liberties; although it was not a major cause of the Revolution, as some have claimed, the irritation it caused was wide and deep.

IF A REBELLION was to come to the American colonies, it seemed only natural that it break out in Massachusetts. Almost from its founding, that colony had been a thorn in England's imperial hide. The Yankees had early turned their attention towards the sea and had so prospered as to become a serious commercial rival of the mother country. During the French and Indian War, known to Europeans as the Seven Years War, New Englanders had traded almost openly with the enemy and had developed smuggling to something akin to a fine art. Massachusetts fitted less into the British scheme of mercantilism than any other North American colony and had made a mockery of the Navigation Acts, statutes designed to funnel colonial trade into the United Kingdom for the financial benefit of British merchants.

George Grenville, called the 'Gentle Shepherd', was anxious to reduce the liabilities of the British government and its debts. When he became prime minister he made an attempt to tidy up the administrative and fiscal system which governed Britain's relations with her American colonies. This new programme was in part a reaction to the lethargic response of the American colonists during the Seven Years War of 1756–63. The ink on the Treaty of Paris had barely dried when the Crown issued the proclamation of 1763, extending the boundaries of the newly acquired province of Quebec down to the Ohio River and prohibiting the further granting of western lands beyond the crest of the Appalachian mountains, and so protecting, it was thought, colonists and Indians from each other. In Grenville's view this had the additional advantage of containing the power and wealth of the seaboard colonies. Catholicism was recognized as the religion of Canada. This provision extending Roman Catholicism in a half-moon around them had enraged the Puritan 'Saints' of New England; the Pope, they felt, had been placed at their back door. And the provision limiting westward expansion had irritated land speculators in the middle and southern colonies, since it thereby deprived them of what they considered to be their rightful spoils of war.

The Proclamation was not intended as a segment of the new colonial policy, but it had proved as noisome as if it had been. And a more formal application came hard on its heels.

England had been forced to bear the brunt of the cost of the war with the French, and it was the general feeling in Parliament that the Americans should pay their share in addition to bearing a portion of the expense of the upkeep of the British force that was to be stationed in the colonies for their protection. It was with this in mind that the Revenue Act of 1764 (sometimes called the Sugar or Molasses Act) was passed; in effect it was a strengthening of statutes already on the books as the Acts of Trade and Navigation. The revenue thus gained was to be used for paying for one-third of the troops stationed in America. Actually this measure lowered the duty on some items, but to Massachusetts it contained one frightening provision—there was to be a more efficient operation of the customs, designed to curtail the smuggling of bold New England mariners. Trade with other nations was restricted and channelled towards England. The Americans felt they needed no protection from British redcoats now that the menace of France had been removed. 'One single Act of Parliament has set people a-thinking, in six months, more than they had done in their whole lives before,' wrote James Otis of Boston. His pamphlet, *The Rights of the British Colonies asserted and proved*, was one of the first written colonial protests against the legislative measures of the mother country.

Before united efforts could be organized against this or the Currency Act of 1764, both issues had been pushed into the background by additional parliamentary legislation. On 22 March 1765, Parliament passed the Stamp Act, requiring stamps on all legal documents, newspapers, pamphlets, almanacs, playing cards, and dice. A similar measure had long been in force in England and was considered a necessary evil. So little were the consequences anticipated that the bill stole through both the House of Commons and the House of Lords with little discussion or debate. The one factor overlooked by its sponsors was that this act affected all the colonies alike and directly touched those colonists who were best able to mould public opinion —the preachers, tavern-keepers, printers, and lawyers.

The first political resistance to the Stamp Act came out of Virginia, fanned into flame by the eloquence of a young country lawyer who bore the name of Patrick Henry. During the course of an address in the House of Burgesses he is reported to have cried, 'Caesar had his Brutus, Charles his Cromwell, and George the Third . . .' When interrupted by shouts of 'Treason! Treason!', Henry waited until the noise had subsided and continued with 'may profit by their example. Sir, if this be treason make the most of it.' A Frenchman travelling through Williamsburg recorded a somewhat different account than the one generally accepted. That night he wrote in his diary:

'*May the 30th.* Set out early from half-way house in the chair and broke fast at York, arrived at Williamsburg at 12 where I saw three negroes hanging at the galous for haveing robed Mr. Walthe of 300 pounds. I went immediately to the Assembly which was seting, where I was entertained with very strong debates concerning dutys that the Parlement wants to lay on the American colonys, which they call or stile Stamp dutys. Shortly after I came in, one of the members stood up and said that he had read that in former times Tarquin and Julus had their Brutus, Charles had his Cromwell, and he did not doubt but some good American would stand up in favour of his Country; but (says he) in a more moderate manner, and was going to continue, when the Speaker of the House rose and, said he, the last that stood up had spoke traison, and was sorey to see that not one of the members of the House was loyal enough to stop him before he had gon so far. Upon which the same member stood up

2. Patrick Henry.
After Sully

Virginian, powerful slogan maker, influential in extending the rebellion to all colonies.

3. William and Mary College, Williamsburg, Virginia *(detail)*

A view of the south façade of the Capitol, the west façade of the Wren building, and the south façade of the Governor's Palace.

Many of the leaders of the Revolution, including Thomas Jefferson, were educated here.

again (his name is Henery) and said that if he affronted the Speaker or the House, he was ready to ask pardon, and he would show his loyalty to His Majesty King George the third at the expence of the last drop of his blood; but what he had said must be attributed to the interest of his country's dying liberty which he had at heart, and the heat of passion might have lead him to have something more than he intended; but, again, if he said anything wrong, he beged the Speaker and the House's pardon. Some other members stood up and backed him, on which that afaire was droped.

May the 31th. I returned to the Assembly to-day, and heard some very hot debates still about the stamp dutys. The whole house was for entering resolves on the records but they differed much with regards the content or purport thereof. Some were for shewing their resentment to the highest. One of the resolves that these proposed, was that any person that would offer to sustain that the Parlement of England had a right to impose or lay any tax or dutys whatsoever on the American colonys, without the consent

4. Oliver forced to resign as Distributor of Stamps in Boston

What happened to Andrew Oliver, secretary and later lieutenant-governor of Massachusetts Bay, after it was learned that he had accepted the post of Distributor of Stamps, triggered similar action in other colonies. Early on the morning of 14 August, an effigy of Oliver was hung on an elm in Hanover Square, soon after to be called Liberty Tree. Later in the day a mob destroyed a newly-built office on Oliver's wharf, looted his house, and burnt his effigy in a great bonfire on Tower Hill. The next day a group of gentlemen called and informed him, according to Governor Bernard's report to the Board of Trade, that if he did not resign 'his House would be destroyed and his Life in Continual Danger'. Without prospect of adequate protection, Oliver wisely agreed to apply for leave to resign. On 17 December, as the broadside announced, he signed an oath of resignation under the Liberty Tree.

In other provinces the Distributors were also forced to resign, sometimes after violent persuasion. In the Bahamas, the local official in New Providence was put into a coffin and lowered into a pit; when the mob began shovelling in the dirt, he yielded and saw the light.

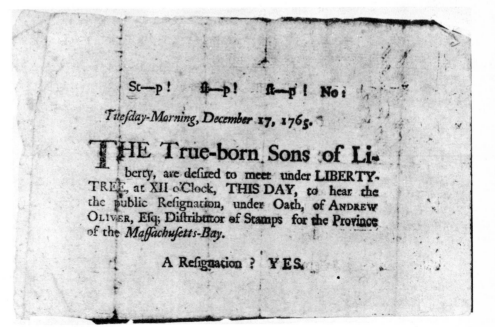

5. The Tory's Day of Judgement. *Elkanah Tisdale*

These Yankee Whigs have had all they can take from an arch-Tory. Bursting out of town meeting, in Trumbull's mock epic M'Fingal, they chase and catch him, and haul him back to the green, where a Liberty Pole has been erected. They fasten a rope to his waistband and pull, until the culprit sees the error of his ways.

M'Fingal, at this altitude, was quite ready to forsake Loyalist opinions and behaviour, but when, returned to earth, he failed to swear full allegiance to his tormentors, the tar bucket and the freshly-plucked goose feathers ready at the foot of the pole were quickly applied, and he was paraded about town in a cart.

6. The Wise Men of Gotham and their Goose. *William Humphrey*

In this famous British Whig cartoon of 1776, Lord North's Tory ministers are shown in the final stage of their struggle to make the American colonial goose lay two golden eggs a day instead of one. The accompanying poem in the corners says they have 'STAMPT upon her Wings and Feet' without effect; now in rage they are about to cut her throat; the poem ends with the dire prediction that blood will come 'pouring from the wound'. The man about to administer the *coup de grâce* is Lord Bute, wearing the Garter; his tartan and Scots cap lingered on in Whig cartoons long after his retirement in 1763. The portly bishop reclining in the chair is probably Markham, Archbishop of York, whose opinions on the American war had made him unpopular with the Whigs. The seven others cannot be exactly identified: the one in ribbon and star may be the King or North; the judge, Mansfield or Bathurst; one of the two lawyers, Wedderburn; others, Sandwich and Germain. One gleefully holds aloft a basket of golden eggs already gathered; others spill out of a bag labelled 'Taxes'. A small dog dishonours a discarded map of North America. Framed on the wall, the British lion is asleep.

16

In Gotham once the Story goes
A Set of Wise-acres arose
Skill'd in the great Politic Wheel
Could pound a Magpie, drown an Eel,
With many Things of worthy Note
At present much too long to quote;
Their District was both far and wide
Which not a little swell'd their Pride
But above all that they possess'd
Was a fine Goose, by all confess'd,
A Rara Avis to behold
Who laid each Day an Egg of Gold
This made them grow immensely rich
Gave them an avaritious Itch,
The Case belongs to many more

They not contented with their store
Would Methods vague and strange pursue
To make the Harmless Bird lay Two,
This Glorious purpose to obtain
About her Neck they put a Chain,
And more their Folly to compleat
They Stampt upon her Wings & Feet,
But this had no Effect at all,
Yet made her struggle, flutter, squall,
And do what every Goose would do
That had her Liberty in view,
When one of more distinguish'd Note
Cry'd D---n her, let us cut her Throat,
They did, but not an Egg was found
But BLOOD came pouring from ye Wound.

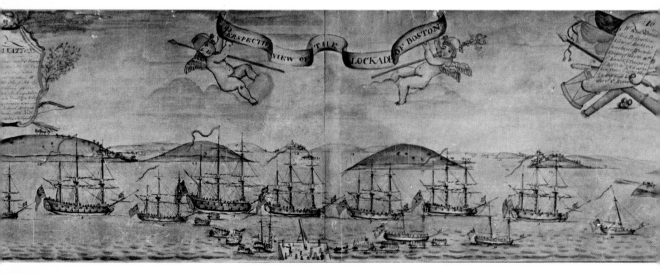

PRSPECTIV VIEW OF THE BLOCKADE OF BOSTON

of the inhabitants thereof, should be looked upon as a traitor, and deemed an enemy to his country: there were some others to the same purpose, and the majority was for entering these resolves; upon which the Governor dissolved the Assembly, which hendered their proceeding.'[1]

Although Virginia had stated its opposition through resolves, it was in Boston that resistance took a violent turn. Mobs rioted through the streets, burning the records of the vice-admiralty court, sacking the home of the comptroller of customs, and looting the mansion of Governor Thomas Hutchinson. Groups of radicals, calling themselves 'Sons of Liberty' after a phrase used in Parliament by Isaac Barré in opposing the passage of the act, began to intimidate stamp masters, insult royal officials, and tar and feather those supporting the measure. Liberty poles were raised, and liberty trees were planted. Economic sanctions, in the form of non-importation agreements, cut imports from England by at least £600,000 in 1765. On 1 November 1765, the day the act was to go into effect, flags were flown at half mast to signify the death of American liberty.

At the instigation of James Otis, Massachusetts sent out a call for a general congress. This Stamp Act Congress sat in New York from 7 October to the 24th of that month. Nine colonies were represented by either formal or informal delegates. New Hampshire, Virginia, North Carolina, and Georgia were not represented, as their assemblies were prevented by their governors from selecting representatives, a manoeuvre that John Adams termed 'ministerial monkery'. The Congress distinguished itself by maintaining a tone of moderation. A fourteen-resolution Declaration of Rights and Grievances displayed their unhappiness. Article V stated the case for the colonists: 'V. That the only representatives of the people of these colonies are persons chosen by themselves, and no taxes ever have been, or can be constitutionally imposed upon them, but by their respective legislatures.'

7. School Street in Salem, Massachusetts. *Joseph Orme*

Already in the year of the Stamp Act, Salem buildings show the prosperity of a flourishing maritime trade with the West Indies and Europe. The great days of her world-wide commerce with Russia, India, China, and the west coast came just after the Revolution.

Salem took a staunch part in pre-Revolutionary dissent, resenting bitterly the restrictions of the Townshend Acts. In 1774, after the harbour of Boston had been closed by the Port Bill, General Gage, the military governor, established his headquarters at Salem and attempted to set up a reconstructed provincial government there; encountering violent opposition, he retired to Boston and the protection of British troops. The first Provincial Congress, elected by voters, met at Salem on 5 October 1774, with John Hancock as president. The Revolution itself might well have begun at Salem, for in February 1775, Gage sent Lieutenant-Colonel Leslie with 200 men to seize cannon that he had heard were in the town. He was stopped at a bridge by a band of armed Patriots, and prudently withdrew. During the war, the great contribution of Salem was to build, arm, equip, and sail a fleet of privateers.

8. Perspective View of Boston Harbour. *Christian Remick*

This painting shows the landing, in October 1768, of the 14th and 29th Regiments, sent by the royal government in answer to a request for protection by Governor Bernard and General Gage after the *Liberty* riot. The view is from the city, towards the Long Wharf where the troops are disembarking, and out beyond to the circle of British ships in the harbour.

Remick was a mariner and a pilot who saw naval service in the Revolution. He also advertised himself in 1769 as performing 'all sorts of drawing in water colours . . . Also, colours pictures to the life'. In the same month, October 1768, he painted the British troops on Boston Common (see plate 10). He it was who hand-coloured copies of Revere's famous engraving of the Boston Massacre in 1770.

In the face of colonial violence and protest, Parliament repealed the act in 1766. In the general jubilation celebrating the repeal, the Americans paid little attention to a trailer act passed the same day asserting that the King and Parliament 'have full power and authority to make laws and statutes of sufficient force and validity to bind the colonies . . . in all cases whatsoever.' The protests seemed to wither. Yet an undercurrent of rebellion flowed swiftly beneath a calm surface; there were those who had seen a degree of colonial unity during the dispute, and some even began to whisper of an unheard-of action—independence—and only waited for an opportunity to reopen the dispute with Mother England.

There was an act passed in March 1765 that had been generally overlooked by the Americans. At the urging of General Thomas Gage, commander-in-chief of royal forces in America, a special measure for America was passed, the Quartering Act of 1765. This statute stated that if local barracks were unavailable or inadequate, troops could be quartered in taverns, inns, uninhabited houses and barns, the rent to be paid by billeting authorities. From time to time the Americans were to provide the soldiers with 'fire, candles, vinegar, and salt, bedding, utensils for dressing their victuals, and small beer or cyder, not exceeding five pints, or half a pint of rum mixed with a quart of water, to each man . . .' There was greatest resistance in Boston and New York, although there were circumventions of the letter of the law in all colonies except Pennsylvania. But the idea that the soldiers were there to force unpopular measures down colonial throats spread and slowly grew like a festering sore.

Parliamentary taxation of the colonies seemed to be too frequent. In 1767 Parliament once again resorted to taxation as a means of raising additional revenues. 'Champagne Charlie' Townshend had become the moving spirit behind a new government headed by the Duke of Grafton and William Pitt. Townshend hinted broadly that he had a new method of taxing the colonies and reducing taxation in England. Parliament took him at his word and passed the so-called Townshend Acts, levying duties on such items as glass, lead, tea, and other items imported into the American colonies. A revised system of vice-admiralty courts was established to try colonials in courts without juries where they could not be freed by their countrymen serving as jurors. In a political sense, the most obnoxious provision was that the revenue gained from the acts was to be used to establish a colonial list out of which governors and judges were to be paid, thereby preventing American assemblies from holding the threat of salary appropriations over the heads of royal officials.

Propagandists filled pages with angry denunciations. John Dickinson of Pennsylvania, wealthy farmer and English-trained lawyer, fascinated with the legal aspects of the quarrel, published a series of letters which he called 'Letters from a Farmer in Pennsylvania', often contradicting himself as the words rolled from his quill. The Massachusetts House of Representatives sent forth a circular letter drafted by that man of angry words, Samuel Adams, declaring that such levies upon the colonies were 'infringements of their natural & constitutional rights'. Tea became a danger to health as newspapers urged the people to give up the stuff lest it cause 'consumptior '. Merchants entered into agreements not to import English goods after 1 January 1769.

The popular John Hancock became a near martyr when his sloop, *Liberty*,

OR THE FUNERAL OF MISS AME-STAMP

9. The Repeal, Or the Funeral of Miss Ame-Stamp. *B. Wilson*

There was enough relief in England at the repeal of the Stamp Act and the hoped-for averting of strife with America to give this print a large sale when it was published on 18 March 1766. The legend beneath goes far to explain the cartoon. 'Mr Stamper', who bears the small coffin of 'Miss Ame-Stamp', dead at twelve months, is Mr George Grenville, author of the Act. The parson leading, funeral sermon in hand, is Dr W. Scott, author of the Anti-Lejanus letters in the *Public Advertiser* for 1765, attacking Lord Bute and his advocacy of American taxation. The two lawyers following him are Wedderburn and Sir Fletcher Norton, carrying black flags decorated with stamps; the thistle and Jacobite white rose on one indicate the anger of the Whigs at the strong anti-American influence of the Scots in the ministry of George III. The numbers indicate the minority vote on repeal in the Houses of Lords and Commons. After Grenville, Lord Bute, in tartan trousers, is chief mourner, followed by four other proponents of the Act, the Duke of Bedford, the weeping Earl Temple, Lord Halifax, and the Earl of Sandwich. Two bishops bring up the rear.

The coffin is to be placed in the family vault, where already are the skeletons of other unpopular taxes of the years 1715 and 1745, with still others named on the tablet: 'Hearth mon[ey]'; 'Ship mon[ey]'; 'Jew Bill', a bill relieving the Jews of disabilities, passed and repealed in 1753. On the wharf are bales of stamps returned from America, and black cloth to dress the mourners.

Beyond the harbour is a joyous contrast: warehouses are baling 'Goods NOW Ship'd for America', and three ships at full sail, named for three supporters of repeal, Rockingham, Grafton and Conway, are about to set sail to resume the trade which had been interrupted by intense American resentment of the Stamp Act. However, the King's reaction to repeal was to say 'It is a fatal compliance'.

A statue of Mr Pitt is the colossal one by Wilton shipped to and erected in Charleston, South Carolina, here baled and ready.

10 . View of Boston Common. *Christian Remick*

John Hancock's mansion on Beacon Street at the top of the Common dominates this scene with the soldiers of the 29th regiment drilling and deploying tents. Bostonians stroll beneath the trees and watch the soldiers. The Beacon itself is in the upper right corner. In 1766, Hancock's great stone house had blazed with light, as fireworks were set off on a stage outside to celebrate the repeal of the Stamp Act, and hogsheads of Madeira were rolled out to the crowd. Two years later another fire lit up the front of the house, as the Sons of Liberty burned before it the boat of the Collector of Customs who had dared to seize Hancock's sloop *Liberty* for smuggling Madeira. Still later, the house became the governor's mansion of the new State of Massachusetts, with Hancock still dispensing hospitality and elegance.

was seized by customs officers because he had not given proper bond before taking on a cargo. James Otis who wrote tirades against customs officials was wounded by one in a tavern brawl. A customs man in Providence was tarred and feathered by a mob when he insisted upon enforcing the laws. In Boston, when a mob surrounded the home of one commissioner, he fired into the crowd, killing a young lad who was promptly given an ostentatious funeral arranged by Sam Adams. In New York there was a clash between soldiers and a mob in what was to become known as the battle of Golden Hill in which 'a number of people [were] wounded, several soldiers bruised, and one badly hurt'.

But the sight of redcoated soldiers walking the streets of Boston gave Sam Adams and his cohorts an opportunity to fan the flames of resentment. Two regiments had been stationed in that port in 1768 when the colony's legislature had refused to withdraw its circular letter stating the Townshend Acts to be unconstitutional. It was in early March that one Samuel Bostwick saw the beginning of the violence which became known as the 'Boston Massacre' that started with a bit of childish banter between the soldiers and a group of workers:

'On Friday, the 2d instant, between ten and eleven o'clock in the forenoon, three soldiers of the 29th regiment, came up Mr. Gray's ropewalke, and William Green, one of the hands, spoke to one of them saying, "soldier will you work?" The soldier replied, "yes." Green said, "then go and clean my

11. John Hancock.
Engraved by C. Shepherd

This handsome, nervous, not overbrilliant, wealthy young man, so much the antithesis of Sam Adams, was one of the latter's most valuable conquests for the Patriot cause.

12. Common-Wealth, The Colossus

William Pitt, created Earl of Chatham in 1766, did indeed seem a colossus to the Americans. In earlier days he had led them with the British to victory over the French in North America; now he championed their cause in the repeal of the Stamp Act and his stand against the other repressive acts of the 1760s. Tory eyes in England saw him differently. The description accompanying another edition of this cartoon reads: 'Colossus, or Pitt on Stilts . . . The Great Commoner, now Earl of C——— is here placed on Stilts, one fishing Sedition in America, or raising the Sence of those brave People against the Stamp Act, the other fixt in the City of London: who was then his true Friend; and two Crutches [Pitt, a lifelong sufferer from gout, was often on crutches], one fixed on his Pension, the other hovering over St. Stevens Chappel . . .' His stilts are labelled 'Popularity, resting on the Royal Exchange and his services to English commerce', and 'Sedition, offering hooks to Americans drowning off New York'. Earl Temple, his great supporter, is in the air blowing bubbles of 'Publick Spirit', 'Honesty', 'Loyalty'. On an island, an Irishman shouts, 'Ah, by Jesus, we will be independent too.' The Puritan hat over Pitt's head suggests his republicanism; the dangling rope, his danger. The verse parodies his name throughout, and refers to his anti-French and pro-American stand, with the refrain 'Doodle-do' soon to be picked up in the Revolutionary song of 'Yankee Doodle'.

s—t house." The soldier swore by the Holy Ghost that he would have recompense, and tarried a good while swearing at Green, who took no further notice of him and then went off . . .'[2]

A short time later, 'about eleven o'clock, A.M. eight or ten soldiers of the 29th regiment, armed with clubs, came to mr. John Gray's ropewalk, and challenged all the ropemakers to come out and fight them. All the hands then present, to the number of thirteen or fourteen, turned out with their wouldring sticks, and beat them off directly. They very speedily returned to the ropewalk, reinforced to the number of thirty or forty, and headed by a tall negro drummer, again challenged them out, which the same hands accepting, again beat them off with considerable bruises.'[3]

The story spread and lost nothing in the telling. Tensions grew taut after a report that on Sunday night soldiers in the streets were swearing 'that if they saw any of the inhabitants of this town out in the street after nine o'clock, they swore by God, they would knock them down, be they who they will'. The bully boys of Boston were beginning to see an opportunity for fun and, according to William Palfrey, a group of youths, after dark on 5 March,

'met in the alley about eight or nine soldiers, some of whom were armed with drawn swords and cutlasses, one had a tongs, another a shovel, with which they assaulted us, and gave us a great deal of abusive language. We then drove them back to the barracks with sticks only; we looked for stones or bricks but could find none, the ground being covered with snow. Some of the lads dispersed, and myself with a few others were returning peaceably home, when we met about nine or ten other soldiers armed with a naked cutlass in one hand and a stick or bludgeon in the other. One of them said, "Where are the sons of bitches?" They struck at several persons in the street and went towards the head of the alley. Two officers came and endeavoured to get them into the barracks. One of the lads proposed to ring the [fire] bell. The soldiers went through the alley, and the boys huzzaed and said they were gone through Royal Exchange lane into King street. I saw two or three snow balls strike the side of the Custom House, near which a sentinel stood.'[4]

The ringing of the fire bell sent many people streaming into the streets. As Thomas Cain ran through the night he

'came up into King street, where they assembled together below the town house (to the best of my knowledge) between thirty and forty persons, mostly youngsters and boys, and then they gave three cheers, and asked where the soldiers were (I imagined they meant them that had insulted them); some of the people assembled being near the sentry at the Custom House door, damn'd him, and I saw some snowballs or other things throwed that way, whereupon the sentry stepped on the steps of the Custom House and loaded his piece, and when loaded struck the butt of his firelock against the steps three or four times, in the interim the people assembled, continuing crying "Fire, fire, and be damned," and some of them drawing near to him he knocked at the Custom House door very hard, whereupon the door was opened about halfway, and I saw a person come out, which I imagined to be a servant without a hat, his hair tied and hung down loose.'[5]

In a matter of minutes, Captain Thomas Preston, officer of the day, led a squad of soldiers to the relief of his sentinel. As the thirteen-man detachment

13. Portrait of John Adams. *Charles Willson Peale*

John Adams was never better defined than in a resolution which he wrote in his historically invaluable diary at the age of twenty, and which he faithfully kept. 'I will rouse up my mind and fix my attention; I will stand collected within myself and think upon what I read and what I see.' His most constantly repeated journal entry is 'At home, thinking.' Lawyer, delegate to the Massachusetts Provincial Congress, representative to the First Continental Congress, framer of the Declaration of Independence and the Constitution, Commissioner to France, Ambassador to England, second president of the United States of America: John Adams moved through them all, collected within himself, thinking in the broadest possible terms.

double-timed through the street, the moonlight glinting on their bayonets, they shouted, 'Where are the damned boogers, cowards, where are your Liberty boys.' William Wyat, a sailor from Salem,

'followed them, and when the officer got there with his men, he bid them face about. I stood just below them on the west wing, and the said officer ordered his men to load, which they did accordingly, with the utmost dispatch, then they remained about six minutes, with their firelocks rested and bayonets fixed, but not standing in exact order. I observed a considerable number of young lads, and here and there a man amongst them, about the middle of the street, facing the soldiers, but not within ten or twelve feet distance from them; I observed some of them, viz., the lads, &c., had sticks in their hands, laughing, shouting huzzaing, and crying fire; but could not observe that any of them threw anything at the soldiers, or threatened any of them. Then the said officer retired from before the soldiers and stepping behind them, towards the right wing, bid the soldiers fire; they not yet firing, he presently again bid 'em fire, they not yet firing, he stamped and said, "Damn your bloods, fire, be the consequences what it will;" then the second man on the left wing fired off his gun, then, after a very short pause, they fired one after another as quick as possible, beginning on the right wing; the last man's gun on the left wing flashed in the pan, then he primed again, and the people being withdrawn from before the soldiers, most of them further down the street, he turned his gun toward them and fired upon them. Immediately after the principal firing, I saw three of the people fall down in the street; presently after the last gun was fired off, the said officer, who commanded the soldiers (as above), sprung before them, waving his sword or stick, said "Damn ye, rascals, what did you fire for?" and struck up the gun of one of the soldiers who was loading again, whereupon they seemed confounded and fired no more. I then went up behind them to the right wing, where one of the people was lying, to see whether he was dead, where there were four or five people about him, one of them saying that he was dead; whereupon one of the soldiers said, "Damn his blood, he is dead, if he ever sprawl again I will be damned for him".'[6]

Three of the mob were killed outright while seven were wounded, two later dying of their wounds. To the radicals and propagandists the affair was a godsend. The funeral of four of the dead was one of the grandest ever held in Boston with the victims buried in a common grave, the stone above them reading:

> Long as in Freedom's cause the wise contend
> Dear to your country shall your fame extend;
> While to the world the lettered stone shall tell
> Where Caldwell, Attucks, Gray and Maverick fell.[7]

One Patrick Carr missed his opportunity for immortality by dying after the funeral. Despite flaring passions and rising tempers, two of the more ardent radicals, John Adams and Josiah Quincy, defended Preston, the British officer, and his men in court after they were charged with murder. Adams and Quincy were determined that their actions were to be based on a respect for the rule of law and were prepared to take considerable personal risks on behalf of this principle. All were acquitted except two of the rank and file, Matthew Kilroy and Hugh Montgomery, who were convicted of manslaughter, and after pleading benefit of clergy were branded on the brawn of the thumb with the letter 'M'. But broadsides condemned the soldiers and every 5 March the anniversary was observed, with Massachusetts preachers thundering forth from their pulpits with such passion-warming sermons as 'Innocent Blood Crying from the Streets of Boston'.

Once again the British government capitulated. In April 1770 the Townshend Acts were repealed, although Townshend was not around to see his work undone, having died in September 1767. The Pitt-Grafton ministry had gone out, succeeded by a government headed by Lord North. North was a politician who believed that his first loyalty was to the Crown, so he found himself forced to support measures of George III with which he did not necessarily wholly agree. It was under North that the Townshend duties had been repealed, although the tax on tea was retained, due to the insistence of

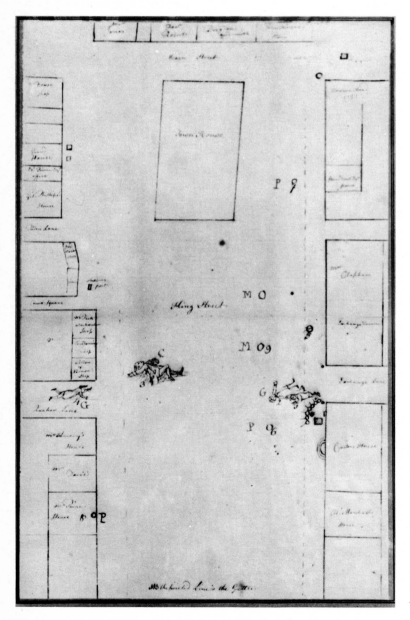

14. Diagram of the Boston Massacre. *Paul Revere*

This manuscript diagram was made by Paul Revere for use in the trial of the British soldiers who fired the shots on 5 March 1770. The accuracy of the diagram is confirmed by the many affidavits taken at the trial; it is very different from Revere's engraving of Pelham's propagandistic drawing of the scene. (See plate 15.)

The buildings surrounding the Town House and King Street are all identified. Four corpses are portrayed, in realistic attitudes. A and G are Attucks and Gray, who died at the feet of the soldiers clustered in front of the Custom House. C is James Caldwell. G is the boy Maverick (G standing for his master, Greenwood), shot in Quaker Lane. Patrick Carr had not yet died when this was made, and he is not represented. The unattached letters are difficult to identify; the P, lower left, is probably Edward Paine, in front of his house. It is not known where Paul Revere was that night; the diagram suggests that he was in King Street.

15. Broadside Account of the Boston Massacre. *Paul Revere*

In this broadside, Paul Revere's famous engraving, 'The Bloody Massacre', is combined with the Boston Gazette article of 12 March 1770, embellished with the coffins of the five victims, also engraved by Revere. The picture is markedly altered from Revere's accurate diagram (see plate 14), to become a Whig propaganda document which Josiah Quincy denounced at the trial of the British soldiers as having added 'wings to fancy'. Here is shown none of the fierce baiting of the huddle of soldiers in front of the Custom House by the angry populace which took place that night, nor the scattered, self-defensive shooting; here a straight line of red-coats fires implacably at a meek, defenceless people, ordered on by Captain Preston, who in reality was in front, risking his life to try to stop them. Crispus Attucks is neither huge nor black. Hand-coloured by Remick, with scarlet coats matching scarlet gore, the prints of this engraving had a powerful effect.

The unsigned article is as inflammatory as the picture. It is entitled 'An Account of a late Military Massacre at Boston, or the Consequences of Quartering Troops in a populous, well-regulated Town'. Its clear purpose is to get the troops withdrawn. This was attained; both regiments were removed to Castle Island.

The drawing for the engraving was made by Henry Pelham, who objected to Revere's use of it, and issued his own engraving of it, under the title 'The Fruits of Arbitrary Powers'. The New-York Historical Society has the only known copy of this broadside.

THE Boston-AND COUNTRY Gazette, JOURNAL.

Containing the freshest Advices, Foreign and Domestic.

No. 770.

MONDAY, January 8, 1770.

THE Committee of Merchants in this Town having by last Night's Post received a Letter from the Committee of Merchants of New-York,

TO THE PRINTERS. THE agreement of the Merchants of this distressed and insulted continent, to with-hold

agreement of the merchants is of that consequence to ALL AMERICA which our brethren in ALL the other governments, and in Great-Britain itself

the king who was to write, 'I am clear there must always be one tax to keep the right, and as such I approve the Tea Duty.'

The years that followed were comparatively quiet, although there was an uncommon colonial interest in smuggling tea, so much so that Thomas Hutchinson noted that even if the smugglers lost one chest of every three, they could still undersell legal tea. Customs officers made themselves unpopular by a more stringent enforcement of the law. One of the most disliked was Lieutenant William Dudington, who cruised about Narragansett Bay in the *Gaspée* making himself generally disagreeable by stopping ships without cause and acting 'more imperious and haughty than the Grand Turk himself'. When the revenue schooner ran aground on 9 June 1772 near Providence, a group of 150 angry townspeople piled aboard, put Dudington and his crew over the side in small boats and burned the ship to the waterline. A royal commission named to investigate the matter could find no one other than a runaway slave to testify. Nothing ever came of the matter other than the realization by the ministry that opposition was not limited to Massachusetts.

In a Boston Town meeting, Sam Adams came up with the idea of a Committee of Correspondence for the exchange of ideas and information with other communities. It seemed a good thing and similar committees sprang up

26

16. Masthead of 'The Boston Gazette', first used 1 January 1770. *Paul Revere*

A seated figure bearing the arms of Britain has her hand on a cage, from which the colonial bird has just flown. The *Gazette* was the chief organ of the Whigs and Patriots of Boston.

17. 'Magna Britannia: her Colonies Reduc'd'. *Benjamin Franklin*

Benjamin Franklin was in England from 1757 to 1775, representing the American Colonies. He used many methods in his long and patient attempt to make the British understand the American point of view. Here he draws a sad cartoon showing Britannia, blinded and dismembered, suffering the fate of the ancient hero, the Byzantine General Belisarius.

throughout the colonies, a number appointing local committees through the lower houses of their legislatures. The Americans became a bit more united in their thinking.

Back in England, the government was more concerned with problems within the East India Company which had fallen on hard times and was on the verge of bankruptcy. The company was too important in the scheme of British imperialism to be allowed to fold. There were 17,000,000 lb of unsold tea rotting in the company's warehouses. In America, tea was so popular a beverage that smugglers had amassed fortunes in 'tea-running'. Of the estimated 7,000,000 lb consumed by the colonists, at least 5,000,000 had been brought in by smugglers. To aid the company, legislation granted the company and its agents a virtual monopoly on tea in the colonies.

Such an arrangement should have delighted the Americans. Under the new arrangement, even with the threepence Townshend duties, the price of tea was lowered to about one-half of its old price. Americans could now slake their thirst with tea that was cheaper than that sold in England and even at less cost than smuggled Dutch tea. The principals affected most were the merchants and the smugglers. These two groups allied themselves with the radicals, and fancied wrongs allowed Sam Adams and his group to use a base from which to build their crusade.

18. Boreas
This freely drawn caricature of Lord North is the only political satire in the Oxford Magazine for 1774. In the lower left corner is a small head inscribed 'Aeolus', who is blowing air against North's back. The legend beneath reads 'I Promise to reduce the Americans'.

On Thursday 16 December 1773, a meeting was held in Boston's Old South Meeting House. Despite a steady rain, nearly 7,000 people crowded in and around the house. There were three tea ships in the harbour whose captains wished to unload, but were thwarted by the attitude of Governor Thomas Hutchinson who refused to grant the necessary clearance until the tea was put ashore. Candles sputtered in the waning light when the Governor's refusal was delivered to the crowd. Merchant John Rowe was heard to murmur, 'who knows, how tea will mingle with salt water?' 'A mob! a mob!' rang through the throng, but Sam Adams rose and restored order; however, a little later he came out with a dramatic statement, 'This meeting can do nothing more to save the country'. It was then:

'Just before the dissolution of the meeting, a number of brave and resolute men, dressed in the Indian manner, approached near the door of the assembly, and gave a war-whoop, and was answered by some in the galleries, but silence was commanded, and a peaceable deportment enjoined until the dissolution. The Indians, as they were then called, repaired to the wharf, where the ships lay that had the tea on board, and were followed by hundreds of people, to see the event of the transactions of those who made so grotesque an appearance. The Indians immediately repaired on board Captain Hall's ship, where they heisted out the chests of tea, and when on deck stove them and emptied the tea overboard. Having cleared this ship, they proceeded to Captain Bruce's, and then to Captain Coffin's brig. They applied themselves so dexterously to the destruction of this commodity, that in the space of three hours they broke up three hundred and forty-two chests, which was the whole number in these vessels, and discharged their contents into the dock. When the tide rose it floated the broken chests and tea insomuch that the surface of the water was filled therewith a considerable way from the south part of the town of Dorchester Neck, and lodged on the shores. There was the greatest care being taken to prevent the tea from being purloined by the populace; one or two being detected in endeavouring to pocket a small quantity were stripped of their acquisitions and very roughly handled. It is worthy of remark that although a considerable quantity of goods were still remaining on board the vessel, no injury was sustained. Such attention to private property was observed, that a small padlock belonging to the captain of one of the ships being broke, another was procured and sent to him. The town was very quiet during the whole evening and the night following. Those who were from the country went home with a merry heart, and the next day joy appeared in almost every countence, some on account of the destruction of the tea, others on account of the quietness with which it was affected. One of the Monday's papers says the masters and owners are well pleased that their ships are thus cleared.'[8]

'Tea Parties' spread like an epidemic. New Yorkers mixed their tea with the waters of the East River; Philadelphians allowed the tea to be landed but saw that it rotted in warehouses; Charlestonians stored it until the outbreak of hostilities and then sold it at auction to help pay for the war effort. Perhaps the most unusual 'Tea Party' later took place in North Carolina at Edenton, where a group of local women participated in what is sometimes called the 'earliest known instance of political activity on the part of American women in the American colonies'. When the news of the Edenton women swearing off the stuff reached London, Arthur Iredell wrote back to his brother, James, in North Carolina:

'Pray are you become Patriotic? I see by the News Papers, the Edenton Ladies have signalized themselves, by their protest ag*t* Tea Drinking—The Name of Johnston I see among others; are their any of my Sister's Relations Patriotic Heroines? Is there a Female Congress at Edenton too? I hope not, for we Englishmen are afraid of the Male Congress, but if the Ladies, we have ever, since the Amasonian Ara, been esteemed the most formidable Enemies, if they, I say, should attack us, the most fatal consequences is to be dreaded. So dextrous in the handling of a Dart, each wound they give is Mortal; whilst we are so unhappily form'd by Nature, the more we strive to

JOHN MALCOM.

Le 25 Janvier 1774 la populace irritée pénétra sans armes dans sa maison. Il blessa plusieurs personnes à coups d'épée: mais les Bostoniens, modérés jusques dans leur vengeance, le saisirent, le descendirent par la fenêtre dans une charrette, ensuite il fut dépouillé, goudronné, emplumé, mené sur la place publique, battu de verges, et obligé de remercier de ce qu'on ne le punissait point de mort, puis on le ramena chez lui sans autre mal.

19. John Malcolm. *F. Godefroy*

Johnny Malcolm was a 'tidewaiter', or minor customs official employed to watch over the unloading of ships. He was also a virulent Loyalist, an odd person whom the pro-British Miss Hulton describes as 'reckond creasy', who had been run out of Carolina and tarred and feathered in Maine before he came to Boston. A scuffle with a Patriot, on 25 January 1774, ended in his barricading himself in his house, near North Square, arming himself with a 'naked sword', and baiting the populace from an upper window. No constable appearing to check the mob, they brought ladders and a cart, lowered him into it, stripped, tarred and feathered him, and carted him about the city, beating him at strategic spots. This was the cruellest of Boston's four recorded tarrings and featherings. However, Malcolm recovered, sent a box of his peeled-off skin, tar, and feathers to England, and received a £200 pension from the government.

29

conquer them, the more the Conquest! The Edenton Ladies conscious of their Superiority, on their Side, by former Experience are willing, I imagine to crush into Atoms, by their omnipotency; the only Security on our Side, to prevent the impending Ruin, that I can perceive is, the probability that there is but few of the places in America who possess so much female Artillerty, as Edenton.'[9]

When details of the Boston 'caper' reached England in February 1774, even those politicians considered to be friends of the colonies were appalled, with Lord Chatham decrying it as 'certainly criminal', while Benjamin Franklin noted from London that the 'violent destruction of the tea seems to have united all parties here'. Parliament struck quickly with the passage of the so-called 'coercive' acts which the colonists were to term 'intolerable'. Between March and June 1774, the Boston Port Act, the Government of Massachusetts Act, the Administration of Justice Act, and the Quartering

Act sped through the House, all but the last applying only to Massachusetts. Not only were they intended to bring Massachusetts to her knees, but to serve as an example to other colonies that should feel restive. The port of Boston was closed to all commerce, royal officials in the colonies were to have their trials transferred elsewhere, and local government was greatly curtailed.

British troops had been stationed in Boston since September 1768, when the customs officers there had begged for protection. By the spring of 1774, General Thomas Gage was in England for his first vacation at home in seventeen years, and had persuaded the Crown that a display of force, coupled with tne authorization to use it, was all that was necessary to quell the colonial disturbances. Gage was named Governor of Massachusetts in place of Thomas Hutchinson and arrived in Boston on 17 May 1774. There was a show of welcome, but cordiality faded when the port of Boston was closed on 1 June.

21. The able Doctor, or America Swallowing the Bitter Draught

In this famous British Whig cartoon, made just after the Boston Port Bill was signed by the King on 31 March 1774, America, stripped to the waist, is being held down by two Tory ministers, probably Thurlow, a drafter of the Bill, and Dartmouth, Colonial Secretary. Lord North, with the Port Bill in his pocket, forces tea down her throat, which she spews back into his face. On the right stands the Solicitor General, Wedderburn, the other drafter, unmistakable in a Scottish kilt and cap, brandishing a sword inscribed 'Military Law'. On the left, Spain, with horror and some glee, points out the scene to France; both hesitate to interfere. Britannia, in the background, leans on her shield and hides her face. In the foreground, the Boston petition, which the House of Commons refused to hear when it was presented by William Bollan, agent for the Council of Massachusetts Bay, lies in shreds. Two interesting features are the salacious interest which the minister at her feet is taking in the victim, suggesting a rape to come rather than treatment by an able doctor, and the fact that, although the Tory ministers repeatedly stated that Boston could be punished without the rest of the colonies being involved, the more prescient Whigs have labelled this resisting victim not Boston, but America.

The able Doctor, or America Swallowing the Bitter Draught.

Other colonies assumed an air of mourning, even Philadelphia, Boston's great commercial rival. Christopher Marshall dipped his pen in gloom and wrote in his diary:

'*June 1st*. This being the day when the cruel act for blocking up the harbour of Boston took effect, many of the inhabitants of this city, to express their sympathy and show their concern for their suffering bretheren in the common cause of liberty, had their shops shut up, their houses kept close from hurry and business; also the ring of bells at Christ Church were muffled, and rung a solemn peal at intervals, from morning till night: the colours of the vessels in the harbour were hoisted half-mast high; the several houses of divine worship were crowded, where divine service was performed, and particular discourses, suitable to the occasion were preached by F. Allison, Duffield, Spreat, and Blair. Sorrow, mixed with indignation, seemed pictured in the countenances of the inhabitants, and indeed the whole city wore an aspect of deep distress, being a melancholy occasion.

4th. This being the birth-day of King George III, scarcely, if any, notice was taken in it in this city, by way of rejoicing: not one of our bells suffered to ring, and but very few colours were shown by the shipping in the harbour; no, nor not one bonfire kindled.'[10]

General Gage was quick to observe the unrest in the country and was soon to send a dispatch to Whitehall: 'Affairs here are worse than even at the Time of the Stamp-Act. I don't mean in Boston, but throughout the Country.' On the other hand, Lord Percy, a general serving under Gage, felt that it was mostly bluff and bluster:

'The people here talk much & do little; but nothing, I am sure, will ever reestablish peace and quiet in this country, except steadiness and perseverance on the part of the Administration. . . . The people in this part of the country are in general made up of rashness and timidity. Quick and violent in their determinations, they are fearful in the execution of them (unless, indeed, they are quite certain of meeting little or no opposition, & then, like all cowards, they are cruel and tyrannical). To hear them talk, you might imagine that they would attack us & demolish us every night; & yet, whenever we appear, they are frightened out of their wits. . . . I am sorry to say that no body of men in this Province are so extremely injurious to the peace

22. Samuel Adams. *John Singleton Copley*

John and Sam Adams were second cousins; 'This brace of Adamses', Governor Shirley called them, and indeed, though at times in sharp opposition, they complemented and braced each other in Revolutionary leadership over the years. John was a landholder in the country town of Braintree, and a Harvard graduate; Sam was a lifelong resident of the city waterfront of Boston, and several times a bankrupt. Fluent of tongue and pen, a shrewd propagandist, passionate, courageous, even rash in the cause of liberty, he was ubiquitous in Boston, equally at home with the aristocratic John Hancock, as they fled from Lexington just before the redcoats, and with his innumerable friends along the docks and in the markets. He was also able to acquit himself well in the august company at Philadelphia when the 'brace of Adamses' enlarged their field to the nation as delegates from Massachusetts to the Continental Congress.

In this fine portrait by Copley, perhaps the greatest of the painters of Revolutionary figures, Sam Adams points to his great love, the Massachusetts Charter, which had for many years allowed 'the right to govern and tax ourselves'. Probably his most important work was done in Boston Town Meeting. 'If the Revolution dawned in Boston, Mr. Adams was its morning star.'

& tranquility of it as the clergy. They preach up sedition openly from their pulpits. (Nay, some of them have gone so far as absolutely to refuse the sacrament to the communicants till they have signed a paper of the most seditious kind, which they have denominated the Solemn League and Covenant.)'[11]

In general, British officers were disgusted with the seeming coddling of the colonists. One observed that the political theories of the New Englanders were a hundred years behind those of England, but he believed that British military might and the jingle of shillings would bring them to their senses. He discovered the women of Boston displayed a better sense of co-operation than did the men. His letter home was printed in the *Bristol Gazette*:

'The workmen at Boston were so mulish, that the General was obliged to sent to Nova Scotia for carpenters and bricklayers to fit up barracks for our accomodations.... The inhabitants of this province retain the religious and civil principles brought over by their forefathers.... With the most austere show of devotion, they are destitute of every principle of religion or common honesty, and are reckoned the most arrant cheats and hypocrites on the whole continent of America. The women are very handsome, but, like old Mother Eve, very frail. Our camp has been as well supplied in that way since we have been on Boston common, as if our tents were pitched on Blackheath. As to what you hear of their taking up arms to resist the force of England, it is mere bullying, and will go no further than words: whenever it comes to blows, he that can run fastest will think himself best off.... We expect to pass the winter very quietly. The Saints here begin to relish the money we spend among them, and, I believe, notwithstanding all their noise, would be very sorry to part with us.'[12]

Not many British officers realized that Boston was no longer standing alone, although there had been signs of unity. First there had been the Committees of Correspondence, designed to keep the spark alive. And out of the New York Committee came a call for delegates to 'meet in a general Congress'. A Providence town meeting became the first official group to propose such a Congress, but perhaps the most significant action came from Virginia, resulting from Thomas Jefferson's resolution for a day of fasting and prayer on behalf of Boston. Governor Dunmore straight away dissolved what he considered an insolent House of Burgesses. Eighty-nine of its members walked down Williamsburg's Duke of Gloucester Street to assemble in the Raleigh Tavern. On 27 May 1774 they suggested that all trade be suspended with Britain and proposed a general congress of all the colonies 'to deliberate on those general measures which the united interests of America may require from time to time'. This was followed by what amounted to an official

23. Paul Revere. *John Singleton Copley*

This is Paul Revere at about the age of thirty, looking up from his work bench as Copley often saw him, holding in his hand one of the beautiful pear-shaped teapots which he was making at that time. He was a very fine craftsman in silver; his numerous other crafts, such as engraving, dental work, bell-making and copper sheathing, supplemented his income. The Whig doctor Thomas Young wrote of him, 'No man of his rank and opportunities in life deserves better of the community. Steady, vigorous, sensible and persevering.' The more aristocratic Patriots trusted him to make long rides bearing important missives, and admitted him to their inner conclaves in the troubled Boston of the Stamp Act and the Tea Party.

Dessiné par le Barbier Peintre du Roi   Gravé par Godefroy de l'Académie Imp.le et Royale de Vienne &c.

24. 'Première Assemblée du Congrès'. *Le Barbier*

The First Continental Congress laid the foundations and passed the resolutions that eventually led to an independence which few if any of its members then desired. On 5 September 1774 fifty-five delegates, elected by the provincial congresses and legislative bodies of the colonies, met in Philadelphia. Georgia was not represented.

The delegates were distinguished leaders in their regions, responsible and experienced. Many had served in the prototype Stamp Act Congress which met in New York nearly ten years earlier. Dr Samuel Johnson characterized them as 'zealots of anarchy', but Chatham's description is more just: 'the most honourable assembly of statesmen since those of ancient Greeks and Romans'.

By October's end the Congress had passed a series of significant statements, including its Declaration and Resolves which provided for a Continental Association to prevent the importation and consumption of British wares, and which denounced the Coercive Acts and other Parliamentary laws and taxes as unconstitutional.

call by the Massachusetts Assembly who suggested that such a meeting be held in Philadelphia on the first of September.

From 5 September to 26 October 1774, fifty-six delegates attended the assembly that was to become known as the First Continental Congress, made up of men who could be termed either radicals or conservatives and moderates. Among the moderates was a tall, silent planter who had already attracted attention and was to be described:

'Ye 3d gentleman Col'o Washington was bred a soldier—a warriour, & distinguished himself in early life before & at ye Death of ye unfortunate but intrepid Braddock. He is a modest man, but sensible & speaks little—in action cool, like a Bishop at his prayers.'[13]

Although Joseph Galloway, a conservative, offered the Pennsylvania State House as a meeting place, the radicals managed enough votes to select Carpenter's Hall, a plain though spacious building, but a choice that was to please the artisans and lesser citizens. Peyton Randolph was elected president while the radical Charles Thomson, who was not a delegate, was the choice for secretary. The Congress was still appointing committees when

Paul Revere clattered into Philadelphia bringing with him the 'Suffolk Resolves', passed by the people of Suffolk County, Massachusetts, and carrying a central theme that 'the people owed an indispensable duty to God and to their country to preserve those liberties for which the fathers had fought and bled'. Despite the opposition of the conservatives, the Congress endorsed the Resolves, convincing John Adams that 'America will support Massachusetts or perish with her'.

The Conservatives made their move when Joseph Galloway of Pennsylvania offered a plan of union that promised a hope of reconciliation with the Mother Country, and the safeguarding of all American rights. But the radicals rallied, defeating the measure by a margin of only one colony, and then, to complete their victory, managed to expunge all mention of Galloway's Plan from the minutes, thereby lending a tone of harmony to the proceedings.

Following this, the body denounced Governor Thomas Gage's efforts to fortify Boston and then passed resolutions condemning the Coercive Acts, and stating that the new government in Massachusetts interfered with basic charter rights; it urged the people to establish their own government, raise troops for their own defence, and to suspend all commerce with England. There was even more of a spirit of co-operation between the two extremes in Congress with the issuing of the document known as the 'Declaration of Rights and Grievances'. Despite professions of loyalty to the King, they condemned Parliament's interference in colonial affairs and declared that body's authority over the colonies to be limited to the supervision of external trade, 'for the purpose of securing the commercial advantages of the Empire'.

Yet the most important and perhaps the most drastic action of the First Continental Congress was the 'Association', a pledge of non-importation and non-consumption. After 1 December 1774, they declared, there should be no further colonial importations from Britain or Ireland, East India Tea from anywhere, or molasses, sugar, coffee, or pimento from the British West Indies, wine from Madeira, or any foreign indigo. All colonial participation in the slave trade should come to a halt. Better to stand the austerity, frugality and the promotion of local manufacture were urged, while the colonists should deny themselves 'every species of extravagance and dissipation, especially all horse-racing, and all kinds of gaming, cock-fighting, exhibitions of shows, plays, and other expensive diversions and entertainments'. Then, after approving petitions to other parts of the empire, the Congress decided that if their grievances had not been redressed a second congress would be held the following May.

John Adams wrote to his beloved Abigail:

'I am anxious to know how you can live without Government. But the experiment must be tried. The evils will not be found so dreadful as you apprehend them. Frugality, my dear, frugality, economy, parsimony, must be our refuge. I hope the ladies are every day diminishing their ornaments, and the gentlemen, too. Let us eat potatoes and drink water; let us wear canvas, and undressed sheepskins, rather than submit to the unrighteous and ignominious domination that is proposed for us.'[14]

By this time, wrath had overflowed into action in New England. General Gage, aware of the growing anger, determined to remove all military sup-

25. General Thomas Gage. *David Martin*

When Gage (1721–87) took office in Massachusetts in May 1774, as Captain-General and Governor, Lord Dartmouth's instructions were to use troops should 'the Madness of the People' or lack of co-operation by provincial officers demand it. He found himself baffled by the situation that developed. After Concord and Lexington, then Bunker Hill with its heavy loss of British troops and officers, he was bitterly criticized by both sides. He was recalled to England and his post was later revoked.

plies out of reach of the rebels. He sent a detachment to seize the powder in the magazine at Charlestown, across the bay from Boston. When the report spread that six men had been killed in the section, men reached for their muskets and set out along the road to Boston:

'rushing forward some on foot some on horseback, at every house Women & children making cartridges, running bullets, making Wallets, baking Biscuits, crying & bemoaning & at the same time animating their Husbands & Sons to fight for their Liberties, tho' not knowing whether they should ever see them again. . . . The Women kept on making cartridges, and after equipping their husbands, bro't them out to the Soldiers which in Crowds passed along & gave them out in handfuls to one and another as they were deficient, mixing Exhortations & Tears & prayers & spiriting the Men in such an unfeminate Manner as even would make Cowards fight. . . . if anything the Women surpassed the Men for Eagerness & spirit in the Defence of Liberty by Arms. For they had no Tho'ts of the Men returning but from Battle, for they all believed the Action commenced between the King's Troops & the Provincials. The Women under this Assurance gave up their Husbands Sons &c to Battle & bid them corageously & manfully & behave themselves bravely for Liberty—commanding them to behave like Men & not like Cowards—to be of good Courage & play the men for our people & for the Cities of our God—& the Lord do as seemeth him good. They expected a bloody Scene, but they doubted not Success & Victory.'[15]

The rumblings of war faded as it was discovered that the rumour was false, and angry men returned to their homes; but there had been demonstrations of violence in other places. Four days later, on Sunday, the news had reached Hebron, Connecticut. The Reverend Samuel Peters, the Anglican minister in that town, observing that 'spiritual iniquity rides in high places', recorded his disgust at the behaviour of his neighbours:

'on their pious Sabbath day, . . . when the preachers and Magistrates left the pulpits &c. for the gun and drum, and set off for Boston, cursing the King and Lord North, General Gage, the bishops and their cursed curates, and the Church of England; and for my telling the Church people not to take up arms, &c., it being high treason, &c. the Sons of Liberty have almost killed one of my church, tarred and feathered two, abused others, and on the 6th day destroyed my Windows, and rent my Cloathes, even my Gown, &c. crying out down with the Church, the rag of Popery, &c. Their rebellion is obvious, and treason is common, and Robbery is their daily devotion.'[16]

When the word got around that Gage was planning to remove the armament and ammunition from Fort William and Mary at Portsmouth, New Hampshire, Paul Revere galloped off to warn the locals who confiscated the cannon and powder. On Sunday, 25 February, Colonel Alexander Leslie with 240 men was detached to Salem to seize military supplies. They sailed to Marblehead and then marched overland some five miles. The word spread quickly, the local artillery was moved over a bridge, shortly before

'The Troops under Col. Leslie arrived at the Bridge, which was a Draw Bridge not far from the No[rth] or young Mr. Barnards Meetinghouse. The provincial Col. Pickering mustered between 30 & 40 under Arms on the other side of the Bridge & drew up the Bridge. A fast Multitude was convened, and

26. The Method of Refining Salt-Petre. *Engraved by Paul Revere*

The making of gunpowder became a crucial necessity to the Americans when war with England cut off their former supply from the mother country. This picture shows four furnaces under a flue. The liquid saltpetre is in the tub (T). The wicker basket serves to drain the dross out of it. Finally, it is ladled into a copper pan (Fig. 1). X is a skimmer used to remove the saltpetre crystals (Fig. 2), and *a* is a windlass to draw up the refined saltpetre into the loft above.

Alarm Guns fired continually. Col. Leslie find*g* the Bridge drawn, ordered his Men to face, seeming to intend to fire on those on the other side. The Men did not face. At length he ordered his man to put off two Gundalos— but the Salemites skuttled them. The Soldiers pricked them with Bayonets &c. At this Inst. the Rev. M*r* Barnard jun. stept up to Col. Leslie; complained that his soldiers abused our pple. told him they were the Agressors & beged him not to fire, for that if they did they would all be cut off. Leslie kept his Troops at the Bridge an hour & half:—at length Col. Leslie pledged his honor that if they would let down the Bridge he would march but thirty rods over it & return without doing any Thing further. The Line was markt, and Col. Pickering with his 40 brave heroes (like Leonidas at Thermopylae) faced the Kings Troops, risked Col. Leslies Honor; the Bridge was let down, Leslie marched over, & while some were on the bridge & others on this side, he halted, ordered them to face about, & so they marched back, returned to Marblehed, & embarked that night for Castle William, without the Canon which they went after. . . . Thus inglorious was the Excursion and Retreat of the Kings Troops.'[17]

The spirit of rebellion had now become an epidemic, racing through the countryside, and like the tentacles of an octopus gathered many new converts within its folds. And the behaviour of the army did little to alleviate the situation. One Sunday in March, near a Boston meetinghouse, a 'parcell of drums and fifes . . . play'd and beat Yanky Doodle the whole forenoon service time, to the great interruption of the congregation'.

But now it was April, carrying a promise of spring, but also a hint of violence. And spring was the time when armies took the field.

2. Rebellion

SINCE EARLY JANUARY General Thomas Gage had been quietly making plans while awaiting the official 'determination from home'. Officers dressed as countrymen had been sent out into the countryside, drawing maps and noting points of strategic importance.

On 14 April 1775, disembarking from the sixteen-gun sloop *Nautilus*, was Oliver De Lancey, bringing a secret dispatch from Lord Dartmouth, Secretary of State for the Colonies. The time had now come, said the Secretary, to take strong action. Reinforcements were promised, and Gage was urged to arrest the leaders of the rebellion. If such strong action, however, should result in the beginning of hostilities, 'it will surely be better that the Conflict should be brought on, upon such ground, than in a riper state of Rebellion'. In other words, Dartmouth seemed to be telling Gage to do something, even if it was wrong. At least the business would be flushed out into the open.

Gage made his preparations. Samuel Adams and John Hancock were at Lexington and there were reported stores of rebel ammunition and ordnances at the village of Concord. It was to be a night march to maintain, as much as possible, the element of surprise. No one realized that the next day's engagements at Lexington and Concord were to mark the opening of the rebellion. Jeremy Belknap later recalled that

'on the night of April 18, they took every imaginable precaution to prevent a discovery. Their meat was dressed on a transport in the harbor. Their men were not apprised of the design, till, just as it was time to march, they were waked up by the sergeants putting their hands on them, and whispering gently to them; and were even conducted by a backway out of the barracks, without the knowledge of their comrades, and without the observation of the sentries. They walked through the streets with the utmost silence. It being about ten o'clock, no sound was heard but of their feet: a dog, happening to bark, was instantly killed with a bayonet. They proceeded to the beach under the new powder-house,—the most unfrequented part of the town; and there embarked on board the boats, which had their oars muffled to prevent a noise, and landed on Phips Farm, where they were met by the infamous Capt. Beeman, and conducted to Concord.

Notwithstanding all this secrecy, the following circumstances contributed to their discovery. Numbers of people were jealous, and kept a vigilant eye upon them. It was observed, that, two days before, general orders were given out that the light infantry and the grenadiers should be excused from duty. The boats were observed to be launched from the transports. In the afternoon of April 18, an uncommon number of officers were seen walking up and down the Long Wharf; and a party of nine rode out of town with their blue surtouts, and passed through Cambridge just before night, riding very slowly; and, being followed by a person who suspected some bad design, they damned him, and told him not to keep so near them. Late in the evening, a light-infantryman was seen in a retail shop with his accoutrements on. These circumstances being communicated to Dr. [Joseph] Warren, he applied to the person who had been retained, and got intelligence of their whole design; which was to seize Adams and Hancock, who were then in Lexington, and burn the stores at Concord. Two expresses were immediately despatched thither, who passed by the guards on the Neck just before a sergeant arrived with orders to stop passengers. Another messenger went over Charlestown Ferry.'[1]

Paul Revere was the messenger who came out of Boston by water:

'On Tuesday evening, the 18th, it was observed that a number of soldiers were marching towards the bottom of the Common. About 10 o'clock, Dr. Warren sent in great haste for me and begged that I would immediately set

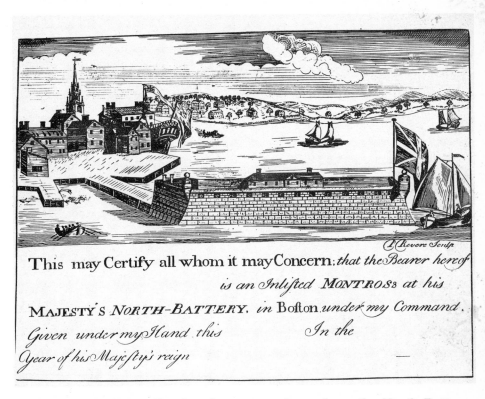

27. Certificate of identification for men on leave from the North Battery, Boston. *Paul Revere*

This engraving by Paul Revere, whose craftsmanship in silver was superior to his work with a burin, gives an unusual view of Boston's North Battery, extending into the shallow waters of the bay. Charlestown, below Breed's Hill and Bunker's Hill, is seen beyond the stern of the anchored vessel. Three boys are diving and swimming off the pier, a favourite playground for North Boston boys, of whom Revere had been one.

Across this body of water to Charlestown, some years later on the night of 18 April 1775, Revere was rowed to begin his famous ride. Behind him in the belfry of Christ Church, here shown, two lanterns hung. 'I agreed with a Colonel Conant and some other gentlemen', Revere wrote to a friend in describing that night, 'that if the British went out by water, we would show two lanthorns in the North Church steeple; and if by land, one.'

This is a certificate of identity to be used on leave by a montross, or artilleryman, stationed at the North Battery, which occupied the site of the present Battery Wharf from the mid-seventeenth century till its destruction at the end of the eighteenth.

off for Lexington, where Messrs Hancock and Adams were, and acquaint them of the movement, and that it was thought they were the objects.

When I got to Dr. Warren's house, I found he had sent an express by land to Lexington—a Mr. William Dawes. . . . I [had] agreed with a Colonel Conant, and some other gentlemen, that if the British went out by water, we would show two lanthorns in the North Church steeple; and if by land, one, as a signal; for we were apprehensive it would be difficult to cross Charles River, or get over Boston Neck. . . .

I then went home, took my boots and surtout, went to the north part of town, where I had kept a boat; two friends rowed me across Charles River. . . . they landed me on the Charleston side. . . . I got a horse of Deacon Larkin. . . .

I set off upon a very good horse; it was then about eleven o'clock and very pleasant. After I had passed Charlestown Neck . . . I saw two men on horse-

28. A Draught of the Towns of Boston and Charlestown. *Montresor*

This carefully drawn manuscript, in watercolours, showing the fortifications made in Boston by the royal troops and around it by the rebel troops after the commencement of the siege, is inscribed to Major-General Earl Percy. Captain John Montresor accompanied Percy on his march to Lexington on 19 April, and as chief engineer quickly rebuilt the bridge across the Charles River which Minutemen had dismantled to prevent troop passage. With Yankee thrift the planks had been stocked on the farther bank; Montresor's men got across and relaid the flooring with little loss of time or delay to the advancing troops.

  Montresor was one of the ablest and most productive map-makers of the Revolution. He made a chief contribution to the high standard of cartographic production both by his own work and by his training of the younger officers under him. In the absence of quick methods of duplication then, a staff of draughtsmen was needed at headquarters; four copies of this map of Boston, nearly identical, are known.

29–32. (*Overleaf*) Four scenes of Lexington and Concord. *Ralph Earl*

The most famous set of historical prints engraved in America, these were sketched by Ralph Earl shortly after 19 April 1775. Amos Doolittle (1754–1832), a silversmith of Cheshire, Connecticut, accompanied Earl. For the scene showing the British retreat from Lexington (the fourth plate) Earl used Doolittle as a model 'to represent one of the Provincials as loading his gun, crouching behind a stone wall when firing upon the enemy'. Later that year Doolittle, a self-taught engraver, transferred Earl's sketches on to copper and coloured the prints; on 13 December 1775 he advertised the set of four scenes in the *Connecticut Journal* 'from paintings made by Ralph Earle'.

29. The Battle of Lexington: Major Pitcairn, on horseback, is directing the fire of the grenadiers on the rapidly dispersing Lexington Provincial Company, of which some have fallen. To the right of the tree in the background is the meeting-house; to the left the tavern from which, Paul Revere recounted, he and a Mr Lowell were carrying a trunk containing Hancock's papers when the British came in sight.

30. A View of the Town of Concord: in the foreground Major Pitcairn is viewing the gathering Provincials mustering on a hill to the east; the commanding officer, Lieutenant-Colonel Smith, whose corpulency is here restricted to his face, is by him. To the extreme left is the meeting-house; behind it the Regulars have discovered and are destroying the stores, scattered on the ground.

31. The Engagement at the North Bridge at Concord: across 'the rude bridge that arched the flood' puffs of smoke rise above the Provincials and the Regulars who initiated the firing. Most of the redcoats have already turned in retreat.

32. A View of the South Part of Lexington: to the right and in the background Lieutenant-Colonel Smith's brigade is in retreat; from the left Earl Percy's force is arriving in support. In the centre Percy and Smith are conferring. In the right centre is one of Percy's two fieldpieces, aimed at the meeting-house in flames. In the foreground are the Minutemen, who kept up a running fire during the entire retreat to Charlestown.

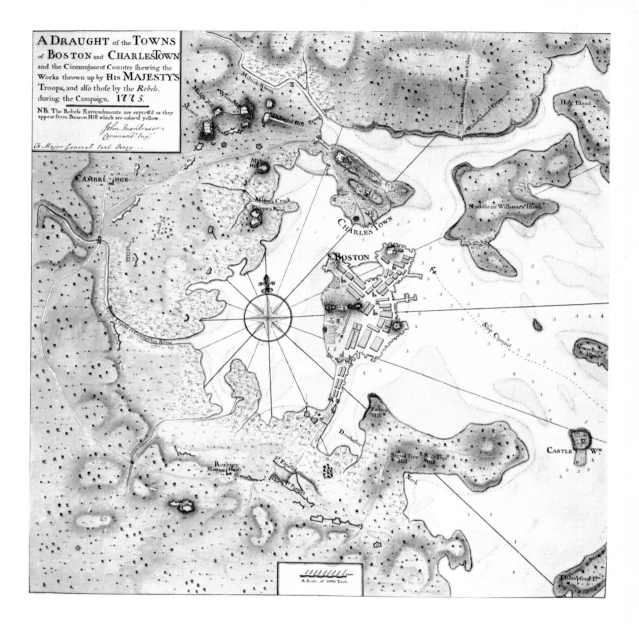

A DRAUGHT of the TOWNS
of BOSTON and CHARLESTOWN
and the Circumjacent Country shewing the
Works thrown up by HIS MAJESTY'S
Troops, and also those by the *Rebels*,
during the Campaign, 1775.

NB. The Rebels Entrenchments are express'd as they
appear from Beacon Hill which are colored yellow.

John Montresor
Command.g Ingr

To Major General Earl Percy.....

CAMBRIDGE

CHARLES TOWN

BOSTON

Naddle or Williams Island

Hog Island

Governors Island

Ship Channel

CASTLE Wm

Foster Hill

Dorchester

Roxbury
Meeting House

Signal Tree Hill

Neck

Thompsons Is.

A Scale of 1000 Yards

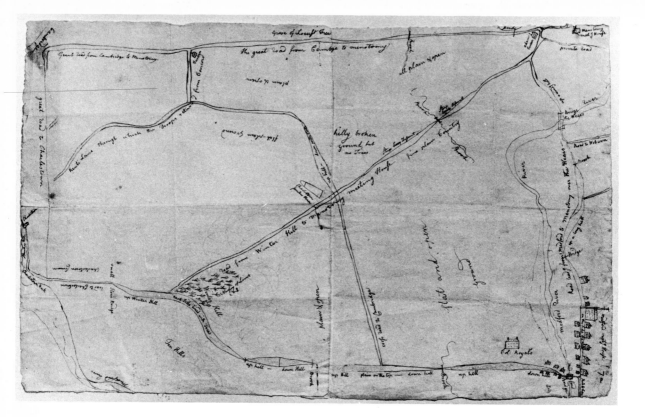

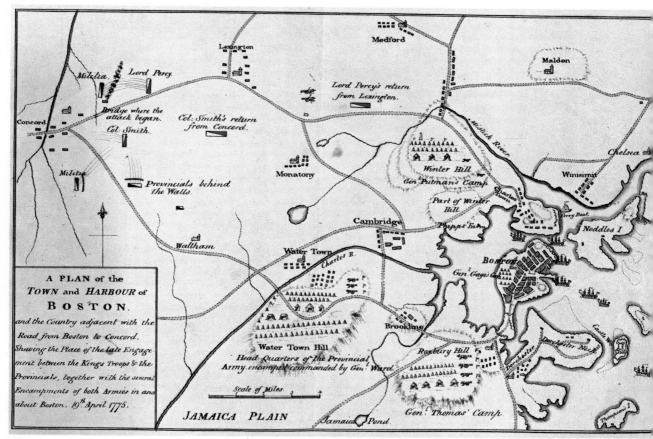

A PLAN of the
TOWN and HARBOUR of
BOSTON.

and the Country adjacent with the
Road from Boston to Concord.
Shewing the Place of the late Engage-
ment between the Kings Troops & the
Provincials, together with the several
Encampments of both Armies in and
about Boston. 19ᵗʰ April 1775.

33. Sketch map of roads between Menotomy and Charlestown

This rough sketch is an impressive example of the way in which ignorance or knowledge of a countryside and its roads can cause or avoid military disaster. If, on his return from Lexington, Percy had not known of Kent's Lane and had instead marched on into the militia who had destroyed the bridge across the Charles River and were waiting in Cambridge, the British, already sorely beset, would have been decimated.

This small, hastily drawn map is one of the treasures of Earl Percy's personal collection in Alnwick.

back, under a tree. When I got near them, I discovered they were British officers. One tried to get ahead of me, and the other to take me. I turned my horse very quick, and galloped towards Charlestown Neck, and then pushed for the Medford road. The one who chased me, endeavouring to cut me off, got into a clay pond. . . . I got clear of him, and went through Medford, over the bridge, and up to Menotomy. In Medford, I awakened the captain of the minute men; and after that I alarmed almost every house, till I got to Lexington. I found Messrs. Hancock and Adams at the Rev. Mr. Clark's; I told them my errand, and enquired for Mr. Dawes. They said he had not been there. . . .

After I had been there about half an hour, Mr. Dawes came. We refreshed ourselves, and set off for Concord to secure the stores, &c. We were overtaken by a young Dr. Prescott, whom we found to be a high son of liberty. . . . I likewise mentioned that we had better alarm all the inhabitants till we got to Concord; the young Doctor much approv'd of it and said he would stop with either of us, for the people between that and Concord knew him and would give the more credit to what we said.

We had got nearly halfway, Mr. Dawes and the Doctor stopped to alarm the people of a house. I was about one hundred rods ahead when I saw two men, in nearly the same situation as those officers were near Charlestown. I called for the Doctor and Mr. Dawes to come up; in an instant I was surrounded by four. . . . The Doctor, being foremost, he came up and we tried to get passed them; but they being armed with pistols and swords, they forced us into the pasture. The Doctor jumped his horse over a low stone wall and got to Concord.

I observed a wood at a small distance and made for that. When I got there, out started six officers on horseback and ordered me to dismount. One of them, who appeared to have the command, examined me, where I came from and what my name was? I told him. He asked me if I was an express. I answered in the affirmative. He demanded what time I left Boston. I told him, and added that their troops had catched aground in passing the river, and that there would be five hundred Americans there in a short time, for I had alarmed the country all the way up. He immediately rode towards those who had stopped us, when all five of them came down upon a full gallop. One of them, whom I afterwards found to be Major Mitchel of the 5th Regiment, clapped his pistol to my head, called me by name and told me that he was going to ask me some questions, and if I did not give him true answers, he would blow my brains out. He then asked me similar questions to those above. He then ordered me to mount my horse, after searching me for arms.

34. The British return from Concord and Lexington

This unsigned manuscript map showing the engagement at Concord of 19 April 1775 and the retreat from Lexington under Earl Percy, whom General Gage sent to support Colonel Smith, is the earliest known plan of the actions which precipitated the Revolution. The encampments of the American militia, with General Ward's headquarters at Watertown, before their removal to Cambridge, show that the map was made within three or four days after 19 April. The 'Bridge where the attack began' (upper left) is that over Mill Brook, where the retreating redcoats fired what they supposed was a parting volley and came under heavy attack by the provincials, hidden behind trees and stone walls. Percy relieved Smith at Lexington (not west of it, as on the plan) and took the lower road through Menotomy towards Cambridge, rather than the upper fork directly to Charlestown.

This map was the personal possession of Earl Percy, later Duke of Northumberland, and was brought by him to Alnwick Castle when he returned to England in 1777, where it remained unknown until the present Duke gave permission for its reproduction in 1969.

He then ordered them to advance and to lead me in front. When we got to the road, they turned towards Lexington. When he had got about one mile, the Major rode up to the officer that was leading me, and told him to give me to the Sergeant. As soon as he took me, the Major ordered him, if I attempted to run, or anybody insulted them, to blow my brains out.

We rode till we got near Lexington meeting-house, when the militia fired a volley of guns, which appeared to alarm them very much. . . . After some consultation, the Major rode up to the Sergeant and asked if his horse was tired. He answered him, he was—he was a Sergeant of Grenadiers and had a small horse. "Then," said he, "take that man's horse." I dismounted, and the Sergeant mounted my horse, when they all rode towards Lexington meeting-house.

I went across the burying-ground and some pastures to the Rev. Mr. Clark's house, where I found Messrs. Hancock and Adams. I told them of my treatment, and they concluded to go from that house towards Woburn. I went with them. . . .'[2]

Fat, lethargic Lieutenant-Colonel Francis Smith had been appointed by General Gage to command the march, but it was John Pitcairn, a major in the Royal Marines and the second in command, who provided the leadership. As they marched through the moonlight, the troops could hear alarm guns off in the distance. They were on edge as they approached Lexington just at dawn. Among those waiting for them on Lexington Green was the American militiaman Sylvanus Wood of Woburn:

'I heard the Lexington bell ring, and fearing there was some difficulty there, I immediately arose, took my gun, and, with Robert Douglass, went in haste to Lexington, which was about three miles distant. When I arrived there, I inquired of Captain [John] Parker, the commander of the Lexington company, what was the news. Parker told me he did not know what to believe, for a man had come up about half an hour before, and informed him that the British troops were not on the road. But while we were talking, a messenger came up and told the captain that the British troops were within half a mile. Parker immediately turned to his drummer, William Diman, and ordered him to beat to arms, which was done. . . .

Parker led those of us who were equipped to the north end of Lexington Common, near the Bedford road, and formed us in single file. I was stationed about in the centre of the company. While we were standing, I left my place and went from one end of the company to the other, and counted every man who was paraded, and just as I had finished, and got back to my place, I perceived the British troops had arrived on the spot between the meeting-house and Buckman's [tavern], near where Captain Parker stood when he first led off his men. The British troops immediately wheeled so as to cut off those who had gone into the meeting-house. The British troops approached us rapidly in platoons, with a general officer on horseback at their head. The officer came up within about two rods of the centre of the company, where I stood, the first platoon being about three rods distant. They there halted. The officer then swung his sword and said, "Lay down your arms, you damned rebels, or you are all dead men—Fire!" Some guns were fired by the British at us from the first platoon, but no person was killed or hurt, being charged only with powder. Just at this time Captain Parker ordered every man to take care of himself. The company immediately dispersed; and while the

35. Revolutionary musket of 1775

This was carried by a Minuteman in the encounter at Lexington.

42

36. Major John Pitcairn

Major Pitcairn (1740–75), of the Royal Marines, was in command of the advance troops that encountered the Minutemen under Captain John Parker on the Lexington green.

company was dispersing and leaping over the wall, the second platoon of the British fired, and killed some of our men. There was not a gun fired by any of Captain Parker's, within my knowledge. I was so situated that I must have known it, had any thing of the kind taken place before a total dispersion of our company.... One member of the company told me, many years since, that, after Parker's company had dispersed, and he was at some distance, he gave them the "guts of his gun".

After the British had begun their march to Concord, I returned to the Common, and found Robert Roe and Jonas Parker lying dead at the north corner of the Common, near the Bedford road, and others dead and wounded. I assisted in carrying the dead into the meeting-house. I then proceeded towards Concord with my gun....'[3]

After they left the village, the British music struck up a jaunty tune as the men shuffled along the road. None had been seriously hurt. At Concord men had gathered. Among the Americans who took down their muskets and scurried to Concord was a twenty-three-year-old corporal, Amos Barrett:

'We at Concord heard they was a-coming. The Bell rung at 3 o'clock for an alarm. As I was then a Minuteman, I was soon in town and found my captain and the rest of my company at the post. It wasn't long before there was other minute companies. One company, I believe, of minute men was raised in almost every town to stand at a minute's warning. Before sunrise there was, I believe, 150 of us and more of all that was there.

We thought we would go and meet the British. We marched down towards Lexington about a mile and a half, and we see them a-coming. We halted and stayed there until we got within about 100 rods, then we was ordered to the about face and marched before them with our drums and fifes a-going and also the British. We had grand music.

We marched into town and then over the North Bridge a little more than half a mile, and then on a hill not far from the bridge where we could see and hear what was a-going on.

What the British came out after, was to destroy our stores that we had got laid up for our army. There was in the Town House a number of entrenching tools which they carried out and burnt them. At last they said it was better to burn the house, and set fire to them in the house—but our people begged of them not to burn the house, and put it out. It wasn't long before it was set fire again, but finally it wasn't burnt. There was about 100 barrels of flour in Mr. Hubbard's malt house; they rolled that out and knocked them to pieces and rolled some in the mill pond, which was saved after they was gone.

When we was on the hill by the bridge, there was about eighty or ninety British came to the bridge and there made a halt. After a while they begun to tear up the plank of the bridge. Major Buttrick said if we were all of his mind, he would drive them away from the bridge; they should not tear that up. We all said we would go. We then wasn't loaded; we were all ordered to load—and had strict orders not to fire till they fired first, then to fire as fast as we could.

We then marched on. Captain Davis's minute company marched first, then Captain Allen's minute company, the one I was in next; we marched two deep; It was a long causeway, being round by the river. Captain Davis had got, I believe, within fifteen rods of the British, when they fired three guns one after the other. I see the balls strike in the river on the right of me. As soon as they fired them, they fired on us—their balls whistled well. We then was all ordered to fire that could fire and not kill our own men. It is strange that there war'nt no more killed, but they fired too high. Captain Davis was killed and Mr. Hosmer and a number wounded. We soon drove them from the bridge. When I got over there was two lay dead and another almost dead. We did not follow them. There was eight or ten that was wounded, and a-running and hobbling about, looking back to see if we was after them.

We then saw the whole body a-coming out of town. We then was ordered to lay behind a wall that run over a hill, and when they got nigh enough, Major Buttrick said he would give the word "fire," but they did not come quite so near as he expected before they halted. The Commanding officer ordered the whole battalion to halt and officers to the front march. The officers then marched to the front. There we lay behind the wall, about 200 of us with our guns cocked, expecting every minute to have the word, "fire". Our orders was, if we fired, to fire two or three times and retreat. If we had fired, I believe that we could have killed almost every officer there was in the front, but we had no orders to fire and there wan't a gun fired.

They stayed about ten minutes and then marched back, and we after them. After a while we found them a-marching back towards Boston. We was soon after them. When they got about a mile and a half to a road that comes from Bedford and Billerica, they was waylaid and a great many killed. When I got there, a great many lay dead and the road was bloody.'[4]

At Lexington, there was relief for the weary redcoats. In response to an earlier request for aid, Lord Percy had been sent out with a detachment to escort the bedraggled column back into Boston. A British naval officer aboard the *Empress of Russia* sent an account back to London:

'Colonel Smith was wounded early in the Action and must have been cut off with all those he commanded had not Earl Percy come to his relief, with the first Brigade; on the Appearance of it [at Lexington] our almost conquer'd Granadiers and light infantry gave three cheers and renew'd the defence with more spirits.

Lord Percys courage and good conduct on this occasion must do him immortal honour. Upon taking the Command he Ordered the Kings own to flank on the right, and the 27th on the left, the R[oyal] Welsh Fusiliers to defend the Rear and in this manner retreated for at least 11 Miles before he reached Charlestown for they could not cross at Cambridge where the bridge is, they haveing tore it up, and fill'd the Town and houses with Arm'd men to prevent his passage; our loss in this small essay amounts to 250 Kill'd wounded and Missing. and we are at present cept up in Boston they being in possession of Roxbury a little Village just before our lines with the Royal and Rebel Centinels within musquet shot of each other. The fatigue which our people pass'd through the Day which I have described can hardly be believ'd, having march'd at least 45 miles and the Light Companys perhaps 60, . . .

The Enthusiastic Zeal with which those people have behaved must convince every reasonable man what a difficult and unpleasant task General Gage has before him, even Weamin had firelocks one was seen to fire a Blunderbuss between her Father, and Husband, from their Windows; there they three with an infant child soon suffered the fury of the day. In another

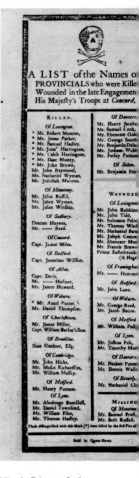

37. A List of the Names of the Provincials who were killed and Wounded in the late Engagement with His Majesty's Troops at Concord, &c.

This unofficial list of the Patriot dead and wounded in the battles of 19 April 1775, was published in Boston and sold immediately after the Concord engagement. Those who fell in the first volley at Lexington are marked with an asterisk.

House which was long defended by 8 resolute fellows, the Granadiers at last got possession when After having run their Bayonets into 7, the 8th continued to abuse them with all the Mort like rage of true Cromwellian, and but a moment before he quitted this World apply'd such epethets as I must leave unmentioned. . . .

The number of Country People who fired on our Troops might be about 5 Thousand ranged long from Concord to Charlestown but not less than 20 Thousand were that day under Arms and on the March to join the Others. their loss we find to be nearly on a footing with our own. three Days have now pass'd without communication with the Country; three more will reduce this Town to a most unpleasant situation for there dependence for provisions was from day to day on supply from the Country that ceasing you may conceive the consequences. preparations are now making on both sides the Neck for attacking and fending.'[5]

The tired troops had camped the night of 19 April on Bunker Hill before being ferried back to Boston. Like an angry flood the rebels poured in to surround Boston. That night their campfires twinkled from the hills, and the following morning pale blue smoke drifted upwards through a blue sky.

The Retreat

From Concord to Lexington of the Army of Wild Irish Asses Defeated by the Brave American Militia

M⁰ Deacon M⁰ Locings M⁰ Mulikens M⁰ Bonds Houses and Barn all Plunder'd and Burnt on April 19.th

38. The Retreat

This unsigned cartoon is evidently one of the few surviving which were made, not by the prolific British Whigs, but by Americans in America. Portraying the Regulars as 'Wild Irish Asses', it emphasizes their plundering and burning of houses on the retreat from Concord on 19 April 1775. The Provincial militia did not advance upon the British in battle formation as here shown, flying the Union Jack with 'Liberty' across the middle; they shot at them from behind trees and stone walls, and from barns and houses. That was why British troops were sent ahead into houses to clear them out and at times set fire to them; this occurred mostly beyond Lexington. Lieutenant Frederick Mackenzie wrote in his diary later, 'Many houses were plundered by the soldiers, notwithstanding the efforts of the officers to prevent it. I have no doubt that this inflamed the Rebels, and made many of them follow us farther than they otherwise would have done.'

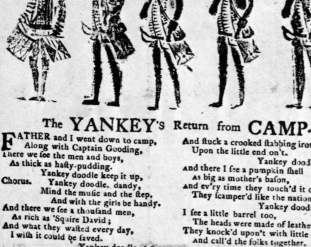

The YANKEY's Return from CAMP.

FATHER and I went down to camp,
 Along with Captain Gooding,
There we see the men and boys,
 As thick as hasty-pudding.
 Yankey doodle keep it up,
Chorus. Yankey doodle, dandy,
 Mind the music and the step,
 And with the girls be handy.
And there we see a thousand men,
 As rich as 'Squire David;
And what they wasted every day,
 I wish it could be saved.
 Yankey doodle, &c.
The 'lasses they eat every day,
 Would keep an house a winter:
They have as much that I'll be bound
 They eat it when they're a mind to.
 Yankey doodle, &c.
And there we see a swamping gun,
 Large as a log of maple,
Upon a ducid little cart,
 A load for father's cattle.
 Yankey doodle, &c.
And every time they shoot it off,
 It takes a horn of powder—
It makes a noise like father's gun,
 Only a nation louder.
 Yankey doodle, &c.
I went as nigh to one myself,
 As 'Siah's underpining;
And father went as nigh again,
 I tho't the deuce was in him.
 Yankey doodle, &c.
Cousin Simon grew so bold,
 I tho't he would have cock'd it:
It scar'd me so, I shrink'd it off,
 And hung by father's pocket.
 Yankey doodle, &c.
And Captain Davis had a gun,
 He kind of clap'd his hand on't,

And stuck a crooked stabbing iron
 Upon the little end on't.
 Yankey doodle, &c.
And there I see a pumpkin shell
 As big as mother's bason,
And ev'ry time they touch'd it off,
 They scamper'd like the nation.
 Yankey doodle, &c.
I see a little barrel too,
 The heads were made of leather,
They knock'd upon't with little clubs,
 And call'd the folks together.
 Yankey doodle, &c.
And there was Captain Washington,
 And gentlefolks about him,
They say he's grown so tarnal proud,
 He will not ride without 'em.
 Yankey doodle, &c.
He got him on his meeting clothes,
 Upon a slapping stallion,
He set the world along in rows,
 In hundreds and in millions.
 Yankey doodle, &c.
The flaming ribbons in their hats,
 They look'd so taring fine, ah,
I wanted pockily to get,
 To give to my Jemimah,
 Yankey doodle, &c.
I see another snarl of men
 A digging graves, they told me,
So tarnal long, so tarnal deep,
 They 'tended they should hold me.
 Yankey doodle, &c.
It scar'd me so, I hook'd it off,
 Nor stop'd, as I remember,
Nor turn'd about 'till I got home,
 Lock'd up in mother's chamber.
 Yankey doodle, &c.

39. The Yankey's Return from Camp

'Yankee Doodle' is one of the best-known American songs, and the only one of the Revolutionary period which is still sung, though never now with the many verses given here, nor the many others now lost. Its origin is unknown, but one version was mentioned in the first American opera, Barton's *The Disappointment*, in 1767, and another is attributed to Dr Shuckberg, a British army surgeon in 1775. Though tune and refrain are older, the words given here are clearly of British authorship, and intended to ridicule the untrained American army forming around Boston, which had a hard time minding 'the music and the step' in its first attempts at drilling. Even a drum is a new experience; the most notable thing about 'Captain Washington' and his 'gentlefolks' is 'the flaming ribbons in their hats'; and the sight of graves for the sick and dying, found in every camp, frightens the rustic into flight. The Americans picked up this satirical ballad cheerfully and made it into a marching song of their own, to fife and drum, almost the only Revolutionary instruments.

Artemus Ward, senior major-general of the Massachusetts militia, suffering from a kidney stone, mounted his horse and jolted down to assume the command of the armed mob surrounding the city. Lord Percy noted that the rebels were 'intrenched up to the chins', while another officer was to feel that 'The Americans are either the cleverest fellows in the world at making strong lines in three or four hours, or the most desperate enemy in defending them'. A British naval surgeon could not bring himself to respect his new enemies:

'There is a large body of them in arms near the town of Boston. Their camp and quarters are plentifully supplied with all sorts of provisions, and the roads are crowded with carts and carriages, bringing them rum, cider, &c. from the neighboring towns, for without New-England rum, a New-England army could not be kept together; they could neither fight nor say their prayers, one with another; they drink at least a bottle of it a day.... This

40. An Appeal for Patriot Troops

This appeal was sent by courier from the Massachusetts Provincial Congress to the towns of Massachusetts and the rest of New England; it was quickly forwarded to the other colonies. It is signed by Dr Joseph Warren, president of the Congress. The response was astonishing. Even before this broadside was issued, by 21 April, two days after Lexington and Concord, the circle of Patriot camps around Boston numbered approximately 9,000 men; by 17 June, when the second battle was fought on Bunker Hill, the American army had grown to 15,000.

In Congreſs, at Watertown, *April* 30, 1775.

Gentlemen,

THE barbarous Murders on our innocent Brethren Wedneſday the 19th Inſtant, has made it abſolutely neceſſary that we immediately raiſe an Army to defend our Wives and our Children from the butchering Hands of an inhuman Soldiery, who, incenſed at the Obſtacles they met with in their bloody Progreſs, and enraged at being repulſed from the Field of Slaughter; will without the leaſt doubt take the firſt Opportunity in their Power to ravage this devoted Country with Fire and Sword: We conjure you, therefore, by all that is dear, by all that is ſacred, that you give all Aſſiſtance poſſible in forming an Army: Our all is at Stake, Death and Devaſtation are the certain Conſequences of Delay, every Moment is infinitely precious, an Hour loſt may deluge your Country in Blood, and entail perpetual Slavery upon the few of your Poſterity, who may ſurvive the Carnage. We beg and entreat, as you will anſwer it to your Country, to your own Conſciences, and above all as you will anſwer to God himſelf, that you will haſten and encourage by all poſſible Means, the Inliſtment of Men to form the Army, and ſend them forward to Head-Quarters, at Cambridge, with that Expedition, which the vaſt Importance and inſtant Urgency of the Affair demands.

JOSEPH WARREN, Preſident, P. T.

army, which you will hear so much said, and see so much wrote about, is truly nothing but a drunken, canting, lying, praying, hypocritical rabble, without order, subjection, discipline, or cleanliness; and must fall to pieces of itself in the course of three months, notwithstanding every endeavour of their leaders, teachers, and preachers, though the last are the most canting, hypocritical, lying scoundrels that this, or any other country ever afforded.'[6]

But despite such contempt, the rebel army held fast in the earthworks around Boston. And every day more straggled in, some armed with little more than their enthusiasm. Among them was a little arrogant man, whose swarthy face belied an active brain. He soon discovered a way to make himself useful. The most critical shortage of the American army was a lack of heavy siege cannon. Knowing that heavy cannon suitable for a siege lay rusting on the dilapidated and lightly garrisoned fort at Ticonderoga at the southern end of Lake Champlain, Benedict Arnold persuaded the Massachusetts Committee of Safety to issue him a commission.

Others had the same idea. A group from Hartford had interested the giant Ethan Allen and his 'Green Mountain Boys' in the same project. While recruiting his force, Arnold heard of Allen's expedition. Boiling with anger, he rode across country to assume command of the assault that he considered to be rightfully his. Allen's force refused to parade with him, and after much argument it was decided that Arnold and Allen should enter the fort side by side. It wasn't much of a conquest. The garrison of forty-five men were described by their own officers as 'old, wore out, & unserviceable', while one of the latest engineering reports had described the fort's walls as 'leaning towards the horizon'. Later, when Ethan Allen wrote his narrative, filled with bombast and noble sentiments, he declared that he had summoned the garrison to surrender 'In the name of the great Jehovah, and the Continental Congress'. Lieutenant Jocelyn Feltham of His Majesty's Twenty-Sixth Foot, and second in command of Ticonderoga, reported it differently. On May 10,

'On which morning about half an hour after three in my sleep I was awaken'd by numbers of shrieks, & words no quarter, no quarter from a number of arm'd rabble. I jumped up about which time I heard the noise continue in the area of the fort. I ran undress'd to knock at Capt. Delaplace's door & receive his orders or wake him, the door was fast. The room I lay in being close to Capt. Delaplace's, I stept back, put on my coat & waist coat & return'd to his room, there being little possibility of getting to the men as there were numbers of rioters on the bastions of the wing of the fort on which the door of my room and back door of Capt. Delaplace's led.

With great difficulty I got into his room, being pursued from which there was a door down by stairs into the area of the fort. I asked Capt. Delaplace, who was now just up, what I should do, & offer'd to force my way if possible to our men. On opening this door, the bottom of the stairs was filled with rioters & many were forcing their way up, knowing the Comm*g* Officer lived there, as they had broke open the lower rooms where the officers live in winter, and could not find them there.

From the top of the stairs I endeavour'd to make them hear me, but it was impossible. On making a signal not to come up the stairs, they stop'd, & proclaim'd silence among themselves. I then address'd them, but in a stile not agreeable to them. I ask'd them a number of questions, expecting to amuse them till our people fired which I must certainly own I thought would

48

have been the case. After asking them the most material questions I could think, viz., by what authority they entered his majesties fort, who were the leaders, what their intent, &c, &c, I was inform'd by one Ethan Allen and one Benedict Arnold that they had a joint command, Arnold informing me he came from instructions rec*d* from the congress at Cambridge which he afterwards show'd me. Mr. Allen told me his orders were from the province of Connecticut & that he must have immediate possession of the fort and all the effects of George the third (those were his words), Mr. Allen insisting on this with a drawn sword over my head & numbers of his follower's firelocks presented at me alledging I was the commanding officer & to give up the fort, and if it was not comply'd with, or that there was a single gun fired in the fort neither man, woman, or child would be left alive in the fort. Mr. Arnold begg'd it in a genteel manner but without success, it was owing to him they were prevented getting into Cap*t* Delaplace's room, after they found I did not command.

Cap*t* Delaplace being now dress'd, came out, when after talking to him some time, they put me back into the room. They placed two sentry's on me and took Cap*t* Delaplace down stairs. They also placed sentrys at the back door, from the beginning of the noise till half an hour after this I never saw a Soldier, tho' I heard a great noise in their rooms and can not account otherwise than that they must have been seiz'd in their beds before I got on the stairs, or at the first coming in, which must be the case as Allen wounded one of the guards on his struggling with him in the guard room immediately after his entrance into the fort. When I did see our men they were drawn up without arms, which were all put into one room over which they placed sentrys and allotted one to each soldier.

Their strength at first coming, that is the number they had ferry'd over in the night, amounted to about 90, but from their entrance & shouting, they were constantly landing men till about 10 OClock when I suppose there were about 300, & by the next morning at least another 100 who I suppose, were waiting the event & came now to join in the plunder which was most rigidly perform'd as to liquors, provisions, &c, whether belonging to his majesty or private property. About noon on the 10th May, our men were sent to the landing at L: George, & sent over next day, then march'd to Albany to Hartford in Connecticut where they arrived on the 22*d*.'[7]

Other British posts of Crown Point and St John's were also taken. Back at Boston the siege had droned on. There were skirmishes and alarums, but not until June was there action of a more spectacular nature. In May British reinforcements had begun to arrive. On 25 May, the *Cerberus*, named for the three-headed mastiff guarding the gates of Hell, dropped her hook in Boston harbour. Aboard were Major-Generals William Howe, Henry Clinton, and John Burgoyne. Some London wit saluted this 'triumvirate of reputation' with:

> Behold the Cerberus the Atlantic plough.
> Her precious cargo, Burgoyne, Clinton, Howe.
> Bow, wow, wow!

Among the hazards that the British suffered were that on either side of Boston were two commanding promontories: Bunker Hill on Charlestown peninsula and Dorchester Heights on Dorchester Neck. Information reached

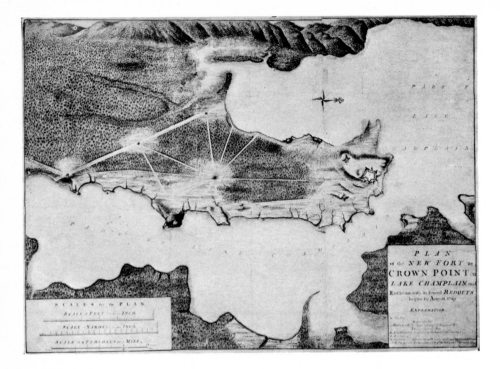

41. Crown Point. *Brasier*

Crown Point on Lake Champlain was a strategic fortress in the Burgoyne campaign, as it had been in the French and Indian War. Under Sir Jeffrey Amherst it was strengthened with enfilading alleys cut through the dense forest to prevent surprise attacks. This beautifully designed and executed plan was made for Amherst in his slow and cautious advance against the French in 1759–60. William Brasier was surveyor and draftsman to the commanding engineer of the campaign, Captain Thomas Sowers, and later to his successor, Captain Henry Gordon.

rebel headquarters in Cambridge that Gage was planning to seize and fortify Dorchester during the night of 18 June. The rebels decided to take the initiative. Using the black of night on 16 June to mask their movement they slipped across to Charlestown Neck and began to throw up crude fortifications. They had been ordered to occupy Bunker Hill, but for some reason they selected Breed's Hill, not so high as Bunker, but nearer Boston. Even as they dug, Gage and his generals were planning the following day's assault on Dorchester Heights, an operation expected to be 'very easy'. John Burgoyne reported the subsequent events:

'On the 17th, at dawn of day, we found the enemy had pushed intrenchments with great diligence during the night, on the Heights of Charlestown, and we evidently saw that every hour gave them fresh strength; it therefore became necessary to alter our plan, and attack on that side.

Howe, as second in command, was detached with about two thousand men and landed on the outward side of the peninsula, covered with shipping without opposition; he was to advance from thence up the hill which was over Charlestown, where the strength of the enemy lay; he had under him Brigadier-general Pigot.

Clinton and myself took our stand (for we had not any fixed post) in a large battery directly opposite to Charlestown, and commanded it, and also reaching the heights above it, and thereby facilitating Howe's attack. Howe's disposition was exceeding soldier-like; in my opinion it was perfect. As his first arm advanced up the hill, they met with a thousand impediments from strong fences, and were much exposed. They were also exceeding hurt by musketry from Charlestown, though Clinton and I did not perceive it until Howe sent us word by a boat, and desired us to set fire to the town, which was immediately done; we threw a parcel of shells, and the whole was instantly in flames; our battery afterwards kept an incessant fire on the heights; it was seconded by a number of frigates, floating batteries, and one ship-of-the-line.

And now ensued one of the greatest scenes of war that can be conceived; if we look to the height, Howe's corps ascending the hill in the face of in-trenchments, and in a very disadvantageous ground, was much engaged; to the left the enemy pouring in fresh troops by thousands, over the land; and in the arm of the sea our ships and floating batteries cannonading before them; straight before us a large and noble town in one great blaze—the church-steeples, being timber, were great pyramids of fire above the rest; behind us, the church-steeples and heights of our own camp covered with spectators of the rest of our army which was engaged; the hills round the country covered with spectators; the enemy all in anxious suspense; the roar of canons, mortars, and musketry; the crash of churches, ships upon the stocks, and whole streets falling together, to fill the ear; the storm of the redoubts, with the objects above described, to fill the eye; and the reflection that, perhaps, a defeat was a final loss to the British empire in America, to fill the mind; made the whole a picture, and a complication of horror and

42. An original Sketch of the Burning of Charlestown & Battle of Bunker Hill. *Taken by a British officer from Beacon Hill, Boston*

This little-known sketch of 1775 shows the spire of the West Meeting House in the foreground, and also the Mill Dam, with people walking on it. To the left and right of the spire are the British warships, *Glasgow* and *Lively*, bombarding the American troops on the Charlestown shore. At the right, the village of Charlestown is burning, below the slopes of Breed's Hill. The sketch was made for Lord Rawdon, and was drawn from Beacon Hill, 138 feet above sea-level. Dr Emmet secured it from a sale of the effects of the Marquis of Hastings, a descendant of Lord Rawdon.

importance beyond any thing that ever came my lot to be witness to. . . . except two cannonballs that went a hundred yards over our heads, we were not in any part of the direction of the enemy's shot.

A moment of the day was critical; Howe's left were staggered; two battalions had been sent over to reinforce them, but we perceived them on the beach seeming in embarrassment what way to march. Clinton then, next for business, took the part without waiting for orders, to throw himself into a boat to head them; he arrived in time to be of service; the day ended with glory, and the success was most important, considering the ascendancy it gave the regular troops; but the loss was uncommon in officers, for the numbers engaged. Howe was untouched, but his aid-de-camp, Sherwin, was killed; Jorden, a friend of Howe's, who came *en gage le de coeur*, to see the campaign (a shipmate of ours on board the Cerberus, and who acted as aid-de-camp), is badly wounded. Pigot is unhurt, but he behaved like a hero. . . . Captain Addison, our poor old friend, who arrived but the day before, and was to have dined with me on the day of the action, was also killed; his son was upon the field at the same time.'[8]

On 2 July 1775, a little over two weeks after the battle, while the British were still licking their wounds, a new American commander rode into Cambridge. The Massachusetts Provincial Congress found that supporting the army around Boston was too expensive and they had implored the Continental Congress to take the army under its wing. Congress had adopted the army and had also selected a new general to command. Primarily because of the influence of John Adams, George Washington was selected. It was a wise political manoeuvre on the part of Adams who wanted to be sure that Virginia entered the fight. The new commanding general didn't think much

43. Sketches identifying figures in Trumbull's 'The Battle of Bunker's Hill'

44. The Battle of Bunker's Hill near Boston. *John Trumbull*

Lord Rawdon, officer of the British Grenadiers, wrote an account of the Battle of Bunker Hill to his uncle on 20 June 1775; he said, 'The famous Doctor Warren, the greatest incendiary in all America, was killed on the spot'; and another officer added, 'He died in his best cloaths'. Here in Trumbull's first and most famous battle scene Warren lies dying on the wind-swept height of Breed's Hill, as the desperate British surge finally reaches the top. President of the Massachusetts Provincial Congress, important member of the Committee of Safety, and the most recently appointed of Washington's major-generals, Warren set out for the Charlestown penin- sula on hearing the alarm in Cambridge without stopping to change his finery. Actually, he did not die sur- rounded by all the great of the battle, as Trumbull has painted him. No one saw him fall; he was killed instantly by a ball in the head. In this picture the mortally wounded British Major Pitcairn is being carried from the field.

John Trumbull, son of the Governor of Connecticut, was an aide-de-camp to General Washington in 1775, and later deputy adjutant-general of the Northern Department under General Gates. After the execution of André in 1780, he was seized as a corresponding adjutant-general, and imprisoned for seven months. In 1786, again at work in West's studio, he painted this picture of Bunker Hill. Adams and Jefferson, ministers after the Revolution in England and France, both sat for Trumbull, and encouraged him to go on to become perhaps the greatest painter of Revolutionary scenes. Though Trumbull used imagination in the construction of his tableaux, he peopled them with persons of whom he had made careful portrait studies. Here, in an engraving of the original begun in 1786, he surrounds Warren with Putnam, Prescott, Parker of Lexington, among the Americans, and Howe, Clinton and Small for the British, and shows the gift for motion, grouping, and feeling which took his pictures to the walls of the United States Capitol.

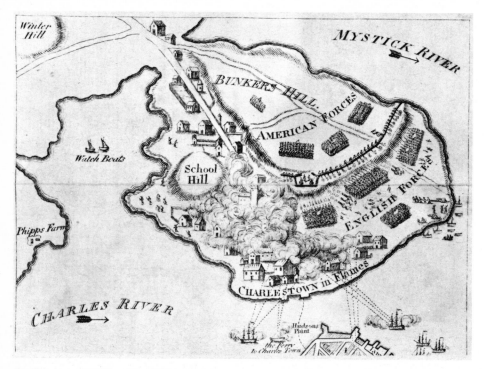

45. Boston and Bunker Hill. *Murray*

This is a plan of Boston and the Charlestown peninsula, with 'Charlestown in Flames' during the battle of 17 July. As in many contemporary maps, there is no differentiation between Breed's Hill and the higher Bunker Hill behind it, which was used by the rebels primarily as a grouping place and a refuge for stragglers. The British 'watch boats' near Charlestown Neck poured a withering fire on the road which made earlier reinforcement difficult and increased the nightmare of later retreat and escape.

Numerous maps of Boston were published in England after Bunker Hill; Murray's map appears to be based on a section of 'Boston and its Environs' made during the siege by Lieut. Richard Williams of the 23rd regiment, published in 1776 by A. Drury, though Murray has many additional details.

of his new command. With the same methodical preparation with which he laid out his crops down in Virginia the General began striving to transform a mob into some semblance of a fighting machine. A chaplain, the Reverend William Emerson, commented:

'There is great overturning in the camp, as to order and authority. New lords, new laws. The Generals Washington and [Charles] Lee are upon the lines every day. New orders from his Excellency are read to the respective regiments every morning after prayers. The strictest government is taking place, and great distinction is made between officers and soldiers. Every one is made to know his place and keep in it, or be tied up and receive thirty or forty lashes according to his crime.

Thousands are at work every day from four till eleven o'clock in the morning. It is surprising how much work has been done. The lines are extended almost from Cambridge to Mystic River, so that very soon it will be morally impossible for the enemy to get between the works, except in one place, which is supposed to be left purposely unfortified to entice the enemy out of their fortresses. Who would have thought, twelve months past, that all Cambridge and Charlestown would be covered over with American camps, and cut up into forts and intrenchments, and all the lands, fields, orchards laid common, horses and cattle feeding on the choicest mowing land, whole fields of corn eaten down to the ground, and large parks of well regulated locusts cut down for firewood and other public uses? This, I must say, looks a little melancholy.

My quarters are at the foot of the famous Prospect Hill, where such great preparations are made for the reception of the enemy. It is very diverting to walk among the camps. They are as different in their form, as the owners are in their dress; and every tent is a portraiture of the temper and taste of the persons, who encamp in it. Some are made of boards, and some of sailcloth. Some partly of one and partly of the other. Again, others are made of stone and turf, brick or brush. Some are thrown up in a hurry, others curiously wrought with doors and windows, done with wreathes and withes in the manner of a basket. Some are your proper tents and marquees, looking like the regular camp of the enemy. In these are the Rhode Islanders, who are furnished with tent-equipage, and every thing in the most exact English style. However, I think this great variety is rather a beauty than a blemish in the army.'9

46. View of the Attack on Bunker's Hill, with the Burning of Charles Town, June 17, 1775. *Millar*
The horrendous flames and thick black smoke billowing up from Charlestown represent an English artist's view of the Battle of Bunker Hill, which made a great impression in London. He has made the slope of Breed's Hill into cliffs, endowed the Americans with a far stronger fortification than they had, and drawn the houses of Boston as he imagined them. This engraving by J. Lodge from Millar's drawing was made for Edward Barnard's *A New, Comprehensive, and Complete History of England*, London, 1783.

In November Thomas Gage was recalled to England and William Howe replaced him as commander-in-chief. Siege operations are, at the best, tedious, and time hung heavy, with the monotony broken only by infrequent raids and desultory bombardments. The weather turned cool and then cold. The occasional cannonades by both armies would bring out spectators who lined the roads and crowded the hills around Boston. January 1776 saw the official beginning of the Continental Army and a restructuring of the mob besieging Boston. To mark the occasion, Washington raised a new flag, 'in Compliment to the United Colonies', an ensign of thirteen red and white stripes with the British Union Jack in the canton. This moment was accompanied with due ceremony, and the American General William Heath noted that the day

'presented a great change in the American army. The officers and men of the new regiments were joining their respective corps; those of the old regiments were going home by hundreds and by thousands. The best arms, such

47. Sir William Howe. *C. Corbett*

When their eldest brother was killed at Ticonderoga in 1758, Sir William Howe wrote to his elder brother Richard, Lord Howe, 'Remember how much our dependence is on you . . . think of a Family whose only hope now is your safety.' This close relationship between the brothers persisted throughout their shared command in the American Revolution; so also did the difference in their characters indicated here. Sir William, like his brother, was an Eton-educated aristocrat, with a record of able military command, some of it won in America. He shared his brother's difficult combination of aims, to conciliate and preserve the colonies, and to maintain British parliamentary supremacy, by force if necessary. He lacked, however, Lord Howe's confidence and strong sense of responsibility. In his leisure hours he was a gambler, a drinker, and a ladies' man. Though he seldom lost a battle when he was in command, he frequently failed to engage in one when the Continental Army might have been taken, preferring to defer action, to recover lost territory, or to follow a design of his own, such as wooing the Loyalists of Pennsylvania. He had allowed the destruction of Burgoyne; he had failed to capture or halt Washington; he had been recalled to England at his own request. Yet he saw nothing inappropriate in being the centre of the extravagant fête, or Meschianza, offered him by his officers at the end of the winter in Philadelphia.

48. *(Overleaf)* Battle of Bunker Hill. *Winthrop Chandler*

Winthrop Chandler, a 'limner' of rural Connecticut, painted this scene from the accounts of his friends in the militia who had taken part in the battle. The viewpoint is from the top of Breed's Hill. The details are graphic; a sailor clings to the rigging of the nearest ship, soldiers are wading to shore from a transport, and British regulars, advancing up the slopes, are falling in deadly combat with Patriot defenders. The topography is inaccurate; three forts surrounding the town are misplaced, with Castle William adjacent to the peninsula instead of across the bay. The forts are flying the Grand Union flag, with its thirteen stripes for the colonies and its British union emblem for the Crown. This flag may have been the result of a conference between Washington and the Continental Congress in October 1775, and therefore not at Bunker Hill. Since it was abolished in June 1777, Chandler probably painted this scene before that date.

Winthrop Chandler is interesting in the Revolutionary Period for two reasons. His work is an effective example of the native tradition in American art, as against that great Anglo-American triumvirate, Copley, Stuart and West. Also, he was an apparently neutral member in a family, like so many in America, fiercely divided in loyalties. His legal guardian, General McClellan, had marched to Lexington with Putnam. He painted with equal care his Patriot brother, Captain Samuel Chandler, with a battle scene behind him, and his cousin, Nathaniel Chandler, son of the famous Loyalist called the 'Honest Refugee', who was in British service during the Revolution.

This view of the Battle of Bunker Hill was painted as a fireboard for the home of Peter Chandler of Pomfret, Connecticut. It is now mounted as an overmantel in the home of Mrs Gardner Richardson, Plaine Hill, Woodstock, Connecticut.

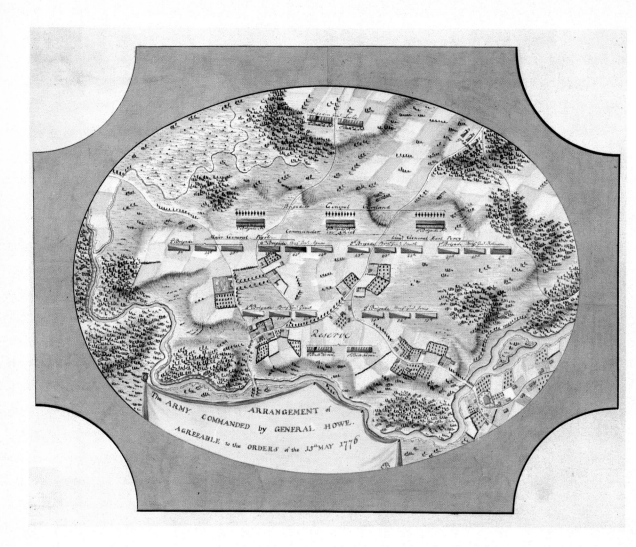

The ARMY ARRANGEMENT of COMMANDED by GENERAL HOWE. AGREEABLE to the ORDERS of the 15th MAY 1776

49. General Howe prepares his troops for the invasion of New York. *Barron*

On a plain near Halifax, Nova Scotia, Howe exercised his troops, including reinforcements from England, in preparation for the expedition to New York. This manuscript plan by the military draftsman Edward Barron was executed for Lord Percy, whose name appears on it with his command.

as were fit for service, were detained from the soldiers who were going home; they were to be paid for; but it created much uneasiness. Such a change, in the very teeth of the enemy, is a most delicate manoeuvre; but the British did not attempt to take any advantage of it.'[10]

And now the streams were frozen thick enough to bear the weight of heavy ordnance. On 24 January 1776 plump Henry Knox waddled into town, bringing with him forty-three cannon and sixteen mortars from Ticonderoga. General Washington now had the artillery to conduct a siege in proper fashion, although there was a 'crying out for powder—powder—ye Gods, give us powder'.

Dorchester Heights near Roxbury commanded the town of Boston, and the occupation of this promontory would result either in bringing on a general action or the evacuation of Boston by the enemy. This was the climax of the policy of containment. The militia was called in, supplies were collected, bandages were prepared, and boats were assembled in the Charles River, the latter in the event of the occupation of Dorchester Heights being successful, when the long projected attack on Boston itself might be carried forward. To

50. The Boston–Albany Road *(detail)*.

Over this road in January 1776 Colonel Henry Knox and his men, with sleighs and oxen, dragged 43 cannon and 14 mortars, captured at Ticonderoga, from Albany, New York, to Framingham, twenty miles west of Boston.

Governor Francis Bernard of Massachusetts had surveys of the roads from Boston to Albany and from Boston to Penobscot, Maine, made by Francis Miller and others. With the exception of two short stretches in New Jersey, they are the most extensive detailed road maps of the colonial period, showing courthouses, taverns, dwellings, and crossroads along the routes.

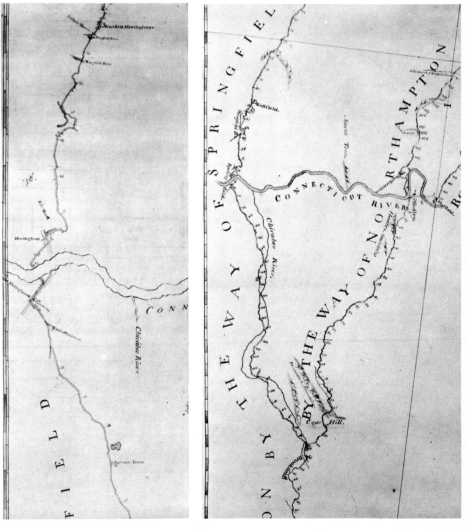

51, 52. Panoramic Sketches of Boston and Vicinity from Mount Whoredom.
  Robertson

'View of Boston Shewing the heights of Dorchester taken from Mount Whoredom, 24*th* Jan*ry* 1776. N*o* 1.'

'N*o* 2: View of the Neck & lines at Boston W*th* the Rebel Works at Roxborough.'

Nos. 3 and 4, not reproduced, extend from Cambridge past Phipps's Farm to the Citadel at Charlestown, 23 February 1776.

In early 1776 Captain-Lieutenant (eventually Lieutenant-General) Archibald Robertson of the Royal Engineers made these five sketches from the vantage point of Mount Whoredom, a lower elevation adjacent to Beacon Hill in Boston. Robertson completed the emplacement of a battery of 32-pounders on the Mount on 1 March. On the night of 4 March Washington achieved the sudden and decisive fortification of Dorchester Heights (shown in sketch No. 1) which closed the shipping lane to Boston and placed the town under its fire power. 'The Materials for the whole Works must all have been carried', noted Robertson in his diary; 'Chandeleers, fascines, Gabions, Trusses of hay pressed and Barrels, a most astonishing nights work must have Employ'd from 15 to 20,000 men.'

A full-scale attack on Dorchester under Earl Percy planned the following evening was thwarted by 'a very tempestuous bad night'; on 6 March General Howe announced the departure for Halifax.

The narrowness of Boston Neck is clearly shown in sketch No. 2; complaints were made that the bowsprits of anchored vessels impeded wagon traffic on the causeway.

Robertson's drawings, paintings, and maps, which he continued to produce throughout the course of the war, show native skill as well as the trained and accurate eye of an engineer and topographer.

divert the attention of the British from these activities, a severe cannonade was initiated by the Americans on 2 March, which the enemy returned with enthusiasm. A council of war was called to fix the time of the occupation. At the suggestion of Colonel Thomas Mifflin, it was decided that the night of 4 March would be appropriate, in that the following day was the anniversary of the Boston 'Massacre' and the troops would exert themselves to greater efforts. On the night of 4 March, the American cannon roared again, throwing a total of 155 shot and 13 shells into the city. It was near seven o'clock when about 2,000 men under General John Thomas marched for Dorchester Heights, followed by 300 carts loaded with fascines and bales of hay. During this time,

'There was an almost incessant roar of cannon and mortars during the night, on both sides. The Americans took possession of Dorchester Heights, and nearly completed their works on both the hills by morning. Perhaps there never was so much work done in so short a space of time. The adjoining orchards were cut down to make the abbattis; and a very curious and novel mode of defence was added to these works. The hills on which they were erected were steep, and clear of trees and bushes. Rows of barrels, filled with earth, were placed round the works. They presented only the appearance of strengthening the works, but the real design was, in case the enemy made an

attack, to have rolled them down the hill. They would have descended with such increasing velocity, as must have thrown the assailants into the utmost confusion, and have killed and wounded great numbers.'[11]

Young John Trumbull, an American brigade major who liked to draw (he became one of the most famous artists of the Revolution), observed the finale:

'Our movement was not discovered by the enemy until the following morning, and we had an interrupted day to strengthen the works which had been commenced the night preceding. During the day we saw distinctly the preparations which the enemy were making to dislodge us. The entire water front of Boston lay open to our observation, and we saw the embarkation of troops from the various wharves, on board the ships, which hauled off in succession, and anchored in a line in our front, a little before sunset, prepared to land the troops in the morning.

We were in high spirits, well prepared to receive the threatened attack. Our positions on the summits of two smooth, steep hills, were strong by nature, and well fortified. We had at least twenty pieces of artillery mounted on them, amply supplied with ammunition, and a very considerable force of well armed infantry. We waited with impatience for the attack, when we meant to emulate, and hoped to eclipse, the glories of Bunker's Hill. In the evening the commander in chief visited us, and examined all our points of

53. Panoramic Sketches of Boston and Vicinity from Mount Whoredom. *Robertson*

'No. 5. Continuation from No. 4 to No. 1, which completes the circle of Boston from the same Point. In this shewn, Chas. Town in Ruins, Bunker's Hill, Noodles Island & that part of the Town call'd North End & New Boston, *7th March 1776.*'

54. Israel Putnam. *John Trumbull*

In this pencil sketch, Trumbull has caught the spirit of 'Old Put' better than the more formal paintings. Putnam was not one of the greatest of the military commanders, but with his indomitable courage, he came near to being the folk hero of the Revolution. One sees him again and again in dangerous and colourful situations: crawling into a wolf den in Connecticut to shoot a marauding wolf 'by the light of his eyes'; rescued from Indian captors just as the torch was about to light his pyre; driving the 125 sheep from Brooklyn across Boston Neck to relieve the city; flinging down his plough when the news of Lexington reached him, and starting for Boston in his farm clothes. He was one of the first four major-generals appointed by the Continental Congress; he commanded at Bunker Hill, and made the first entry into Boston after the siege. He was less successful on Long Island; in the New York and New Jersey campaigns, Washington found him insubordinate. He died of a stroke in 1779.

preparation for defense. Soon after his visit, the rain, which had commenced, increased to a violent storm, and heavy gale of wind, which deranged all the enemy's plan of debarkation, driving the ships foul of each other, and from their anchors, in utter confusion, and thus put a stop to the intended operation.'[12]

Frustrated by the elements, and with Bunker Hill still green in his memory, General Howe decided to follow the orders he had received earlier in the year and evacuate Boston. On 17 March the troops left the town, unmolested by the Americans who allowed them to leave on Howe's assurance that he would not burn the town. The fleet tarried in the harbour until 27 March, and then spread their sails for Halifax, Nova Scotia. There it was hoped that the troops could refresh themselves, take on provisions and supplies, and receive the promised reinforcements from England while General Howe planned his next campaign.

Washington, feeling that New York would be the most logical place for the next British strike, sent troops marching for that town almost as soon as the white sails of the enemy fleet disappeared over the horizon. On 2 April 1776 British anchors were dropped in the harbour of Halifax. A good harbour, Halifax nevertheless proved unsuitable for troop cantonments.

Provisions were scarce and prices high. The navy found it difficult to secure the pitch, tar, and other naval stores so necessary for the maintenance of ships. Victuallers kept the army fairly well supplied with food, but the navy, for a short time, was forced to go on two-thirds rations.

Idle troops found it easy to discard discipline and Howe exercised them by repairing docks, making cartridges, and working on fortifications. While some officers amused themselves by hunting, the general busied himself drawing up plans for an assault upon New York. Intelligence reported that Washington, travelling as a 'private Gentleman', had already arrived in that city and was superintending the construction of fortifications. Some troops were detached to Quebec to relieve that garrison, at the time undergoing siege by the rebels. When Howe had word that he would soon receive a large reinforcement, he began to embark his troops aboard transports. Late in the afternoon of 11 June the wind fell around to the north-east and the convoy upped anchor and set its sails for New York.

Eleven days later, Richard, Lord Howe, newly appointed to command the fleet on the North American station, arrived in Halifax, only to learn that his brother, the General, had already sailed. Ambrose Serle, civilian secretary to Lord Howe, commented on the harbour:

'The Country, about the Mouth of the Harbor, appeared very rugged and barren in some Parts, & in others wholly covered with Trees and lofty Pines, which looked above the Rest like so many Pinnacles or Steeples of Churches. The Smell of the Land & of the Spruce-trees was very pleasant, after so long a Voyage, in which we had no better Effluvia than the Hold of a crouded Ship, or at best the Smell of Ropes & Tar. We had no divine Service this Day. In the Evening, we sailed out of the Harbour, in order to join the Fleet and Troops.

As I did not go up to the Town, and therefore could only view it and the Harbor at a Distance, I can say nothing of them but by Report. The Town is very irregularly & poorly built, and depends upon the Fleet & Army for its principal Support. So large a Fleet & Army, as were lately there, drained the Province of Provisions, & even the Farmers' breeding Stocks. Meat was at the Rate of 1/- a Pound; & it was a Favor to purchase it so. The Price of an Egg is Sixpence. The Harbor is certainly capacious, & said to be one of the finest & best in the World. We sailed out of the Harbor in a fine Evening; the Light House bearing about a League to the Westward, which made a very splendid appearance, contrasted with the Darkness of the Night.'[13]

But in the meantime, there had been high adventure in Canada, for both rebel and redcoat.

3. Thrust to the North

55. General Richard Montgomery

Commander of one branch of the two-pronged invasion of Canada in 1775, he was on the American side by choice, not birth. He reluctantly accepted the Continental Congress's appointment as their second brigadier-general in 1775, performed brilliantly at Chambly and St John's, took Montreal, and lost his life at Quebec.

To the north, Canada sprawled like a wilderness harlot, flourishing a beckoning finger to the rebellious colonies. Already there was talk of that province becoming the fourteenth in insurrection. The key was Quebec, and from the beginning there had been many who advocated the taking of that citadel. The Continental Congress had procrastinated, but finally in the fall of 1775 there had been authorization for two spearheads to strike north. One column, under the leadership of young Irish-born Brigadier-General Richard Montgomery, who had served in Canada during the Seven Years War, was to drive north from Lake Champlain, take Montreal and then swing eastward to Quebec. Farther to the east, the other column, under Benedict Arnold, was to thrust its way through the wilderness, along the Kennebec and Chaudière rivers, to make a junction with Montgomery's command before Quebec. By early September, Montgomery had laid siege to St John's, the fortress guarding the entrance from Lake Champlain into the Sorel River and the water route to the St Lawrence. Ethan Allen, no longer in command of the Green Mountain Boys, was dispatched on a scouting and recruiting expedition towards Montreal. His ambition flamed forth, fired by a dream of freshening his laurels by capturing Montreal. A makeshift army of British regulars and Canadian militia sallied out to meet him. Those recruits taken up by Allen quickly melted off through the forest. Allen was captured and later sent in irons to England.

To facilitate his operations, Montgomery sent a party down to besiege the fort at Chambly, twelve miles towards Montreal from St John's. This stronghold surrendered on 19 October, thereby cutting off communications with the St Lawrence and providing valuable stores and powder for the primary operation at St John's. On 2 November that post surrendered.

A New York officer described the last days of the siege:

'On Saturday, the 28th ultimo, the main body of the Army decamped from the south, and marched to the north side of the fort, under the command of General Wooster. We were joined in the evening by General Montgomery, and the same night we began to throw up a breastwork (on an eminence which entirely commanded the enemy's work,) in order to erect a battery of cannon and mortars; this battery they kept continually pelting at with grape shot and shells, but without doing us the least injury, until Wednesday morning, when we opened our battery, consisting of three twelve and one nine-pounders, three mortars, and as many cohorns, with which we kept up an almost incessant blaze on them the great part of the day, and likewise from our battery on the east side of the river, which the enemy returned with great spirit. Late in the afternoon, I received a message from General Montgomery, ordering me to cease firing until further orders; these orders were extremely disagreeable to me, when I saw some of my men bleeding before my eyes, and dying with the wounds they had received.

On our ceasing to fire, the General ordered a parley to be beat, and sent in an Officer to demand a surrender of the fort. Two officers soon after returned

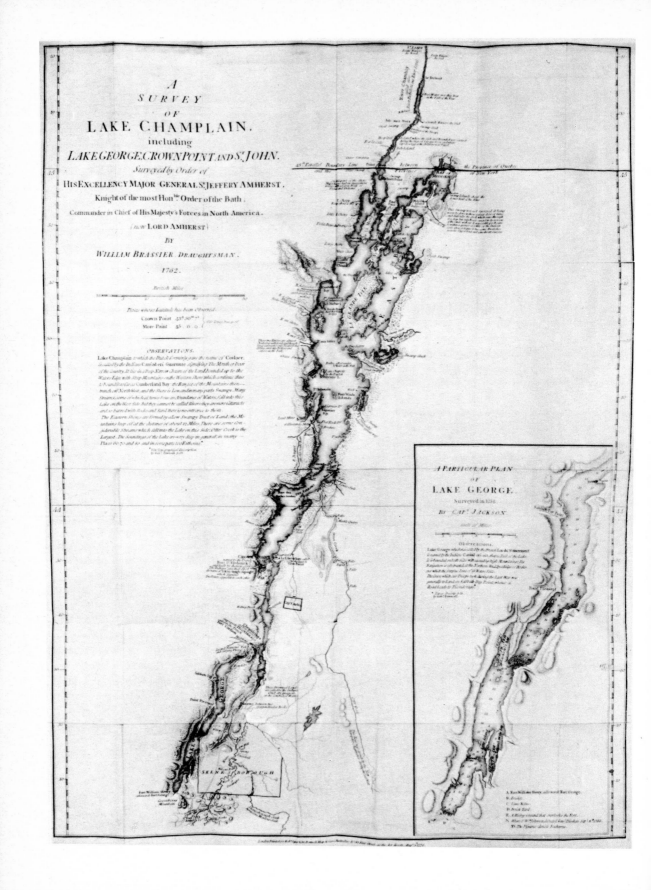

A
SURVEY
OF
LAKE CHAMPLAIN,
including
LAKE GEORGE, CROWN POINT and St. JOHN.
Surveyed by Order of
HIS EXCELLENCY MAJOR GENERAL St JEFFERY AMHERST,
Knight of the most Hon.ble Order of the Bath.
Commander in Chief of His Majesty's Forces in North America.
(NOW LORD AMHERST)
BY
WILLIAM BRASSIER DRAUGHTSMAN.
1762.

A PARTICULAR PLAN
OF
LAKE GEORGE
Surveyed in 1756
BY CAP.t JACKSON

56. A Survey of Lake Champlain, including Lake George.
William Brasier

William Brasier (his own spelling of his name on numerous manuscript maps) was 'draughtsman in the office of ordnance' for Amherst during the French and Indian War. This fine map, first published in 1776 and later revised, was the best printed map of the two lakes during the Revolution; it was printed separately and appeared in Sayer and Bennett's *American Military Pocket Atlas* (1776), published for the use of officers, and in Faden's *North American Atlas*.

with him, and were led blindfold through the camp to the General's tent, where a pretty long conference was held, and they promised the General an answer from the commanding officer the next morning; which promise they complied with. The answer imported, that if they should receive no relief within four days, he would then send in some proposals. The General replied, that he must have an explicit answer next morning, and the garrison must remain prisoners of war, at all events; and that if they had any intention to renew hostilities they need signify it by firing a gun, as a signal. This, though unpalatable, they were at length obliged to digest, as you see by the capitulation. . . .

I have been all day at the Fort, examining the stores, and we are to begin our march to Montreal this morning and my fingers and senses are so benumbed with cold, that I can scarcely write at all, owing to a northeasterly wind and plenty of snow, which is now falling in abundance.'[1]

By 12 November Montgomery was before Montreal. With his promise of generous terms the city surrendered, and the Americans marched in the following day. The way was now open for a strike down the St Lawrence to Quebec where he was to be joined by Arnold's force.

Arnold had returned to Boston from the conquest of Lake Champlain, restless and planning methods further to enhance his stature. He proposed a Canadian campaign to Washington, who saw in the fiery and determined

57. St John's, on the Sorel River. *Anburey*

St John's was an important fort and staging point on the Richelieu or Sorel River above the Chambly Rapids, with a short land route to Montreal and naval facilities for expeditions to and from Lake Champlain. It was the first British fort which General Richard Montgomery had to take on his way in September 1775 from captured Ticonderoga to the hoped-for capture of Quebec. Garrisoned by 700 men under Major Preston, St John's put up a stiff resistance. After a two-month siege and the capitulation of Fort Chambly at the rapids, Preston had to surrender; the Americans were delighted to find in the fort 'seventeen pieces of brass artillery . . . two royal howitzers, several mortars, cohorns, and a considerable number of iron cannon'. They went on to capture Montreal.

little man an almost ideal leader for such a project. Big, bluff Daniel Morgan of Virginia was given the command of the three rifle companies that were to go along with the battalion of volunteers. On 13 September 1775 they marched. Among those who were disappointed at not being selected for the

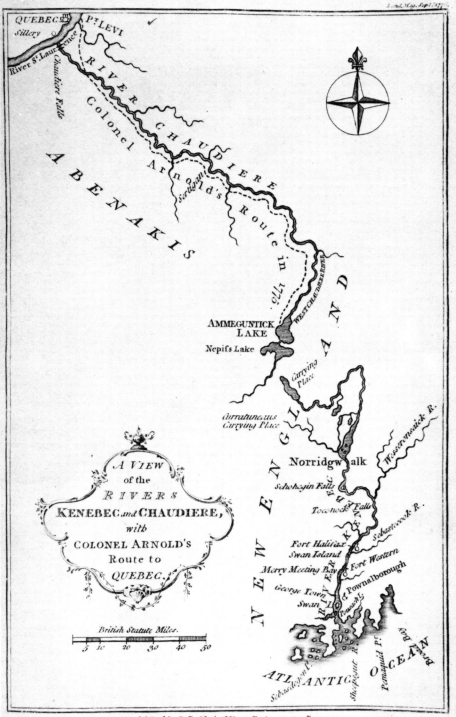

58. Benedict Arnold's route to Quebec, 1775

The expedition of Colonel Arnold to Quebec was a constant and desperate struggle against difficulties of terrain, bitter cold, and hunger. Of nearly 1,100 men, most of them young and filled with enthusiasm and patriotism, fewer than 700 reached Quebec. Planned to be part of a two-pronged attack, Arnold's contingent had to wait for ammunition until the arrival of Montgomery.

Arnold knew the account of Montresor, who had made the same journey in the winter of 1760 and drew maps of the route in 1761. But he did not know the number and length of portages through 'a direful howling wilderness, not describable'.

On 9 November after a most hazardous journey, the expedition reached the St Lawrence; but by 27 November, when Montgomery arrived with 300 men and desperately needed equipment, the garrison in Quebec had increased to over 1,700 soldiers.

adventure was Jesse Lukens who walked along with the men as far as Lynn, nine miles from Cambridge:

'Here I took leave of them with a *wet eye*. The drums beat and away they go as far as Newburyport by land, from there they go in sloops to Kennebec River, up it in Batteaux, and have a carrying place of about forty miles over which they must carry on their shoulders their batteaux and baggage, scale the walls [of Quebec] and spend the winter in joy and festivity among the sweet nuns.'[2]

Fort Western, nearly sixty miles up the Kennebec, was the staging area. On 25 September Captain Dan Morgan, a 'large, strong-bodied personage, [who] gave the idea history has left us of Belisarious', led an advance unit. Among those who embarked in the batteaux was a Connecticut Major with the fascinating name of Return Jonathan Meigs. Two days later he recorded in his journal:

29th. In the morning contined our route up the river. At 11 o'clock, A.M., arrived at Fort Halifax, which stands on a point of land between the river Kennebeck and the river Sebastecock. This fort consists of two large block-houses, and a large barracks, which is enclosed with a picket fort. I tarried half an hour at the fort—then crossed the river to a carrying-place, which is 97 rods carriage—then proceeded up the river, which falls very rapidly over a rocky bottom 5 miles, and encamped. . . .

[*October*] *2d.* In the morning proceeded up the river, and at 10 o'clock arrived at Scohegin Falls, which is a carrying place of 250 paces, which lies across a small island in the river. Here I waited for my division to come up, and encamped on the west side of the river, opposite the island, with Captain Goodrich. It rained in the night. I turned out, and put on my clothes, and lay down again, and slept well till morning. . . .

3d. Proceeded up the river to Norridgewalk. On my way I called at a house, where I saw a child of 14 months old. This is the first white child born at Norridgewalk. At 7 o'clock in the evening, a little below Norridgewalk, my battoe filled with water, going up the falls. Here I lost my kettle, butter and sugar, a loss not to be replaced here. At Norridgewalk are to be seen the vestiges of an Indian fort and chapel, and a priest's grave. There appears to have been some intrenchment, and a covered way through the bank of the river for the convenience of getting water. This must have been a consider-able seat of the natives, as there are large Indian fields cleared. . . .

7th. Continued our march up the river, and at 12 o'clock arrived at Carra-tuncas carrying-place. Here the river is confined between two rocks, not more than forty rods wide, which lie in piles 40 rods in length on each side of the river. These rocks are polished curiously in some places, by the swift running of the water. The carrying-place here is 433 paces in length. . . .

22d. Continued our route up the river about three miles. In our way we passed 2 portages, or carry-places, each 74 perches. Our whole course this day is only 3 miles, owing to the extraordinary rise of the river the last night. In some parts of the river the water rose 8 feet perpendicular, and in many places overflowed its banks, and filled the country with water, which made it very difficult for our men that were on shore to march.

23d. In the morning continued our march, though very slow, on account of the rapidity of the stream. A number of our men that marched on shore, marched up a river that came from the westward, mistaking it for the main river, which, as soon as we discovered, we despatched some boats after them. The river now falls fast. Here a council was held, in which it was resolved that a captain, with 50 men, should march with all despatch by land to Chaudiere pond, and that the sick of my division and Captain Morgan's, should return back to Cambridge. At this place the stream is very rapid, in passing which, five or six battoes filled and overset, by which we lost several barrels of provisions, a number of guns, some clothes and cash. . . .

26th. Continued our route, and soon entered a pond, about two miles across, and passed through a narrow strait, only 2½ perches wide, and about four rods long; then entered another small pond about a mile over, and then through a narrow straight, about a mile and a half long, to a third pond three miles wide; then passed through a narrow strait, and entered a fourth pond, about a quarter of a mile wide; then entered a narrow crooked river about three miles in length, to a carrying-place, 15 perches across, to a pond about 15 perches across, and encamped in the northeast side, upon a high hill, which is a carrying-place. These ponds are surrounded with mountains. . . .

59. View of the Falls of the Chaudière. *G. B. Fisher*

Of the many marches through the wilderness made during the Revolutionary War, none matched for hardship and difficulty of terrain the struggle of Arnold and his men up the Kennebec River, across a snowy height, and down the Chaudière to the St Lawrence opposite Quebec. This aquatint, with a few Indians the only human figures, captures the wildness of the scene. Abner Stocking could write in Maine, 'The forest was stripped of its verdure, but still appeared to me beautiful'; but by the time they were hunting for the Chaudière on the great carrying-place, Dr Senter was recording, 'Our bill of fare for last night and this morning consisted of the jawbone of a swine, destitute of any covering.' But finally, with immense triumph: 'Twenty miles only from this to the settlements. Lodged at the great falls this night.'

November 1st. Continued our march through the woods—marching this day exceedingly bad. This day I passed a number of soldiers who had no provisions, and some that were sick, and not in my power to help or relieve them, except to encourage them. One or two dogs were killed, which the distressed soldiers eat with good appetite, even the feet and skins. This day, on our march upon the banks of the Chaudiere, we saw several boats, which were split upon the rocks, and one of Captain Morgan's men was drowned. The travelling this day and yesterday very bad, over mountain and passes. . . .

4th. In the morning continued our march. At 11 o'clock arrived at a French house, and were hospitably used. This is the first house I saw for 31 days, having been that time in a rough barren, uninhabited wilderness, where we never saw human being, except our own men. Immediately after our arrival, we were supplied with fresh beef, fowls, butter, pheasants, and vegetables. This settlement is called Sertigan. It lies 25 leagues from Quebec. . . .

10th. I marched down to Point Levi and joined the detachments.

11th, 12th and 13th. I was at Point Levi. Nothing extraordinary happened, except that a deserter came in to us from Quebec, by whom we were informed that Col. M'Lean had arrived from Sorel with his regiment. I had forgot to mention that the Lizard frigate arrived a few days before our arrival at Point Levi. On the evening of this day, at nine o'clock, we began to embark our men on board 35 canoes, and at 4 o'clock in the morning we got over and landed about 500 men, entirely undiscovered, although two men of war were stationed to prevent us. We landed at the same place that General Wolfe did, in a small cove, which is now called *Wolfe's Cove*. Soon after our landing, a barge from the Lizard frigate came rowing up the river. We hailed her, and ordered her to come in to the shore. They refusing, we fired upon them. They pushed off shore, and cried out. After parading our men on the heights, and sending a reconnoitering party towards the city, and placing sentries, we marched across the plains of Abram, and took possession of a large house, which was formerly owned by General Murray, and other houses adjacent, which were fine accomodations for our troops.

14th. This morning employed in placing proper guards on the different roads to cut off the communications between the city and country. At 12 o'clock the enemy surprised one of our advanced sentries and made him prisoner. The guard soon discovered the enemy, and pursued, but were not able to overtake them. We rallied the main body, and marched upon the heights near the city, and gave them three huzzas, and marched our men fairly in their view; but they did not choose to come out to us. They gave us a few shots from the ramparts. We then returned to our camp. This afternoon they set fire to the suburbs, and burned several houses. This evening Col. Arnold sent a flag to the town, with a demand of the garrison, in the name and behalf of the United Colonies. As the flag approached the walls, he was fired upon, contrary to all rule or custom on such occasions. We constantly lie on our arms to prevent surprise.'[3]

During the gruelling march through the wilderness, one of Arnold's divisions had returned and now Arnold felt he had not enough men to take the town and that he was short on artillery, small arms, or ammunition. He retired up-river to Pointe aux Trembles to await the coming of Montgomery. The junction was made on 3 December, and two days later the combined force took up positions before the walls of Quebec. The men struggled

60. A Plan of Quebec. *Rocque*

This plan shows the fortifications around Quebec at the time of the English capture in 1759. North is to the right.

with the frozen ground in erecting siege lines, and finally turned to the expedient of throwing up snow works to lend an illusion of protective works.

Sir Guy Carleton, Governor of Canada, had slipped down the St Lawrence under the cover of night, just before Montreal surrendered to Montgomery. He wasn't impressed by the procedures utilized by the rebels:

'The seventh a woman stole into town with letters addressed to the principal merchants, advising them to an immediate submission and promising great indulgence in the case of their compliance. Enclosed was a letter to me in very extraordinary language and a summons to deliver up the town.'[4]

As the siege wore on, the Americans who had struggled in misery through the wilderness, lived in unaccustomed luxury, some sleeping in fine houses in such suburbs as St Rochs. Sergeant John Pierce did not elaborate but made a laconic observation that 'a certain officer of the field keeps with the nuns'. But enlistments would be running out on the first of the year, and Montgomery realized that if he was to make an effective move it would have to be soon. He waited for a snowstorm to blanket the movement of his troops as they launched an attack against the town.

Inside the town, one of the British defenders kept a diary which he labelled a 'Memorandum':

'*11 Dec*r. 1/2 after 4 in the morning threw in 49 Shells. This morning they threw some Letters into the Garrison fixed upon wood Arrows. They were wrote in French, reflecting upon General Carleton for putting their prisonr in Irons, and extremely insolent. This evening they threw in 47 Shells. . . .

15th. This morning about 8 o'Clock the enemy opened a small Battery opposite Saint Johns Gate about 800 yards from the walls with 4–12 and 1–6 Pounder. Their range was for the Ursulines Convent and the provision Store, about 10 o'Clock a flag of truce came to the Palace Gate but was not admitted. The fire on both sides was extremely warm for about 9 Hours when the enemy ceased occasioned by our dismounting their cannon. They threw in 8 Shells from a Howitzer at their Battery. . . .

17th. This morning a woman was killed by the centry in the Ordnance yard, she being with some of the enemy and the centry at the right angle of La Potars Bastion was wounded in the Head by some of the enemy's riflemen and died a short time after. about 12 o'Clock a man came from Point Levy in a canoe and says that there are but 50 of the enemy there, but he was sent back immediately. at 1/2 after 2 they threw in 15 small Shells from their Battery, one of them set fire to a House, but soon extinguished.

20th. This morning a woman came in from Old Lovelle with 3 Letters from our officers prisoners, informing us that the Canadians of Chamblee [with Montgomery] are dissatisfied and it is expected they will retire in a few days. The woman tells us that there are a great number of the Enemy in Saint Rocks. This evening we fired a great quantity of Shells into Saint Rocks, one of them set fire to a House which set fire to 3 more. . . .

61. A View of the City of Quebec. *Hervey Smith*

In this view, to the extreme right is the Charles River; to the left, the Heights of Abraham extend behind the citadel. Behind the city, between it and the Charles River, were the encampments of Montgomery and Arnold in the winter of 1775–6; Arnold crossed to the Quebec side several miles up the river to the left.

23rd. This day orders were gave for the Garrison to sleep in their Cloathes till further Orders. The British and French militia were ordered on fatigue to get the Lizard and Hunters Guns upon the Lines to complete the Flanks. this evening a deserter from the enemy came in at S*t* Johns Gate and confirms the intention of the enemy to storm us. . . .

29th. This evening a deserter came in at Palace Gate gives account that they are 3000 men and that they will attack us in a few days. . . .

31st. [Heavy snowfall]. This morning the enemy threw in a great quantity of Shells. about 1/4 before 5 an alarm was gave the enemy having attacked Sault de Matelot with 600 men under the command of Colonel Arnold. They advanced to the Barrier through a constant fire from the Palace Gate the Block House and the Sally port Guards. The guard not being in readiness and the Captain, one Macloud of the Royal Emmigrants being in Liquor they passed it and throwing in a body of men into some Houses facing Mr Limburners. They kept a constant fire at it to deter the Garrison from defending the Barrier, while they should pass the Barrier but it was vigorously defended by Lieut*t* Colonel Caldwell and some Militia in the interim. Capt*n* Law advanced with his party to the Sault de Matelot where he was in a manner prisoner for some minutes, he entering into a House w[h]ere some of the [American] Officers were assembled and seeing it impossible to retire he availed himself of a method by telling them he was come to treat of a capitulation (Arnold who received a wound on their advance had escaped over the ice being carried by 2 men on one of their scaling Ladders) they then took him up into a garrett when Capt*n* McDougall was sent with a reinforcement to Capt*n* Law. he surrounded the House and took them all prisoners being 47. Colonel Caldwell advancing and Capt*n* Law in their rear threw the enemy into such a panic that they threw down their arms and begged for mercy.

an attack was likewise made by 700 men under the command of Gen*l* Montgomery at Pres de Ville. after sending about 200 men to make a feint at Cape Diamond and Saint Johns, but our cannon made them soon retire, he drew up his men on Mr. Drummonds Wharf and sent an officer to reconnoitre the Barrier who advanced almost to touch it (our guns being masked and our people being under cover he could not observe them) he retired then. about 50 of them advanced to a narrow pass facing the Barrier and were within 20 yards of it when they received a general discharge of Cannon and Musquetry which mowed them down like grass. They immediately retired, the driftiness of the snow enabling them to carry off their dead and wounded except 9 who were too near the Barrier. a 6 *pr* Brass Gun was took at the Slip opposite the Hotel de Dieu. a Major who guarded it observing the Sortie left it and escaped with his men over the river. a party was sent out about 9 oClock to set fire to the Houses in Saint Rocks and the Intendants Palace to prevent any reinforcements coming to the enemy. about 11 oClock a party was sent out to set fire to Mr. Grants House which they executed with very little resistance and upon their return they found 2 royals and 3 Coehorns with 33 live Shells which the enemy had hid in a House. . . .

1st Jany. [1776] Upon viewing the Dead, General Montgomery, His Aid de Camp Captain Cheeseman and Capt*n* Hendricks of the rifle men was discovered. Montgomery had received a Shot thro' the Left Cheek and thro' both legs with Musquetry. this afternoon about 3 oClock an Officer came over the river from Beauport to Sault de Matelot imagining the lower town

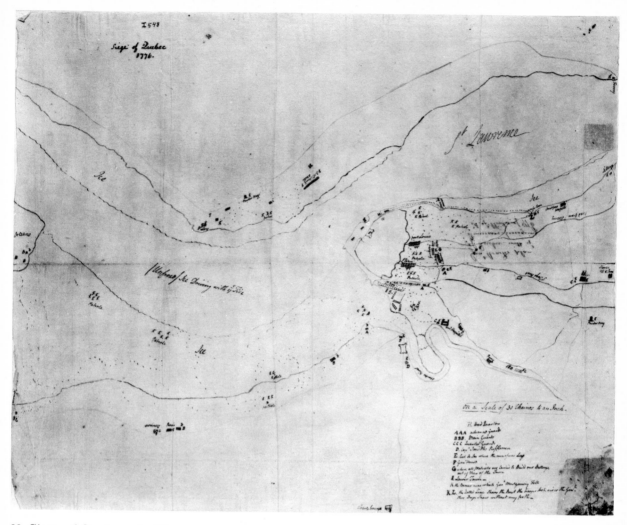

62. Siege of Quebec. *Antill*

The map is endorsed 'Genl. Arnold's Plan of Quebec with the Americans Besieging it Winter 1776'. In the bottom right corner is 'E Antill lt'. This manuscript sketch shows (A,B,C) the location of the American forces, (D) the location of Captain Smith's riflemen, the powder magazine, (K,L) the pathless route through deep snow taken by General Montgomery and his men, and (K) the barrier near which Montgomery fell on 31 December 1775. The south on the plan is at the top.

was taken, but was took prisoner himself. about 5 oClock Monsr Lanadiere, aid de Camp to his Excelly General Carleton with Major Meigs one of the prisoners went out to the enemy with a flag of truce to desire the prisoners Baggage to be sent in, but was refused conference they being persuaded the lower town was taken, notwithstanding the majors telling them of his being taken prisoner and of General Montgomery's death.'[5]

The assault on Quebec had ended in a dismal failure. From his hospital bed Benedict Arnold wrote to his sister, 'I have no thought, of leaving this proud town, until I first enter it in triumph.' He continued the siege, even as his men drifted off across the snow-covered terrain, making their way back home. Despite a drop in the temperature to twenty-eight degrees below zero, he clung doggedly to his ambitious scheme of subduing the town. Those

63. Col. Arnold Wounded at Quebec. *T. Hart*

This engraved portrait of Arnold, with a small view of the Quebec assault in the background, does not share the sharp-faced quality of most of his other portraits. If it is questionable as a likeness, it was at least drawn very soon after the event depicted. It is as difficult for words as for the brush to capture the complex personality of Arnold. Nowhere did he show the brilliance of his reckless courage and his flashing initiative more clearly than in this first Canadian campaign, in his leadership across the wilderness, and in his construction and manoeuvring of the first American fleet. Yet always he misses his goal. Even the British pay him no more than £6,000 for his treason. He acts in reprisal for personal injuries, real or imagined, and so in the end betrays the cause for which he had fought so brilliantly.

inside the town suffered, but seemed to have little trouble getting fuel. And towards the end of March Arnold was complaining, 'We labour under almost as many difficulties as the Israelites did of old, obliged to make bricks without straw.' As the first days of spring scampered by, provisions ran short and smallpox, 'that fatal disorder', ran through camp like a flame.

On 1 April, General David Wooster, whom Montgomery had left in command at Montreal, came down the river with heavier guns and ammunition and assumed direction of the siege. Arnold, miffed, requested, and was granted, permission to return to Montreal. Wooster, a country-looking fellow who considered a day wasted unless he had paid his homage to Bacchus, soon had 'thrown everything into confusion'. On 1 May, Wooster was relieved by General John Thomas who decided that the siege should be raised. Even as he was making preparations, three British transports were spotted breaking through the soft ice in the river and were soon dropping anchor off Quebec. Reinforced with the troops aboard these vessels, Carleton sallied forth onto the Plains of Abraham; the Americans fled, many crying out bitterly because of the loss of their plunder.

Near the middle of May the American garrison at The Cedars, a post of 400 men forty-five miles south-west of Montreal, was attacked by a combined force of Canadians and Indians. A relief force marching to their aid was ambushed. Major-General John Sullivan was appointed to replace John Thomas, and on the same day that he arrived, Thomas died of smallpox, his body 'obliged to be interred that day—he was so mortified'.

Sullivan rashly threw his troops against the British at Trois Rivières, a post now commanded by John Burgoyne who had returned from a trip to England. Sullivan was driven off, leaving behind on the field some twenty-five dead and 200 of his men taken prisoners. On the seventeenth he joined Arnold at St John's and then fell back down Lake Champlain to Ticonderoga.

At St John's, Carleton halted his pursuit of the Americans. Beyond the water barrier of Lake Champlain there were three armed vessels, three schooners, and a sloop that could wreak havoc among a troop-laden flotilla of small boats. And there were no roads around the lake. A number of pre-fabricated flatboats had been sent out from England, but not enough. The square-rigged *Inflexible* and the schooners *Maria* and *Carleton* were dismantled in the St Lawrence and manhandled overland to St John's to be reassembled. A massive, ungainly raft was constructed, fitted with guns, and christened the *Thunderer*.

At the far end of the lake hammers were also ringing out in the forest. Benedict Arnold was building a fleet to add to the *Royal Savage*, a sloop

64. The Death of General Montgomery at Quebec. *John Trumbull*

Trumbull's painting is a spirited, snow-swept tableau, accurate in portraiture, less so in the placement of those present. Montgomery and Arnold, before Quebec, waited for a night of snowstorm, made two feints and attacked the Lower Town simultaneously, Montgomery from the river side, Arnold from the rear. The approach along the river was very narrow; going fearlessly ahead with his advance guard Montgomery encountered withering fire at the first barrier, a fortified house, and was instantly killed.

Lieutenant Ogden supports the dying general; Colonel Donald Campbell, behind him, holds the flag. The Indian chief with upraised tomahawk was known by the name of Colonel Louis. Major Meigs and Captain Hendricks are at bottom left: Colonel Thompson of Pennsylvania to the right. Several of the Americans are in red coats because Montgomery had dressed his men in British winter uniforms captured at Montreal.

65. The *Royal Savage*

The schooner *Royal Savage* was the flagship of Captain Jacobus Wynkoop, commodore of the small American fleet on Lake Champlain in the spring of 1776; later he was superseded by Arnold. The flag in this drawing is said to be the earliest surviving picture of the Jack and Stripes. In the Battle of Valcour Island the ship was grounded by Captain Hawley to escape capture; it later exploded. Its former name was the *Royal George*, which made its renaming a bit of political satire.

formerly called after George III. By the time the sounds of construction were stilled there were, in addition to the *Royal Savage*, the *Revenge*, the sloops *Enterprize* and *Liberty*, the cutter *Lee*, seven gondolas, *Boston, New Haven, Providence, New York, Jersey, Success* and *Spitfire*, and three heavily armed row galleys, *Washington, Trumbull*, and *Congress*, mounting a total of ninety guns.

By 11 October, Arnold had his fleet behind a cape on Valcour Island, a half mile off the western shore of Lake Champlain. The British fleet swept proudly down the lake, a brisk wind bellying its sails, trailed at some distance by 500 batteaux filled with soldiers. Arnold reported the action of 11 October:

'Yesterday morning at eight o'clock, the enemy's fleet, consisting of one ship, mounting sixteen guns, one snow, mounting the same number, one schooner of fourteen guns, two of twelve, two sloops, a bomb-ketch, and a large vessel (that did not come up), with fifteen or twenty flat-bottomed boats or gondolas, carrying one twelve or eighteen pounder in their bows, appeared off Cumberland Head. We immediately prepared to receive them. The galleys and Royal Savage were ordered under way; the rest of our fleet lay at an anchor. At eleven o'clock, they ran under the lee of Valcour, and began the attack. The schooner, by some bad management, fell to leeward, and was first attacked; one of her masts was wounded, and her rigging shot away. The captain thought it prudent to run her on the point of Valcour, where all the men were saved. They boarded her, and at night set fire to her.

At half-past twelve, the engagement became general, and very warm. Some of the enemy's ships, and all their gondolas beat and rowed up within musket-shot of us. They continued a very hot fire, with round and grape shot, until five o'clock, when they thought proper to retire to about six or seven hundred yards' distance, and continued the fire till dark.

The Congress and the Washington have suffered greatly; the latter lost her first lieutenant killed, captain and master wounded. The New York lost all her officers, except the captain. The Philadelphia was hulled in so many places, that she sank in about one hour after the engagement was ended. The whole killed and wounded amounted to about sixty. The enemy landed a large number of Indians on the island and each shore, who keep an incessant fire upon us, but do little damage. The enemy had, to appearance, upwards of one thousand men in batteaux, prepared for boarding. We suffered much for want of seamen and gunners. I was obliged, myself, to point most of the guns on board the Congress, which, I believe, did good execution. The Congress received seven shot between wind and water; was hulled a dozen times; had her mainmast wounded in two places, and her yard in one. The Washington was hulled a number of times; her mainmast shot through, and must have a new one. Both vessels are very leaky and are repairing. . . . it was thought prudent to return to Crown Point, every ammunition being three fourths spent and the enemy greatly superior to us in ships and men. . . .

Colonel Wiggleworth in the Trumbull, got under way; the gondolas and small vessels followed; and the Congress and the Washington brought up the rear. The enemy did not attempt to molest. Most of the fleet is this minute come to an anchor. The wind is small to the southward. The enemy's fleet is under way to leeward, and beating up.'[6]

Three days later Arnold completed the story in a second dispatch:

'We remained no longer at Schuyler's Island than to stop our leaks, and mend the sails of the Washington. At two o'clock, P.M., the 12th, weighed anchor, with a fresh breeze to the southward. The enemy's fleet at the same time got under way; our gondola made very little way ahead. In the evening the wind moderated, and we made such progress, that at six o'clock next morning we were about of Willsborough, twenty-eight miles from Crown Point. The enemy's fleet were very little way above Schuyler's Island; the wind breezed up to the southward, so that we gained very little by beating or rowing at the same time the enemy took a fresh breeze from the northeast, and by the time we had reached Split Rock, were alongside of us. The Washington and Congress were in the rear, the rest of our fleet were ahead, except two gondolas, sunk at Schuyler's Island. The Washington galley was in such a shattered condition, and had so many men killed and wounded, she struck to the enemy, after receiving a few broadsides.

We were then attacked in the Congress galley by a ship mounting twelve eighteen-pounders; a schooner, a fourteen sixes; and one of twelves sixes, two under our stern, and one on our broadside, within musket-shot. They kept up an incessant fire upon us for about five glasses, with round and grape shot, which we returned as briskly. The sails, rigging, and hull of the Congress was shattered and torn in pieces, the first lieutenant and three men killed, when, to prevent her from falling into the enemy's hands, who had seven sail around me, I ran her ashore into a creek ten miles from Crown Point, on the east side, when, after saving our small-arms, I set her on fire, with four gondolas, with whose crews I reached Crown Point, through the woods, that evening, and very luckily escaped the savages, who waylaid the road in two hours after we passed. At four o'clock yesterday morning, I reached this place [Ticonderoga], exceedingly fatigued and unwell, having been without sleep or refreshment for near three days.'[7]

Realizing that he was unable to defend Crown Point with the 200 survivors and four vessels under his command, Arnold had burned that place before falling back on Ticonderoga. His arrival threw the garrison there into a strange contrast of bravado and fright. Captain John Lacey of the Pennsylvania troops was both proud and outraged with the men:

'On the morning of the 28th of October, word was brought by our scouts and look-out boats on the lakes that the enemy were approaching both by land and water. A general alarm was fired, and every one hurryed to his post. All was bustle; the whole camp presented a terrific blaze of fire arms issuing from every quarter to prepare for battle, which was momently expected to

66. Ticonderoga and its Dependencies. *John Trumbull*

The immediate result of the almost total destruction of Arnold's little flotilla was British victory; the eventual outcome was defeat of Carleton's plan to reach Howe in New York after eliminating American opposition. The necessity of building a fleet strong enough to deal with Arnold and clear the way for transportation of the army delayed Carleton's start until mid-fall; it gave Gates time enough to assemble a new force to replace the shattered remnants after the retreat from Quebec and to strengthen the fortifications at Ticonderoga. Carleton was not prepared for a winter campaign.

Burgoyne returned to capture Ticonderoga the next year.

John Trumbull was barely twenty when he made this map in 1776; he had so impressed Washington at Boston that the general appointed him colonel. At Ticonderoga Gates made him deputy adjutant-general. For this 1841 engraving in his *Autobiography*, he added some details to his on-the-spot sketch, which is in the Connecticut State Library.

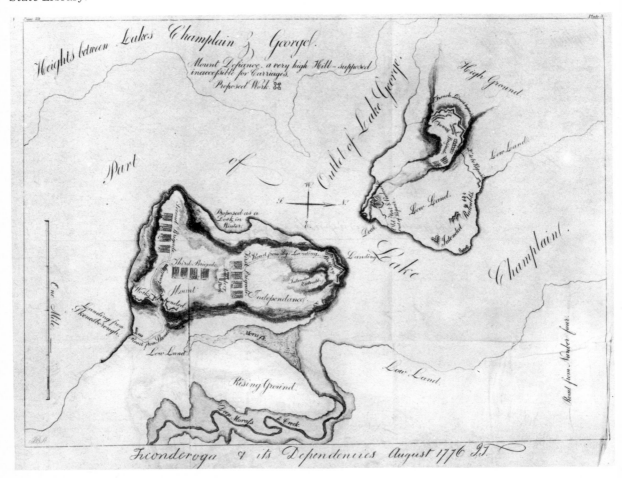

78

67. General Guy Carleton

Carleton, governor of the province of Quebec and commander-in-chief of the British army in Canada, lost Montreal, saved Quebec, and unsuccessfully invaded upper New York in 1776. He replaced Sir Henry Clinton in New York in 1782 and was reappointed governor of Canada in 1786.

commence. Collom after collom presented their fronts along the lines, with fixed bayonet, whose glissining fire arms reflected the bright raise of the sun presented a luster from their tablits more radient than the sun itself. What mind could resist a flash like this! The sounds of the drums to arms, the reports of the alarm cannon, and the crye of the sergeants to the men in hurrying them from their tents of "Turn out! Turn out!" would make even a coward brave. These were, however, the times that tryed mens souls, and here only the sunshine and summer soldier srunk from the expected conflict.

I will throw a vail over some names, who but the evening before bosted over a glass of grog what feats they intended to do on the approach of the enemy, now srunk with sickning apathy within the cover of their tents and markees, never appeared to head their men, leaving their tasks to their subalterns to perform. On finding at least the enemy had made a halt, and that this movement was only a reconitering from them, they came out as boald soldiers as ever, complaining only of a little sick headake. . . .

I viewed the men and observed their countenances with pleasure to be animated and not a ray of fear depicted in the face of any of them, and am confident had the enemy made an attack at that time, they would not have dishonoured either themselves or their country. Their view, however, was otherwise, perhaps to trye us, and, to make a view of our camp, situation and strength, no doubt Gen. Burgoin, who commanded Crown Point, was with his suit on the point of some of the mountains with glasses overlooking our encampment, fortifications and troops, and not very well liking our position and appearance, towards the close of the day the British army retired, not having come nearer to us than what we call Half Way Point, three miles from Ticonderoga, but from which we and they had a fair view of each other. As the enemy approached, our scouts and pickets retired without firing. Within supporting distance of our lines, they halted for their reception.

Nothing worth noticing after this affair took place between the enemy and our army, and on the 13th of November we received information they had evacuated Crown Point and gown over the lake toward St. Johns, giving up the further contest for the present. . . . Here ended the Northern Campaign for the year 1776.'[8]

Sir Guy Carleton, surveying the situation and knowing full well that winter would be upon him and that supply lines would be long and difficult to maintain, had given the order to pull back into Canada and more comfortable winter quarters. On the surface, the whole affair had been a disaster for the Americans, but Benedict Arnold's stubbornness in denying Lake Champlain to the enemy had averted even greater disaster. But, for the present, all thoughts of gaining Canada as a fourteenth colony had to be shelved. And soon there was to be a heartwarming victory far to the south that would lift rebel spirits.

4. Charleston, 1776

NEW ENGLAND, as a theatre for military activity, was not popular with many of those Englishmen concerned with England's prosperity as well as their own fortunes. Already there were cries that the war had 'begun at the wrong end'. Others argued that the British Army was not strong enough to roll over all the colonies and crush them in one giant operation. Economic interests dictated a serious consideration of a southern campaign. The products of the semi-tropical south fitted better into the scheme of British mercantilism, and already one Robert Herries was suggesting military operations in an area where tobacco could be picked up to allow him to fulfil contracts with the Farmers General of France.

Others insisted that the southern colonies, because of their rural nature, would be easier to conquer, and because of their attachment to the Crown the people would readily return to their allegiance, furnishing supplies for the British Army as the rebellion was put down in the northern colonies. Much optimism had been generated by the reports of southern governors: Lord Dunmore in Virginia, Josiah Martin in North Carolina, Lord William Campbell in South Carolina, and Sir James Wright in Georgia. All declared that the majority of the people in their governments were loyalist in sentiment and those who did not answer a call to the King's Standard surely would not fight on either side.

Of the southern governors, Josiah Martin of North Carolina was the most persistent and optimistic in his arguments. The Scots Highlanders in the area around Cross Creek (present-day Fayetteville) and the former Regulators of the back country would flock to the colours if only allowed the opportunity. He suggested that a detachment of the regular army be landed in his colony to co-operate with the loyalists and subdue North Carolina. Then, with the military striking overland and with the Navy sweeping in from the sea, Charleston, the most important port in the South, could be easily taken. With a base from which to operate, the southern colonies could then be overrun one at a time.

But there had already been near-disaster in Virginia. Their new Scots governor, John Murray, Earl of Dunmore, seemed to feel that the rebellion was little more than the actions of a few 'young men of good Parts, but spoil'd by a strange, imperfect desultory kind of Education which has crept into Fashion all over America'. Contemptuous of such individuals, he had rashly seized, on 20 April 1775, the twenty casks of gunpowder stored in the colony's magazine at Williamsburg and touched off a small rebellion. Marching men had crowded the roads to the capital until restrained by men of milder tempers after Dunmore had agreed to pay the worth of the powder.

He had stirred restlessly in the Governor's Palace until 8 June when, after receiving the news of Lexington and Concord, he had fled during the small hours to the protection of the frigate *Fowey*, anchored in the York River off Williamsburg. Indulging his flair for pomposity, he issued proclamations aimed at stirring up the Indians on the western frontier, and striking a blow at the planters by issuing a call for slaves to desert their masters and enlist in his regiment of 'loyal Ethiopians'. Hovering in the Chesapeake, Lord Dunmore raided plantations, carried off tobacco, harassed fishing vessels and, in general, made a nuisance of himself. And, or so the story ran, when he released 160 of those whom he had taken prisoner, he retained two fair maidens, 'detained as bedmakers to his Lordship'.

68. Portrait of Governor Dunmore.
Sir Joshua Reynolds
John Murray, the 4th Earl of Dunmore, was the royal governor of Virginia at the outbreak of the Revolution. He escaped to a warship in Chesapeake Bay. After the British regulars were defeated by local Patriots at Great Bridge he burned Norfolk in retaliation on 1 January 1776.

Here he is painted in his tartan finery against a romantic background.

Then this fribbling governor took post at Norfolk, already termed by the rebels a 'nest of Tories'. He established a post nine or ten miles up the Elizabeth River where a long causeway and bridge across a swamp lent it the name of 'Great Bridge'. Colonel William Woodford, with about 900

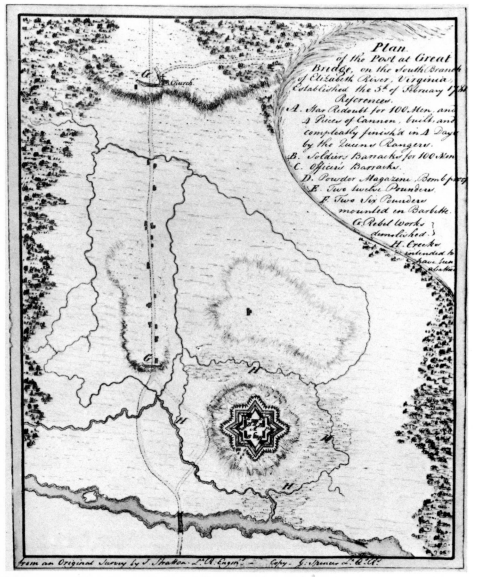

69. Plan of the Post at Great Bridge. *George Spencer*

At Great Bridge, south of Norfolk, on the morning of 9 December 1775, British troops, despatched from Norfolk by Governor Dunmore's orders, attacked Colonel William Woodford's forces, which had entrenched themselves on the opposite side of the Elizabeth River from a British outpost. The British did not succeed in dislodging them.

Over five years later, in 1781, Benedict Arnold sent Lieutenant-Colonel John G. Simcoe of the Queens Rangers to the support of a detachment of the 14th Regiment that had been harassed at Great Bridge by a body of rebels. This manuscript plan is by George Spencer, one of Simcoe's lieutenants who drew many maps of the Rangers' encounters 'on the spot'. The original coloured map with the interesting detail of a star redoubt by James Stratton of the Royal Engineers is in the Library of Congress.

Virginia and North Carolina troops, mostly militia, took a position on the far side of the bridge. Woodford persuaded a Negro to carry across the tale that he had only 300 men under his command. Dunmore, despite protests, ordered the rebels dislodged. On Saturday 9 December 1775, shortly after the drums had rattled out the reveille, Dunmore's 60 British regulars, accompanied by 230 sailors, loyalists, and black troops, and led by Captain Charles Fordyce, started across the causeway. Among them was an officer who signed himself simply as 'J.D.', and who sent an account of Dunmore's operations to the Earl of Dumfries. Captain Fordyce, he said,

'fell covered with 11 wounds on the Morning of the 9th of Decr. in an absurd, ridiculus & unnecessary Attack (in all our Opinion) which our little Detachmt, consisting of 121 rank & file, were ordered by the Governor to make on a strong Body of the Rebels, consisting of upwards of 1000, as securely intrenched against any Numbers as Nature or Art could place them, & were composed of people of all Nations, mostly rifle-men, who lived in the Mountains & back parts of Virginia & Carolina, the most hardy warlike people in America, frequently at War with their Neighbours the Indians; regularly inlisted & disciplined, formed into 2 regiments, & sent down to stop some little progress which we had made, to please his Lordship, in this part of the Country successfully, tho' in direct opposition to common Prudence & common Sense.

Our little Detachment having marched many Miles into a Country unknown to us, covered with thick Woods against strong Bodies of Rebels, who for some time dispersed at our Approach, but at last had the Resolution to attack us in passing through a thick Wood, where near four hundred of them lay concealed; Their Fire was badly directed, only wounding some of our people: we did not give them time for a second, but rushing in with our Bayonets, they only gave us an opportunity of killing five or six of them, and

70. Virginia and part of Maryland. *J. Bew*

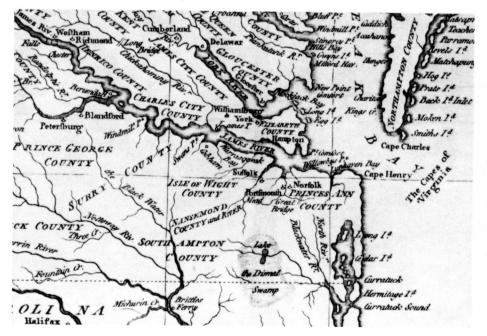

taking double the Number Prisoners among whom were two Colonels leading Men. Upon this Defeat, the Town of Norfolk, the largest in Virginia, & the two neighbouring Counties laid down their Arms, & took the oath of Allegiance.

The News of this reaching Williamsburg, the Capital, fifty Miles distant, where the two Regiments were quartered, they were immediately sent down to oppose us. Certain Intelligence being received of their Approach, his Lordship gave Orders for the Town of Norfolk to be fortified, an operation of three Months, tho' he could reasonably expect five Days. & to be defended by us altho' ten times our Number would have been insufficient. Our only hope was therefore in a little Wooden Fort, which we immediately erected; at a Pass called the Great Bridge, twenty Miles from Norfolk, the only inlet by Land from the Rest of the Colony to those two Counties; & which we defended for many Days against all their Efforts & Numbers, & might with some little Precautions have done so still; but as they could not force us, His Excellency (& certainly he excells all Men as a General) wisely proposed to us, to pass the Bridge & dislodge them from their Intrenchments; we hinted to him as far as Delicacy in our Situation would permit, the Absurdity & extravagant Folly of so unnecessary an Attempt—it was in vain—The Scotch Pedlars have been better judges, their Counsel prevailed.

We passed the Bridge exposed to the Enemy, drove in their Out-Posts and advanced towards their Entrenchments, over a narrow Causeway which led from the Bridge through a Morass at the end of which they were securely posted. The Approach to it was so narrow we were obliged to march up by files; & by a Curve in the Causeway & Breastworks on the opposite Side of the Morass on our Right, we were flank'd & our Rear almost equally exposed as our Front; in less than ten Minutes that we were exposed to the Enemy's Fire; upwards of Seventy of our little Detachment were killed & wounded; After doing as much as Men do in such a Situation, Capt. Leslie who commanded the Party, ordered the remainder to carry off the wounded into the Fort.

We knew their Situation well, & knew that it was impenetrable, but we had long seen that we were under the Guidance of Folly, & that sooner or later we should be forced into some Scrape. Capt. Fordyce fell within four Yards of their Breastwork & Stockade seven Feet high, with loop Holes to fire through, some of the Grenadiers fell against it; my Division which was next to Fordyce's five only, out of twenty two escaped; it was my Fate to be of the small Number unhurt. Lieutenants Napier, Leslie & Bates fell, the last is still living a Prisoner with the Enemy; the Rebels behaved with the greatest Humanity, ceasing to fire when we were retreating with the wounded, as also to fifteen that fell into their Hands; they have since informed us that eight of them are dead, but that they have still some Hopes of a Corporal who has seventeen Balls through him.

They paid the greatest respect to poor Fordyce's Body, burying it with all the Honours of War. They call him the brave Fordyce, & say his Death would have been that of a Hero, had he met it in a better Cause. They were astonished at Men marching up with such Courage, or rather Madness to certain Death. They had only one Man wounded slightly in the Hand.

We are now retired on board Ship, cut off from all Communications from the Shore. The Rebels took possession of Norfolk, but that flourishing Town is now laid in Ashes: we set Fire to it under the Cannon of the Men of War, a

71. Flora MacDonald. *Richard Wilson*

In January 1776, a beautiful Scotswoman rode with her husband from door to door of the Highland emigrants along the upper Cape Fear River in North Carolina, exhorting them to join the King's standard and march against the American rebels. This was Flora MacDonald, who, in 1746, had conveyed the fugitive Prince Charles Edward from Benbencula to Portree in the Hebrides, disguised as her maid, with all the zeal for the House of Stuart which she now displayed for George III. Flora, her husband Allan MacDonald, and several children had come from Skye in 1774, only the year before, forced away by the impossible rents of the Scottish lairds. With their neighbours, they formed the earliest and largest homogeneous group of Loyalists to go into battle against the Patriot militia.

Conduct equally absurd with the former, as the Rebels meant to have done it themselves, & indeed were so obliging as to assist us in it, by setting fire to the greatest part of the Town that was not in our reach; it cost us three or four Men, & could answer no other Purpose than that of taking the inhumanity of the Action off their Shoulders upon our own.

His Lordship has much to answer for—besides sacraficing a handfull of brave Men, he has ruined every Friend of Government in this Colony, & done the Cause much Disservice, but indeed if You know anything of him, & who ever must be sensible how equal he is to move in the Sphere he is placed in, & to the Character he has assumed.—We were sent here at his Request as a Guard to his Person & it was never supposed we were to act but on the devensive; what is to become of us next I can form no Opinion; if we do not receive any Instructions from the Commander in Chief before our Provisions are out, we must try some more friendly Shore. We are ignorant of what is going on at Boston, as we have not heard from there these four Months, nor from England later—I have little Hopes of it. . . . Before Harmony is established in this Quarter of the Globe your Lordship will probably hear of some broken Heads.—I left you about this time last year, since then it has been a rather rugged Life.'[1]

Dunmore lay off the charred post of Norfolk until early February, and lingered in Chesapeake Bay until the summer fevers threatened to wipe out the remainder of his little force. By August he had joined the British fleet off New York and was rewarded for failure with an appointment as governor of the Bahamas, where he sold a number of his 'loyal Ethiopians' into slavery. There he continued to nourish his dreams of martial splendour and managed to dismiss the memories of past mistakes from his mind.

In North Carolina, premature actions had also resulted in failure. Josiah Martin, impressed by the 'pressing and reiterated assurances' of the loyalists, decided that the proper moment was at hand and called for the King's Friends to make their move. Two seasoned British officers of Scots birth, Lieutenant-Colonel Donald MacDonald and Captain Donald McLeod, had earlier been sent into North Carolina seeking recruits for the Royal Emigrant Regiment. Martin had appointed MacDonald a brigadier-general of militia 'for the time being', while McLeod was designated a second-in-command with the rank of lieutenant-colonel.

The loyalists were not so enthusiastic as Martin anticipated. The Highlanders came out, but the back-country Regulators appeared loath to take up arms. Those who did come into Cross Creek became disenchanted when promises made to them were not kept, and the majority straggled home, plundering as they went.

In the meantime, the Whigs were taking steps and calling out the militia. They were not a particularly impressive lot. Janet Schaw, an Englishwoman visiting North Carolina, sniffed as she witnessed their drill:

'Their exercise was that of bush-fighting, but it appeared so confused and so perfectly different from anything I ever saw, I cannot say whether they performed well or not; but this I know that they were heated with rum till capable of committing the most shocking outrages. They at last however assembled on the plain field, and I must really laugh while I recollect their figures: 2000 men in their shirts and trousers, preceded by a very ill-beat drum and a fiddler, who was also in his shirt with a long sword and a cue at his hair, who played with all his might. They made indeed a most unmartial appearance. But the worst figure there can shoot from behind a bush and kill even a general Wolfe.'[2]

Colonel James Moore, commanding the newly raised First Regiment of North Carolina Continentals, began to close in on Cross Creek. After a show of bluster to gain time, MacDonald slipped out of Cross Creek and began his march for the coast, expecting to make a junction with the British squadron in Cape Fear. Moore manoeuvred his troops so as to force the loyalists to march by way of the Widow Moore's Creek bridge where the militia of Colonels Richard Caswell and Alexander Lillington had been stationed.

MacDonald fell ill and McLeod assumed the command. The rebels abandoned their position on the near side of the creek and fell back across the stream to prepared earthworks, supported by two ancient artillery pieces they had affectionately dubbed 'Old Mother Covington and her daughter'. The flooring of the bridge was removed and stringers greased with soft soap and tallow. One of the loyalists, a fellow by the name of McLean, did not know of this latest move:

'Intelligence was brought that Casswell had marched at 8 oClock the Night

72. North Carolina (detail). *Jonathan Price and John Strother*

Moore's Creek (also called 'Widow Moore's Creek') flows from the northeast into the Black (or South) River about ten miles above the juncture of Black River and Cape Fear. The main road from Cross Creek (Fayetteville) to Wilmington crosses it.

before & had taken possession of the Bridge upon Widow Moore's Creek, a party went to examine his abandoned Camp & found there some horses and Provisions which the Precipitancy of their March made them leave behind them, that evening Mr. Hepburn was sent to the Enemy's Camp with offers of Reconciliation upon their returning to their duty and laying down their Arms, who upon his return to Camp informed us that Casswell had taken up his Ground 6 Miles from us upon Widow Moores Creek & that he thought it very Practicable to attack them, a Council of War being immediately called it was unaminously agreed that the Enemy's Camp should directly be attacked.

73. Plan of the Town of Cross Creek in Cumberland County, North Carolina.
C. J. Sauthier

Cross Creek was the obvious location for the Loyalist troops to assemble in February 1775. They went on from there to their defeat at Moore's Creek Bridge. Cross Creek was at the head of navigation on the Cape Fear River and was the trading centre for an area recently settled by Highland Scots like Flora MacDonald and her husband Allan. These Highlanders felt more closely bound by their belief in the divine right of kings and by ties to Great Britain than by any allegiance to the province whither they had immigrated. Not all the inhabitants were Tory, however; back-country Whigs had gathered at Cross Creek on 20 June 1775 and passed resolutions to 'go forth and be ready to sacrifice our lives and fortunes to secure freedom and safety!' And in 1783 the citizens changed the name of the town to Fayetteville, the first community so honouring the Marquis de Lafayette.

Sauthier (1736–1802), one of the ablest surveyors and map-makers of the Revolutionary period, made a series of ten maps of towns in North Carolina, the only province so well represented in the colonial period. Brought to America in 1767 by Governor Tryon, Sauthier was a native of Strasbourg who had already written a fine manuscript work on architecture and landscaping. He accompanied Tryon to New York in 1771 and there made a number of important maps.

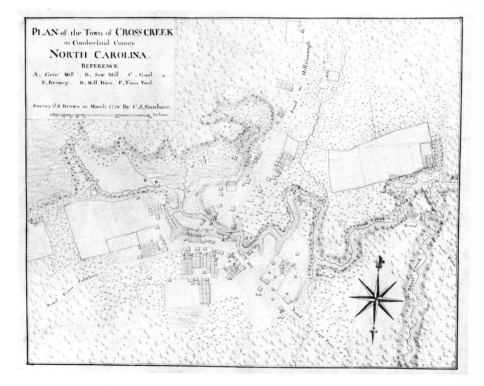

The Army was immediately ordered under Arms and about one oclock Tuesday Morning the 27th. We March'd six Miles with 800 Men, in the front of our Encampment was a very bad swamp, which took us a good deal of time to pass so that it was within an hour of Daylight before we could get to their Camp, upon our entering the Ground of their Encampment, we found their fires beginning to turn weak & concluded that the Enemy were Marched.

Our Army entered their Camp in three Columns but upon finding that they left their ground, orders were directly given to reduce the Columns and form the Line of Battle within the verge of the Wood (it not being yet day) and the Army should retire a little from the Rear in order to have the Wood cover us from the sight of the Enemy the word of Rallement being King George and the Broad Swords.

Upon hearing a shot on the plain in our front betwixt us & the bridge the whole Army made a Halt & soon thereafter at the end of the Bridge it being still dark, the Signals for an Attack was given, which was three cheers, the Drum to beat, the Pipes to play. the Bridge lying above a Cannon Shot in our front upon the deep Miry Creek Mr. McLean with a party of about 40 Men came Accidently to the Bridge, he being a Stranger & it being still dark he was challenged by the Enemies Centinels they observing him sooner than he observed them. He answered that he was a friend, they asked to whom; he replyed to the King; Upon his making this reply they squatted down upon their faces to the Ground. Mr. McLean uncertain but they might be some of our own people that had Crossed the Bridge, challenged them in Gallic to which they made no answer, upon which he fired his own piece & ordered his party to fire, upon which the firings turned more general in that place.

Capt Donald McLeod & Capt. John Campbell repaired to the Bridge and endeav'g to cross they were both killed & most of the Men that followed them: during the time of the firing the most of the Country born Army began to runaway & could not be made to stand their Ground the Loyalists excepted, the people being called away from the Bridge and we retired with the Army to Camp, where when we arrived we found we had but two barrels of flour to serve the whole Army, that the Men were not to be keeped together & that the Officers had no Authority of the Men. A Council of War being instantly called it was proposed that the Army should retire to Crosscreek & there fortify ourselves till Gov.r Martin's pleasure should be known. . . .'[3]

The refugees from the battle were rounded up and imprisoned or given their paroles. Yet, Governor Martin, although suffering the pangs of chagrin, still maintained that the defeat had been but a 'little check'. In London, the *Gentleman's Magazine* agreed with the governor in that the Americans had 'only reduced a body of their own people, supported by no one body of regular troops'. Only the *Annual Register* was astute enough to direct the attention of its readers to the fact that the colony had been able to raise an estimated 10,000 men and warned that the loyalists could not be expected to rise again so quickly, and went on to note: 'They had encountered Europeans [the Highlanders] (who were supposed to hold them in the most sovereign contempt, both as men and soldiers) and defeated them with an inferior force.'

And so it was that Henry Clinton, when he arrived in early March, dis-

74. Sir Peter Parker. *L. T. Abbott*

Sir Peter Parker, who in 1799 became Admiral of the Fleet, was the son of an admiral, the father of an admiral, and the grandfather of an admiral. In October 1775, he was given the command of a small squadron for North America, with the *Bristol* as flagship. Sailing from Portsmouth in December, he encountered bad weather, and reached Cape Fear in May. After his disastrous defeat in Charleston harbour, Parker joined Lord Howe in the attack on Long Island. In 1777, now rear-admiral, he was made commander at Jamaica, where he remained until returning to England in 1782 with the Comte de Grasse as his prisoner. As Admiral of the Fleet, he was chief mourner at Lord Nelson's funeral. His grandson Peter, a naval captain, was killed in the War of 1812 on the banks of Chesapeake Bay.

covered only the silent pine trees awaiting him rather than a strong loyalist force. He was forced to wait until early May before the last of the fleet from Ireland finally straggled in, weary and sore from the buffetings they had endured by the heavy seas. Even with the reinforcements under Lord Cornwallis, Clinton, as early as 3 May, had decided that an invasion of North Carolina was now impracticable, while an assault against Charleston would be 'exceedingly difficult'. He had even gone so far as to report to Lord George Germain that the taking of that port would do little towards the re-establishment of order. Georgia, because of the onset of the sultry season, was out of the question.

Clinton had set his mind on operations in Chesapeake Bay. A vague dispatch from General Howe suggested that his force was not needed immediately to the northward, but gave him no real instructions as to when or where to make a junction with him. He seemed to wish that some action take place in the southern colonies and indicated that to him Charleston was a port of considerable importance. Then there was intelligence that the defensive works of Charleston were as yet incomplete. Because of the sum total of all this, it was not too difficult for Admiral Sir Peter Parker to persuade Clinton that a strike should be made against the South Carolina port after all.

The Charlestonians had been working on fortifications at a rather leisurely pace, but the work had been pushed forward once it was known that

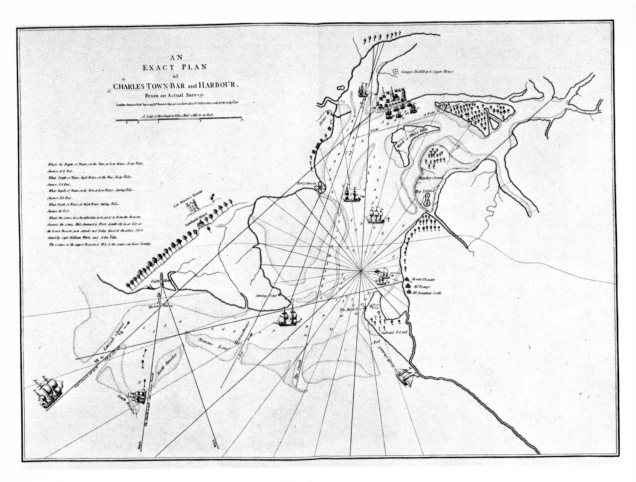

75. An Exact Plan of Charles-Town-Bar and Harbour

This chart of Charleston harbour was published in London before news of the successful defence of Fort Sullivan reached England. The only structure on Sullivan's Island is a 'Pest House'. The inaccuracy of the survey, in spite of its interesting landmarks for guidance to navigation, can be seen by a comparison with Des Barres's chart of 1777 and Leitch's 1774 view of the town.

a British force was in the south. There was jubilance in the town when Major-General Charles Lee had been assigned as commanding general of the Southern department. This spindly-shanked general, a former officer in the British Army, had a reputation that gave him an aura of almost a new Joshua. Some were irritated by Lee's eccentricities, and C. C. Pinckney grumbled, 'General Lee appears very clever, but is a strange animal; however . . . we must put up with ten thousand oddities in him on account of his abilities and his attachments to the rights of humanity.' Not knowing just what the British objective was to be, Lee had frittered away much of his time in Virginia and North Carolina before making his way down to Charleston.

Charleston lay on the end of the peninsula formed by the confluence of the Ashley and Cooper Rivers. Between the tip of the peninsula and the sea lay eight miles of harbour. Two islands flanked either side of the harbour's mouth: on the east there was Sullivan's Island, on the west, James Island. Sullivan's Island, which lay like a half-closed fist, was the site for the primary defensive work of the Carolinians. North-east, towards the Atlantic, lay Long Island, separated by an inlet known locally as the 'Breach'. In command of the fort was Colonel William Moultrie and his Second South Carolina Regiment of Continentals. The British had dallied too long and had missed the heavy spring tides; this, in turn, meant that they had to remove the heavy guns from the ships of the line so that they could negotiate the massive bar that lay across the mouth of the harbour.

By 1 June the British fleet dropped anchor in Bull's Bay, and three days later lay off Charleston bar. Clinton's troops were landed on Long Island and by 15 June all were ashore, camped amongst the palmettos and myrtle bushes. When the fleet began their attack, the troops were to ford the 'Breach' and drive overland against the fort on Sullivan's Island. They began to search for the fords that had been reported; there were none, the water ranging from seven to eight feet deep. By 21 June the fleet was across the bar, and the twenty-third was fixed as the day for the joint attack. When the wind shifted in the morning, the signals were hauled down and the fleet continued rocking in their anchorage in Five Fathom Hole. Signals fluttered again in the rigging on 27 June, but again were pulled down when the wind went 'flying suddenly round to the northward'.

The following day, Tuesday 28 June, conditions once again appeared favourable. Clinton was signalled, and at 11.15 the warships weighed anchor

76. An Exact Prospect of Charles Town

This view of Charleston as seen from the opposite bank of the Cooper River identifies the chief buildings and fortifications by letter: A. the Granville bastion at the point of the peninsula, B. the court house, C. the council-chamber, D. the meeting-house, E. St Philip's Church, F. the custom-house, G. the secretary's office, and H. Craven's bastion. Four other bastions are not shown on this plan; the chief defence at the time was Fort Johnson on James Island at the entrance to the harbour.

The bar across that spacious entrance seldom allowed passage of ships of over 200 tons' burden; yet at the time of the Revolution, maritime activity was heavy and the produce of the coastal plantations in rice and indigo as well as the trade in peltry from a thousand miles into the continent were brought to Charleston for export. 'Here', notes the commentary in the *London Magazine* which accompanies the 'Exact Prospect', 'the rich people have handsome equipages, the merchants are opulent and well bred . . . everything conspires to make this town the politest, as it is one of the richest in America.'

The engraving was based on Bishop Roberts' painting of 1737–8, which was first engraved by W. H. Toms in 1739.

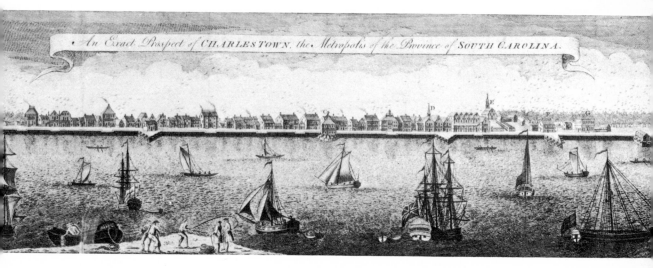

An Exact Prospect of CHARLESTOWN, the Metropolis of the Province of SOUTH CAROLINA.

and lumbered up before the fort, letting go their anchors, with springs on their cables. Earlier that morning, Colonel Moultrie, cursing his gout, had ridden out to check the force stationed to oppose any attempt by Clinton to cross the 'Breach'. He recorded his recollections of that sultry June day:

'On the morning of the 28th of June, I paid a visit to our advance-guard (on horseback three miles to the eastward of our fort) while I was there, I saw a number of the enemy's boats in motion, at the back of Long Island, as if they intended a descent upon our advanced post; at the same time, I saw the men-of-war loose their topsails; I hurried back to the fort as fast as possible; when I got there the ships were already under sail; I immediately ordered the long roll to beat, and officers and men to their posts: We had scarcely manned our guns, when the following ships of war came sailing up, as if in confidence of victory; as soon as they came within the reach of our guns, we began to fire; they were soon a-breast of the fort . . . let go their anchors, with springs upon their cables, and began their attack most furiously about 10 o'clock, A.M. and continued a brisk fire, till about 8 o'clock, P.M.

The ships were, the Bristol, of 50 guns, Commodore Sir Peter Parker: the captain had his arm shot off, 44 men killed and 30 wounded.
The Experiment, 50 guns: the captain lost his arm, 57 men killed and 30 wounded.
The Active, 28 guns: 1 lieutenant killed, 1 man wounded.
The Sole-bay, 28 guns: 2 killed, 3 or 4 wounded.
The Syren, 28 guns.
The Acteon, 28 guns: burnt: 1 lieutenant killed.
The Sphynx, 28 guns: lost her bowsprit.
The Friendship, 26 guns; an armed vessel taken into service.
The Thunder-Bomb had the beds of her mortar soon disabled; she threw

77. A N.b.E. View of the Fort on the Western end of Sulivans Island . . . 28th of June 1776

A N.b.E. View of the Fort on the Western end of Sulivans Island with the Disposition of His Majesty's Fleet Commanded by Commodore Sir Peter Parker Kn. &c &c &c. during the Attack on the 28.th of June 1776. which lasted 9 hours and 40 minutes.

A. The Active 28 Guns Capt. Williams. B. Bristol Commodore Sir Peter Parker Kn. &c. &c. &c. of 50 Guns, Capt. Morris. C Experiment 50 Guns Capt. Scot. D Solebay 28 Guns Capt. Simons. E Syren 28 Guns Capt. Fourneau. F F. The Acteon of 28 Guns Capt. Atkins and Sphynx of 20 Guns Capt. Hunt on a Shoal the latter got off but the Acteon was burnt by our selves the next Morning as it was impossible to get her off. G H. The Thunder Bomb Capt. Reed with the Friendship Armed Vessel of 28 Guns Capt. Hope. I I Mount Pleasant. K Hog Island. L Sulivans Island and Fort. M A Narrow Isthmus. N An Armed Hulk to defend the Isthmus. O The Continent P. The Myrtle Grove. Q. The Western end of Sulivans Island & Fort Erected upon a Peninsula.

LONDON. Engrav'd & Publish'd according to Act of Parliament Aug.st 20.th 1776. by W.m Faden Corner of St Martins Lane Charing Cross.

To Commodore Sir Peter Parker Kn. &c. &c. &c. This View is Most humbly Dedicated and Presented by L.t Colonel Tho.s James R.l R. of Artillery June 30.th 1776.

78. William Moultrie. *Charles Willson Peale* (?)

Moultrie (1730–1805), then colonel of the 22nd South Carolina Regiment, was in command of the fort on Sullivan's Island, at the mouth of Charleston Harbour, in June 1776, when word came that the British fleet under Sir Peter Parker and a force of three thousand under General Clinton were approaching Charleston. The fort was not finished. General Lee insisted on a bridge of hogsheads for retreat; it sank. 'I never was uneasy on not having a retreat, because I never imagined the enemy could force me to that necessity', wrote Moultrie in his *Memoirs*; and to Captain Lempriere, who told him the British men-of-war would knock down his fort in half an hour, he replied, 'Then we will lay behind the ruins and prevent their men from landing.' This stubborn courage, plus the fortunate grounding of three of the British ships, produced one of the few 'miracle' victories of the Americans which put life into the Revolution.

her shells in a very good direction; most of them fell within the fort, but we had a morass in the middle, that swallowed them up instantly, and those that fell in the sand in and about the fort, were immediately buried, so that very few of them bursted amongst us: At one time, the Commodore's ship swung around with her stern to the fort, which drew the fire of all the guns that could bear upon her: we supposed he had the springs of her cables cut away: The words that passed along the plat-form by officers and men, were "mind the Commodore, mind the two fifty gun ship:" most of all the attention was paid to the two fifty gun ship, especially the Commodore, who, I dare say, was not at all obliged to us for our particular attention to him; the killed and wounded on board those two fifty gun ships confirm what I say. During the action, Gen. Lee paid us a visit through a heavy line of fire, and pointed two or three guns himself; then he said to me, "Colonel, I see you are doing very well here, you have no occasion for me, I will go up to town again," and then left us.

When I received information of Gen. Lee's approach to the fort, I sent Lieut. [Major] Marion, from off the plat-form, with 8 or 10 men, to unbar the gate-way, (our gate not being finished) the gate-way was barricaded with pieces of timber 8 or 10 inches square, which required 3 or 4 men to remove each piece; the men in the ships tops, seeing those men run from the plat-form concluded "we were quitting the fort," as some author mentions: Another says, "we hung up a man in the fort, at the time of the action;" that idea was taken from this circumstance; when the action began, (it being a warm day) some of the men took off their coats and threw them upon the top of the merlons, I saw a shot take one of them and throw it into a small tree behind the plat-form, it was noticed by our men and they cried out "look at the coat." Never did men fight more bravely, and never were men more cool; their only distress was the want of powder; we had not more than 28 rounds, for 26 guns, 18 and 26 pounders, when we begun the action; and a little after, 500 pounds from the town, and 200 pounds from Captain Tufft's schooner lying at the back of the fort.

There cannot be a doubt, but that if we had had as much powder as we could have expended in the time, that the men-of-war must have struck their colors, or they would certainly have been sunk, because they could not retreat, as the wind and tide were against them; and if they proceeded up to town, they would have been in much worse situation: They could not make any impression on our fort, built of palmetto logs and filled in with earth, our merlons were 16 feet thick, and high enough to cover the men from the fire of the tops. The men we had killed and wounded [12 men killed and 24 wounded] received their shots mostly through the embrasures.

An author, who published in 1779, says "the guns were at one time so long silenced, that it was thought the fort was abandoned; it seems extraordinary that a detachment of land forces were not in readiness on board the transports, or boats, to profit from such an occasion."

The guns being so long silent, was owing to the scarcity of powder which we had in the fort, and to a report that was brought me, "that the British troops were landed between the advance-guard and the fort;" it was upon this information, that I ordered the guns to cease firing, or to fire very slow upon the shipping; that we should reserve our powder for the musketry to defend ourselves against the land forces, there being a great scarcity of powder at this time.

At one time, 3 or 4 of the men-of-war's broadsides struck the fort at the same instant, which gave the merlons such a tremor, that I was apprehensive that a few more such would tumble them down. During the action, three of the men-of-war, in going round to our west curtain, got entangled together, by which the Acteon frigate went on shore on the middle ground; the Sphinx lost her bowsprit; and the Syren cleared herself without any damage; had these three ships effected their purpose, they would have enfiladed us in such a manner, as to have driven us from our guns: It being a very hot day, we were served along the plat-form with grog in fire-buckets, which we partook of very heartily: I never had a more agreeable draught than that which I took out of those buckets at the time; it may be very easily conceived what heat and thirst a man must feel in this climate, to be upon a plat-form on the 28th June, amidst 20 or 30 heavy pieces of cannon, in one continual blaze and roar; and clouds of smoke curling over his head for hours altogether; it was a very honorable situation, but a very unpleasant one.

During the action, thousands of our fellow-citizens were looking on with anxious hopes and fear, some of whom had their fathers, brothers, and husbands in the battle; whose hearts must have been pierced at every broad-side. After some time our flag was shot away; their hopes were then gone, and they gave up all for lost! supposing that we had struck our flag,

A N.W.b.N. View of CHARLES TOWN from on board the Bristol Commodore Sir Peter Parker Knt. &c. &c. taken in Five Fathom Hole the day after the Attack upon Fort Sulivan by the Commodore & his Squadron, which Action continued 9 hours & 40 minutes.

A. Charles Town, B. Ashley River, C. Fort Johnston, D. Cummins's Point, E. Part of Five Fathom Hole where all the Fleet rode before & after the Attack of Fort Sulivan, F. The Station of the headmost Frigate the Solebay, two Miles & three quarters from Fort Sulivan Situated to the Northward of G. N.s. Cummins's Point D & F. Johnston, C. bears nearly N & S, H. Part of Mount Pleasant, J. Part of Hog Island, K. Wando Riv. L. Cooper Riv. M. James Island, at the Southern Point is Fort Johnston opposite the Center of Mount Pleasant Three Miles and a ¼ distance, N. Breakers on Charles Town Bar, O. Rebels Schooner of 12 Guns.

To Commodore Sir Peter Parker Knt. &c. &c. &c. This View is Most humbly Dedicated and presented by Lt. Colonel Thos. James Rl. Rl. of Artillery, Five Fathom Hole South Carolina, June 29th. 1776.

79. A N.W.b.N. View of Charles Town . . . taken in Five Fathom Hole the day after the Attack upon Fort Sulivan

This view was made aboard Commodore Peter Parker's flagship the *Bristol* by Lieutenant-Colonel Thomas James of the Royal Artillery.

and had given up the fort: Sergeant Jasper perceiving that the flag was shot away, and had fallen without the fort, jumped from one of the embrasures, and brought it through a heavy fire, fixed it upon a sponge-staff, and planted it upon the ramparts again: Our flag once more waving in the air, revived the drooping spirits of our friends; and they continued looking on, till night had closed the scene, and hid us from their view; only the appearance of a heavy storm, with continual flashes and peals like thunder; at night when we came to our slow firing (the ammunition being nearly quite gone) we could hear the shot very distinctly strike the ships: At length the British gave up the conflict: The ships slipt their cables, and dropped down with the tide, and out of the reach of our guns. When the firing had ceased, our friends for a time, were again in an unhappy suspense, not knowing our fate; till they received an account by a dispatch boat, which I sent up to town, to acquaint them, that the British ships had retired, and that we were victorious.

Early the next morning was presented to our view, the Acteon frigate, hard and fast aground; at about 400 yards distance; we gave her a few shot, which she returned, but they soon set fire to her, and quitted her: Capt. Jacob Milligan and others, went in some of our boats, boarded her while she was on fire, and pointed two or three guns at the Commodore, and fired them; then brought off the ships bell, and other articles, and had scarcely left her, when she blew up, and from the explosion issued a grand pillar of smoke, which soon expanded itself at the top, and to appearance, formed the figure of a palmetto tree; the ship immediately burst into a great blaze that continued till she burnt down to the water's edge.

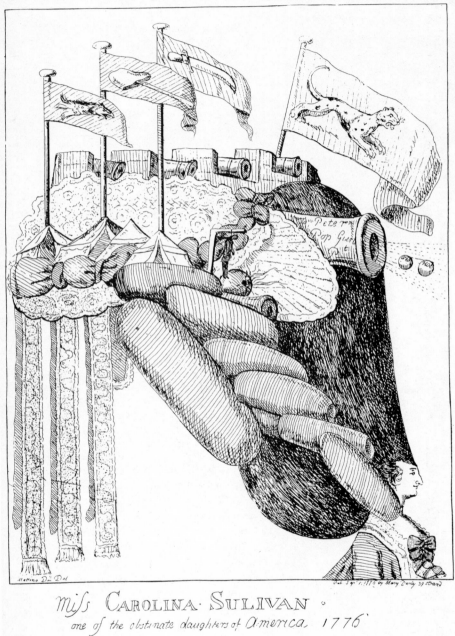

Miss CAROLINA SULIVAN.
one of the obstinate daughters of America. 1776

80. Miss Carolina Sulivan

This cartoon, like the similar earlier satire on Bunker Hill, takes its rise from a London series caricaturing the fantastic hairstyles of fashionable women of the day, in Mary Darly, *Comic Prints of Characters, Caricatures, Macaronis, Etc*, London, 1776.

96

The other ships lay at the north point of Morris' Island we could plainly see they had been pretty roughly handled, especially the Commodore.

The same day, a number of our friends and fellow citizens, came to congratulate us on our victory and Governor Rutledge presented Sergeant Jasper with a sword, for his gallant behavior; and Mr. William Logan a hogshed of rum to the garrison, with the following card. ''Mr. William Logan, presents his compliments to Col. Moultrie and the officers and soldiers on Sullivan's Island, and beg their acceptance of a hogshed of old Antigua rum, which being scarce in town at this time, will be acceptable.'' Mr. Logan's present was thankfully received. A few days after the action, we picked up, in and about the fort, 1200 shot of different calibers that was fired at us, and a great number of 13 inch shells.'[4]

One British army officer reported the damage to men and ships:

'The next Morning at day break we expected to have seen the Battle renewed, instead of which We observed the Ships returning to their former Station in a very shattered Condition. The Bristol a 50 gunn ship had lost her mizzen & main mast. The Experiment another 50 has likewise suffered much; the frigates but little as the whole fire of the Battery was principally aimd att the large ships. Capt. Morris of the Bristol lost one Arm, the other hand shattered, He is since dead. Capt. Scott of the Experiment lost an arm & I fear will not live. Lt. Pike of the Active killed; One Midshipman & about 200 Men killd & wounded—there was 2 fifty Gunn Ships, 5 frigates & a Bomb of the Invincible British Navy defeated by a Battery which it was supposed would not have stood one Broadside—this will scarce be believ'd in England.

81. The morning after the engagement on Sullivan's Island. *Lt Henry Gray*

This detail of Lieutenant Gray's watercolour drawing confirms the palmetto-and-earth structure of the fort, unlike the stylized engravings with their stonework and embrasures. In the background dispatch vessels sail to Sir Henry Clinton's camp on Long Island.

But when we come seriously to consider the Nature of the Attack & the disadvantages under which the Ships labour'd, the consequences is not so surprising. The Battery was made of palmito trees of a stringy tough Substance, so that not a single shott could do any mischief, but what went through the Embrazures. The Ships were all 800 yds distance & tho' very little Wind, there was a great Swell. On the contrary, the Rebels had a steady mark, & att that distance hull'd the Ships almost every Shott, & their Shott being mostly 32 & 42 pounders pierc'd them thru' & thru': Their first & 3d Shott dismounted 2 guns, & killed 7 Men on board the Bristol.'[5]

Even as the Americans celebrated, the carpenters aboard the British ships lying in Five Fathom Hole plied their tools in repairing the battered vessels. Clinton's troops remained on Long Island, making the best of their lot of 'sand, salt pork, grog, snakes and mosquitoes'. Although no one doubted the courage of British sailors, the military argued among themselves as to why Parker had not sailed past Sullivan's Island to make a direct attack upon the city. Not until 21 July, nearly four weeks after the engagement before Sullivan's Island, did Clinton's troops come aboard the transports. Once re-embarked, they set sail for New York under the convoy of the *Solebay*. The majority of the fleet remained behind until they were again seaworthy. Not until 2 August did they once again make their way across Charleston bar. That same day the news of the Declaration of Independence reached the city.

The Charlestonians were in the mood to receive such a document as, indeed, were most of the southern colonies. They had met a supposedly invincible enemy and had sent them home with their tails between their legs.

When it was reported that Sir Peter Parker had suffered indignity when a cannon ball passed so close to his rear that 'the commodore had his breeches tore off, his backside laid bare', a satirical song was published in London. It ran:

A NEW WAR SONG

By

Sir Peter Parker

Tune: 'Well Met, Brother Tar.'

My Lords, with your leave
An account I will give
That deserves to be written in meter;
For the Rebels and I
Have been pretty nigh—
Faith! almost Too Nigh for Sir Peter.

With much labour and toil
Unto Sullivan's Isle
I came fierce as Falstaff or Pistol,
But the Yankees ('od rot 'em)
I could not get at 'em:
Most terribly maul'd my poor Bristol.

Bold Clinton by Land
Did quietly stand
While I made a thundering clatter;
But the channel was deep,
So he could only peep
And not venture over the water.

D'el take 'em; their shot
Came so swift and so hot,
And the cowardly dogs stood so stiff, sirs,
That I put the ship about,
And was glad to get out,
Or they would not have left me a skiff, sirs!

Now bold as a Turk
I proceed to New York,
Where with Clinton and Howe you may find me.
I've the wind in my tail,
And am hoisting my sail,
To leave Sullivan's Island behind me.

But my lords, do not fear
For before the next year,
(Altho' a small island could fret us,)
The Continent whole
We shall take, by my soul,
If the cowardly Yankees will let us.[6]

5. New York

82. New York, as it was when his Majesty's Forces took Possession of it in 1776. *C. J. Sauthier*

This manuscript map of lower Manhattan Island is of exceptional interest because it shows the fortifications built to defend the city from impending British attack in 1775–6, and the area west of Broadway destroyed by the fire of 17 September.

GENERAL WILLIAM HOWE had sailed from Halifax in the *Greyhound*, an aptly named vessel, for she soon outdistanced the remainder of the fleet, arriving off Sandy Hook on 25 June. Prospects were not encouraging, for the rebels had allowed little grass to grow under their feet. The town bristled with half-moon batteries and other fortifications. Rebel picks and spades were applied even more vigorously when the first white sails of the British fleet crept over the horizon. The *Greyhound* rocked in the gentle swells as the general awaited not only his own transports but reinforcements from England, including German mercenaries hired from the indigent princes of the various German states who were to become generally known as the Hessians.

The British general planned to make his initial landing on Gravesend Bay, but Engineer Archibald Robertson and other general officers persuaded him that such an undertaking would be hazardous until he received the troops from home. Between ten and eleven o'clock on the morning of 2 July,

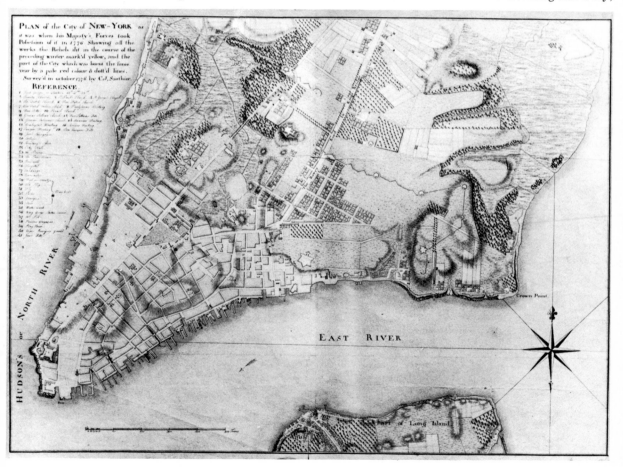

three men-of-war stood in through the Narrows and dropped anchor off the 'watering place' on Staten Island, first lobbing in a few shells to test rebel resistance. The following day transports hove to and began to disembark their human cargoes. Although dissuaded from his original plan of landing on Long Island, Howe still considered that place his primary area of operations. He made plans as he awaited reinforcements.

On 9 July 1776, repeated rebel huzzas floated across the water to pique British ears. Washington had issued orders that the brigades be drawn up at six that evening to hear the reading of a new document but recently arrived from the Continental Congress in Philadelphia. A member of the general's staff recorded his impressions:

'*July 9*. Agreeable to this day's orders the Declaration of Independence was read at the head of each Brigade, and was received by three Huzzas from the Troops, every one seeming highly pleased we were separetd from a King, who was endeavoring to enslave his once royal subjects. God grant us success, in this, our new Character.'[1]

After they were dismissed, a number of the soldiers rushed down to the Battery to indulge themselves in a bit of celebration. Their objective was an equestrian lead statue erected by the Americans after the repeal of the Stamp Act. Lieutenant Isaac Bangs of the Massachusetts militia was among those who watched the fun:

'Last night the statue on the Bowling Green representing George Ghwelps alias George Rex was pulled down by the populace. In it were four thousand pounds of lead and a man undertook to take ten ounces of gold from the superfices, as both man and horse were covered with gold leaf; the lead we hear is to be run up into musket balls for the use of the Yankees, when it is hoped that the emanations from the leaden George will make . . . deep impressions in the bodies of some of his redcoated and Tory subjects. . . .'[2]

83. View of the Narrows between Long Island & Staaten Island with our Fleet at Anchor & Lord Howe coming in—taken from the height above the Waterg. Place Staaten Island 12*th* July 1776. *Robertson*

84. The Destruction of the Royal Statue in New York. *François Xavier Habermann*

The gilded statue of George III was erected in Bowling Green by order of the New York General Assembly in August 1770 to express its loyalty to the king after the repeal of the Stamp Act. Six years later emotions had changed.

On 9 July 1776 some of the troops, with many civilians, broke through the gates of the iron fence that surrounded the statue, pulled it down, hacked off the head, and carried off the trunk to the sound of fife and drum beating out the 'Rogues March'. Later the lead was moulded into bullets; Captain John Montresor removed the head from display in a New York tavern and shipped it to Lord Townshend.

The amusing fabrication presented in this engraving, implying that the action was committed by slaves whose masters looked on complacently, secure from retaliation by authorities, is without foundation.

And when he heard that the lead was to be melted down into bullets, Ebenezer Hazard was led to quip to Horatio Gates, 'His [George III's] troops will probably have melted majesty fired at them.' Rebel spirits soared a bit more when, on 1 August, Sir Peter Parker's battered fleet limped in. When the *Bristol*, Parker's flagship, let its anchor chain go, one Englishman saw dire consequences: 'The arrival of a crippled ship and a defeated officer, at *this time*, was very unwelcome; for it infused *fresh spirits* into the rebels, and showed them that ships were sometimes obliged to retreat from batteries.'

But all of this was but martial fluff, perhaps to ease apprehensions as the forests of masts grew out in the harbour. Lord Howe had followed his brother from Halifax, and added his considerable fleet. Both brothers had come to America with hopes of conciliation, and limited authority to treat with the rebels; they were too late. A letter which they sent to 'Mr. Washington' requesting a meeting was refused because they had not used 'General'; they met, to no purpose, only with his aides. Disappointed, they resumed their roles as leaders of the attack.

Sir George Collier, commander of the frigate *Rainbow*, arrived in early

August after a voyage of thirteen weeks from England. He had escorted a considerable detachment of weary and seasick Hessians:

'We at last arrivd at our place of Destination & have joind our Friends: a bad pilot run my Ship aground at the entrance of the River leading to New York, but fortunately the Water was smooth & little Wind, so that we got off without little Damage. . . .

Every thing breathes the Appearance of War. The Number of Transports are incredible. I believe there are more than 500 of different kinds, besides the Kings ships—a Force so formidable would make the first Power in Europe tremble; Gen*l* Howes Army, with the Reinforcements we have bro't him, consists of 23 thousand effective Men, besides an Artillery more considerable than were ever brought before into the Field—We have various Accounts of the Rebels, some make over 60 thousand others not more than half that number; but let their Force be what it will, it never can stand

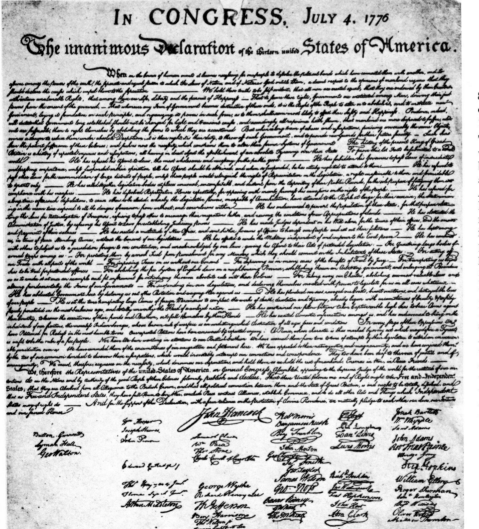

85. The Declaration of Independence.
Thomas Jefferson
The Declaration, written in two weeks by Jefferson and amended slightly by Adams and Franklin, has turned out to be a memorable document in the history of political theory. It places the fate of a nation, pledging 'our lives, our fortunes, and our sacred honour', firmly on the side of the so-called Age of Reason, leading to the way of thought of the modern age, and turns its back on traditionally constituted authority in kings and established institutions. It asserts that it is 'self-evident' to human reason that men are created essentially equal, and have natural rights to 'life, liberty, and the pursuit of happiness'.

86. Thomas Jefferson. *Rembrandt Peale*

Thomas Jefferson's great part in the American War of Independence was a portion of a greater struggle to which his life was devoted. He stated it best in his successful campaign for the presidency in 1800: 'I have sworn upon the altar of God eternal hostility against every form of tyranny over the mind of man.' Thoughts on the natural and essential rights of man had matured in his mind before he was called upon to bring them forth in the nation's crisis, and what John Adams called his 'peculiar felicity of expression' had been carefully developed, nurtured both by his philosophical convictions and by his passionate love of music and of ordered and beautiful architecture.

More surprising in this natural aristocrat was his faith in the people as controllers of their own destiny. He was ahead of his time in his wish to free the slaves, to educate all at public expense, to give a voice to minorities, to free trade, to limit executive and legislative power, and to liberate the present from the tyranny of the past. To Jefferson, the Revolution was prelude to the creation of a nation based on practical ideals.

87. **The Manner in which the American Colonies Declared themselves Independent of the King of England, throughout the different Provinces on July 4, 1776.** *Hamilton*

Americans think of the first Fourth of July as a day of hilarious excitement. Yet this engraving, made to illustrate Barnard's *New, Complete and Authentic History of England* in 1790, is probably a truer picture of the first readings of the Declaration of Independence. One man tosses his tricorn hat in a cheer, but most of the listeners are intent and serious, as were the writers, when, 'in the course of human events', they found it behoved them to give account of their conduct to the civilized world. Celebrations came later.

against veteran Troops commanded by the best Officers in Europe & supported by a responsible Fleet of Thirty Men of War of different Ships.'[3]

Sir George proved a good prophet. But first soldiers of both armies cowered in their shelters the night of 21 August, when lightning ripped across a velvet black sky, and for three terrifying hours hurricane force winds rumbled and rolled about the city. Howe chose the following morning to make his move. At eight in the morning small boats played like so many water-bugs as they ferried men across to Gravesend on Long Island. Washington began to bring men over from Manhattan Island as British transports began to move in. By 25 August Howe had around twenty thousand troops on Long Island, supported by forty pieces of artillery, more than twice the number the Americans could throw into battle. Sir James Murray, a Scots officer, had experienced humiliation in South Carolina and was happy to have an opportunity to redeem his pride:

'Upon the 22nd (a few days after the arrival of the Hessians) we landed upon Long Island without the smallest opposition. At a little village called Flat

Bush, which unfortunately lay contiguous to a wood, they made their first appearance. During three days that we halted there, they kept up a constant kind of dirty firing, in the course, of which we had about 30 men killed and wounded.

Upon the 26th in the evening we at last received orders to proceed. We were about three miles distant from the works which they had erected at the corner of this Island, which commanded the town of New York, and which was absolutely necessary for us to be in possession of. Imagining that we should attempt a passage by the shortest way, they had brought 5 or 6,000 men to oppose us upon a hill which overlooked a village, and in the woods adjoining to the road.

The enterprise of that night certainly reflects the highest honour upon the General, and it will probably be attended with the happiest and most extensive consequences. The Light Infantry and Grenadiers followed by upward of 2/3 of the British Army took a cross road to the right, marched several miles about, and by an unaccountable negligence on the part of the enemy, past the wood which stretches quite across the island and by means of which they chiefly expected to detain us, and almost within sight of their works, in the morning before they were apprized of our arrival. . . .

Upon a signal given the Hessians advanced in front from the village, as the rest of the British troops under General Grant had done some time before, along the sea coast up on the left; so that they were hemmed in upon every quarter. . . .

88. View of New York

To the extreme right, seen from the Hudson River, is the Battery at the southernmost tip of Manhattan Island, with the Fort to its left, surmounted by the Governor's House. To the right of the ship, below the Fort, is the Custom House. To the extreme left of the view are the wharves with the steeple of Trinity Church towering above on the bluff. Continuing to the right are other churches: Lutheran, Middle Dutch, Wall Street Presbyterian, French Eglise du St. Esprit, and South Dutch. The flag and cupola of City Hall are to the left of South Dutch. This view from the *Atlantic Neptune* was probably originally drawn about 1773.

We fell in with them upon the heights, which over looks the village of Bedford and Brocland, the latter of which was defended by their works. The situation of the country was entirely after their own heart covered with woods and hedges, from which they gave us several heavy fires. No soldiers ever behaved with greater spirit than ours did upon this occasion. An universal ardor was diffused throughout every rank of the army. . . .

Two companies suffered by an unfortunate mistake which might have created a good deal of confusion. They took a large body of the rebels dressed in blue for the Hessians, and received a fire from them at a very small distance, before they discovered their mistake. The two captains Neilson and Logan were killed on the spot.

Quite upon the left, near the seaside, there was a marsh, across which several of them, I believe, effected their escape. The two brigades under General Grant secured however, the greater part of them, tho', by all accounts, they were at one time a little staggered with the heavy fire from the woods, with which they were every where surrounded. Thus repulsed on every quarter, they appear to have been an easy prey to the Hessians, who took and killed and drowned great numbers of them with the loss of six men only. It requires better troops than even the Virginia riflemen who make much opposition on one side when they know their retreat is cut off on the other. It is impossible to ascertain the loss on their side. 12 or 1500 prisoners and above 2,000 killed and wounded is the present calculation and by no means exaggerated. Our loss is very trifling, considering the nature of the country, 230 or 240 killed and wounded, many of them very slightly.'[4]

British troops pursued the fleeing Americans as far as the works on Brooklyn Heights. Howe, perhaps remembering the redcoated bodies sprawled on the slope of Bunker Hill, halted his eager troops and set them to work throwing up siege lines, although several hours of daylight still remained.

89. View of the City of New York taken from Long Island. *Saint-Mémin*

As the British and Hessians looked across Long Island Sound in 1776 at the city they were about to take, the view would not have differed greatly from this one, drawn and etched twenty years later by Charles Balthazar Julien Févret de Saint-Mémin, French artist who came in 1793 to New York and made there several of the most beautiful views of the period.

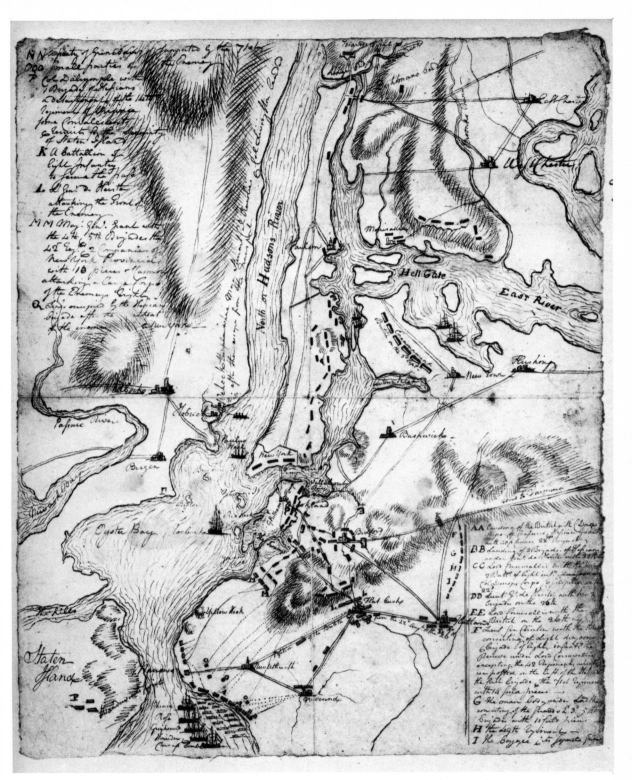

90. Battle of Long Island, August 1776

This anonymous manuscript sketch shows in detail, with accompanying legends, the movements of the British troops from 22 August, when they landed below The Narrows, to their positions early in September.

In his report the general admitted that it required repeated orders to keep the troops from charging the rebel fortification, but explained that following 'the dictates of prudence rather those of vigor', he had called a halt 'as it was apparent the lines must have been ours at a very cheap rate, by regular approaches, I would not risk the loss that might have been sustained in the assault. . . .' His men were bitter, but fell to with their spades.

The day after the battle a north-easter blew in with considerable fury. Entrenchments filled with water, ammunition became soaked, and fires were quickly drowned by the downpour forcing the gulping of soggy, raw provisions. But the storm prevented the British naval vessels from sailing up the East River and cutting off a retreat. Washington decided to pull his men back over into New York, but his general orders were so worded as to deceive the enemy and suggested merely a shift in troop positions. The small boats used were manned by seamen from the New England port of Marblehead. Young Benjamin Tallmadge was active on that misty 29 August:

'Gen. Washington commenced recrossing his troops from Brooklyn to New York. To move so large a body of troops, with all their necessary appendages, across a river full a mile wide, with a rapid current, in face of a victorious, well disciplined army, nearly three times as numerous as his own, and a fleet capable of stopping the navigation, so that not one boat could have passed over, seemed to present most formidable obstacles. But, in face of these difficulties, the Commander-in-Chief so arranged his business, that on the evening of the 29th, by 10 o'clock, the troops began to retire from the lines in such a manner no chasm was made in the lines, but as one regiment left their station on guard, the remaining troops moved to the right and left and filled up the vacancies, while Gen. Washington took his station at the ferry, and superintended the embarkation of the troops. It was one of the most anxious, busy nights that I ever recollect, and being the third in which hardly any of us had closed our eyes in sleep, we were all greatly fatigued. As the dawn of the next day approached, those of us who had remained in

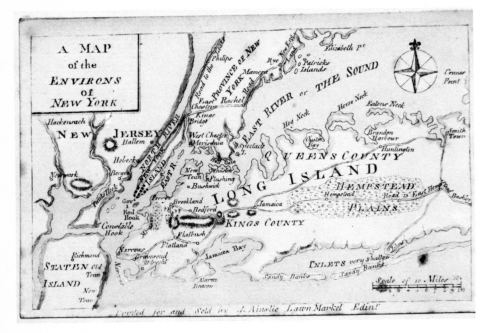

91. A Map of the Environs of New York. *J. Ainslie*

This map, showing the seat of war in 1776, was printed in Edinburgh for Scots following the events in America. It is with other maps in the collection of General Earl Percy.

92. News from America, or the Patriots in the Dumps

This engraving illustrated an article in the *London Magazine* for 1 December 1776 concerning the British victory on Long Island and capture of New York, and maintaining that extravagant rejoicing was foolish and premature. On the steps are Mansfield and North triumphantly showing a long despatch signed 'How', with Bute and King George III behind them. On the ground, a group of patriots making gestures of distress, with Wilkes the most prominent, surround a disreputable-looking, weeping America in a Liberty cap. The two ministers at right are Sandwich, with a List of the Navy, and probably Germain. In the background is the sea.

the trenches became very anxious for our own safety, and when the dawn appeared there were several regiments still on duty. At this time a very dense fog began to rise, and it seemed to settle in a peculiar manner over both encampments. . . .

When the sun rose we had just received orders to leave the lines, but before we reached the ferry, the Commander-in-Chief sent one of his Aids to order the regiment to repair again to their former station on the lines. Col. Chester immediately faced to the right about and returned, where we tarried until the sun had risen, but the fog remained as dense as ever. Finally, the second order arrived for the regiment to retire, and we very joyfully bid those trenches a long adieu. When we reached the Brooklyn ferry, the boats had not returned from their last trip, but they very soon appeared and took the whole regiment over to New York; and I think I saw Gen. Washington on the ferry stairs when I stepped into one of the last boats that received the troops. I left my horse tied to a post at the ferry.

The troops having now all safely reached New York, and the fog continuing as thick as ever, I began to think of my favorite horse, and requested leave to return and bring him off. Having obtained permission, I called for a crew of volunteers to go with me, and guiding the boat myself, I obtained my horse and got some distance before the enemy appeared in Brooklyn.'[5]

Outraged British officers blamed Howe for allowing Washington to escape. Sir George Collier, in his cabin aboard the *Rainbow*, allowed his pen to express the disgust in his soul:

'The having to deal with a generous, merciful *forbearing* enemy, who would take no unfair *advantages*, must have been highly satisfactory to General Washington, and he was certainly very deficient in not expressing his gratitude to General Howe for his *kind* behaviour towards him. Far from taking the rash resolution of *hastily passing* over the East River . . . and *crushing at once* a frightened, trembling enemy, he generously gave them time to recover from their panic,—to throw up *fresh works*,—to make new arrangements,—and to recover from the torpid state the rebellion appeared in from its late shock.

For *many succeeding* days did our brave veterans, consisting of twenty-two thousand men, stand on the banks of the East River, like Moses on Mount Pisgah, looking at their promised land, little more than half a mile distant. The Rebel's standards waved insolently in the air, from many different quarters of New York. The British troops could scarcely contain their indignation at the sight and at their own *inactivity*; the officers were *displeased and amazed*, not being able to account for the strange delay.'[6]

But there was little elation in Washington's army; they had been beaten into the ground. They vented their frustrations and humiliation upon the inhabitants, plundering at every opportunity, while many others caught a case of 'cannon fever and very prudently skulked home'. Some remembered the cruelty of the Hessians and felt their courage melt within them. And even as they looked back on their day of terror, an exultant British officer was boasting of the triumph of British arms:

'Rejoice, my friend, that we have given the Rebels a d—d crush. . . . The Hessians and our brave Highlanders gave not quarter, and it was a fine sight to see with what alacrity they dispatched the Rebels with their bayonets after we had surrounded them so that they could not resist. . . . it was a glorious achievement, my friend, and will immortalize us and crush the rebel colonies. . . . We took care to tell the Hessians that the rebels had resolved to give no quarter to them in particular, which made them fight desperately, and put all to death that fell into their hands.'[7]

On the night of 3 September, the *Rose*, convoying thirty boats, sailed in almost arrogant fashion past American batteries and dropped anchor in Wallabout Bay. This in itself was enough to convince Washington that New York could not be defended and his army was open to encirclement. Howe planned to cut off the American army by a flanking action. A detachment under General Clinton was to cross the East River, force the rebel works at Kipp's Bay, and turn Washington's left flank. On 15 September 1776 Francis, Lord Rawdon was in the boats with Clinton's force:

'We embarked in Newtown Creek and, as soon as we got into the East River, formed the line, and pushed directly for Kipp's Bay. As we approached we saw the breastworks filled with men, and two or three large columns marching down in great parade to support them. The Hessians, who were not used to this water business and who conceived that it must be exceedingly uncomfortable to be shot at whilst they were quite defenceless and jammed so close together, began to sing hymns immediately. Our men expressed their feelings as strongly, though in a different manner, by damning themselves and the enemy indiscriminately with wonderful fervency.

The ships had not as yet fired a shot, but upon a signal from us, they began the most tremendous peal I ever heard. The breastworks were blown to pieces in a few minutes, and those who were to have defended it were happy to escape as quick as possible through the neighboring ravines. The columns broke instantly, and betook themselves to the nearest woods for shelter. We pressed to shore, landed, and formed without losing a single man, As we were not without artillery, upon an island where the enemy might attack us with five times our number, and as many cannon as he thought proper, it was necessary to attain some post where we might maintain ourselves till we were reinforced, which we knew could not be done quickly. We accordingly attacked and forced a party of the rebels from the Inchenberg, a very commanding height, taking from them a new brass howitzer, some waggons of ammunition, and the tents of three or four battalions who were encamped on it.'[8]

93. The *Phoenix* and the *Rose* attacked by fireships in 1776

Two British warships, the *Phoenix* and the *Rose*, penetrated the defences of New York harbour and caused severe disappointment to the Americans early in the struggle for the city. Shore batteries had been strengthened in preparation at Paulus Hook and at Greenwich, and the defenders hoped to prevent the invader's entrance to the Hudson. Lord Howe's fleet dropped anchor in the harbour on 3 July 1776; the troops disembarked on Staten Island on 5 July. Just a week later, on 12 July, the *Phoenix* and the *Rose* sailed up the Hudson as far as Tappan Bay; neither heavy bombardment from the shore batteries nor the attack by fireships shown in this picture availed to stop them.

This engraving in the *Atlantic Neptune* is based on a painting by Sir James Wallace, who was present at the action.

95. The Declaration of Independence submitted to the Congress, 2 July 1776. *Trumbull*

Thomas Jefferson is laying the draft of the Declaration on the table before Hancock; standing with him are the other members of the committee, Benjamin Franklin to the right, John Adams to the left, Connecticut's Roger Sherman and New York's Robert Livingston between. Forty-eight figures are in the painting, thirty-six drawn directly from life on to the canvas, which Trumbull carried around with him for eight years. He began the painting in Paris in 1786, after consultation with John Adams and with Thomas Jefferson, who drew a sketch of the hall on the ground floor of the State House for him. Trumbull's purpose was to 'preserve the resemblance of the men who were the authors of the memorable act'. Those who did not sign are omitted, and fifteen signers are not represented because they were not present at the vote or had died before the painter could portray them.

94. Landing of the English Troops at New York. *Habermann*

On the morning of 15 September 1776 British troops landed on Manhattan Island. The main body of the army under Sir Henry Clinton crossed East River in transports from Newtown Creek on Long Island to Kip's Bay (present 34th Street) after a vigorous bombardment by several warships had caused the Patriot troops to flee in confusion from their poorly constructed entrenchments. 'So terrible and so incessant a roar of guns few even in the army and navy had ever heard before', wrote Ambrose Serle, secretary to Lord Howe. '. . . The Rebels were apparently frightened away by the horrid din.' General James Robertson with a strong detachment invested the town, but after delay long enough to enable the American soldiers in lower Manhattan to escape and join Washington's main forces at Harlem. The troops in transports from the main fleet did not land until the next day.

Habermann's engraving is fictitious; neither the countryside at Kip's Bay nor the Battery were lined with buildings such as these.

Washington pulled up his tired and frightened troops to Harlem Heights. It was a good defensive position, but he lay awake that night wondering if his men would stream away from this strong-point as they had from the earthworks on Kipp's Bay. His answer came the following day. Among those who were engaged that sultry fall morning was a private from Connecticut. He later remembered that,

'The next day, in the forenoon, the enemy, as we expected, followed us "hard up," and were advancing through a level field; our rangers and some few other light troops, under the command of Colonel Knowlton, of Connecticut, and Major Leitch of (I believe) Virginia, were in waiting for them. Seeing them advancing, the rangers, &c. concealed themselves in a deep gully overgrown with bushes; upon the western verge of this defile was a post and rail fence, and over that the aforementioned field. Our people let the enemy advance until they arrived at the fence, when they arose and poured in a volley upon them. How many of the enemy were killed and wounded could not be known, as the British were always as careful as Indians to conceal their losses. There were, doubtless, some killed, as I myself counted nineteen ball-holes through a single rail of the fence at which the enemy were standing when the action began. The British gave back and our people advanced into the field. The action soon became warm. Colonel Knowlton, a brave man, and commander of the detachment, fell in the early part of the engagement. It is said, by those who saw it, that he lost his valuable life by unadvisedly exposing himself singly to the enemy. . . . Major Leitch fell soon after, and the troops who were then engaged, were left with no higher commanders than their captains, but they still kept the enemy retreating.

Our regiment was now ordered into the field, and we arrived on the ground just as disagreeable to them as it was agreeable to us at that period of the war. We soon came to action with them. The troops engaged, being reinforced by our regiment, kept them still retreating, until they found shelter under the cannon of their shipping, lying in the North river. We remained on the battle ground until nearly sunset, expecting the enemy to attack us again, but they showed no such inclination that day. The men were very much fatigued and faint, having had nothing to eat for forty-eight hours,—at least the greater part were in that condition, and I among the rest. While standing on the field, after the action had ceased, one of the men near the Lieut. Colonel, complained of being hungry; the Colonel, putting his hand into his coat pocket, took out a piece of an ear of Indian corn, burnt as black as coal. "Here," said he to the man complaining, "eat this and learn to be a soldier." '9

Measured in terms of military spectacles, the battle of Harlem Heights wasn't much of a contest. In Washington's words, it was a little more than a 'brisk little skirmish' in a barley field, but after the shame of Kipp's Bay it was a great boost to sagging American morale. And the British did not take advantage of the obvious weakening of the American army because of the departure of men seeking their own chimney corners. On 21 September, Howe and his troops had a near disaster to occupy their minds. Frederick Mackenzie, a lieutenant in the Royal Welsh Fusiliers, was among those who attempted to extinguish the racing flames that broke out a little after midnight:

'From a variety of circumstances which occurred it is beyond a doubt that the town was designedly set on fire, either by some of those fellows who concealed themselves in it since the 15*th* Instant, or by some Villains left behind for that purpose. Some of them were caught by the Soldiers in the very act of setting fire to the inside of empty houses at a distance from the fire; many were detected with matches and combustibles under their Clothes, and combustibles were found in several houses. One Villain who abused and cut a woman who was employed in bringing water to the Engines, and who was found cutting the handles of water buckets, was hung up by the heels on the spot by the Seamen. One or two others who were found in houses with fire brands in their hands were put to death by the enraged Soldiery and thrown into the flames.

It is almost impossible to conceive a Scene of more horror and distress than the above. The Sick, The Aged, Women, and Children, half naked were seen going they knew not where, and taking refuge in houses which were at a distance from the fire, but from whence they were in several instances driven a second and even a third time by the devouring element, and at last

98. The triumphal entrance of the King's troops in New York. *Habermann*

With the arrival of the British the character and population of New York changed rapidly and drastically. 'There were not 3,000 left when the King's troops took possession', reported the *Connecticut Gazette* (New London) 7 March 1777; 'and of these above half are Dutch and German traders . . . the rest, composed of aged, sick and such persons as refused to enter into the measures of the Congress.' Tory adherents flocked in from all sides; obstructions and barricades were cleared and the city became the British headquarters for the remainder of the war. Widespread troop looting, during which the rifled contents of the King's College library were hawked for a dram to three drams a volume, was quickly and severely repressed by the Commandant, General James Robertson.

Habermann's engravings showed little knowledge of what American cities looked like; they were printed to capitalize on the widespread interest in Europe over the revolt of the American colonies.

99. The terrible fire in New York. *Habermann*

Shortly after midnight on 20 September 1776, five days after the British investment of New York, a fire broke out near Whitehall Slip in a wooden house or groggery on a wharf. It spread rapidly, and by midday had consumed some 493 buildings between Broadway and Hudson River before it was controlled by soldiers of the 5th Brigade and seamen sent ashore by Lord Howe. 'A most horrid attempt was made by a number of wretches', wrote Sir William Howe to Germain on 23 September, 'to burn the town of New York, in which they succeeded too well, having set it on fire in several places with matches and combustibles that had been prepared with great art and ingenuity.'

The fire was a heavy loss to the British, who had expected to house the troops there for the coming winter. General Greene had strongly recommended burning the town to Washington, who wrote 'Providence, or some good honest fellow, has done more for us than we were disposed to do for ourselves.' Sauthier's plan of New York (plate 82) shows the destroyed area.

in a state of despair laying themselves down on the Common. The terror was encreased by the horrid noise of the burning and falling houses, the pulling down of such wooden buildings as served to conduct the fire, (in which the Soldiers & Seamen were particularly active and useful) the rattling of above 100 waggons, sent in from the Army, and which were constantly employed in conveying to the Common such goods and effects as could be saved;—The confused voices of so many men, the Shrieks and cries of the Women and children, the seeing the fire break out unexpectedly in places at a distance, which manifested a design of totally destroying the City, with numberless other circumstances of private misery and distress, made this one of the most tremendous and affecting Scenes I ever beheld.

The appearance of Trinity Church, when completely in flames was a very grand sight, for the Spire being entirely framed of wood and covered with Shingles, a lofty Pyramid of fire appeared, and as soon as the Shingles were burnt away the frame appeared with every separate piece of timber burning, until the principal timbers were burnt through, then the whole fell with a great noise.'[10]

Perhaps it was the fire that led Howe to allow Washington to remain un-molested on Harlem Heights for almost a month. In fact, the soldiers almost forgot they had been shooting at each other just a couple of weeks earlier:

'. . . they were so civil to each other, on their posts, that one day, at a part of the creek where it was practicable, the British sentinel asked the American, who was nearly opposite to him, if he could give him a chew of tobacco: the latter, having in his pocket a piece of a thick twisted roll, sent it across the creek, to the British sentinel, who after taking off his bite, sent the remainder back again.'[11]

On 12 October, Howe moved. His first landing was on Throg's Neck, a peninsula jutting two miles out in Long Island Sound, and to the rear and the left of the American lines. But upon this occasion Washington had antici-pated him, and there were men entrenched and waiting. On the 18th, just one day after he had put ashore his last boatload of troops, Howe re-embarked his men and put them ashore at Pell's Point, just below New Rochelle. Captain Henry Duncan, Lord Howe's flag captain aboard the H.M.S. *Eagle*, wrote in his journal:

'About three o'clock Saturday morning, the 12th, the troops were embarked in the flat boats and batteaux, to the number of between four and five thousand men; the guards and 42nd regiment, between fourteen and fifteen hundred men, were embarked on board sloops under my direction. At day-break in the morning the boats set off, and no sooner had they put off, with an amazing strong tide, but it came on a fog equal to pitch darkness, with now and then an interval of light for a few seconds. The boats were put off; to attempt to stop them would have been very dangerous, for the headmost boats must have anchored, and the boats that followed would in all prob-ability run foul of them, to the imminent danger of sinking each other; the admiral, therefore, rather chose to run the risk of passing Hell Gate with all the boats in that rapid tide and dark fog.

I went astern and ordered all the boats to move forward. Soon after their putting off, a galley towing one of the artillery boats, in endeavouring to cross a vessel lying in the passage, towed her athwart hawse; the boat ran directly up her cable, and overset instantly. Many of the people were picked up; there were three field-pieces lost, and I suppose five or six people. There were very few people in the flat boats that ever been through or knew any-thing of the passage of Hell Gate. This made the danger much the greater. To keep the starboard shore was the safest passage; straight through carried them upon the rocks, and the larboard shore would have brought them under the fire of the enemy, perhaps without being able to land or retreat; but the boats got all luckily through, the one instance only excepted, and arrived at Frog Point, the place of their destination, about nine o'clock, where they landed without opposition.

They marched about two miles and a half in the country, but were there stopped very unexpectedly by a bridge being broke down across a small rivulet, and a causeway tore up that led across a morass.

Our people remained in this situation, with the sentinels popping at each [other], from the time of landing to the 18th October, when very early in the morning the flat boats all assembled and embarked between four and five thousand troops, with which they proceeded round Frog Point and landed on Myers' Neck in East Chester with opposition. The ground was very

100. The Royal Navy in New York har-bour, 1776
This beautifully engraved chart of the approaches to New York City and the lower Hudson River shows also by hachur-ing the elevations and contours of the land on either side of the river better than on any previous map. The chart, prepared for the *Atlantic Nep-tune* and the royal navy, gives the sound-ings in the river and its approaches as well as the location of British naval vessels up the Hudson in late 1776.

116

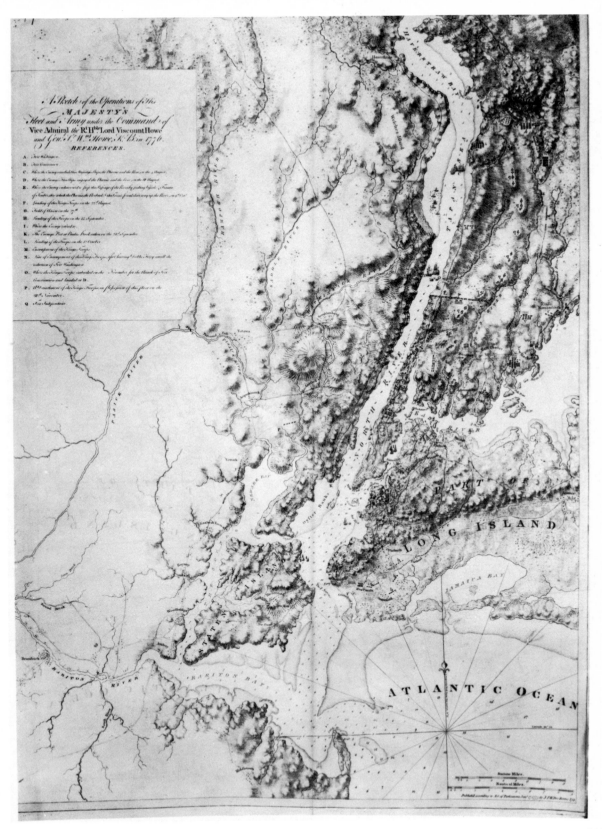

117

favourable for an attempt of that kind: a considerable part of the army marched across the Neck, not more than one or one and a half miles, and got within pistol-shot of the landing-place, although the passage by water could not be less than five or six miles.'[12]

Once again, Howe adopted a leisurely pace as he made his way towards the enemy, although he was delayed briefly by a small force under the command of John Glover. The British crawl had allowed Washington time to better his own position. Leaving garrisons at Forts Washington and Lee on the Hudson, Washington ordered the remainder of his army into Westchester to take post at White Plains. It was a strong position on the heights above the village, anchored on the left by a swamp and on the right by the Bronx River. Off to the right rose Chatterton's Hill. One American officer wrote such a graphic account of the subsequent battle that his story was published in several newspapers:

'Last Monday, the 28th, we received intelligence that the enemy, with their whole body. were advancing towards us. The army was immediately alarmed, and part of General Wadsworth's brigade, with some of the regiments under General Spencer (consisting in the whole of five or six hundred men), were sent out as an advanced party to skirmish with the enemy and harass them in their march. We marched on to a hill about one mile and a half from our lines, with an artillery company and two field pieces, and placed ourselves behind walls and fences in the best manner we could to give the enemy trouble. . . .

Once the Hessian grenadiers came up front of Colonel Douglass's regiment, and we fired a general volley upon them at about twenty rods distance, and scattered them like leaves in a whirlwind; and they ran off so far that

101. East View of Hell Gate. *T. A. Williams*

This peaceful scene, drawn by T. A. Williams in 1775, contrasts with the naval activity there in the fall of 1776. From the elevation at Morrisania ('5' on the plate) Washington looked across Harlem River on 17 November and saw to the north the disastrous defeat and capture of Greene's forces at Fort Washington.

The artist's position in this picture is on Long Island near Horn Hook, looking across the islands to the Bronx.

East View of Hell Gate, in the Province of New York.

Lond. Mag. Apr. 1778.

W A Williams del 1775

| 1 Hoorn's Hook. | 3 Hancock's Rock. | 5 Morrisena. | 7 Pinfold's Place. | 9 The Pot. | 11 The Frying |
| 2 The Gridiron. | 4 The Mill Rock. | 6 Bahannas Island. | 8 Hallet's Point. | 10 The Hogs back. | Pan. |

102. Operations of the King's army . . . 12th October to the 28th of November 1776 . . . The Engagement on the White Plains *(detail). C. J. Sauthier*

Washington's army was encamped in northern New York (Manhattan) Island between Fort Washington and Knightsbridge when Howe began a movement to cut off his rear communications. The American army, except for the troops at Fort Washington, then moved north in two detachments, one by the road paralleling Bronx River to White Plains, the other entrenching itself along the ridge of land by the Hudson. For the whole map see plate 104.

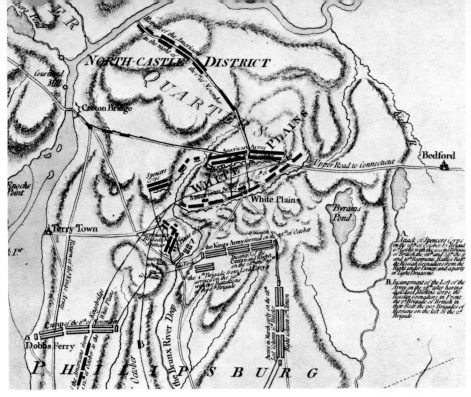

some of the regiment ran out to the ground where they were when we fired upon them and brought off their arms and accoutrements and rum, that the men who fell had with them, which we had time to drink with before they came on again.

They formed at a distance, and waited until their artillery and main body came on, and they advanced in solid columns against us, and were gathering all around us, ten to our one, Colonel Douglass's and Silliman's regiments fired four or five times on them as they were advancing and then retreated, but not until the enemy began to fire on their flanks. Colonels Silliman, Douglass and Arnold behaved nobly, and the men gained much applause. . . .

The scene was grand and solemn; all the adjacent hills smoked as though on fire, and bellowed and trembled with a perpetual cannonade and fire of field pieces, howitzers and mortars. The air groaned with streams of cannon and musket shot. The hills smoked and echoed terribly with the bursting of shells; the fences and walls were knocked down and torn to pieces, and men's legs, arms and bodies, mangled with cannon and grape shot all around us. I was in the action, and under as good advantage as any man, perhaps, to observe all that passed, and write these particulars of the action from my own observations. No general action was designed on our part, and I believe that one thousand men were never, at one time, engaged with the enemy. They came on the hills opposite our lines and halted, and after cannonading for a short time, they became very still and quiet.

On the 31st it was observed that they had near finished four or five batteries which they had erected against us and as our ground, near the center of the town of White Plains, was not good, being overlooked by the neighboring hills, the generals, last night, drew off most of the troops from the lines there, and this morning the guards and sentries burned the town and forage around it and came off about nine o'clock. We carried off all our stores, and planted our artillery on the hills about a mile and a half back of the center of the town. The enemy advanced this forenoon on to the ground we had left, but as soon as they came over the hill we saluted them with our cannon and field pieces, and they advanced no further. Our sick and wounded are sent out eight or ten miles. Our men are in good spirits, and with much patience endure great hardships and fatigue. Their main body now lies over against us, and they have formed no lines across the country, as yet, below us. Their light horse may possibly scour across as far as the river, but how that is we cannot determine. All things seem to be quiet at Fort Washington.'[13]

Again, Sir William Howe failed to follow up his advantage. He waited around for three days until he was reinforced by two brigades under Lord Percy and General Knyphausen's division of Hessians just off their transports. Now that he could overwhelm Washington by a sheer force of numbers, he proposed to attack the American lines on 31 October, only to be frustrated by a heavy rainstorm. During the dark hours of 1 November, Washington slipped out of his lines to take up a strong defensive position at North Castle behind the Croton River, some five miles away. Howe now fell back to Dobb's Ferry on 5 November, a position that put him between the American Army and Fort Washington and allowed him to pose a threat to Fort Lee.

Forts Washington and Lee had been built on the high cliffs above the Hudson as a means of controlling the river traffic. Vessels of the Royal Navy had proved them ineffective as they sailed almost insolently past the forts. Now they were isolated, yet remained as a symbol of rebel defiance. Congress had urged that the forts should not be given up; a council of war held in mid-October concurred with this opinion. The two forts were under the command of Nathanael Greene who had almost demanded that they be held and, against his own better judgement, Washington had gone along with this advice. The fort belied its appearance and was not the citadel its defenders claimed it to be. Yet one Hessian officer thought it formidable:

'The enemy had erected a fort on a high rocky elevation, which seemed fortified by nature itself, which they called Fort Washington. Human skill had also been employed to make it very strong. Without possession of this fort, we could not keep up communications with New York, nor could we think of advancing any farther, much less get quiet winter quarters.'[14]

Fort Washington was under the command of Colonel Robert Magaw. He was confident that he could hold his post 'till the end of December', and then, if pressed, could take off its garrison and stores to the Jersey shore. Greene agreed. No one, however, seemed to worry that the post's only water supply was the Hudson River, 240 feet below the rocky heights.

The formalities of war were carried through on 14 November, when Howe's adjutant, Lieutenant-Colonel Paterson, accompanied by a drummer, came up to the fort under the protection of a flag. To his demand that the garrison surrender or be put to the sword, Magaw's reply was that 'he did not expect inhumanity from Englishmen, and that he would defend the place to the last extremity'. The bombardment began the following morning, from batteries on the east side of the Harlem River and from the frigate *Pearl* in the Hudson. Years later, Ichabod Perry remembered this opening barrage:

'There was one little circumstance which took place which I believe no

103. A Topographical Map of the North Part of New York Island. *C. J. Sauthier*

After the inconclusive battle of White Plains, Howe decided to attack Fort Washington. On 16 November he launched a four-pronged attack, by (A) General Knyphausen and his Hessians from the north, (C) Generals Matthews and Cornwallis across Harlem River from the east, (B) Lieutenant-Colonel Stirling by transports down Harlem River, and (D) a feint by Lord Percy from the south at Gowan's Pass. Percy's movement, planned only as a diversion, became the major attack; it was the finest achievement in his short but able military career. With personal intrepidity and leadership, he broke through three lines of fortifications on Harlem Heights on the way and stormed the fort against the main body of defenders, who had been forced back into it by the other three attacks. The whole of Manhattan Island was now under British control. For the Continental army it was a disastrous defeat; 2,634 prisoners were taken, with large supplies of guns, ammunition, and stores.

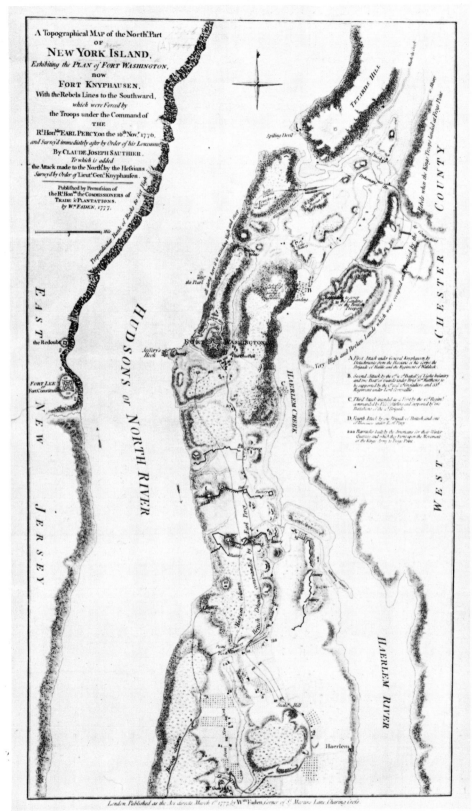

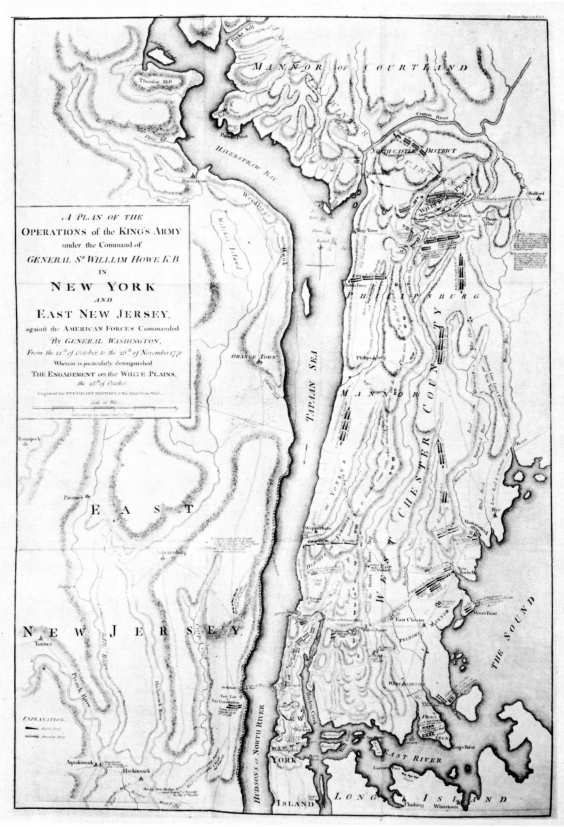

A PLAN OF THE
OPERATIONS of the KING'S ARMY
under the Command of
GENERAL Sr. WILLIAM HOWE K.B.
IN
NEW YORK
AND
EAST NEW JERSEY,
against the AMERICAN FORCES Commanded
By GENERAL WASHINGTON,
From the 12th of October, to the 28th of November 1776.
Wherein is particularly distinguished
THE ENGAGEMENT on the WHITE PLAINS,
the 28th of October.
Engraved for STEDMAN'S HISTORY of the American War.

104. Operations of the King's army . . . 12th October to the 28th of November 1776 . . . The Engagement on the White Plains. *C. J. Sauthier*

When Howe began transporting his army by East River to Frog's Neck and to Pell's Point and Myers Point on the Sound, Washington concentrated both detachments, almost 15,000 men, behind the lines at White Plains between 12 and 25 October. He sent out small groups which slowed Howe's advance, but the British attacked with superior strength on 28 October. Washington withdrew north of the Croton River to a position that Howe felt was too strong for further pursuit; he decided to turn his attention to Fort Washington. Howe withdrew to Dobbs Ferry on the Hudson and then south to the Fordham Heights. Washington crossed the Hudson to New Jersey, leaving part of his army under Greene to guard against a British march into New England.

historian has before mention'd that is, when the British was throwing shells from their howitzs' and dropping them just over our breast-works, we had a small dog that would watch them and whenever he saw one strike the ground, he would run and catch the fuse in his mouth, and hold it with his feet on the shell, till he pull'd it out and so stop it from exploding, He had the good luck to serve several that way which made to the amusement of the spectators, but at length he fail'd. While he was in the act of trying to get out the fuse, the shell explod'd and the poor dog went to atoms. It is possible that the little dog by his exertion saved some human lives but lost his own.'[15]

Robert Auchmuty, loyalist and former Admiralty judge in Boston, now a refugee in England, received a graphic description of the taking of the two forts on the Hudson:

'The honour of reducing this important place was solicited by General Knyphausen, in which he was indulged by General Howe. Everything therefore being prepared, agreeable to the most masterly disposition, the attack was begun at daybreak on Saturday morning the 15th instant. A

105. The Landing of the British Forces in the Jerseys on the 20th of November 1776 under the command of the Rt Honl Lieut Genl Earl Cornwallis. *Davies*

Two days after the surrender by Colonel Magaw of Fort Washington with almost 3,000 men and much equipment and ammunition, General William Howe moved with uncharacteristic rapidity to surprise Fort Lee, almost directly across the Hudson. The troops under Cornwallis ascended the Palisades on the night of 19 November and reached the fort unopposed; it had been hurriedly evacuated. Washington, at Hackensack, had been hastily informed by General Greene, in command at the Fort, that the British were approaching; he saw the situation was hopeless and immediately ordered retreat.

The script and style of this unsigned watercolour is that of Captain Thomas Davies of the Royal Regiment of Artillery, who had made a signed drawing of the attack on Fort Washington a few days before. As an artillery officer he noted the ferrying of cannons across, their unloading, and their being dragged up the precipitous slope.

detachment of Hessians with cannon marched round from General Howe's army from Kingsbridge along the clear road (which you will remember is a kind of causeway) through a hollow way, commanded on both sides by very steep craggy hills on which the rebels had redoubts, which enfiladed the whole length of the valley. The Hessians with great firmness marched through this way until they came to the north end of the steep mountain on the Harlem River, on the left side, which they began to climber up, notwithstanding the heavy fire from the rebels on the top of the hills, and after very great difficulties and labours gained the summit; which as soon as the rebels saw they ran away towards the fort with great precipitation.

At the same time that this Hessian detachment marched around by Kingsbridge, the 43rd and 71st, two Highland regiments, pushed over Harlem or Kingsbridge River in flat bottomed boats about two miles and a half below Kingsbridge, and directly opposite to the most rugged and steep part of the mountain, where the rebels had raised no works, thinking it utterly impossible for any human being to climb up a rocky precipice nearly perpendicular. There however these brave North Britons landed, and with incredible labour scrambled up by means of small bushes growing out through the cracks of the rocks on the side of the mountain; all the while sustaining a heavy fire from the rebels at the top; which as soon as they had reached, they began a very spirited attack upon the rebels, who were in the bushes on top of the mountains, driving them from behind trees and rocks; and by this means greatly facilitating the operations of the Hessians, who had very hard work, some to scramble over the rocks, and fight all the way, in order to make way for others who was to drag their cannon along a very steep road, commanded on all sides. All these difficulties were at last overcome by firmness, patience, and the most manly perseverance, and they had the pleasure of soon dispersing all the rebels they could find in their route, who ran towards the fort in the utmost panic.

These operations you will observe were on the north and east side of the rebels' works. But the success would, in all human probability, have been very precarious, had it not been for Lord Percy's attack on the very strong lines on the heights of the Harlem side; in which the chief body of the rebels had planted themselves. For at the same instant that the Hessians and Highlanders began their attack, his Lordship with the brigades under his command attacked the lines with singular bravery, rushing into them with the greatest fury, and driving the rebels from line to line, and from work to work, till he had got them crammed up in the fort, before the Hessians could get to it with their cannon.

About one o'clock this was the situation of the wretches, who seeing themselves surrounded on all sides by the troops with fixed bayonets, and the cannon within two hundred paces, sent out a white flag, begging that the general would not fire upon them, for that they were consulting about surrendering, which they were not long about. By 4 o'clock they had laid down their arms, delivered themselves up prisoners, and the troops took possession of the fort, with everything in it. . . .

General Howe, I think, on the morning of the 20th instant landed 5,000 men under the command of Lord Cornwallis up the North River on the Jersey shore, a few miles above the other famous fortification, called Fort Constitution or Fort Lee. His Lordship immediately marched to attack this place, and got to it by 1 o'clock the same day, but found that it had been evacuated by the rebels so precipitately that the pots were left absolutely boiling on the fire, and the tables spread for dinner of some of their officers.

In the fort they found but twelve men, who were all dead drunk. There were forty or fifty pieces of cannon found loaded, with two large iron sea mortars and one brass one, with a vast quantity of ammunition, provisions and stores, with all their tents standing. His Lordship finding this pressed forward as quick as he could toward Hackensack new bridge. But the people belonging to the fort had the heels of him. However, on the road he met with 3 or 4,000 fresh hands coming from Newark to assist in garrisoning the forts. To these gentry the troops distributed a couple of rounds, and sent them a scampering, leaving behind them several brass field pieces and their baggage; and as they marched along, found the roads thick strewed with muskets, knapsacks, etc. . . .

The southern people will no more fight than the Yankees. The fact is that their army is all broken to pieces, and the spirits of their leaders and their abettors is also broken. However, I think one may venture to pronounce that it is well nigh over with them. All their strongholds are in the hands of his Majesty's troops. All their cannon and mortars, and the greatest part of their stores, ammunition, etc. are gone. The people in the country almost universally sick of it, in a starving condition, and cannot help themselves, And what is to become of them during the approaching inclement season God only knows.'[16]

New York was lost. Washington could no longer make a stand. He began to pull back through the Jerseys. Howe felt confident enough to dispatch an expedition to occupy Narrangansett Bay. Among the British officers was Alexander Cochrane:

'You will have heard of our leaving New York with the rest of the fleet under Sir Peter Parker & Commodore Hotham, and the land forces which amounted to about 6000 under General Clinton & Lord Piercey upon a private expedition which proved to be Rhode Island, where we arrived about a Month ago and effected our Landing the next day without any Opposition, the Rebels having entirely left the Island. (I mean their Troops, for the whole Inhabitants are Rebels.)

A day or two after our arrival we were sent about 15 Miles above the Town to assist in blocking up the Rebel Admiral Hopkins and his Squadron which consists of a 32, one 30, & one 28 gun Frigate, & a 16 gun brig, and a few sloops & Schooners. If you will look at any draught of the Coast you will perceive their cituation. The Rebels now lay up at Providence—We lay between Hope Island and the Main. There is a Frigate lays up above us in the passage from Patience and Connecticut, and below us the Renown between Rhode Island and Providence is guarded by Frigates. And at Town the two Commodores lay ready to run out in Case they attempt to make their escape. I think they are pretty safe for this Winter.'[17]

To many it appeared that the war was just about over. Some British soldiers were beginning to think of home, while some officers were sending to England for items that might make their occupation duty in the restored colonies more comfortable.

6. The Jersey Campaign

FOR THE BRITISH, the conquests of Forts Washington and Lee had seemed easy. One soldier chortled,

'On the appearance of our troops, the rebels fled like scared rabbits, and in a few moments after we reached the hill near their entrenchments, not a rascal of them could be seen. They have left some poor pork, a few greasy proclamations, and some of that scoundrel Common Sense man's letters, which we can read at our leisure, now that we have got one of the "impregnable redoubts" of Mr. Washington's to quarter in. . . . We intend to push on after the long-faces in a few days.'[1]

Rebel faces were indeed long, and none longer than that of the commander-in-chief. Cold rain fell, turning roads into soggy quagmires over which ragged, weary men dragged their ill-clad feet. There was no way to make a stand; the picks and shovels lost at the Hudson River forts so depleted the supply of the American Army that they could not even dig entrenchments. The general gloom of his men grew darker as the story circulated of a conversation supposedly between Washington and Joseph Reed, his adjutant. When Colonel Reed observed that if the eastern counties of Pennsylvania were subdued by the British the back counties would submit without a struggle, Washington, or so the story ran, passed his hand over his throat and said, 'My neck does not feel as though it was made for a halter. We must retire to Augusta County, in Virginia, . . . and, if overpowered, we must pass the Allegheny Mountains.'

Cornwallis had crossed the Hudson and was in full cry in pursuit. There was nothing for Washington to do but continue the flight across Jersey and get the Delaware River between his army and the enemy. Matters worsened every day. He reached Brunswick, New Jersey, but the New Jersey and Maryland militia brigades kept on going, seeking the comforts of home. Even as Washington looked deeper into the pit of despair, the vanguard of Cornwallis's army appeared on the far side of the Raritan River and American gunners played a smart cannonade to cover the army's withdrawal. The pursuit slowed, for Howe had ordered Cornwallis to halt at the Raritan. The British chafed with restlessness until the commanding general jogged down to Brunswick to give the word to take up the chase again. Washington gained the time to cross his baggage, stores, sick and wounded, as well as to collect or destroy every boat on the Delaware for seventy miles above Philadelphia. He controlled the river passage. He started back to Princeton, but discovering that the British were again marching forward under Howe's personal command, he once more fell back towards the river. Captain Enoch Anderson of the Delaware Continentals commanded the rear guard:

'We continued on our retreat—our regiment in the rear, and I, with thirty men, in rear of the regiment, and General Washington in my rear with pioneers—tearing up bridges and cutting down trees to impede the march of the enemy. I was to go no faster than General Washington and his pioneers. It was dusk before we got to Trenton.'[2]

It was cold on Sunday 8 December, when Cornwallis, leading the vanguard of Howe's army, pushed into Trenton. They arrived just in time to see the last of the Americans rowing across to the Pennsylvania shore. Thirty-seven rebel guns mounted on the south bank saluted Howe's men as they came up. The British pitched camp and sat waiting, waiting for Washington to make his next move.

When Washington crossed the river, Charles Lee stubbornly remained behind at White Plains with the twenty-five hundred Continental troops under his command. But the American situation had grown so desperate that the presence of these forces was now imperative. The eccentric Lee was now feeling so superior to the commander-in-chief that he seemed to feel it degrading to have to serve again under Washington. The commander-in-chief prostrated himself in humiliation, trying to urge his subordinate to come forward with his men. 'Do come on,' he begged, 'your arrival may be happy, and if it can be effected without delay, may be the means of preserving a City, whose loss must prove of the most fatal consequences to the cause of America.'

On 4 December, Lee bestirred himself and crossed the Hudson at King's Ferry, having written earlier, 'I am going into the Jerseys for the salvation of America.' He had proceeded as far as Morristown via Pompton, but by 12

106. Gray's Ferry, Schuylkill River, Pennsylvania

At the time of his dramatic recrossing of the Delaware River in December 1776 to win his victories at Trenton and Princeton, Washington conscripted the ferrymen up and down the river to help with the moving across of men and supplies. This is a typical ferry of the time; the ferry is halfway across the river, to the right of a pontoon footbridge.

AN EAST VIEW of GRAY'S FERRY. on the RIVER SCHUYLKILL.

December his troops had marched no farther than Bernardsville. The Continentals were ordered towards Germantown under General John Sullivan, his second-in-command. Accompanied by a guard of fifteen men and his aides, Lee stopped over at a tavern kept by a widow at Basking Ridge, three miles from the encampment of his troops. The following morning, in dressing gown and slippers, he sat in his room at the tavern writing a letter to his friend, Horatio Gates, in which he took the opportunity of flailing Washington and inflating his own value:

'The ingenious manoeuvre of Fort Washintong has unhing'd the goodly fabrick We have been building—there never was so damn'd a stroke—*entre nous*, a certain great man is most damnably deficient—he has thrown me into a situation where I have my choice of difficulties—if I stay in this Province I risk myself and Army and if I did not stay the Province is lost for ever.'[3]

Even as Lee wrote, danger came galloping down the lane. Lieutenant-Colonel William Harcourt, on a British patrol, had discovered that Lee had stopped at the tavern with but a thin guard. Captain James Wilkinson, an aide, was with the American general:

'General Lee was engaged in answering Gates' letter, and I had risen from the table and was looking out an end window down a lane about one hundred yards when I discovered a party of British dragoons turn a corner of the avenue at a full charge.

Startled by this unexpected spectacle, I exclaimed, "Here, Sir, are the British cavalry!"

"Where?" replied the general, who had signed his letter in the instant.

"Around the house," for they had opened files and encompassed the building.

General Lee appeared alarmed, yet collected, and his second observation marked his self-possession: "Where is the guard?—damn the guard, why don't they fire?" and after a momentary pause, turned to me and said, "Do, Sir, see what has become of the guard?"

The woman of the house at this moment entered the room and proposed to him to conceal himself in a bed, which he rejected with evident disgust. I caught up my pistols which lay on the table, thrust the letter he had been writing into my pocket, and passed into a room at the opposite end of the

107. Occupation of Newport. *Robert Cleveley*

In December 1776 General Howe sent a strong force under his two lieutenant-generals, Sir Henry Clinton and Earl Percy, by transports through Long Island Sound to occupy Rhode Island. A fleet of larger war ships under Sir Peter Parker sailed south of Long Island; the British seized Newport in an amphibious assault and occupied it until October 1779. Howe recalled Clinton to New York and left Percy in command. Early in 1777 he called on Percy to send him 1,500 men for the New Jersey campaign; Percy sent only 1,100, claiming that a greater number would leave him with inadequate defence against hostile attacks. This occasioned a sharp reprimand from Howe. Percy, who had just inherited six baronies and was one of the wealthiest young noblemen in England, requested and received permission to retire. On 5 May 1777 he left Newport for England. There, although both he and his father, the Duke of Northumberland, had favoured conciliation before the war, he made in the House of Lords a defence of the conduct of British officers and urged vigorous prosecution of the war. He took back with him as his personal secretary C. J. Sauthier, who had made some of the finest maps of the Revolution.

Robert Cleveley (1747–1809) was a maritime painter who attained distinction for his scenes of naval action. He was referred to as 'Robert Cleveley of the Navy'; he probably had an appointment at Deptford but no naval commission.

house, where I had seen the guard in the morning. Here I discovered their arms, but the men were absent. I stepped out of the door and perceived the dragoons chasing them in different directions, and receiving a very uncivil salutation, I returned into the house.

Too inexperienced immediately to penetrate the motives of this enterprise, I considered the *rencontre* accidental, and from the terrific tales spread over the country of the violence and barbarity of the enemy, I believed it to be a wanton murdering party, and determined not to die without company. I accordingly sought a position where I could not be approached by more than one person at a time, and with a pistol in each hand, I awaited the expected search, resolved to shoot the first and second person who might appear, and then appeal to my sword. I did not remain long in this unpleasant situation, but was apprised of the object of the incursion by the very audible declaration, "If the General does not surrender in five minutes, I will set fire to the house"; which after a short pause was repeated with a solemn oath; and within two minutes I heard it proclaimed, "Here is the general. He has surrendered." A general shout ensued, the trumpet sounded assembly, and the unfortunate Lee mounted on my horse, which stood ready at the door, was hurried off in triumph, bareheaded, in his slippers and blank coat, his collar open, and his shirt very much soiled from several days use.'[4]

To many British soldiers, the capture of Charles Lee was almost a prelude to victory, and one newspaper reported that 'a band or two of music played all night to proclaim their joy for this important occasion' and they celebrated 'by making his horse drunk, while they toasted their King until they were in the same condition'. Many believed that Lee had been responsible for those little successes that the Americans had been able to gain. Washington mourned the loss of Lee, for he too felt the former British officer to have been a great asset to the rebel forces. Yet the Americans were not so despondent as they should have been. One young Brigade-Major even described the retreat with a bit of a lilt:

'You ask me our Situation; it has been the Devil, but it is to appearance better. About 2,000 of us have been obliged to run damn'd hard about 10,000 of the Enemy. Never was finer lads at a retreat than we are. 'Tis said the

108. Battle of Princeton. *William Mercer*

General Hugh Mercer was sent with a detachment to destroy the Stony Brook bridge south of Princeton on the main road from Trenton. On a hill near William Clark's house, shown in the right background, they encountered the 17th regiment and a troop of the 16th mounted dragoons under Colonel Mawhood that had been quickly diverted from their march to join Cornwallis at Trenton. The detachment was driven back and dispersed; General Washington arrived with reinforcements, rallied the troops, and routed the British. General Mercer, mortally wounded, is shown in the centre of the painting fallen from his white horse; he was carried to, and died later in the house of Thomas Clark, situated behind the viewpoint from which the scene is painted. Washington is on a charger; two mounted officers by him are probably Generals Greene and Cadwallader.

The British Lieutenant-Colonel William Harcourt wrote after the Battle of Princeton, 'They [the Americans] possess . . . extreme cunning, great industry . . . and a spirit of enterprise upon any advantage . . . though it was once the fashion of this army to treat them in the most contemptuous light, they are now become a formidable enemy.'

William Mercer, the son of General Mercer, copied this painting from one (now lost) by Charles Willson Peale who was present at the battle under Cadwallader, or from the painting by James Peale, Charles Peale's brother, which is now in the Princeton University Library.

109. The Capture of General Lee.
Hamilton

In this strange episode of 11 December 1776 in the career of the erratic General Charles Lee, a young cornet of cavalry named Banastre Tarleton makes his first appearance in the history of the Rebellion. He it was whom Colonel Harcourt sent ahead at a gallop, with his advance guard of five men, towards the tavern where they had been informed that Lee was. 'I went on at full speed', Tarleton wrote to his mother, 'when perceiving two sentrys at a door and a loaded wagon, I pushed at them, making all the noise I could . . . I fired twice through the door of the house and then addressed myself to this effect: . . . "if he [Lee] would surrender himself, he and his attendants should be safe, but if not, . . . the house should be burnt and every person without exception should be put to the sword"'. While Tarleton was called to the back door on a false alarm, Lee emerged from the front and surrendered to a sentry. A French colonel was captured with him. 'This is a most miraculous event', concluded young Tarleton; 'it appears like a dream.'

Enemy are bound for N. York Via South Amboy; it wants Confirmation. I wish it may be true. No fun for us that I can see; however, I cannot but think we shall drub the Dogs. Those gone for New England will meet their Deserts. I hope, sure I am, the Lads of that Country will not behave in the dam'd cowardly, rascally manner the people of this Country have. Never mind, all will come right one of these days.'[5]

The almost headlong flight of the American Army and the capture of Charles Lee convinced Howe that the time had come to retire into winter quarters and rest on his laurels. Fourteen thousand troops were distributed in a long chain of posts stretching from Staten Island to Princeton. Along the Delaware there were garrisons stationed at Pennington, Bordentown, Trenton, and, for a short while, Burlington. So confident was he of a quiet winter that Howe granted Cornwallis permission to return to England to visit his ailing wife. Before he returned to the comforts of New York, Howe issued orders to the officers of the various garrisons 'to exert themselves in preserving the greatest regularity and strictest discipline in their respective quarters particularly attending the protection of the inhabitants and their property in their several districts'. Commanding officers apparently paid little attention to this directive. It had been a hard campaign and the rank and file seemed determined to take their fun where they found it, especially the Hessians who felt they were entitled to all the spoils of war. And every incident was played up by the Americans. It made good propaganda, yet there was always more than a germ of truth in the accounts:

'The progress of the British and Hessian troops through New-Jersey has been attended with such scenes of desolation and outrage as would disgrace the most barbarous nations. Among inumerable instances, the following are authenticated, in such a manner as leaves no doubt of their truth:

William Smith, of Smith's farm, near Woodbridge, hearing the cries of his daughter, rushed into the room and found a Hessian officer attempting to ravish her. In an agony of rage and resentment, he instantly killed him, but the officer's party came upon him, and he now lies mortally wounded at his ruined, plundered dwelling.

On Monday morning they entered the house of Samuel Stout, Esq., in Hopewell, where they destroyed his deeds, papers, furniture, and effects of every kind, except what they plundered. They took every horse away, left his house and farm in ruins, injuring him to the value of three thousand pounds in less than three hours. Old Mr. Phillips, his neighbour, they pillaged in the same manner, and then cruelly beat him.

On Wednesday past three women came down to the Jersey shore in great distress; a party of the American Army went and brought them off, when it appeared that they all had been very much abused, and the youngest of them, a girl about fifteen years of age, had been ravished that morning by a British officer.

A number of young women in Hopewell, to the amount of sixteen, flying before the ravaging and cruel enemy, took refuge on a mountain near Ralph Hary's, but information being given of their retreat, they were soon brought down into the British camp, where they have been kept ever since.

The fine settlements of Maidenhead and Hopewell are entirely broken up; no age nor sex have been spared; the houses are stripped of every article of furniture, and what is not portable is entirely destroyed. The stock of cattle and sheep are drove off; every article of clothing and house linen seized and carried away. Scarce a soldier in the Army but has a horse loaded with plunder. Hundreds of families are reduced from comfort and affluence to poverty and ruin, left at this inclement season to wander through the woods without house or clothing.

If those scenes of desolation, ruin, and distress, do not rouse and animate every man of spirit to revenge their much-injured countrymen and country-women, all virtue, honour, and courage must have left this country, and we deserve all that we shall meet with, as there can be no doubt the same scene will be acted in this Province [Pennsylvania] upon our property, and our beloved wives and daughters.'[6]

But plundering was no one-way street. Charles Stedman, once a student at the College of William and Mary, but now a British officer, although admitting that 'no sooner had the army entered the Jerseys, than the business (we say business for it was a perfect trade) of plunder began. The friend and the foe, from the hand of rapine, shared alike', also noted that 'at the same time it is to be noticed, that the American troops were suffered to plunder the loyalists, and to exercise with impunity every act of barbarity on that unfortunate class of people; frequently inflicting on them scourges and stripes'.

One volunteer with Washington in the flight across the Jerseys carried a pen that was mightier than his sword. Thomas Paine had spent his spare time writing a sequel to his *Common Sense* and on 19 December had published *The Crisis* in Philadelphia. His words rang like a bell:

'These are the times that try men's souls: the summer soldier and the sunshine patriot will, in this crisis, shrink from the service of his country; but he that stands it NOW, deserves the thanks of man and woman. Tyranny, like Hell, is not easily conquered; yet we have this consolation with us, that the harder the conflict the more glorious the triumph. What we obtain too cheap, we esteem too lightly. 'Tis dearness only that gives everything its value. Heaven knows how to set a proper price upon its good; and it would be

110. Take Your Choice! *Cartright*

John Cartright, 'the father of Parliamentary reform', vigorously advocated American independence. He had served ten years as a young naval officer in Newfoundland; upon his return to England in 1770 he turned to politics. As the crisis in the Empire worsened, his sympathy for the colonies strengthened. In 1774 appeared his *American Independence*; he published an enlarged edition the following year with a draft bill for Parliament's settling the problems with the colonies. It also included a map of 'British America' with details of proposed new territories west of the Appalachians, such as Choctawria west of Georgia and South Carolina, and Chicasawria west of North Carolina and Virginia. He extended his attack on Parliament in 1776, detailing its evils and advocating reforms in *Take Your Choice!* This diagram served as the frontispiece to the work.

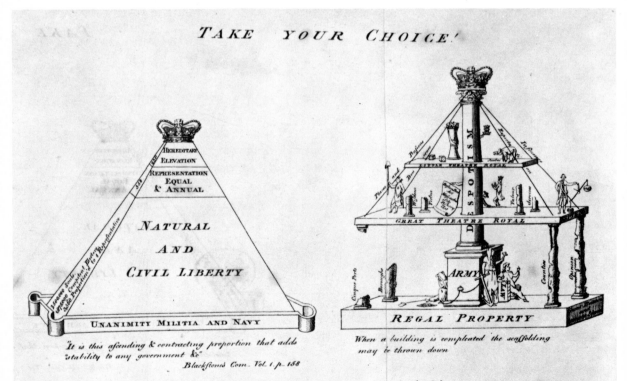

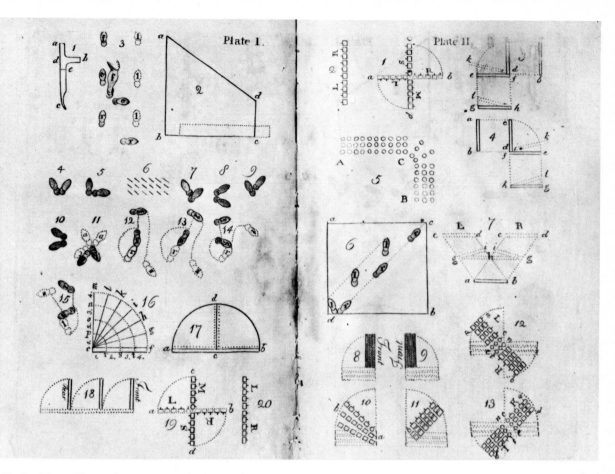

Plate I.

Plate II.

111. An Easy Plan of Discipline for a Militia. *Timothy Pickering*

This clear, concise codification of essentials, including organization, elementary foot-drill, and company movements, was published in 1775. Plate I shows, 1. a trenching and all-purpose tool, 2. how to wrap a cartridge in brown paper, 3. positions of the feet when firing three ranks deep, 7–8. right face, 9–10. left face, 11. about face, 12–13. to the rear, march; Plate II, 1. wheeling by line, 5. wheeling by column of ranks, and 6. oblique march.

strange indeed, if so celestial an article as FREEDOM should not be highly rated. . . . Would that Heaven might inspire some Jersey maid to spirit up her countrymen, and save her fair fellow sufferers from ravage and ravagement.'[7]

The soul of George Washington had indeed been tried, but events were beginning to take on a temporary brightness. His army was increasing faster than his men deserted. John Sullivan brought in 2,000 of Lee's men, although the captured general had crossed over into the Jerseys with 5,000. Horatio Gates brought in 500, all that remained out of seven regiments. A regiment of German immigrants came in. John Cadwalader led in 1,000 Philadelphia Associators. The American commander-in-chief would soon have 6,000 men, but he knew that he would have to act quickly. Many enlistments would be expiring at the end of the year, and the general mood of the men was such that they would return home as soon as they were free.

Washington decided to attack Trenton. This garrison was the terminal of the string of the British posts across Jersey, and there were also signs that the enemy intended using that point as a jumping off place for an invasion of Pennsylvania.

He initiated a campaign to throw the Hessian commander, Colonel Johann Gottlieb Rall, off guard by subjecting the garrison to a series of harassing raids. The Hessians became jittery. Rall didn't. The arrogant colonel was contemptuous of the 'Country clowns'. And he had a cure for the jitters—his bottle. So certain was he that he would not be molested that he had parked his artillery before his headquarters rather than in positions commanding the approaches to the town. After the subsequent battle, a Hessian diary was found and published in a newspaper:

'December 13, 1776. We marched to Trenton and joined our two regiments of Rall and Kniphausen, in order to take up a fort for winter quarters here, which are wretched enough. This town consists of about one hundred houses, of which many are mean and little, and it is easy to conceive how ill it must accomodate three regiments. The inhabitants, like those at Princeton, are almost all fled, so that we occupy bare walls. The Delaware, which is here extremely rapid, and in general about two ells deep, separates us and the rebels. We are obliged to be constantly on our guard, and do very severe duty, though our people began to grow ragged and our baggage is left in New York. Notwithstanding we have marched across this extremely fine province of New Jersey, which may justly be called the garden of America, yet it is by no means freed from the enemy, and we are insecure in flank and rear. This brigade had uncontestably suffered the most of any, and we now lie at the advanced point, and as soon as the Delaware freezes we may march over and attack Philadelphia, which is about thirty miles distant. My friend Sheffer and myself lodge in a fine house belonging to a merchant, and we have empty rooms enough. Some of the servants of the inhabitants remain here; last evening I gave one a box on the ear for his sauciness; I bid him bring me a candle, and he replied, if I wanted candles, I should have brought them with me. I was furnished with a candle, but nothing else. Here is no wine, except Madaira at three shillings and six pences sterling a bottle. On the third instant Capt. Weiterhausen, of the grenadiers, was shot at Brunswick bridge by a rebel, who had concealed himself under the bridge. The Capt, had wrote by the last packet to his wife, desiring her to follow him to America. . . .

The 16th the rebels came over the river in boats, but effected nothing.

The 18th seventy rebels came over the water, and we were obliged to turn out. But they only carried off a family who went willingly, with three cows and some furniture.

The 19th one of the English lighthorse was twice badly wounded by a troop of rebels near Maidenhead.

The 21st a horseman shot dead.

The 23rd Count Donop wrote to us from Bordentown, desiring us to be on our guard, for that he was certain of being attacked.

The 24th the enemy actually attacked our grenadiers last night, but without success. two Highlanders and a grenadier were wounded. We have not slept one night in peace since we came to this place. The troops have laid on their arms every night, but they can endure it no longer. We give ourselves more trouble and uneasiness than is necessary. That men who will not fight without some defense before them, who have neither coat, shoe nor stocking, nor scarce any thing else to cover their bodies. and who for a long time have not received a farthing of pay, should dare attack regular troops in open country, which they could not withstand when they were posted amongst rocks and in the strongest intrenchments, is not to be supposed.'[8]

134

All surgeons were called in by Washington, should their services be needed. Doctor Benjamin Rush arrived on 21 December:

'I visited Genl. Washington in company with Col. Jos. Reed at the Generals quarters about ten miles above Bristol, and four from the Delaware. I spent the night at a farm house near to him, and the next morning passed near an hour with him in private. He appeared much depressed, and lamented the ragged and dissolving state of his army in affecting terms. I gave him assurance of the disposition of Congress to support him, under his present difficulties and distresses. While I was talking to him, I observed him to play

112. Operations of General Washington, against the Kings Troops in New Jersey

On Christmas night Washington crossed the Delaware at Mckonkey Ferry, nine miles above Trenton, his army ferried through drifting ice floes by Glover's Marbleheaders, who had saved his army that summer in the evacuation of Long Island. Early in the morning of 26 December the Continentals fell on the insolently unprepared Colonel Johann Rall in Trenton. The Hessians were routed; a thousand were taken prisoner and Rall was mortally wounded. Washington returned to Pennsylvania but crossed the Delaware again to Trenton with augmented forces. Cornwallis, however, had hurried to New Brunswick from New York and marched with 6,000 troops to the outskirts of Trenton by 2 January. It was too late for Washington to ferry his troops across the river without heavy loss; that night, leaving his campfires burning, he marched east to Allentown and north to Princeton. Cornwallis, outflanked and outmanoeuvred, angrily set out in pursuit. Washington turned left at Kingstown to a tactically safe encampment at Morristown.

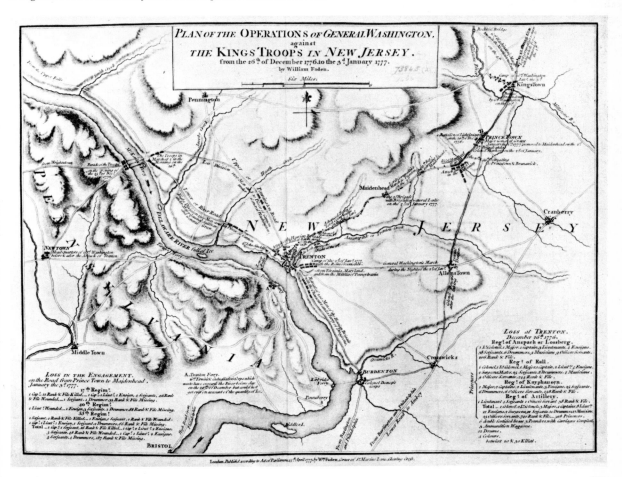

with his pen and ink upon several small pieces of paper. One of them by accident fell upon the floor near my feet. I was struck with the inscription upon it. It was "Victory or Death". . . . I had reason to believe here, that in my interview with Genl. Washington, he had been meditating upon his attack upon the Hessians at their posts on the Jersey side of the Delaware, for I found that the countersign of his surprise of Trenton was "Victory or Death." '9

The attack was set for the day after Christmas. One of Washington's aides speculated that 'They make a great deal of Christmas in Germany, and no doubt the Hessians will drink a great deal of beer and have a dance to-night. They will be sleepy tomorrow morning. Washington will set the tune for them about daybreak.' Among those who assembled was young John Greenwood:

'A day or two after reaching Newton we were paraded one afternoon to march and attack Trenton. If I recollect aright the sun was about half an hour high and shining brightly, but it had no sooner set than it began to drizzle or grow wet, and when we came to the river it rained. Every man had sixty rounds served out to him, and as I then had a gun, as indeed every officer had, I put the number which I received, some in my pockets and some in my cartridge-box.

Over the river we then went in a flat-bottomed scow, and as I was with the first that crossed, we had to wait for the rest and so began to pull down fences and make fires to warm ourselves, for the storm was increasing rapidly. After a while it rained, hailed, snowed, and froze, and at the same time blew a perfect hurricane; so much so that I perfectly recollect after putting the rails on to burn, the wind and fire would cut them in two in a moment, and

113. Amputation techniques. *Lorenz Heister*

This rather formal picture of doctors in curled wigs and frock coats amputating limbs gives a small idea of the sufferings of the wounded and sick in the American Revolution. Not only were general anaesthetics for surgery unknown, but the most elementary medicines were in short supply, as were blankets, bedding, dry accommodations, food, and doctors, surgeons and nurses themselves.

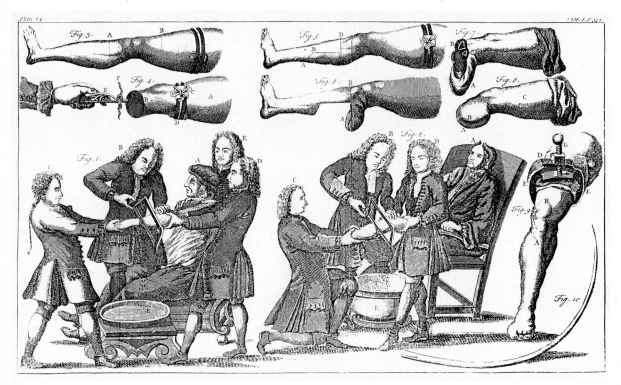

when I turned my face towards the fire my back would be freezing. However, as my usual acuteness had not forsaken me, by turning round and round I kept myself from perishing before the large bonfire. The noise of the soldiers coming over and clearing away the ice, the rattling of the cannon wheels on the frozen ground, and the cheerfulness of my fellow-comrades encouraged me beyond expression, and, big coward as I acknowledge myself to be, I felt great pleasure, more than I do now in writing about it.

After our men had all crossed—and there were not, as I could see, more than 200 of us—we began an apparently circuitous march, not advancing faster than a child ten years old could walk, and stopping frequently, though for what purpose I know not. During the whole night it alternately hailed, rained, snowed, and blew tremendously. I recollect very well that at one time, when we halted on the road, I sat down on the stump of a tree and was so benumbed with cold that I wanted to go to sleep; had I been passed unnoticed I should have frozen to death without knowing it; but as good luck always attended me, Sergeant Madden came and rousing me up, made me walk about. We then began to march again, just in the old slow way, until the dawn of day, about half-past seven in the morning.

I have heard that we surprised the enemy, if we did, they must have been a lazy, indolent set of rascals, which is nothing to the credit of a regular army, as the English called themselves. But any who would even suppose such a thing must indeed be ignorant, when it is well known that our whole country was filled with timid, designing tories and informers of all descriptions, and our march was so slow that it was impossible but that they should be apprised of it. It was likewise asserted at the same time that the enemy were all drunk; if they were, it shows there was no good discipline among those brave, regular troops. If they were drunk, I can swear that we were all sober to a man; not only sober, but nearly half dead with cold for want of clothing, as, putting the storm to one side, many of our soldiers had not a shoe to their feet and their clothes were ragged as those of a beggar. I am certain that not a drop of liquor was drunk during the whole night, nor, as I could see, even a piece of bread eaten. . . .

Between seven and eight- o'clock, as we were marching near the town, the first intimation I received of our going to fight was the firing of a 6-pound cannon at us, the ball from which struck the fore horse that was dragging our only piece of cannon, a 3-pounder. The animal, which was near to me as I was in the second division on the left, was struck in its belly and knocked over on its back. While it lay there kicking the cannon was stopped and I did not see it again after we passed on.

As we advanced, it being dark and stormy so that we could not see very far ahead, we got within 200 yards of about 300 or 400 Hessians who were paraded, two deep, in a straight line with Colonel Roll, their commander, on horseback, to the right of them. They made a full fire at us, but I did not see that they killed any one. Our brave Major Sherburne ordered us to fall back about 300 yards and pull off our packs, which we accordingly did and piled them by the roadside. "Now, my boys," says he, "pass the word through the ranks that he who is afraid to follow me, let him stay behind and take care of the packs!" Not a man offered to leave the ranks, and as we never went back that way, we lost all our packs: at least I never heard anything of mine, and I had in it a beautiful set of blue clothes, turned up with white and silver laced. As we had been in the storm all night we were not only wet through and through ourselves, but our guns and powder were wet also, so that I do not believe one would go off, and I saw none fired by our party.

When we were all ready we advanced, and, although there was not more than one bayonet to five men, orders were given to "Charge bayonets and rush on!" and rush on we did. Within pistol-shot they again fired point-blank at us; we dodged and they did not hit a man, while before they had time to reload we were within three feet of them, when they broke in an instant and ran like so many frightened devils into the town, which was a short distance, we after them pell-mell. Some of the Hessians took refuge in a church at the door of which we stationed a guard to keep them in, and taking no further care of them for the present, advanced to find more, for many of them had run down into the cellars of the houses. I passed two of their cannon, brass 6-pounders, by the side of which lay seven dead Hessians and a brass drum. The latter article was, I remember, a great curiosity to me and I stopped to have a look at it, but it was quickly taken possession of by one of our drummers, who threw away his own instrument. At the same time I obtained a sword from one of the bodies, and we then ran on to join our regiment, which was marching down the main street toward the market. Just before we reached this building, however, General Washington, on horseback and alone, came up to our major and said, "March on, my brave fellows, after me!" and rode off.

After passing a number of dead and wounded Hessians we reached the other side of town and on our right beheld about 500 or 600 of the enemy paraded, two deep, in a field. By the time we were marching in grand division which filled up the street, but as we got opposite the enemy we halted and filing off two deep, marched right by them—yes, as regular as a Prussian troop. When we reached the end of their line we were ordered to wheel to the right, which brought us face to face six feet apart, at which time, though not before, I discovered they had no guns, which they had laid down. A few minutes afterwards a number of wagons came behind us, into which the guns were placed, and the next thing ordered was to disarm the prisoners of their swords, with one of which every man was provided; these we also put into the wagons, but compelled the enemy to carry their cartridge-boxes themselves. Our regiment was ordered to conduct them down to the ferry and transport them over to the other side, so we began the march, guarding the flanks on both sides of the road.

The Hessian prisoners, who were all grenadiers, numbered about 900. . . . The scow, or flat-bottomed boat, which was used in transporting them over the ferry, was half a leg deep with rain and snow, and some of the poor fellows were so cold that their underjaws quivered like an aspen leaf. On the march down to the boats, seeing some of our men were so much pleased with the brass hats they had taken from the dead Hessians, our prisoners, who were besides exceedingly frightened, pulled off those that they were wearing, and, giving them away, put on the hats which they carried behind their packs. With these brass hats on it was laughable to see how our soldiers would strut,—fellows with their elbows out and some without a collar to their half-a-shirt, no shoes, etc.'[10]

It was a happy and proud American army that recrossed the Delaware into Pennsylvania. Two divisions of Washington's army that were supposed to have crossed the river on the same night as the attack on Trenton had

114. Gunnery

This diagram by the Philadelphia engravers James Thackara and John Vallance is copied, with slight modification, from one of several similar diagrams in earlier eighteenth-century treatises on artillery. The plate appears in the eighth volume of the *Encyclopedia*, an ambitious undertaking published in Philadelphia between 1790 and 1798.

Except aboard ship and in forts, cannon of this size were infrequently used. Three-pounders, referred to frequently in journals and letters in the text, were more practical instruments for use in troop movements along the primitive colonial roads and through unpathed terrain.

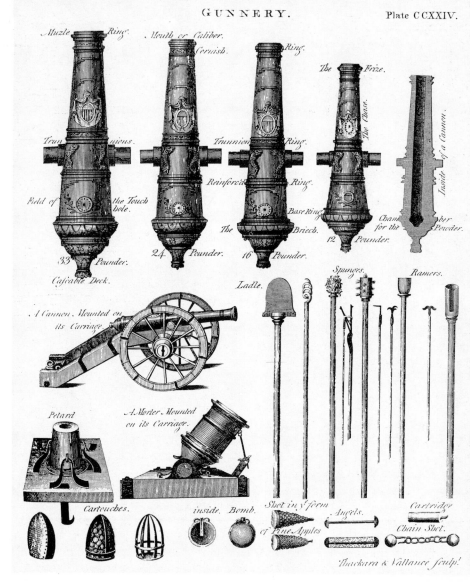

finally made it across and were now on the far side. Washington made plans to ferry his men back to Jersey. The town of Brunswick was his objective, for it was the principal British storehouse and the taking of it would isolate the British garrison at Princeton. His ambition swelled by victory, the General thought 'a fair opportunity is offered of driving the enemy entirely from, or at least to the extremity of, the province of New Jersey'. A number of officers kept a record of the subsequent events, but by far the most graphic was by an American non-commissioned officer whose only identification was 'Sergeant R———':

'Three or four days after the victory at Trenton, the American army re-crossed the Delaware into New Jersey. At this time our troops were in a destitute and deplorable condition. The horses attached to our cannon were without shoes, and when passing over the ice they would slide in every

139

direction, and could advance only with the assistance of the soldiers. Our men too, were without shoes or other comfortable clothing; and as traces of our march towards Princeton, the ground was literally marked with the blood of the soldiers' feet. Though my own feet did not bleed, they were so sore that their condition was little better.

While we were at Trenton, on the last of December, 1776, the time for which I and most of my regiment had enlisted expired. At this trying time General Washington, having now but a little handful of men and many of them new recruits in which he could place but little confidence, ordered our regiments to be paraded, and personally addressed us, urging that we should stay a month longer. He alluded to our recent victory at Trenton; told us that our services were greatly needed, and that we could now do more for our country than we ever could at any future period; and in the most affectionate manner entreated us to stay. The drums beat for volunteers, but not a man turned out. . . .

The General wheeled his horse about, rode in front of the regiment, and addressing us again said, "My brave fellows, you have done all I asked you to do, and more than could be reasonably expected; but your country is at stake, your wives, your houses, and all that you hold dear. You have worn yourselves out with fatigues and hardships, but we know not how to spare you. If you will consent to stay only one month longer, you will render that service to the cause of liberty, and to your country, which you probably never can do under any other circumstances. The present is emphatically the crisis, which is to decide our destiny." The drums beat a second time. The soldiers felt the force of the appeal. One said to another, "I will remain if you will." Others remarked, "We cannot go home under such circumstances." A few stepped forth, and their example was immediately followed by nearly all who were fit for duty in the regiment, amounting to about two hundred volunteers. An officer enquired of the General if these men should be enrolled. He replied, "No! men who will volunteer in such a case as this, need no enrolment to keep them to their duty."

When we were about commencing our march for Princeton, Lord Cornwallis [whose leave had been cancelled because of Trenton] left that place with the intention of attacking, and at one blow cutting off the rebel army. He appeared near Wood Creek on the Assanpink river, where a skirmish took place at the bridge over the creek. The Hessians were placed in front of the British troops, and endeavoured to force the bridge. They retired, and we were left undisturbed for the night.

Leaving our fires kindled to deceive the enemy, we decamped that night, and by a circuitous route took up our line of march for Princeton. General Mercer commanded the front guard of which the two hundred volunteers composed a part. About sunrise of the 3rd January 1777, reaching the summit of a hill near Princeton, we observed a light-horseman, as we view an object when the sun shines directly in our faces. Gen. Mercer observing him, gave order to the riflemen who were posted on the right to pick him off. Several made ready, but at that instant he wheeled about, and was out of their reach.

Soon after this as we were descending a hill through an orchard, a party of the enemy who were entrenched behind a bank and a fence, rose and fired upon us. Their first shot passed over our heads cutting the limbs of the trees under which we were marching. At this moment we were ordered to wheel. As the platoon which I commanded were obeying the order, the corporal who

140

stood at my left shoulder, received a ball and fell dead on the spot. He seemed to bend forward to receive the ball, which otherwise might have ended my life. We formed, advanced, and fired upon the enemy. They retreated eight rods to their packs, which were laid in a line. I advanced to the fence on the opposite side of the ditch which the enemy had just left, fell on one knee and loaded my musket with ball and buckshot. Our fire was most destructive; their ranks grew thin and the victory seemed nearly complete, when the British were reinforced. Many of our brave men had fallen, and we were unable to withstand such superior numbers of fresh troops.

I soon heard Gen. Mercer command in a tone of distress, "Retreat!" He was mortally wounded and died shortly after. I looked about for the main body of the army which I could not discover—discharged my musket at part of the enemy, and ran for a piece of wood, at a little distance where I thought I might shelter. At this moment Washington appeared in front of the American army, riding towards those of us who were retreating, and exclaimed

115. Recruits. *W. H. Bunbury*

The contrast between the smart young recruiting sergeant and the sorry material he collected in the streets of London provided the subject of many cartoons. Here the characterization of the recruits about to be shipped off to ports unknown, and of the youth leering from below 'The Old Fortune' tavern sign is Hogarthian. Britain's fighting manpower was greatly overextended at this period; the purchase of the services of the Hessians was a grim necessity.

This stipple engraving by Watson and Dickinson is based on a simpler line engraving by W. H. Bunbury of about 1770.

RECRUITS.

London. Publifh'd Jan.ʳ 1ˢᵗ 1780. by Watfon & Dickinfon Nᵒ 158. New Bond Street.

"Parade with us, my brave fellows, there is but a handful of the enemy, and we will have them directly." I immediately joined the main body, and marched over the ground again.

O, the barbarity of man! On our retreat, we had left a comrade of ours whose name was Loomis from Lebanon, Ct., whose leg was broken by a musket ball, under a cart in a yard; but on our return he was dead, having received several wounds from a British bayonet. My old associates were scattered about groaning, dying and dead. One officer who was shot from his horse lay in a hollow place in the ground rolling and writhing in his blood, unconscious of anything around him. The ground was frozen and all the blood which was shed remained on the surface, which added to the horror of this scene of carnage.

The British were unable to resist this attack, and retreated into the College, where they thought themselves safe. Our army was there in an instant, and cannon planted before the door, and after two or three discharges, a white flag appeared at a window, and the British surrendered. They were a haughty, crabbed set of men, as they fully exhibited while prisoners, on their march to the country. In this battle, my pack, which was made fast by leather strings, was shot from my back, and with it went what little clothing I had. It was, however, soon replaced by one which belonged to a British officer, and was well furnished. It was not mine long, for it was stolen shortly afterwards.

Immediately after the battle an officer observing blood on my clothes said, "Sergeant R——— you are wounded?" I replied "No," as I never expected to be injured in battle. On Examination I found the end of my forefinger gone, and bleeding profusely. When and how it happened I never knew; I found also bullet holes in the skirts of my coat, but, excepting the slight wound of my finger, was not injured.

In this battle and that of Trenton, there were no ardent spirits in the army, and the excitement of rum had nothing to do in obtaining the victories. As I had tried powder and rum on Long Island to promote courage, and engaged here without it, I can say that I was none the less corageous here than there.

The Army retreated to Pluckemin mountains. The weather was extremely cold, and we suffered greatly from its severity. ... The inhabitants manifested very different feelings towards us, from those exhibited a few weeks before, and were now ready to take up arms against the British. At Morristown I was sick of the small-pox and many of our little army died there of that disease.'[11]

Morristown, a village of about fifty houses, lay with its back up against Thimble Mountain. It was an easy place to defend and sudden sallies could be made against the enemy at Elizabethtown, Newark, or Amboy. Washington, shortly after establishing his headquarters in Freemason's Tavern on the north side of the village green, confidently wrote, 'I shall draw the force on this side of the North River together at Morristown, where I shall watch the motions of the Enemy and avail Myself of every favourable Circumstance.'

It was cold at Morristown, and there was smallpox, but the air was warmed by the brags and boasts of the ragged soldiers as they huddled around campfires.

7. Thrust from the North

116. General John Burgoyne. *Engraved by J. Chapman*

They called him 'Gentleman Johnny'. His troops loved him, and even for his enemies he had a certain fascination. Like his snowy linen and resplendent uniforms, everything he did, even his defeat, had style.

ON 6 MAY 1777 the frigate *Apollo*, fresh in from England, dropped anchor in the St Lawrence opposite Quebec. On board was 'Gentleman Johnny' Burgoyne, his dispatch case stuffed with plans and his heart brimming with ambition. He had returned to England for the winter and on 28 February 1777 had submitted a grand plan of conquest which he had entitled 'Thoughts for conducting the war from the side of Canada'. He had never shown this new draft to Sir William Howe, perhaps because the commanding general had earlier expressed his disapprobation of a similar plan. Burgoyne had constructed his scheme on two presumptions, namely that the New England militia would not turn out to fight in New York and that the Canadians would flock to the support of the king. And he held no fear of the opposition, ridiculing the rebel army as a 'preposterous parade of military arrangement'.

When the plan was shown to Carleton, the latter was deeply hurt and humiliated at being superseded in command by a soldier sometimes called 'General Swagger', and almost immediately dispatched his resignation to London. Burgoyne's plan was complicated and involved a three-pronged movement of troops. He expected that Howe would send a detachment of troops up the Hudson to gain control of the river as far as Albany. A smaller group, led by Lieutenant-Colonel Barry St Leger, was to strike inland through the Mohawk Valley from Fort Oswego on Lake Ontario. The primary body under Burgoyne was to sweep majestically southward from Canada by way of Lake Champlain, Ticonderoga, Skenesborough, Fort Anne, Fort Edward, and Saratoga to make a junction with the other two units at Albany, thus cutting the colonies in two and mortally injuring their effort. Just why Howe, in embarking his army for the conquest of Philadelphia, was allowed to enter upon an action so contrary to Burgoyne's plan has been a matter of long debate. Lord George Germain approved both plans, and failed to impress upon Howe at the proper time that Burgoyne might well need strong support from the south.

By 20 June, Burgoyne had assembled his army on Cumberland Point on Lake Champlain. It was a great, cumbersome machine, ill-designed for a march through the wilderness, numbering nearly 8,000 men, composed of three British brigades and a like number of Hessian brigades under the command of Major-General Baron von Riedesel. Only 250 Canadians and 400 Indians had joined. Over 1,500 horses were needed to transport the baggage (thirty of the two-wheeled carts carried Burgoyne's own resplendent wardrobe), the 138 pieces of artillery and the women of the army. These last included not only camp followers but a number of gentle ladies, such as Major Ackland's pregnant wife, and the Baroness von Riedesel, dainty and vivacious, who had come to be with her husband, and who travelled through this appalling wilderness and into captivity in a calèche, with her three small daughters, aged seven, three and one. Before he left Montreal, the general was shocked to see a newspaper account of his plans that was so accurate that it could have been 'copied from the Secretary of

143

State's letter'. Nevertheless, by 27 June Burgoyne was at Crown Point, making preparations, and three days later his general orders read:

'The Army embarks tomorrow to approach the Enemy. We are to contend for the King and the Constitution of Great Britain, to vindicate the Law and to relieve the Oppressed. A Cause in which His Majesty's Troops and those of the Princes His Allies will feel equal Excitement.

The Services required on this particular Expedition are critical and conspicuous. During our progress occasions may occur, in which neither difficulty nor labour nor life are to be regarded. THIS ARMY MUST NOT RETREAT.'[1]

Ticonderoga was the first obstacle, although 'Mad Anthony' Wayne had termed the fort 'the last place in the world that God made . . . the ancient Golgotha or place of skulls'. Inside the fort were 3,000 Americans com-

117. General Burgoyne addressing the Indians at their War Feast in Canada. *Woodruff*

At St John's in June 1777, before starting south on his campaign, General Burgoyne addressed the 400 Indians of the Iroquois nations who had joined his composite army. They must have been bewildered by his elegant phraseology and by the rules he laid down for them: no bloodshed except in combat; no harm to old men, women, children, or prisoners; no scalps, except from the dead in battle; no killing of the wounded; no wholesale ravaging of the country. When news of this appeal reached the House of Commons, Edmund Burke ridiculed it: 'Suppose there was a riot on Tower Hill. What would the keeper of his Majesty's lions do? Would he not fling open the dens of the wild beasts, and then address them thus: "My gentle lions—my humane bears—my tender-hearted hyenas, go forth! But I exhort you, as you are Christians and members of civil society, to take care not to hurt any man, woman or child."'

manded by Generals Arthur St Clair and Anthony Wayne. One Pennsylvania officer wasn't impressed with the garrison, classing them as 'a set of low, griping, cowardly, lying rascals'. There was one great weakness: Sugar Loaf Hill, or Mount Defiance, an eminence within easy cannon shot of, and overlooking, the fort. It was thought beyond human ability to drag cannon up the steep slopes. General William Phillips, an old artilleryman, recognized the possibilities for the British. On 15 July:

'Lieutenant Twiss, the commanding engineer, was ordered to reconoitre Sugar Loaf Hill on the south side of the communication from Lake George into Lake Champlaign, part of which the light-infantry had taken possession of last night; he reported this hill to have the entire command of the works and buildings, both at Ticonderoga and Mount Independence, of about 1400 yards from the former, and 1500 from the latter; that the ground might be levelled so as to receive cannon, and that a road to convey them, though extremely difficult, might be accomplished in twenty-four hours. . . .

Upon this report of Lieutenant Twiss, it was determined that a battery should be raised on this post, for light twenty-four pounders, medium twelves, and eight inch howitzers, which very arduous undertaking is now carrying on so rapidly, that there is little doubt but it will be compleated and ready to open upon the enemy tomorrow morning. Great praise is due to the zeal and activity of General Phillips, who has the direction of this operation: he has expeditiously conveyed cannon to the summit of this hill, as he brought it up in that memorable battle of Minden, where, it is said, such was his anxiousness in expediting the artillery, that he split no less than fifteen canes in beating the horses; at which battle he so gallantly distinguished himself, by the management of his artillery, as totally to rout the French.'[2]

When St Clair discovered that the enemy had occupied Sugar Loaf Hill and his garrison now lay under the ugly black muzzles of their artillery, Ticonderoga was evacuated without firing a shot. Burgoyne, leaving all but fifty-two guns, set out in pursuit; his progress slowed by the rebels, who destroyed bridges and felled trees across the roads. On the morning of 7 July, the British caught up with the Americans in the thick forests near Hubbardstown. The rebels were driven off, but not before they had given one Hessian officer a healthy respect for their fighting ability when at home, in the wilderness:

'In the open field the rebels are not of much count, but in the woods they are redoubtable. At the present time we are almost continually marching through, and living in, forests. It is on such occasions that the rebels lurk in the woods and dart from tree to tree. In their ability to hit an object . . . their riflemen are terrible. The latter wear a short white shirt over their clothes, the sleeves being bordered by a number of rows of white linen fringes. A rebel invariably looks for protection to his musket, which is very long. They load their guns with three small and three somewhat larger bullets; bad enough for him whom they hit. Nearly all of those wounded in the affair at Hubert-Town had three or four wounds—all caused by one shot.'[3]

At Skenesborough, Burgoyne allowed himself to be persuaded by the loyalist Philip Skene, eager to improve his property, to hack a road through the wilderness to Fort Edward on the Hudson, instead of sailing down Lake

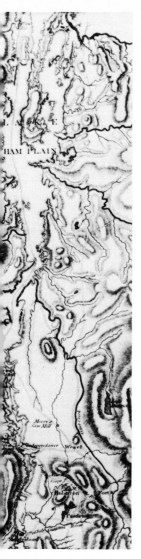

118. Country in which the Army under L*t*** General Burgoyne acted in the Campaign of 1777.** *Medcalfe* In this map Medcalfe shows by bold hachuring the mountainous and difficult terrain through which Burgoyne had to lead his army. South of Skenesborough, the land was swampy, roadless, and the way impeded by huge trees felled by Schuyler's foresters.

A Prospective View of the BATTLE foug
under the command of Genᴸ JOHNSON & 2500 French & Indians under the command of Gᴸ

FIRST ENGAGEMENT

Lake George
Lymans Fort
Saratoga
Hosock
Mohawks
Albany
Mʳ Scylers House
Green Bush
Kenderhook
Claverack
Livingstons Manor
Camptown
Coats Kill
Mountaine
Martin Hoffmans House
Sopas
The Halfway Islands
New Windsor
Pakepsy
The Glass House 100 by 80 f
Vis Kill
Sugar Loaves
Antonys Nose
Col. Moores Folly
Entrance High Lands
Tappan Sea
Corbits Point
Dubss Ferry
Stepping Stones
Scale of Miles for the Length of the River
16   32
Hudsons River
New York
Scale of Miles for the Width of the River
1   2   3

A Plan of Lymans now called Fort Edward

Lake George

A Plan of Fort William Henry

Samuel Blodget delin.

119. The American method of bush fighting (detail). Thomas Jefferys

Forest guerrilla warfare was almost as important in the Revolution as it was in the French and Indian War. This engraving shows two such attacks near Lake George by Canadians and Indians under General Dieskau on English and colonial troops under General William Johnson on 5 September 1755.

'Both the Canadians and Indians became invisible to our Men, by squatting below the undergrowth of Shrubs, and Bushes, or by concealing themselves behind the Trees', wrote Samuel Blodget, a sutler from Boston who was an eye-witness and drew a 'Prospective Plan of the Battle fought near Lake George', of which Jefferys made this copy; he called it 'A prospective view . . .' The detail of the left section shows the ambuscade of the English in which Ephraim Williams and the Mohawk chief Henrick were killed.

George. The territory was dense forest and swamp; the Americans felled huge trees and flooded the land to increase the excruciating labour. It took 24 days to travel 23 miles, while the enemy gained much needed time.

The Indians also gave the British trouble. Even the Hessians, who had earned for themselves a reputation for cruelty, were disgusted with the conduct of their savage allies. One Hessian officer wrote:

'Our Indians, whom we brought with us from Canada, and who, while they were supposed to be Christians, or nearly so, have since behaved like hogs.

146

When it comes to plundering they are on hand every time; and most of them have remained at Ticonderoga and Skenesborough. While here they filled themselves with rum in true military style. But few of their leaders remain true; and after every campaign they get "full", and remain in that condition until they reach home, when they begin to brag of their deeds while away.'[4]

And it was the Indians who furnished the Americans with one of their choicest bits of propaganda. It began when a scouting party of Indians returned to camp. One, Wyandot Panther, carried a scalp of long and lustrous hair, still dripping blood. It had belonged to a Miss Jane McRae who had been making her way to see her fiancé, a loyalist lieutenant, David Jones. Burgoyne, fearful of a desertion of his red allies, did not punish the guilty savages, which gave credence to the rumour that the British general was paying for scalps. Later, it led to an exchange between the American General Horatio Gates and Burgoyne. On 2 September, Gates was to make the charge:

'That the savages of America should in their warfare mangle and scalp the unhappy prisoners who fall into their hands, is neither new or extraordinary; but that the famous Lieut General Burgoyne, in whom the fine gentlemen is united with the soldier and the scholar, should hire the savages of America to scalp Europeans and the descendants of Europeans: nay more, that he should pay a price for each scalp so barbarously taken, is more than will be believed in England until authenticated facts shall in every gazette convince mankind of the truth of this horrid tale.

Miss M'Crea, a young lady lovely to the sight, of virtuous character and amiable disposition, engaged to be married to an officer in your army, was with other women and children taken out of a house near Fort Edward,

120. General Horatio Gates. *Murray*

Gates was an Englishman of humble birth; he retired to America to farm, and on the outbreak of the Revolution decided to embrace the Patriot cause.

121. A View of a Saw Mill & Block House upon Fort Anne Creek the property of Gen*l* Skeene. *Anburey*

It was from this sawmill at Skenesborough in 1776 that Benedict Arnold obtained the logs to build his fleet on Lake Champlain. Anburey made here one of his most effective pictures, which he himself called 'a very romantic view'. Wilderness country, waterfall, and Indians are all here, as is a great cascade of logs. Later the Americans returned and burned the mill and the blockhouse.

carried into the wood, and there scalped and mangled in the most shocking manner. Two parents with their six children, [were] all treated with the same inhumanity while quietly residing in their once happy and peaceful dwelling. The miserable fate of Miss McCrea was partly aggravated by her being dressed to receive her promised husband; but met her murderers employed by you. Upwards of one hundred men, women and children have perished at the hands of these ruffians, to whom it is asserted, you have paid the price of blood.'

Indignation flowed from Burgoyne's pen in his answer:

'It has happened, that all my transactions with the Indian nations last year and this, have been open, clearly heard, distinctly understood and accurately minuted by very numerous, and many parts, very prejudiced audiences. So diametrically opposite to the truth is your assertion that I have paid a price for scalps, that one of the first regulations established by me at the great Council in May, and repeated and enforced, and invariably adhered to since, was that the Indians should receive compensation for prisoners, because it would prevent cruelty, and that not only such compensations should be withheld, but a strict account demanded for scalps. These pledges of Conquest—for such you well know they will never esteem them—were solemnly and peremptorily prohibited to be taken from the wounded and even the dying, and the persons of aged men, women and children, and prisoners were pronounced sacred even, in assaults.

Respecting Miss McCrea; her fall wanted not the tragic display you have laboured to give it, to make it as sincerely abhorred and lamented by me, as it can possibly be by the tenderest of her friends. The fact was not pre-meditated barbarity, on the contrary, two chiefs who had brought her off for the purpose of security, not of violence to her person, disputed who should be her guard, and in a fit of savage passion in the one in whose hands she was snatched, the unhappy woman became the victim. Upon the first intelligence of the events, I obliged the Indians to deliver the murderer into my hands, and tho to have punished him by our laws and principles of justice would have perhaps been unprecedented, he certainly should have suffered an ignominious death, had I not been convinced, by circumstances and observation beyond the possibility of a doubt, that a pardon under the terms I prescribed and they accepted, would be more efficacious than an execution to prevent similar mischiefs. The above instance excepted, your intelligence respecting cruelties of the Indians is absolutely false.'[5]

Gates had but recently been appointed commander to succeed General Philip Schuyler. Schuyler was not liked by the New Englanders, and the militia from that area refused to answer his calls. One Massachusetts unit had turned round and gone home after they arrived at camp and discovered Schuyler to be in command. Despite Schuyler's statement, 'What could induce General St Clair and the general officers with him to evacuate Ticonderoga, God only knows,' Surgeon James Thacher, accompanying the wounded to Albany, heard the current rumour:

'It may be deemed ludicrous that I should record a rumor so extravagantly ridiculous as the following, but it has received too much credence to be altogether omitted. It has been industriously reported, that generals Schuyler and St. Clair acted the part of traitors to the country, and that

122. The Closet

Here reproduced are three insets from a large and complicated Whig cartoon which takes its title from a scene not here shown where the King is closeted with his advisers, including the Devil.

In the uppermost inset Indians are using a tomahawk on a prostrate person. Beside this is the murder of Jane McCrea by an Indian sent to escort her to her fiancé, an officer in Burgoyne's army. Behind her, Esopus burns, a village destroyed by General Vaughan after Clinton's campaign up the Hudson in October 1777. Next is an inset containing more Indian atrocities: a man on a spit, a skull, a scalped head, cannibalism. In the final inset, Burgoyne leads unarmed men with their hands tied. Gates pursues him with an American flag.

they were paid for their treason by the enemy in *silver balls*, shot from Burgoyne guns into our camp, and that they were collected by order of General St. Clair and divided between him and General Schuyler.'[6]

Congress selected Horatio Gates to be commander of the Northern Department, pouring salt into Schuyler's wounded vanity, for the two men disliked each other intensely. John Adams wrote to his wife, Abigail:

'In the northern department they begin to fight. . . . I presume Gates will be so supported that Burgoyne will be obliged to retreat. He will stop at Ticonderoga, I suppose, for they maintain posts although we cannot. I think we shall never defend a post until we shoot a General. After that we shall defend posts, and this event, in my opinion, is not far off. No other fort will ever be evacuated without an inquiry, nor any officer come off without a court martial. We must trifle no more. We have suffered too many disgraces to pass unexpiated. Every disgrace must be wiped off.'[7]

Gates appeared to be in no great hurry to take over his new command. By the time he arrived in Albany on 19 August, the tide had already begun

Oswego, on the south shore of Lake Erie, was St Leger's base in his operations in the Mohawk Valley in support of Burgoyne's invasion from Canada. Here he retreated after his unsuccessful expedition. With portages, the Oswego River provided river transportation for supplies and men to the Mohawk.

to reverse itself. Burgoyne had settled in at Fort Edward, still confident that his grand scheme of conquest was working smoothly.

On 25 July, Lieutenant-Colonel Barry St Leger had landed far to the west at Oswego on Lake Ontario. The following day he put his troops in motion towards what was expected to be a relatively easy task, for the Mohawk Valley, though sparsely inhabited frontier country, was felt to be a loyalist stronghold. So confident had been St Leger that he had sent his baggage

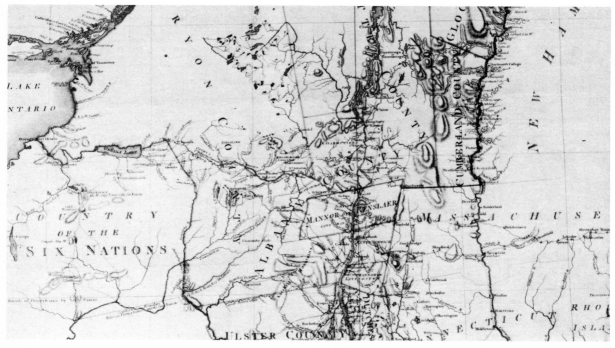

125. Fort Stanwix.
John Williams

Fort Stanwix, built in 1758 by General Stanwix with provincial troops, was at the 'great carrying place' or portage at Oneida station between the headwaters of the Mohawk and Oswego rivers. The plan is interesting as an example in its simplest form of the classic star-shaped fort, with projections enabling the garrison to make an enfilading fire upon attackers attempting to scale the walls.

In August 1777 Barry St Leger besieged it unsuccessfully. The patriot defenders had impeded his approach for days by felling trees and obstructing the waterway while they strengthened the defences of the fort.

124. A Map of the Province of New York *(detail)*.
Sauthier

This detail includes the area of the expedition of St Leger from Oswego to Fort Stanwix (Fort Schuyler), the Mohawk Valley, and the final stages of Burgoyne's campaign after he reached the Hudson River.

Sauthier made numerous surveys for Governor William Tryon in the province of New York between 1771 and 1775. This is a reduction of the finest map of any province made in the colonial period, Sauthier's great chorographic map of New York.

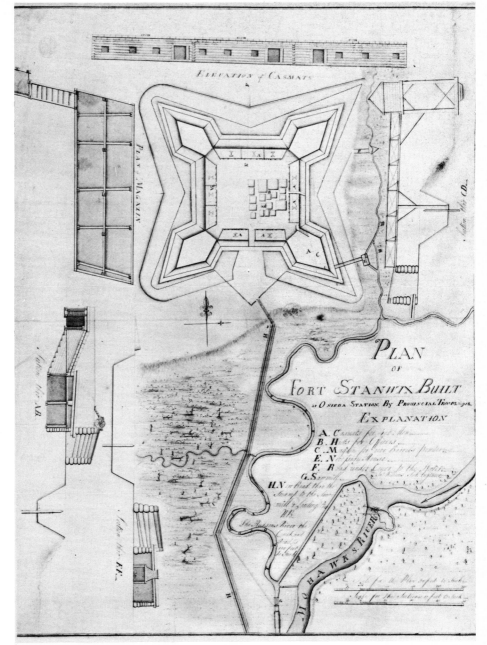

with Burgoyne, to be reclaimed when the two forces made their junction at Albany.

The first obstacle on the road to Albany was Fort Stanwix at the 'Great Carrying Place', the portage between the Mohawk and Wood Creek, the latter stream emptying into Lake Ontario. The fort had been renamed Fort Schuyler, but was usually referred to by its old name. In command was tall, young Colonel Peter Gansevoort of the Third New York Regiment. His second-in-command was nine years older, 'a bold enterprizing young fellow', by the name of Marinus Willett. Trees were felled by Wood Creek, the level of the walls was raised, and women, children, and invalids were evacuated.

Marinus Willett was to write a narrative of the siege which was later printed in newspapers:

'On Saturday evening, August 2d, five batteaus arrived with stores for the garrison, about the same time we discovered a number of fires a little better than a mile from the N. West corner of the Fort. The stores were all got safe in, and the troops, which were a guard to the batteaus, marched up. The Captain of the batteaus, and a few of his men, delaying their time about the boats, were fired on by a party of Indians, which killed one man and wounded two; the Captain himself was taken prisoner.

Next morning the enemy appeared at the edge of the woods, about a mile below the Fort, where they took post, in order to invest it on that quarter, and to cut off the communication from the country; from whence they sent in a flag, who told us of their great power, strength and determination, in such a manner as gave us reason to suppose they were not possessed of strength sufficient to take the fort. Our answer was, a determination to support it. All day on Monday we were much annoyed by a sharp fire of musketry from the Indians and German Rifle-men, which, as our men were obliged to be exposed on the works, killed one and wounded seven. The day after, the firing was not quite so heavy, and our men under better cover, all the damage was, one man killed by a rifle ball. . . .

Wednesday morning there was an unusual silence; we discovered some of the enemy marching along the edge of the woods downward. About eleven o'clock three men got into the Fort, who brought a letter from General Harkaman, of the Tryon County Militia, advising us he was at Eriska (eight miles from the Fort) with part of his militia, and proposed to fight his way to the Fort for our relief—in order to render him what service we could in his march—it was agreed that I should make a sally from the Fort with two hundred and fifty men, consisting of one half of Gansevoort's and one half of Massachusetts men, and one field piece (an iron three pounder).'[8]

This 'Harkaman' was a middle-aged, square-built Dutchman with black hair and dancing eyes whose real name was Nicholas Herkimer. St Leger discovered the advance and a trap was laid at a place called Oriskany, meaning 'Field of Nettles' in the Oneida language. A newspaper account reported Herkimer's exploit:

'Last Wednesday about nine o'clock an engagement ensued between a part of the militia of Tryon county under the command of General Herkimer, and a party of Savages, Tories and regulars, about half way between Eriska and Fort Stanwix. It lasted till three o'clock in the afternoon, when the enemy thought proper to retire, leaving General Herkimer master of the field; unluckily however, the General and some valuable officers got wounded and killed in the beginning. This however did in no ways intimidate the ardor of the men; and the General, although he had two wounds, did not leave the field until the action was over; he seated himself down on a log, with his sword drawn, animating his men. The enemy on this occasion lost some of their chief men. . . .

About one o'clock the same day Col. Gansevours, having received information of General Herkimer's march, sent Lieut. Col. Willett out with 200 men, to attack an encampment of the enemy, and thereby facilitate General Herkimer's march to the fort. In this the Col. succeeded; for after an engagement of an hour he had completely routed the enemy, took one Captain and four privates prisoners. The baggage taken was very considerable; such as money, bear skins, officer's baggage, and camp equipage: one of the soldiers had for his share a scarlet coat, trimed with gold lace to the full, and three laced hats. . . . When the Col. returned to the fort he discovered 200 regulars in full march to attack him, he immediately ordered his men to prepare for battle, and having a field piece with him, Capt. Savage of the Artillery so directed its fire as to play in conjunction with one out of the fort; these, with a brisk fire from the small arms, soon made these heroes scamper off with great loss. Col. Willett then marched with his booty into the Fort, where he arrived at four the same day, having not a single man killed or wounded.'[9]

On Friday 8 August a flag approached the fort with a message summoning its defenders to surrender and declaring that if not, 'the consequences to the garrison, should it fall into their hands, must be terrible; that the Indians were very much enraged on account of their having a number of their chiefs killed in the late actions, and were determined, unless they got possession of the fort, to go down the Mohawk River, and fall upon the inhabitants'. The reply was 'that such proceedings would ever remain a stigma upon the name of Britain; but for our parts, we were determined to defend the fort'. That evening a council of field officers decided that Willett and a Lieutenant Stockwell, 'a good woods-man', should slip out and go for aid.

When Willett and Stockwell reached German Flats they discovered that Schuyler had earlier detached Benedict Arnold and a force who had started on the march to relieve Fort Stanwix. Arnold, fearing he was outnumbered by the enemy, resorted to subterfuge. Knowing that the Indians held the mentally retarded in some awe, he approached one such person, Hon Yost Schuyler, a nephew of Herkimer's, who had been captured and sentenced to death for participation in a Tory plot. A chief, or 'Sachem', was also enlisted and sent forward with Yost to spread the word that a large army was marching to the relief of Fort Stanwix. When they arrived at that post, St Leger had pushed his siege lines within one hundred and fifty yards of the walls. Schuyler began to spread rumours among the Indians. Years later the results were still being repeated:

'The Indians being thus thoroughly alarmed, the chief, who was in the secret, arrived as if by mere accident; and in the mysterious manner of that people began to insinuate his countrymen, that a bird had brought him great intelligence, of great moment. This hint got their curiosity afloat; and excited a series of anxious enquiries. To these he replied in hints, and suggestions, concerning warriours in great numbers, marching with the utmost rapidity, and already far advanced. In the mean time he had dispatched two or three young warriors in the search for intelligence. These scouts, who had received their cue, returned, as they had been directed, at different times; and confirmed, as if by accident also, all that had been said by Schuyler, and the Sachem. The Indians, already disgusted with the service, which they found a mere contrast to the promises of the British commanders, and their own expectations, and sore with the loss they had sustained in the battle with General Herkimer, were now so completely alarmed, that they determined upon an immediate retreat. . . .

In a mixture of rage and despair, he [St Leger] broke up his encampment with such haste, that he left his tents, cannon, and stores, to the besieged. The flight of this army (for it could not be called a retreat) was through a deep forest and the spongey soil. . . . The Sachem, who had been partner with Schuyler in the plot, accompanied the flying army. Naturally a wag, and pleased to see the garrison rescued from their danger, he engaged several of the young men to repeat, at the proper intervals, the cry "they are coming." This unwelcome sound, you will easily believe, quickened the march of the fugitives whenever it was heard. The soldiers threw away their packs; and the commanders took care not to be in the rear. . . . After much fatigue, and at least an equal degree of mortification, they finally reached the Oneida lake; and there, probably, felt themselves for the first time secure from the pursuit of their enemies.'[10]

Disaster struck again, even before Burgoyne had received the news of St Leger's defeat. Supplies were running low for the army that struggled through the tangled wilderness. Off to the left lay the 'Hampshire Grants', an area that was later to become the state of Vermont. The Grants had not suffered the ravages of marching armies and there were, or so the reports ran, provisions in plenty in the area. A detachment of 150 Brunswick dismounted dragoons, fifty picked British marksmen, 150 provincials, fifty-six loyalists, and eighty Indians was placed under command of a Hessian Lieutenant-Colonel, Friedrich Baume. His mission was to disrupt enemy operations, gather dragoon horses, recruit loyalists, and bring in all horses, cattle, and carriages that he could lay his hands on.

What Burgoyne did not know was that the little force in the Grants had now risen to nearly 1,500 men united under the command of John Stark. On 14 August, as he moved towards the town of Bennington, Baume heard that there was a large group at Bennington, 'but are supposed to leave it on our approach'. The following day it had rained, soaking the weary men as they slogged over the soggy ground. Lieutenant Glich was happy when,

'the morning of the sixteenth rose beautifully serene; and it is not to the operation of the elements alone that my expression applies. All was perfectly quiet at the out posts, not an enemy having been seen, nor an alarming sound heard, for several hours previous to sunrise. So peaceable, indeed, was the aspect which matters bore, that our leaders felt warmly disposed

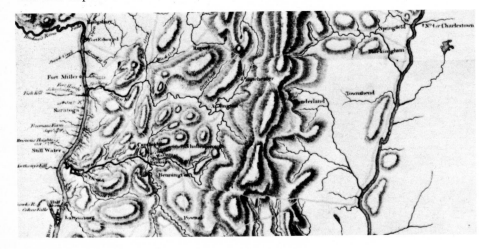

126. Lieutenant-Colonel Baum's expedition to Bennington (detail). *Medcalfe*

This shows the route along the Hoosick River by which Baum and his dismounted Hessian dragoons, clumsily attired in ponderous boots, made their way with their Indian and Canadian escort towards Bennington. Only a remnant returned.

154

to resume the offensive, without waiting the arrival of the additional corps for which they had applied; and orders were already issued for the men to eat their breakfasts, preparatory to the more active operations. But the arms were scarcely piled, and the haversacks unslung, when symptoms of a state of affairs different from that which had been anticipated, began to show themselves, and our people were recalled to their ranks in all haste, almost as soon as they had quitted them. From more than one quarter scouts came to report, that columns of armed men were approaching; though whether with friendly or hostile intention, neither their appearance nor actions enabled our informants to ascertain.

It has been stated, that during the last day's march our little corps was joined by many of the country people; most of whom demanded and obtained arms, as persons friendly to the royal cause. How Colonel Baume became so completely duped as to place reliance on these men, I know not; but having listened with complacency to their previous assurances, that in Bennington a large majority of the populace were our friends, he was some how or other persuaded to believe, that the armed bands, of whose approach he was warned, were loyalists on their way to make tender of their services to the leader of the king's troops. Filled with this idea, he dispatched positive orders to the outposts, that no molestations should be offered the advancing columns; but that the pickets retiring before them should join the main body, where every disposition was made to receive either friend or foe. Unfortunately for us, these orders were but too faithfully obeyed. About half past nine o'clock, I, who was not in the secret, beheld, to my utter amazement, our advanced parties withdraw without firing a shot, from thickets which might have been maintained for hours against any superiority of numbers; and the same thickets occupied by men whose demeanor, as well as their dress and style of equipment, plainly and incontestably pointed them out as Americans.

I cannot pretend to describe the state of excitation and alarm into which our little band was now thrown. With the solitary exception of our leader, there was not a man among us who appeared otherwise than satisfied that those to whom he had listened were traitors.... [but he] remained convinced of their fidelity....

Now then, at length, our leader's dreams of security were dispelled....

If Col. Baume had permitted himself to be duped into a great error, it is no more than justice to confess, that he exerted himself manfully to remedy the evil, and avert its consequences. Our little band, which had hitherto remained in column, was instantly ordered to extend, and the troops lining the breastworks replied to the fire of the Americans with extreme celerity and considerable effect. So close and destructive, indeed was our first volley, that the assailants recoiled before it, and would have retreated, in all probability, within the woods; but ere we could take advantage of the confusion produced, fresh attacks developed themselves, and we were warmly engaged on every side, and from all quarters....

It was at this moment, when the heads of columns began to exert themselves in rear of our right and left, that the Indians who had hitherto acted with spirit and something like order, lost all confidence, and fled. Alarmed at the prospect of having their retreat cut off, they stole away, after their own fashion, in single files, in spite of the strenuous remonstrances of Baume, and of their own officers, leaving us more than ever exposed, by the

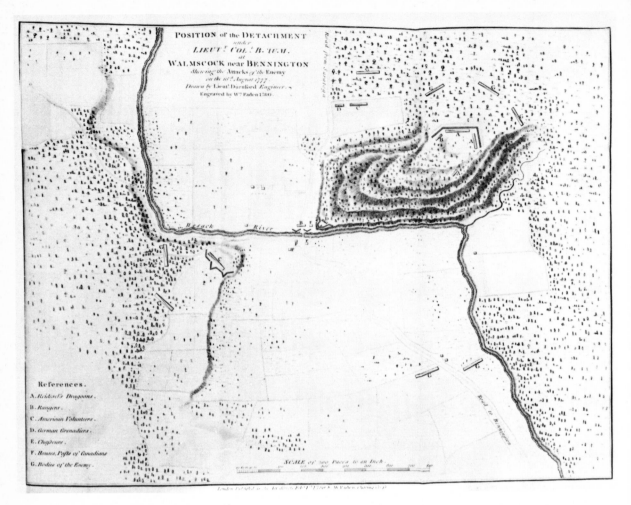

127. Baum's defeat at Walmscock (Walloomsack) near Bennington on 16 August 1777

The position of the detachment under Lieutenant-Colonel Baum, sent by Burgoyne to gather supplies, cattle, and horses for his army, is shown just prior to the attack by General John Stark.

'In the night [of 13 August] I was informed by express', wrote Stark to General Gates, 'that there was a large body of the enemy on their march in the rear of the Indians ... On the 16th in the morning I pursued my plan, detached Colonel Nichols with 200 men to attack them in the rear. I also sent Colonel Herrick with 300 men in the rear of their right ... The remainder of my little army I pushed up in the front, and in a few minutes the action began ... The enemy was obliged to give way, and leave all their field pieces and all their baggage behind them ... We pursued them till dark.'

abandonment of that angle of the intrenchments which they had been appointed to maintain. .... The vacancy, which the retreat of the savages had occasioned, was promptly filled up by one of our field pieces, whilst the other poured destruction among the enemy in front, as often as they showed themselves in the open country, or threatened to advance. ....

The solitary tumbril, which contained the whole of our spare ammunition, became ignited, and blew up with a violence which shook the ground under our feet, and caused a momentary cessation in firing, both on our side and that of the enemy. But the cessation was only for the moment. The American officers, guessing the extent of our calamity, cheered their men to fresh exertions. They rushed up the ascent with redoubled ardor, in spite of the

156

heavy volley which we poured in to check them; and finding our guns silent, they sprang over the parapet, and dashed within our works.

For a few seconds the scene ensued defies all power of language to describe. The bayonet, the butt of the rifle, the sabre, the pike, were in full play; and men fell, as they rarely fall in modern war, under the direct blow of their enemies. But such a struggle could not, in the nature of things, be of long continuance. Outnumbered, broken, and somewhat disheartened by late events, our people wavered, and fell back, or fought singly and unconnectedly, till they were either cut down at their posts, obstinately defending themselves, or compelled to surrender. . . . Col. Baume, shot through the body by a rifle ball, fell mortally wounded; and all order or discipline being lost, flight or submission was alone thought of.'[11]

Baume had written to Burgoyne on 14 August, informing him of the unexpected number of troops gathered at Bennington. The general had dispatched another German, Lieutenant-Colonel von Breymann, who began a laborious march through the wilderness. This was a mistake by the commanding general, for the Hessians were notoriously slow marchers through forest. Breymann had reached the bridge at the mill at Van Schaick's when he first made contact with the rebels. He reported to Burgoyne:

'I was scarcely 600 paces from the bridge when I noticed through the woods a considerable number of armed men (some of whom wore blouses and some jackets), hastening towards an eminence on my left flank. I called Colonel Skene's attention to it, and received from him the reply that these men were loyalists. But upon his riding up towards them and calling to them, the matter was soon explained, for instead of returning an answer, they fired upon us. . . .

The troops did their duty, and I know of no one who doubts this fact. After our ammunition was all expended, and the artillery in consequence ceased firing, nothing was more natural than to suppose that the enemy would be encouraged to renew the attack. Under this supposition I hastened, with a number of men, to the cannon in order to take them away. By this movement most of my men were severely wounded. The horses were either dead or in a condition which prevented them from moving from the spot. In order, therefore, not to risk anything (as I was unable to return the enemy's fire, my ammunition being exhausted), I retreated on the approach of darkness, destroyed the bridge, had as many of the wounded as possible brought thither that they might not be captured, and, after a lapse of half an hour, in company with Colonel Skene, pursued my march and reached Cambridge toward twelve o'clock at night. Here, after taking precautionary measures, I remained during that night, and marched thence at daybreak of the 17th of August to the camp.'[12]

At Bennington, John Burgoyne had suffered his first personal setback and it was even more humiliating in that it had been administered by that ludicrous body of soldiers classed as militia. To Lord George Germain he explained that the Hampshire Grants 'abound in the most active and most rebellious race of the continent, and hang like a gathering storm on my left'.

The victorious rebels celebrated with parades and rejoicing, and their commander, John Stark, became an instant hero. Some more sober souls saw the intervention of Divine Providence, and Captain Peter Clark mused that the battle was 'equal to Bunker Hill excepting there was not so many

128. A Real American Rifle Man
This picture of an American soldier, with 'Liberty' or death (skull and cross-bones) on his cap and CC (for Continental Congress) on his pouch, appeared in John Murray's *Impartial History of the War in America*, published in London.

cannon. . . . The Lord of Hosts sent them off in such haste they left their all and run'. Others held different opinions as to the cause for the defeat. The Baroness Riedesel, who was accompanying her German General husband through the wilderness, sniffed as she wrote in her journal, 'It is very true, that general Burgoyne liked to make himself easy, and that he spent half his nights in singing and drinking, and diverting himself with the wife of a commissary, who was his mistress, and who was as fond of Champaign as himself.' And when he heard that the New Hampshire Board of War had rewarded Stark with a new uniform, one British officer felt compelled to quip, 'Either the General was *Stark* naked or Congress stark mad.'

And now Burgoyne faced Horatio Gates on the Hudson above Saratoga. Gates was popular with the New England militia and they came in with much greater enthusiasm than they had for Schuyler. General William Heath was not impressed with some of these reinforcements:

'As to the ability of this body of men I cannot fully determine. The greater part that I saw appeared able, but it is more probable that there were some advanc'd in life, and some lads, and a number of negroes (the latter were generally able bodied, but for my own part I must confess I am never pleased to see them mixed with white men).'[13]

Despite the affection the New Englanders held for him, Horatio Gates was not a particularly inspiring man in appearance. Burgoyne referred to him as an 'Old Midwife', while his own men spoke of 'Granny Gates'. A German officer later described him as a man 'who wears his thin, gray hair cut round, is still lively and friendly, and almost always wears spectacles'.

On the high ground called Bemis Heights (named for the man who kept a tavern in its shadow), Gates had his men dig in, for it had now become evident that 'Gen. Burgoyne designs to risque all upon one rash stroke'. Burgoyne had indeed crossed the Hudson on a bridge of boats to the west bank and was determined to fight his way through Gates' army to Albany. On the approach of the enemy, Daniel Morgan's Virginia riflemen and Henry Dearborn's New Hampshire regiment, with the troops of Benedict Arnold in reserve, were ordered out to bring on the action, with Morgan manoeuvring his men by the use of a 'turkey call'. Captain Wakefield, of Dearborn's light infantry, remembered the opening scenes:

'The riflemen and light infantry were ordered to clear the woods of the Indians. Arnold rode up, and with his sword pointing to the enemy emerging from the woods into an opening partially cleared, covered with stumps and fallen timber, addressing Morgan, he said, "Colonel Morgan, you and I have seen too many redskins to be deceived by that garb of paint and feathers; they are asses in lions' skins, Canadians and Tories; let your riflemen cure them of their borrowed plumes."

And so they did; for in less than fifteen minutes the "Wagon Boy," with his Virginia riflemen, sent the painted devils with a howl back into British lines. Morgan was in his glory, catching the inspiration of Arnold, as he thrilled his men; when he hurled them against the enemy, he astonished the English and Germans with the deadly fire of his rifles.

Nothing could exceed the bravery of Arnold on this day; he seemed the very genius of war. Infuriated by the conflict and maddened by Gates' refusal to send reinforcements, which he repeatedly called for, and knowing he was meeting the brunt of the battle, he seemed inspired with the fury of a demon.'[14]

The effect of this action on the opposing side was noted by Lieutenant Anburey:

'The Indians were running from wood to wood, and just as soon as our regiment had formed in the skirts of one, several of them came up, and by their signs were conversing about the severe fire on our right. Soon after the enemy attacked us, and at the very first fire the Indians run off through the woods.

As to the Canadians, little was to be depended upon their adherence, being easily dispirited, with an inclination to quit as soon as there was an appearance of danger; nor was the fidelity of the Provincials to be relied on who had joined our army, as they withdrew on perceiving the resistance of the Americans would be more formidable than expected. The desertion of the Indians, Canadians, and Provincials, at a time when their services were most required, was exceedingly mortifying.'[15]

Lieutenant William Digby felt the full fury of the battle:

'About 9 o'clock we began our march, every man prepared with sixty rounds of cartridges and ready for instant action. We removed in three columns, ours to the right on the heights and farthest from the river in thick woods. A little after 12 our advanced pickets came up with Colonel Morgan and engaged, but from the great superiority of fire received from him—his numbers being much greater—they were obliged to fall back, every officer being either killed or wounded except one, when the line came up to their support and obliged in his turn to retreat with loss. . . .

To an unconcerned spectator, it must have had the most awful and glorious appearance, the different battalions moving to relieve each other, some being pressed and almost broke by their superior numbers. This crash of cannon and musketry never ceased till darkness parted us, when they retired to their camp, leaving us master of the field; but it was a dear victory, if I can give it that name, as we lost many brave men. The 62nd had scarce ten men a company left, and other regiments suffered much, and no very great advantage, honor excepted, was gained by the day.

On its turning dusk, we were near firing on a body of our Germans, mistaking their dark clothing for that of the enemy. General Burgoyne was everywhere and did everything that could be expected of a brave officer, & Brigadier General Fraser gained great honor by exposing himself to every danger. During the night we remained in our ranks, and tho' we heard the groans of the wounded and dying, yet could not assist them till morning, not knowing the position of the enemy, and expecting the action to be renewed at daybreak.'[16]

The battle swayed back and forth, with one side pushing the other, who would then push back. Alexander Scammel, leading his New Hampshire regiment, winced as 'A Ball passed through the Breech of my Gun and another through my overalls and just escaped my Legg, whilst my Sergt Major had both the Cords of his Ham cut off with a Ball by my side.' And so intense was the struggle that a British officer speculated that 'The Rebels were in general drunk, a piece of policy of their General to make them fight.' One young German could see that little had been gained by the fight other than, 'The action to-day has caused the house of a poor farmer to become famous; for it has give to this day's engagement the name of the "Battle of Freeman's House".'

Lieutenant Anburey was in command of a burial detail and his heart grew sick within him:

'. . . on seeing fifteen, sixteen, and twenty buried in one hole. I however observed a little more decency than some parties had done, who left heads, legs and arms above ground. No other distinction is paid to officer or private, than the officers are put in a hole by themselves. Our army abounded with young officers, in the subaltern line, and in the course of this unpleasant duty, three of the 20th regiment were interred together, the age of the eldest not exceeding seventeen. This friendly office to the dead . . . was nothing to the scene in bringing in the wounded; the one were past all pain, the other in the most excruciating torments, sending forth dreadful groans. They had remained out all night, and from the loss of blood and want of nourishment, were upon the point of expiring with faintness: some of them begged they might lay and die, others again were insensible, some upon the least movements were put in the most horrid tortures, and all had near a mile to be conveyed to the hospitals; others at their last gasp, who for want of our timely assistance must have inevitably expired. These poor creatures, perishing with cold and weltering in their blood, displayed such a scene, it must be a heart of adamant that could not be effected by it, even to a degree of weakness.

In the course of the late action, Lieutenant Harvey, of the 62d, a youth of sixteen, and a nephew to the Adjutant-General of the same name, received several wounds, and was repeatedly ordered off the field by Colonel Anstruther, but his heroic ardor would not allow him to quit the battle, while he could stand and see his brave lads fighting beside him. A ball striking one of his legs, his removal became absolutely necessary, and while they were conveying him away, another wounded him mortally. In this situation the Surgeon recommended him to take a powerful dose of opium, to avoid a seven or eight hours of the most exquisite torture; this he immediately consented to, and when the Colonel entered the tent with Major Harnage, who were both wounded, they asked whether he had any affairs they could settle for him? his reply was, "that being a minor, every thing was already adjusted:" but he had one request, which he had just life enough to utter, "Tell my uncle I die like a soldier!" '[17]

After the battle of Freeman's Farm, Burgoyne seemed to wilt, and to bury his ambitions along with his officers and men. Matters drifted from bad to worse, and the general had his men cutting trees and building fortifications, chancing the random shots sent winging their way by American riflemen. He was hoping to hear from Sir Henry Clinton who had been left in command of New York when Sir William Howe had sailed off on an expedition to take Philadelphia.

While the two armies stirred restlessly in the heights around Saratoga, Clinton at last made his move. Sailing up the Hudson, he landed his troops with the objective of attacking Forts Montgomery and Clinton, guarding the great log and chain boom across the river. Governor George Clinton, meeting with the New York legislature at Esopus, hastily dissolved that body and hurried to Fort Montgomery, calling out the militia as he sped across country.

The American surgeon James Thacher later heard of the attack and subsequent events:

'Fort Montgomery, and Fort Clinton, are near to each other, on the western bank of the Hudson. They have been considered of great importance as defensive posts, against the passage of the enemy up the river. In addition to these forts, a strong boom, and an iron chain of immense size, were stretched across the river, and a frigate and two gallies were stationed above them. . . . it unfortunately happened that most of the continental troops were necessarily called off to join Gates' army. The forts were defended by Governor George Clinton, and his brother James Clinton, of New York, having about six hundred militia men, a force greatly inadequate to the defence of the works.

The enemy came up the river, landed, and appeared unexpectedly, and demanded a surrender of the forts, which being absolutely refused, were taken by assault, though not without a firm and brave resistance. General James Clinton received a bayonet wound in his thigh, but he and the Governor with a part of the garrison made their escape, leaving about two hundred and fifty men killed, wounded and prisoners. The enemy suffered a severe loss of three field officers killed, and their dead and wounded is estimated at about three hundred.

General Putnam, who commanded at Peekskill in the vicinity, having a small force only to guard the deposit of stores, was obliged to retire, and the

129. Saratoga, 17 October 1777. *Stedman*

At Saratoga ended Burgoyne's expectations of heroic military achievement and his scheme, always highly speculative, of being able to isolate New England from the other colonies. On 13 September, with almost a month's delay after Bennington, he moved south along the east bank of the Hudson and crossed the river a few miles above Saratoga. Six miles to the south Gates waited passively for him near Stillwater on Bemis Heights, a high table-land, dropping down to the Hudson a few hundred yards away on one side and on the other to a roadless, precipitous, forested terrain. At Freeman's Farm the two armies met in a bloody but indecisive battle on 19 September. In a final desperate attempt to drive Gates's army back and break through to Albany, Burgoyne again attacked the Americans on 7 October in the Second Battle of Freeman's Farm. He failed. Retiring to Saratoga on 10 October (not 10 September, as in the title on the map), he vacillated indecisively instead of retreating to Canada. By 17 October, surrounded by Gates's army and unable to escape across the Hudson because of heavy militia forces gathered on the opposite bank, he surrendered.

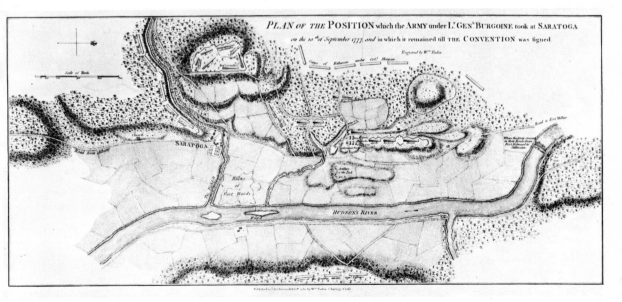

161

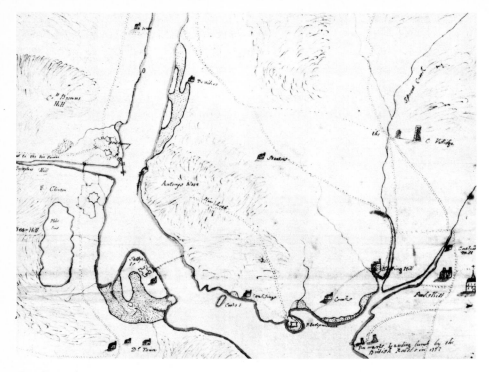

130. Fortifications along the Hudson River Highlands *(detail). T. Machin*

The Americans in 1777 placed four chains or booms across the Hudson to impede British navigation, as shown in this map by Captain Thomas Machin, who helped to construct and emplace them. Machin shows also in detail the roads, fortifications, and homes of the region, with names of the owners. The lowest chain was between Stony Point and Verplanck's Point. Below Stony Point is King's Ferry, where in October 1777 Sir Henry Clinton disembarked and took the road behind Thunder Mountain (Donderberg) to Forts Montgomery and Clinton, which he captured and where he destroyed the chain and boom, as shown in the map. At West Point was another chain, still preserved at the Academy; and between Plum Point and Potipot Island was a log boom (chevaux de frise) with large spikes to prevent ramming by vessels.

Thomas Machin (1744–1816) was appointed 2nd Lieutenant of the New York Artillery on 18 January 1776 and promoted on 1 January 1777 to Captain-Lieutenant in Lamb's 2nd Battalion of Artillery. In 1779 he accompanied General George Clinton, to whom he dedicated this map, on the expedition against the Indians to the Genessee country and later went with General Sullivan's expedition of which he made a sketch.

barracks, stores and provisions, to a very considerable amount, fell into the hands of the enemy and were destroyed. With wanton cruelty they set fire to the houses and buildings of every description, and spread ruin and devastation to the extent of their power. To consummate their destructive scheme, General Vaughan destroyed by conflagration, the beautiful town of Esopus, with the church, and every other building it contained. . . .

They are well apprised of the disastrous and desperate situation of their boastful General Burgoyne, and if they dare not march to his relief, they can cowardly retaliate by conflagration with impunity. It is the prevalent opinion here, that by taking advantage of the wind and tide, it is in the power of Sir Henry Clinton to convey his forces to this city [Albany] within the space of five or six hours, and having arrived here, a march of about twenty miles will carry him without opposition to Stillwater, which must involve General Gates in inexpressible embarrassment and difficulty, by placing him between two armies, and thereby extracting Burgoyne from his perilous situation. We have been tremblingly alive to this menacing prospect, but our fears are in a measure allayed by the following singular incident.

After the capture of Fort Montgomery, Sir Henry Clinton dispatched a messenger by the name of Daniel Taylor, to Burgoyne, with the intelligence; fortunately he was taken on his way as a spy, and finding himself in danger, he was seen to turn aside and take something from his pocket and swallow it. General George Clinton, into whose hands he had fallen, ordered a severe dose of emetic tartar to be administered; this produced the happiest effect as respects the prescriber, but it proved fatal to the patient. He discharged a small silver bullet, which being unscrewed, was found to enclose a letter from Sir Henry Clinton to Burgoyne. "Out of thine own mouth thou shalt be condemned." The spy was tried, convicted and executed. The following is an exact copy of the letter enclosed.

Fort Montgomery, October 8th, 1777

Nous voici—and nothing between us but *Gates*. I sincerely hope this *little* success of ours may facilitate your operations. In answer to your letter of the 28th of September by C. C. I shall only say, I cannot presume to order, or even advise, for reasons obvious. I heartily wish you success.

Faithfully yours,

H. CLINTON

To General Burgoyne'[18]

But Clinton had come with too little and too late and indicated that he could come no farther. The nerves of Burgoyne's troops grew frayed, as he was to note:

'From the 26th of September to the 7th of October, the armies were so near, that not a night passed without firing, and sometimes concerted attacks, on our advanced picquets; no foraging party could be made without great detachments to cover it; it was the plan of the enemy to harass the army by constant alarms and their superiority of numbers enabled them to attempt it without fatigue to themselves. . . . I do not believe that either officer or soldier ever slept during that interval without his cloaths, or that any general officer, or commander of a regiment, passed a single night without being upon his legs occasionally at different hours and constantly an hour before daylight.'[19]

By 4 October Burgoyne, in council with his officers, had made up his mind. Leaving 800 men to guard the supplies, he hoped to flank the American army, get into its rear, and make a dash for Albany. He refused to heed the advice of his generals that he withdraw to a stronger position until he had at least made a reconnaissance in force. Between eleven and twelve o'clock on the morning of 7 October, Burgoyne moved out with 1,500 men and ten artillery pieces, the time chosen so that he could have the cover of darkness should he be forced to withdraw late in the afternoon. Among those alerted was Ebenezer Mattoon, a young American artillery officer, when:

'About one o'clock of this day, two signal guns were fired on the left of the

British army which indicated a movement. Our troops were immediately put under arms, and the lines manned. At this junction Gens. Lincoln and Arnold rode with great speed towards the enemy's lines. While they were absent, the picket guards on both sides were engaged near the river. In about half an hour, Generals Lincoln and Arnold returned to headquarters, where many of the officers collected to hear the report, General Gates standing at the door.

Gen. Lincoln says, "Gen. Gates, the firing at the river is merely a feint; their object is to your left. A strong force of 1500 men are marching circuitously, to plant themselves on yonder height. That point must be defended, or your camp is in danger."

Gates replied, "I will send Morgan and his riflemen, and Dearborn's infantry."

Arnold says, "That is nothing, you must send a strong force."

Gates replied, "Gen. Arnold, I have nothing for you to do; you have no business here."

Arnold's reply was reproachful and severe.

Gen. Lincoln says, "You must send a strong force to support Morgan and Dearborn, at least three regiments."

131. View of General Burgoyne's Camp on the Hudson River, September–October 1777. *Anburey*

Burgoyne's army took post on 20 September on the west bank of the Hudson, three miles above Stillwater. This drawing shows Brigadier-General Simon Fraser's funeral procession on the right.

Samuel Woodward, a volunteer under Gates, recalled the circumstances leading to Fraser's death during the battle of Baemus (Bemis) Heights on 7 October: 'Soon after the commencement of the action, General Arnold . . . said to Colonel Morgan, "That officer upon a grey horse is of himself a host, and must be disposed of."' Soon after, bullets began to fly around Fraser, and his aide urged him to withdraw. 'Fraser replied, "My duty forbids me to fly from danger", and immediately received a bullet through his body.' He survived until the next day and was buried that evening, as he requested, at the top of the nearby hill. 'We saw the generals and their staffs take part in the services', wrote Baroness Riedesel: 'Cannon balls constantly flew around and over the heads of the mourners.' General Gates later sent apologies for the unwitting bombardment of the funeral.

132. Lady Harriet Acland crossing the Hudson to attend her wounded husband, prisoner in the American camp. *Robert Pollard*

General Burgoyne's army, in its rough journey from the St Lawrence to Saratoga, was accompanied by an extraordinary number of women. Of these, the most aristocratic and two of the most heroic were the Baroness Riedesel and Lady Harriet Acland, the pregnant wife of Major John Dykes Acland. The inscription on the plate of this aquatint reads: 'In the unfortunate Action between G.[en.] Burgoyne and G.[en.] Gates Oct. 7, 1777, Major Acland was wounded and made Prisoner, when his Lady received the news she formed the heroic Resolution of delivering herself into the hands of the Enemy that she might attend him during his Captivity . . . She rowed down Hudson River in an open boat towards the American Camp, but night coming on before she reached their outposts the Guards on duty . . . threatened to fire upon her if she moved until morning. . . . She was compelled to wait on the water half dead with anxiety and terror. The morning put an end to her distress, she was received by Gen. Gates & restored to her husband with that politeness and humanity her sex, quality & Virtues so justly merit.'

Two regiments from Gen. Larned's brigade, and one from Gen. Nixon's were then ordered to that station and to defend it at all hazards. Generals Lincoln and Arnold immediately left the encampment and proceeded to the enemy's lines. . . .

During this time, a tremendous firing was heard on our left. We poured in upon them our canister shot as fast as possible, and the whole line, from left to right, became engaged. The smoke was very dense, and no movements could be seen; but as it soon arose, our infantry appeared to be slowly retreating, and the Hessians slowly advancing, their officers urging them on with their hangers. . . .

They advanced with a quick step, firing as they came on. We returned them a brisk fire of canister shot, not allowing ourselves time even to sponge our piece. In a short time they ceased firing and advanced upon us with trailed arms. At this juncture Arnold came up with a part of Brooks' regiment and gave them a most deadly fire, which soon caused them to face about and retreat with a quicker step than they advanced.

The firing had now principally ceased on our left, but was brisk in front and on the right. At this moment Arnold says to Col. Brooks (late governor of Massachusetts), "Let us attack Balcarras's works."

Brooks replied, "No. Lord Auckland's [Ackland] detachment has retired there, we can't carry them."

"Well, then, let us attack the Hessian lines."

Brooks replies, "With all my heart."

We all wheeled to the right and advanced. No fire was received, except from the cannon, until we got within eight rods, when we received a tremendous fire from the whole line. But a few of our men, however, fell. Still advancing, we received a second fire, in which a few men fell, and Gen. Arnold's horse fell under him, and he himself was wounded. He cried out, "Rush on, my brave boys!" After receiving the third fire, Brooks mounted their works, swung his sword, and the men rushed into their works. When we entered the works, we found Col. Bremen dead, surrounded with a number of his companions, dead or wounded. We still pursued slowly, the fire, in the mean time, decreasing. Nightfall now put an end to this day's bloody contest. During the day we had taken eight cannon and broken the centre of the enemy's lines.

We were ordered to rest until relieved from the camps. The gloom of the night, the groans and shrieks of the wounded and dying, and the horrors of the whole scene baffle all description.'[20]

Among those who experienced all the horrors of war, yet fired no gun that day, was the Baroness Riedesel, wife of the German general:

'About two o'clock in the afternoon, the firing of cannon and small arms was again heard, and all was alarm and confusion. My husband sent me a message telling me to betake myself forthwith into a house which was not far from there. I seated myself in the calash with my children, and had scarcely driven up to the house when I saw on the opposite side of the Hudson River five or six men with guns, which were aimed at us. Almost involuntarily I threw the children on the bottom of the calash and myself over them. At the same instant the churls fired, and shattered the arm of a poor English soldier behind us, who was already wounded, and was also on the point of retreating within the house.

Immediately after our arrival a frightful cannonade began, principally directed against the house in which we had sought shelter, probably because the enemy believed, from seeing so many people flocking around it, that all the generals made it their headquarters. Alas! it harbored none but wounded soldiers, or women! We were finally obliged to take refuge in a cellar, in which I laid myself down in a corner not far from the door. My children lay down on the earth with their heads upon my lap, and in this manner we passed the entire night. A horrible stench, the cries of the children, and yet more than all this, my own anguish, prevented me from closing my eyes. On the following morning the cannonade again began, but from a different side. I advised all to go out of the cellar for a little while, during which time I would have it cleaned, as otherwise we would all be sick. They followed my suggestion, and I at once set many hands to work, which was in the highest degree necessary; for the women and children, being afraid to venture forth, had soiled the whole cellar. . . .

I had just given the cellars a good sweeping, and had fumigated them by sprinkling vinegar on burning coals, and each one had found his place prepared for him—when a fresh and terrible cannonade threw us all once more into alarm. Many persons, who had no right to come in, threw themselves against the door. My children were already under the cellar steps, and we would all have been crushed, if God had not given me strength to place myself before the door, and with extended arms prevent all from coming in; otherwise every one of us would have been severely injured.

Eleven cannon balls went through the house, and we could plainly hear them rolling over our heads. One poor soldier, whose leg they were about to amputate, having been laid upon a table for this purpose, had the other leg taken off by another cannon ball, in the very middle of the operation. His comrades all ran off, and when they again came back they found him in one corner of the room, where he had rolled in his anguish, scarcely breathing. I was more dead than alive, though not so much on account of my own danger as for that which enveloped my husband, who, however, frequently sent to see how I was getting along, and to tell me he was still safe. . . .

In this horrible situation we remained six days. Finally, they spoke of capitulating, as by temporizing for so long a time our retreat had been cut off. A cessation of hostilities took place, and my husband, who was thoroughly worn out, was able for the first time in a long while, to lie down upon a bed. . . .But about one o'clock in the night some one came and asked to speak to him. It was with the greatest reluctance that I found myself obliged to awaken him. I observed that the message did not please him, as he immediately sent the man back to headquarters and laid himself down again considerably out of humor.

Soon after this General Burgoyne requested the presence of all the generals and staff officers at a council of war, which was to be held early the next morning; in which he proposed to break the capitulation, already made with the enemy, in consequence of some false information just receivd. It was, however, finally decided that this was neither practicable nor advisable; and this was fortunate for us, as the Americans said to us afterwards that had the capitulation been broken off we all would have been massacred; which they would have done the more easily as we were not over four or five thousand men strong, and had given them time to bring together more than twenty thousand. . . .

At last my husband sent to me a groom with a message that I should come to him with our children. I, therefore, again seated myself in my dear calash; and in the passage through the American camp I observed with great satisfaction that no one cast at us scornful glances. On the contrary, they all greeted me, even showing compassion on their countenances at seeing a mother with her little children in such a situation. I confess that I feared to come into the enemy's camp, as the thing was so entirely new to me.'[21]

In the negotiations, Burgoyne outsmarted Horatio Gates. Rejecting the

133. The Engagement on Lake Champlain at Valcour Island. *H. Gilder*

On 11 October 1776 the British fleet under Captain Pringle of the Royal Navy, manned with experienced seamen and gunners, cornered the Americans twenty miles north of Crown Point in a channel between Valcour Island and the west shore of Lake Champlain. 'It was', wrote Admiral Mahan, 'the strife of pigmies for the prize of a continent.'

Gilder's painting shows the situation at the end of the day. Arnold's flagship, the *Royal Savage*, was disabled and beached; its crew scrambled ashore on the island. Twenty-two British gunboats lined the entrance to the channel (i). Both gunboats and the schooner *Carleton* (j), damaged by American fire, withdrew. The Maria (l), with Captain Pringle and Sir Guy aboard, and the *Inflexible* (k) waited until morning for the annihilation of the enemy. But that night Arnold, by a bold and skilful manoeuvre, rowed his fleet out with muffled oars, undetected in the mist, between the island and the British. Not until morning was the escape discovered; the pursuit was only partially successful. 'This retreat did great honor to Gen. Arnold', wrote Lieutenant Hadden of the Royal Artillery, in charge of one of the gunboats. Only three American ships escaped; Arnold beached and burned five boats at Crown Point and reached Ticonderoga with their crews. 'On the whole', wrote Arnold to General Schuyler, 'I think we have had a very fortunate escape.' (See pp. 76–7, Chapter 3.)

134. A View of Ticonderoga, from a point on the North Shore of Lake Champlain. *James Hunter*

The artist is looking south, with Fort Ticonderoga to the right; Fort Independence is around the curving wooded east bank to the left. Connecting the two forts at the narrowest point may be seen a boom and bridge made of bateaux and planks. Beyond is South Bay and the outlet of Lake George. In the foreground are a whaleboat-like vessel with a mounted howitzer and other smaller boats with troops.

The reduction of the two forts was essential to Burgoyne's plan in his advance towards Albany; the British under General William Phillips advanced on the west shore towards Ticonderoga, the Hessians under General Riedesel upon Independence. The British mounted a secret battery of heavy ordnance on a hill, Mount Defiance, at the outlet of Lake George, which the Americans thought unscalable. The battery could lay a withering fire down on both forts and made them untenable. On the night of 5 July General Arthur St Clair wisely evacuated his troops in Ticonderoga across the pontoon bridge, and escaped. The women and children, the sick, and large stores of artillery and equipment were loaded aboard two hundred bateaux. The British, alerted by the unplanned firing of Fort Independence, crossed the bridge in pursuit and caught up with the retreating Americans at Hubbardton, where an indecisive skirmish with St Clair's rearguard occurred. The British gunboats broke through the boom and caught up with the American flotilla at Skenesborough, where they captured the valuable equipment and made some prisoners.

James Hunter, an assistant engineer in Burgoyne's army, survived Burgoyne's surrender, for he made a map of northern Lake Champlain signed and dated 1780, now in the William L. Clements Library.

135. (Overleaf) The Surrender of General Burgoyne at Saratoga, New York, 17 October 1777. *Trumbull*

In the centre stands Major-General Horatio Gates; to his left in the painting is General John Burgoyne, with his sword, politely returned by Gates. In the background, above Burgoyne's hand, is the face of Major-General Friedrick Adolf Riedesel; in front of the cannon is Colonel Daniel Morgan, then of the 11th Virginia Regiment, clad in buckskin.

The painting, despite Trumbull's title, does not represent the actual surrender of the British forces, at which Lieutenant-Colonel James Wilkinson, Deputy Adjutant-General of the Northern Department, representing Gates, was the only American staff officer present. After the soldiers had laid down their arms, General Burgoyne and his staff, accompanied by Wilkinson, rode to General Gates's headquarters and there were entertained at a sumptuous dinner. Later the British troops marched between parallel lines of American soldiers; after that Burgoyne and Gates emerged from headquarters and the formal military protocol of offering the sword to the victor and of its return took place. Careful as Trumbull was in his effort to make accurate portraits, this did not always extend to the dress. Wilkinson wrote that Burgoyne wore 'a rich royal uniform, and Gates a plain blue frock'.

John Trumbull first planned the painting in 1786, but did not start this small oil until 1816. In 1824 he completed the large, heavy-handed replica of it now in the Rotunda of the Capitol.

136. Hudson's River From Chambers, Looking toward the north gate of the Hudson Highlands.
Alexander Robertson

This hand-coloured aquatint gives a view of the highlands at the north end of Tappan Sea, which was under British naval control for most of the war after August 1776.

Alexander Robertson (1772–1841), a watercolour landscape painter, came to New York from Scotland in 1792 and with his older brother Archibald founded the Columbian Academy of Painting. Alexander was later Librarian (1812) and Keeper (1820) of the American Academy.

terms offered by the American general, Burgoyne submitted a 'Convention', a rather bizarre document in the annals of military history. This proposal allowed the British all the honours of war, and a free passage to Great Britain 'on condition of not serving again in North America during the present condition'. To the consternation of the Americans, and the amazement of the British, Gates accepted the proposals after making only minor changes. And Gates was pleased enough to write to his wife, 'If old England is not by this lesson taught humility, then she is an obstinate old slut, bent on her ruin.' Lieutenant Digby, who had left Canada with such high hopes, was humiliated:

'About ten o'clock, we marched out according to treaty, with drums beating & the honors of war, but the drums seemed to have lost their former inspiring sounds, and though we beat the Grenadiers march, which not so long before was so animating, yet then it seemed by its last feeble effort as almost ashamed to be heard on such an occasion.

As to my own feelings, I cannot express them. Tears (though unmanly) forced their way and if alone, I could have burst to give myself vent. I never shall forget the appearance of their troops on our marching past them; a dead silence universally reigned through their numerous columns, and even then they seemed struck with our situation and dare scarce lift up their eyes to view British troops in such a situation. I must say their decent behaviour during the time (to us so greatly fallen) merited the utmost approbation and praise.

The meeting between Burgoyne and Gates was well worth seeing. He paid Burgoyne almost as much respect as if he was the conqueror; indeed, his noble air, tho' prisoner, seemed to command respect from every person. A party of light dragoons were ordered as his guard, rather to protect his person from insults than any other cause.

Thus ended all our hopes of victory, honor, glory &c., &c., &c. Thus was Burgoyne's army sacrificed to either the absurd opinions of a blundering ministerial power, the stupid inaction of a general [Howe] who, from his lethargic disposition, neglected every step he might have taken to assist

137. The Generals in America doing nothing, or worse than nothing

A year and a half after the surrender of Burgoyne at Saratoga, this cartoonist in the Westminster Magazine is still angry at Sir William Howe, at ease with cards and bottles, for not coming to Burgoyne's aid. The letter ordering him to do so lies unseen or unopened at his feet.

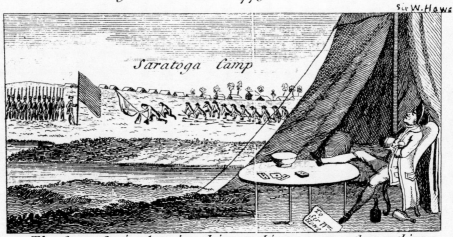

The Generals in America doing nothing, or worse than nothing.

their operations, or lastly, perhaps, his own conduct in penetrating so far, as to be unable to return, tho' I must own my partiality to him is great. . . .'[22]

The Continental Congress refused to honour the Convention of Saratoga, reasoning that although the surrendered army would no longer fight in America, they could relieve troops stationed in England who would replace them in America. The news of the surrender spread through the country, leaving in its wake ringing bells and the boom of cannon as they fired joyous salutes. To the loyalists, who had ventured their all on British might, the world seemed to have tumbled down around their ears. In New York one loyalist officer observed, 'News that General Bergoyn is taken & every man is put on a long fase.' Another wrote,

'I wish not to survive the destruction of this place, or its capture by the Rebels. . . . From everything I see, America seems to be intentionally given up, and the interests and glory of Britain sacraficed to party and a junto of villains within her own bowels. . . . Rebellion, which a twelvemonth ago was really a contemptible pigmy, is now in appearance become a giant more dreadful to the minds of men than Polyphemus of old, or the Sons of Anak.'[23]

So great was the gloom in New York that few considered the victories won in Pennsylvania by Sir William Howe.

138. Encampment of the Convention Army at Charlotte Ville in Virginia. *Anburey*

From January 1779 to October 1780 the troops of General Burgoyne were quartered in barracks near Charlottesville, Virginia. From their first encampment near Boston they were marched in the fall of 1778 back across the Hudson and Potomac Rivers and reached their destination shortly after Christmas. The weather was bitter and neither food nor lodging was adequate. Both Baroness Riedesel and Major Anburey have left vivid accounts of the privations.

8. The Fall of Philadelphia

IN THE PRECEDING MONTHS Sir William Howe had had a difficult choice before him. It was a decision of major importance: should he go to the aid of Burgoyne on the Hudson, or should he devote his attention to Pennsylvania, resume the fight with Washington and capture the nearest thing to a capital city held by the Americans? The problem was greatly increased by slowness of communication across great distances. It also involved the complex question of what constituted the winning of a war in this huge and formless land, where resistance was diffused rather than concentrated, and where defeated bands of rebels could melt away into forests, regroup, and attack again. Lord George Germain, Secretary of State for the Colonies, had approved Burgoyne's plan calling for a junction of the forces of Burgoyne and Howe at Albany, an operation designed to isolate the New England states from the rest of the country, allowing the British to roll up the remainder at their leisure. But Germain had also approved, less than six weeks later, a subsequent scheme by Howe to concentrate on the capture of Philadelphia before going to the aid of the troops on the Hudson. Then, around the first of July, dispatches had come from Burgoyne, reporting that all was well. There was also the consideration that if Burgoyne's expedition were successful, he, and not the commanding general, would gather the victor's laurels. Howe, despite the protests of Sir Henry Clinton, made up his mind: he would sail for Philadelphia. He rationalized that if Washington moved northward to meet the threat of Burgoyne, Howe could come in on his tail and catch the entire American army between the two British armies.

Washington was apprehensive, watching British developments with an uneasy eye. Reports indicated that Burgoyne was moving grandly down from Canada, especially after St Clair evacuated Ticonderoga without firing a shot. He shifted his forces to sites that would allow them to dash up the Hudson with the least effort should the British in New York move in that direction. To aid recruiting in the northern states he sent two popular New England generals, Benjamin Lincoln and Benedict Arnold, to the northern theatre. And on the suggestion of the Continental Congress he had weakened his own command by sending Daniel Morgan and his riflemen northward.

Howe began embarking troops aboard transports in the first part of July, confusing the American commander-in-chief even more. It would seem that the troops would have been happy to leave New York. A loyalist, Nicholas Cresswell, reported a rather repulsive city:

'Now all these Ditches and fortified places [of the rebels] are full of stagnate water, damaged sour Crout and filth of every kind. Noisome vapours arise from the mud left in the docks and slips at low water, and unwholesome smells are occasioned by such a number of people being crowded together in so small a compass almost like herrings in a barrel, most of them very dirty and not a small number sick of some disease, the Itch, Pox, Fever, or Flux, so that altogether there is a complication of stinks enough to drive a person whose sense of smelling was very delicate and his lungs of the finest contexture, into a consumption in the space of twenty-four hours. If any author who had an inclination to write a treatise upon stinks and ill smells, he never could meet with more subject matter than in New York, or anyone who had abilities and inclinations to expose the vicious and unfeeling parts of human nature or the various means, that are used to pick up a living in this world, I recommend New York as a proper place to collect his characters. Most of the former inhabitants that once possessed this once happy spot are utterly ruined and from opulence reduced to the greatest indigence, some in the Rebels' Jails by force, others by inclinations in their Armies.'[1]

By 8 July Howe had loaded his troops aboard some 260 vessels, and then,

'returned to New York, and after spending a fortnight in dalliance with Mrs. Loring [the reputedly obliging wife of Joshua Loring, a loyalist appointed commissary of prisoners by Howe], while the troops were lying on board the transports crowded together in the sultry heat of summer, he went on board his brother's ship [the *Nonsuch*], and orders were given for sailing.'[2]

In New York there were left some seventeen battalions, some cavalry, and the loyalist provincial troops under the overall command of Sir Henry Clinton. Howe's invasion force consisted of 15,000 officers and men, including two regiments of cavalry. On 23 July, the fleet upped anchor and stood out to sea by Sandy Hook where Ambrose Serle 'viewed the Light-House, a stinking edifice, by means of the oil and the Provincials stationed in it'. Once under way, the convoy ran into rough weather; thunderstorms were frequent, lightning striking several vessels and doing some damage. Standing in through the Virginia Capes, the fleet swept up Chesapeake Bay, loosing their anchor chains at Head of Elk, Maryland.

139. A section of a First Rate Ship of War, Showing its various Timbers and Apartments
Howe's fleet ascending the Chesapeake numbered over 280 sail, including transports and auxiliaries. Four 64-gun ships of the line (naval vessels with 60 guns or more) accompanied the flotilla, with one 50-gun ship and 10 smaller fully equipped vessels of war.

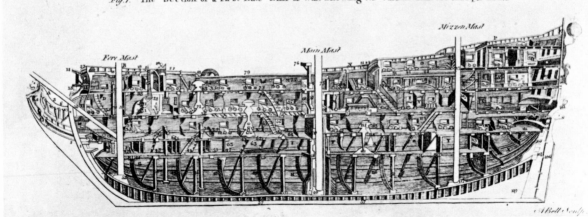

Fig. 1. The Section of a First Rate Ship of War, Shewing its various Timbers and Apartments

140. A Sketch of the Navigation from Swan Point to the River Elk. *Hunter*

Howe's fleet was two hundred miles from the capes when Washington heard that it was sailing up Chesapeake Bay. The troops began disembarking at Head of Elk on 25 August; hundreds of horses had died on the long and stormy voyage from New York, and General William Howe scoured the country for horses while the troops advanced slowly up either side of the river.

A note on this manuscript map in Lord Howe's own hand tells us that it was by Captain John Hunter. Hunter (1735–1821), master of the *Eagle*, Howe's flagship, had been present aboard the *Neptune* at the taking of Quebec in 1759; he made a number of charts of the coast from New York to Florida, including at least three of the Delaware River. One of these was published in the *Atlantic Neptune*.

Even as Howe prepared his army for the march on Philadelphia, Washington's indecision was brought to an abrupt conclusion with the intelligence that the British were disembarking, and their obvious objective was Philadelphia. He set out to block the approaches. His army had been gradually reinforced by new detachments and, counting the militia, now numbered about 16,000 men, although the figure was flexible because of the militia's habit of coming and going as they pleased. On 4 August, the general rid his forces of surplus baggage with the order:

'In the present marching state of the army, every incumbrance proves greatly prejudicial to the service; the multitude of women in particular, especially those who are pregnant and have children, are a clog upon every movement. The Commander in Chief therefore earnestly recommends

173

it to the officers commanding brigades and corps, to use every reasonable method in their power to get rid of all such as are not absolutely necessary; the admission or continuance of any, who shall, or may come to the army since its arrival in Pennsylvania, is positively forbidden, to which point the officers will give particular attention.'[3]

To bolster flagging American spirits, Washington paraded his army through Philadelphia, and to compensate for the lack of uniforms every man was instructed to wear a sprig of green in his hat as an 'emblem of hope', while the drums and fifes were ordered to play a quickstep, 'but with moderation, that the men may step to it with ease; and without *dancing* along, or totally disregarding the music'. The show was a success, although John Adams noted of the troops, 'They don't hold up their heads quite erect, nor turn out their toes so exactly as they ought. They don't all cock their hats, and such as do, don't all wear them the same way.'

Brandywine Creek became the obvious place to check the British advance. The stream scrambled along between steep banks and was deep enough to force the British to use the fords. Unfortunately, there were many fords. If the enemy were not stopped here, there was no other natural obstacle between them and Philadelphia.

Washington selected Chad's Ford as the logical crossing. The divisions of Nathanael Greene and Anthony Wayne, supported by most of the artillery, were posted along the creek just south of Chad's. General William Maxwell and 800 men were deployed on the far side of the stream with orders to 'bring on the action' should the British advance. By 11 September the British were encamped at Kennett Square, five miles west of Chad's Ford. Howe's plan was to send a division of 5,000 men under General Knyphausen to make a diversionary feint at Chad's, while Howe himself accompanied Cornwallis' 'Grand Division', of around 12,500 rank and file, their mission being to march upstream, cross at one of the fords, and come in on the flank of the American army. The scheme was almost a mirror image of the tactic the British general had used on Long Island.

Included in Knyphausen's division was a detachment of riflemen commanded by Major Patrick Ferguson. Ferguson, called 'Bull Dog' by his fellow officers, had invented a remarkable breech-loading 'rifle-gun', and had been given a special command to test it under combat conditions. While he and his corps lay concealed in the skirts of wood in front of Knyphausen's division:

'We had not lain long . . . when a rebel officer, remarkable by a hussar dress, passed towards our army within a hundred yards of my right flank, not perceiving us. He was followed by another dressed in dark green or blue, mounted on a bay horse, with a remarkably large cocked hat.

I ordered three good shots to steal near . . . and fire at them, but the idea disgusted me. I recalled the order. The hussar in returning made a circuit, but the other passed again within a hundred yards of us, upon which I advanced from the woods towards him.

On my calling, he stopped, but after looking at me, proceeded. I again drew his attention and made signs to him to stop, but he slowly continued his way. As I was within that distance at which in the quickest firing I could have lodged half-a-dozen balls in or about him before he was out of my reach, I had only to determine. But it was not pleasant to fire at the

174

back of an unoffending individual, who was acquitting himself very cooly of his duty, so I let him alone.

The day after, I was telling this story to some wounded officers who lay in the same room with me, when one of our surgeons, who had been dressing the wounded rebel officers, came in and told us they had been informing him that General Washington was all that morning with the light troops and only attended by a French officer in a hussar dress, he himself dressed

141. Progress of the British Army. *John André*

This simplified drawing of the route taken by the British from Elk River to Philadelphia, showing the chief engagements with enemy forces in their advance, summarizes almost a score of detailed plans made by André. Many of these are in the journal which he kept on the march, now in the Huntington Library; many other maps, made during his career in America, are in widely scattered libraries. His cartographic skill was but one of his many talents cut short by his untimely death.

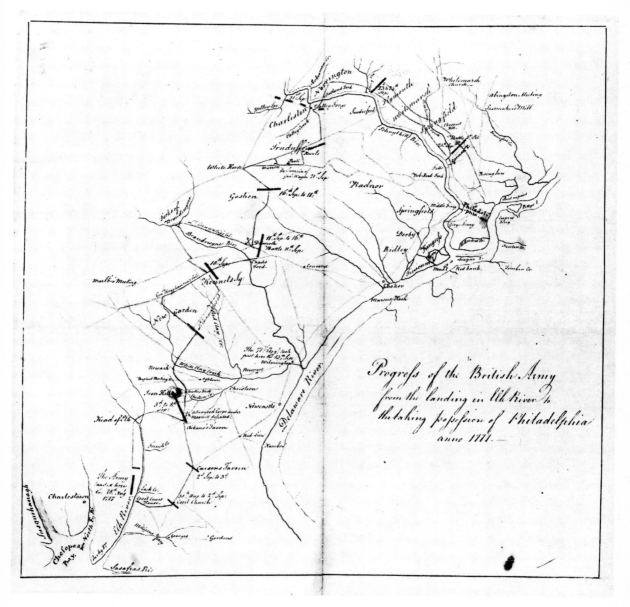

and mounted in every point as above described. I am not sorry that I did not know at the time who it was. Farther this deponent sayeth not, as his bones were broken a few moments after.'[4]

Sometime later, Ferguson wrote home (using his left hand) to describe the initial onset of the battle against 'such a set of base runaways never before presumed to disgrace a Gentleman's profession':

'The Army March'd to the attack in two Columns, one under G: Howe (at the head of which was all the light infantry of the Army, follow'd by all the Grenadiers) attack'd the right of the Rebels: The other under General Knyphausen (Hessian) at the head of which my little Corps had the Honour to be, attack'd in front. Gen. Knyphausen, when I ask'd his orders, was pleased to desire me to take my own way. . . .

As our Column took the direct road and had only four Miles to March whilst Gen: Howe made a circuit of 15. We had the whole body of their light troops (riflemen, light infantry &ct.) on hand who occupied every strength and had erected various breast works to stop us in front and annoy us in flank in the course of our March.

The first party we had to do with was an advanced Post of 150 Men and some light horse who threw away their fire and ran off, with the loss of three or four men and a horse whom we shot flying: their numbers encreased as we advanced and in the course of two hours my lads underwent the fire of 2000 men who were kind enough to fire in general in the air and run away. The Queen's Rangers, Americans commanded by Rachael Wemyss' husband seconded us with spirit and . . . we kept them undisturbed and clear'd the way for them as fast as they could follow us.

My Lads were so fatigued with dashing after the Rebels over all surfaces that I found it necessary to leave one half by turns in the rear with the

142. The Battle of Paoli. *Xavier della Gatta*

'The terror that flieth by night' had full meaning for General Anthony Wayne's Pennsylvania Continentals at midnight on 20 September 1777. Encamped near Paoli, sleepily stirring around their campfires in preparation for a march to harass the British crossing of the Schuylkill, they had no warning of the stealthy approach of General Grey's battalion of light infantry, forbidden to fire a shot. Suddenly the flash of British bayonets was everywhere among the confused and terrified Americans. Major Samuel Hay wrote, 'The annals of the age cannot produce such a scene of butchery'; and commented sadly that he now had left in his unit 'just half the men we had on the ground fit for duty'.

There are very few night scenes among contemporary Revolutionary paintings. This and the next picture were painted by the Italian artist Xavier della Gatta in 1782, possibly in England, probably on commission for some British officer who had been an eyewitness.

143. The Battle of Germantown. *Xavier della Gatta*

If this picture, as is supposed, was painted from an eyewitness account, the witness failed to impress upon the artist the density of the early morning fog which even caused two American divisions to fire upon each other. Nor did the witness do justice to the Chew House; he mentioned its stone construction and the urns on its roof, but did not convey the quality which made Colonel Knox call it a 'castle', and advise against bypassing it. 'This house of Chew's was a strong stone building . . .,' wrote Colonel Pickering, who was with Washington, 'having windows on every side, so that you could not approach it without being exposed to a severe fire . . . Several of our pieces, six-pounders, were brought up within musket shot of it, and fired round balls at it, but in vain.' The painting does show, however, the flanking action attempted by the Americans. Their defeat at Germantown came so near to being a victory in a general attack upon a British army that it left them in high spirits.

Column of March and work my way with the others—which as our whole detachment was under 90 men was no great command: however by avoiding the road, gaining their flanks, on keeping up a rattling fire from the ground or by bullying them we still got on:—when my 30 Lads advanced to a breast work of 100 yards in extent, well lined with men whose fire they received at twelve yards and when every body thought they were all destroyed, they Scrambled into the breast work and the Dogs ran away, leaving even their Hatts and Shoes by the way:—We were stop'd from following them by a heavy flanking fire from a very extensive breast work at 80 yards distance. I threw my party immediately on the ground, but Wemyss's, who had kept the road, being close to my rear, came under a part of it and had a fourth part of his Men and officers killed and wounded—this fire continued for some minutes very heavy until we Sicken'd [of] it, after which upon the Signal to rise my Lads . . . Sprung up and not one hurt: Such is the great advantage of an Army that will admit of being loaded and fired on the ground without exposing the men, that I threw my people on the ground under pretty smart firing Six times that morning without losing a man, although I had 1/4 part of those with me kill'd or wounded before I was disabled.

When we came in view of the Rebel Army, our Column formed the line in readiness of advance whenever General Howes attack begun. The line was much harrassed by a fire from a wood 200 yards in front to which my Lads advanced, unsupported, and drove the Rebels first from the Skirt of the wood, then from a breast work within it, and then out of it entirely, after which they mentained themselves at the further skirt of it for half an hour without any assistance, 1/4 of a Mile in front of any other troops.

The Rebels attempted to flank us and Collect a powerful fire round us, but they Scarse could discover us, but by the Smoke, and when they came to show themselves, our Balls rattled among them so quick and with so good a meaning that they mostly withdrew. At last, however, they lined a fence on our left flank which made it necessary to change our ground to an opposite fence from whence we amused them for some time untill being out-flank'd on that side too, from their great Superiority in Numbers, I got Wounded, after which I gave my part orders to break and run untill they were a little under Cover of a Swell of the ground, when to their eternal honour upon the first Signal they rally'd again, and threw themselves upon the ground; they were soon after supported.'[5]

Even as the artillery duel continued at Chad's Ford, Howe and Cornwallis were leading the flanking column across the Brandywine above its fork. Light troops, ranging off on the flanks,

'passed by the ford where now is "Wistar's Bridge." The Wistar farm was then owned by John Brinton. He was an eccentric, daring little man, and a furious Whig, somewhat intemperate in his habits; . . . he was so extravagant in his deportment, when excited by liquor, that he was commonly called "Crazy Johnny." When the companies aforesaid approached his house, he greated them with a hearty "Hurrah for General Washington!" They immediately arrested him, and treated him very roughly. They threatened to kill him instantly, if he did not *Hurrah for King George*. They prevailed, after some time, to make him say *Hurrah for King George*—but he immediately added—WASHINGTON! Finding him utterly unmanageable,

144. The Taking of Miss Mud I'land

The importance of the capture of the fort on Mud Island, 15 November 1777, was that it opened the Delaware River to the British, and made it possible to supply Sir William Howe and his troops in winter quarters in Philadelphia. Admiral Howe had a stubborn fight on his hands. In this cartoon, published in London before the news of the final victory reached England, America straddles a cannon on a pentagonal fort-shaped island, and fires another; her hair is elaborately dressed with two flags, the striped 'Don't tread on me' flag, and the Union flag. Howe's ships, surrounding the island, are all named; the *Isis* and the *Merlin* were lost in the battle. The *chevaux de frises* impeding shipping in the river are also shown.

they plundered his house, and took him with them, as a prisoner, to Philadelphia, where he was detained a long time and treated with great severity.'[6]

At Benjamin Ring's tavern, where Washington had estabiished his headquarters, a puzzled general pondered conflicting reports that a British column was marching on a flanking movement. He became convinced that there might be some validity to the vague reports when Squire Thomas Cheney forced his way into the building and reported activity upstream. John Sullivan was sent to oppose this possible threat, while the divisions of Lord Stirling and Adam Stephen were rushed forward in support. Greene, Wayne, and Maxwell were to entertain the British at Chad's Ford. When he finally received word that the British were indeed engaging the Americans in the neighbourhood of Birmingham Meeting House, the general looked around for a guide to lead him to the action by the shortest route. He seized upon a resident of the neighbourhood, one Joseph Brown,

'an elderly man, and extremely loth to undertake that duty. He made many excuses, but the occasion was too urgent for ceremony. One of Washington's aides dismounted from a fine charger, and told Brown that if he did not instantly get on his horse, and conduct the General by the nearest and best route to the place of action, he would run him through on the spot.

Brown thereupon mounted, and steered his course towards Birmingham Meeting House, with all speed—the General and his attendants being close on his heels. He said the horses leapt all the fences without difficulty, and was followed in a like manner by the others. The head of Gen. Washington's horse, he said, was constantly at the flank of the one on which he was mounted; and the General was continually requesting to him, *"Push along, old man" – "Push along, old man."*

When they reached the road, about half a mile west of Dilworthtown, Brown said the bullets were flying so thick that he felt very uncomfortable; and as Washington no longer required, nor paid any attention to his guide, the latter embraced the first opportunity to dismount and make his escape.'[7]

A Young Quaker boy, Joseph Townshend, was fascinated with the British army and gawked at such a spectacle of martial splendour, especially the Hessians, many of whom 'wore their beards on their upper lips, which was a novelty in that part of the country'. Leaning on a rail fence, he and his companions were

'amusing ourselves with the wonderful curiosity before us, [when] to our

145. Battle of Brandywine. 11th Septr 1777

Washington placed the main body of his army at Chad's Ford on deep Brandywine Creek (bottom left of map) to stop Howe's march to Philadelphia; Howe's strategy was to make a strong surprise flanking movement in order to destroy the rebel forces by a pincer attack. Neither succeeded; but Howe's plan came perilously close to success. Early on the morning of 11 September 5,000 British and Hessian troops under Knyphausen approached Chad's Ford in a feint (B, bottom left) to hold the rebels while 7,500 troops under Cornwallis made a fifteen-mile circuitous march north and then back towards the rear of the rebel forces. Not until 2 p.m. did Washington learn of Cornwallis's approach; he then hurried Nathanael Greene north towards Birmingham meeting-house to reinforce the troops already engaged. Cornwallis (A) met and drove back the Americans across the road from the meeting-house. Knyphausen was able to cross Chad's Ford against weakened opposition. Greene's men prevented a rout at Birmingham but retreated past Dilworth. Howe failed to pursue his advantage, probably because his men were too exhausted.

great astonishment and surprise the firing of musketry took place; the advanced guard . . . having arrived at the street road, and were fired upon by a company of Americans, who were stationed in the orchard north of Samuel Jones' brick dwelling house.

The attack was immediately returned by the Hessians, by their stepping

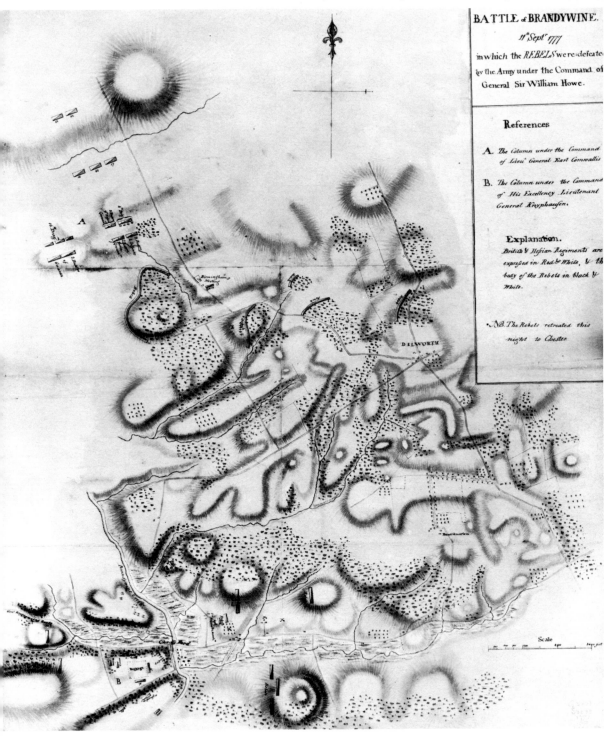

BATTLE of BRANDYWINE.

11th Septr 1777

in which the REBELS were defeated by the Army under the Command of General Sir William Howe.

References

A. The Column under the Command of Lieut General Earl Cornwallis

B. The Column under the Command of His Excellency Lieutenant General Kniphausen.

Explanation.

British & Hessian Regiments are expressed in Red & White, & the body of the Rebels in Black & White.

NB. The Rebels retreated this night to Chester.

up the bank of the road alongside the orchard, making the fence a breast work through which they fired upon the company who made the attack. From the distance we were from them (though in full view until the smoke of firing covered them from our sight,) I was under no apprehension of danger, especially when there was such a tremendous force coming on and ready to engage in the action; nevertheless, I concluded it best to retire. . . .

I then made the best of my way through the crowd until I arrived at the aforementioned bars on the road, which opened into the field of Amos Davis, where I was met by several companies of soldiers, who were ordered into the field to form and prepare for the approaching engagement—the opening of the bars was not of sufficient width to admit them to pass with that expedition the emergency of the case required. A German officer on horse back ordered the fence to be taken down, and as I was near the spot, I had to be subject to his requirings as he flourished a drawn sword over my head with others who stood by; on the removal of the second rail I was struck with the impropriety of being active in assisting to take the lives of my fellow beings, and therefore desisted proceeding any further in obedience to his command. The hurry was so great, and so many rushing forward under arms, I found no difficulty in retiring undiscovered. . . .

It was now a time of seriousness and some alarm among them—the battle had commenced in earnest—little was to be heard but the firing of musketry and the roaring of cannon from the parties. It appeared that those on horseback were some of the principal officers of the British army with their aids. . . . Among them was General Howe. He was mounted on a large English horse much reduced in flesh, I suppose from their being so long confined on board the fleet between New York and Chesapeake Bay, which was about six weeks, occasioned by contrary winds, &c. The general was a large portly man, of coarse features. He appeared to have lost his teeth, as his mouth had fallen in. As I stood alongside I had a full opportunity of viewing him as he sat on horseback, and to observe his large legs and boots, with flourishing spurs thereon.

While the officers were in consultation, and we viewing them together with smoke issuing from the cannon and musketry, we heard a tremendous roaring of cannons, and saw the volume of smoke arising therefrom at Chadd's Ford. General Knyphausen having discovered that the engagement was on with the front of Howe's army at the meeting house, he immediately forced the troops under his command across the Brandywine, and the whole of General Washington's army in that station were routed from their breastworks and different positions they had taken to impede the march of the British. From these circumstances General Washington concluded it prudent to effect a retreat which took place accordingly.'8

The retreat was saved from becoming a rout by the troops of Nathanael Greene who covered the withdrawal. That night the army fell back on Chester where they regrouped. Even as they marched, one young British officer was thinking of the exhilaration of battle; and feeling relief that it ended:

'I should have written to thee, O Imperial! Consider the pain of the contusion! What excessive fatigue—a rapid march from four o'clock in the morning till four in the eve. when we engaged till dark. We fought. Describe the battle. 'Twas not like those of Covent Garden or Drury Lane. Thou hast seen Le Brun's paintings and the tapestry perhaps at Blenheim; are these natural resemblances? Pshaw! quoth the *captain, en un mot.* There was a most infernal fire of cannon and musquetry; smoke; incessant shouting; "Incline to the right! Incline to the left! Halt! Charge!" &c. The balls ploughing up the ground; the trees cracking over one's head; the branches riven by the artillery; the leaves falling as in autumn, by the grapeshot, the affair was general.

The masters on both sides showed conduct. The action was brilliant. Mr. Washington retreated (i.e., run away,) and Mr. Howe remained master of the field.

We took four pieces of cannon and a howitzer. . . . I took a night cap, lined with fur, which I find very comfortable in the now "hot summer evenings in my tent." A ball glanced about my ancle and contused it; for some days I was lifted off and on horseback in Men's arms.'[9]

As Washington manoeuvred his army, Anthony Wayne was ordered to move his Pennsylvania Continentals to the rear of the enemy with a view of harassing the British should they attempt to cross the Schuylkill River. Wayne took a position near the Paoli Tavern and not too far from his own home. Major-General Sir Charles Grey was given the task of eliminating this threat in an action that was to earn him the sobriquet of 'No Flint Grey'. One British officer left an account of the night's action in his journal:

'As soon as it was dark, the whole battalion got under arms. Major-General Grey then came up to the battalion, and told Major Maitland, who commanded, that the expedition was going on a night expedition to try and surprise a camp, and that if any of the men were loaded, they must immediately draw their pieces. The major said the whole of the battalion was always loaded; and that if he would only allow them to remain so, he (the major) would be answerable that they did not fire a shot. The general then said if he could place that dependence on the battalion, they should remain loaded, but firing might be attended with very serious consequences. We remained loaded, and marched at eight in the evening to surprise General Wayne's camp.

We did not meet a patrol or vidette of the enemy till within a mile or two of the enemy, where our advanced guard was challenged by two videttes. They challenged twice, fired, and galloped off at full speed. A little further on there was a blacksmith's forge; a party was immediately sent to bring the blacksmith, and he informed us that the picket was only a few hundred yards up the road. He was ordered to conduct us to the camp; we had not marched a quarter of a mile when the picket challenged, fired a volley, and retreated. General Grey then came to the head of the battalion, and cried out—"Dash on, Light Infantry!" and without saying a word the whole battalion dashed into the wood, and guided by the straggling fire of the picket, that was followed close up, we entered the camp, and gave such a cheer as made the woods echo.

The enemy were completely surprised, some with arms, others without. running in all directions in the greatest confusion. The light infantry bayoneted every man they came up with. The camp was immediately set on fire, and this, and the cries of the wounded, formed altogether one of the most dreadful scenes I ever beheld. Every man that fired was instantly put to death. Captain Wolfe was killed, and I received a shot in my right hand, soon after we entered the camp. I saw the fellow present at me, and was running up to him when he fired. He was immediately killed. The enemy were pursued for two miles. I kept up till I grew faint from blood. and was obliged to sit down. Wayne's brigade was to have marched at one in the morning to attack our battalion while crossing the Schuylkill river, and we surprised them at twelve. Four hundred and sixty of the enemy were counted the next morning, lying dead, and not one shot was fired by us,— all done with the bayonet. We had only twenty killed and wounded.'[10]

This 'Paoli Massacre' removed the threat of Wayne, and Howe began an almost indolent march towards Philadelphia, at a pace so leisurely that his men had ample time to plunder the countryside. He drew Washington off by a feint at Reading Furnace, an American depot, then marched straight

146. The Flight of the Congress

One of the few cartoons hostile to the Americans. This engraving was published in London by William Hitchcock on 20 November 1777, during the brief but happy time when Howe's occupation of Philadelphia was known, but the news of Burgoyne's surrender had not reached London, as it did on 2 December. It depicts the flight of the Continental Congress from Philadelphia to York, Pennsylvania. The animals have been chased out of the Cave of Rebellion by the lion, Howe. The Liberty tree is hung with paper currency. The ass wearing a lion's skin is the president, Hancock. The stag, labelled 'V——D', is Van Dyke, a New York patriot. In the air, the German eagle clutches the rattlesnake, Independence; the owl flies away, carrying a missive 'Louis Baboon à Paris', representing Franklin on his mission to France.

THE FLIGHT of the CONGRESS.

Impatient of Imperial sway,
The Wild Beasts of America,
In Congress met, disclaim'd allegiance.
And to the As profess'd obedience,
With such New Leader, feeling bold,
No wonder they disdain'd the Old.

Resolving roundly, one and all,
In the good cause, to stand or fall,
Then herding, underneath the Tree,
Of Treason, alias Liberty;
They boast the Baboon King's alliance,
And at their own, hurl mad defiance.

Their foul revolt, their Monarch hears,
And strait upon the plain appears,
Aloud, the British Lion roars;
Aloft the German Eagle soars;
When Lo,'midst broken Oaths and curses,
The Rebel rout at once disperses.

Publish'd Nov.r 1777 by Wm. Hitchcock. No.3 Birchin Lane.

147. 'Passage d'York sur la Susquehanna'. *E. C. V. Colbert*

This is Wright's Ferry across the Susquehanna on the road from Philadelphia to York, Pennsylvania. By this road the Congress fled at the approach of Howe; the young Lafayette, newly arrived in Pennsylvania, saw them crossing the ferry. It must have been a slow business, since Colbert, travelling in 1798, said that it took him an hour to get across.

Colbert was a French aristocrat exiled during the Revolution.

Appartient au Comte Paul de Leusse.

for Philadelphia with nothing to impede him. Young Robert Morton, a lad in his teens, and a loyalist at heart, had watched the flight of the Continental Congress:

'*Sept. 19.*—This morning, about 1 o'clock, an Express arrived to Congress, giving an account of the British Army having got to Swedes Ford on the other side of the Schuylkill, which so alarmed the Gent'm of the Congress, the military officers and other Friends to the general cause of American Freedom and Independence, that they decamped with the utmost precipitation, and in the greatest confusion, insomuch that one of the Delegates, by name of Fulsom [of New Hampshire] was obliged in a very *Fulsom* manner to ride off without a saddle. Thus we have seen the men from whom we have received, and from whom we still expected protection, leave us to fall into the hands of (by their accounts) a barbarous, cruel, and unrelenting enemy.'[11]

A British officer recorded the triumphant entry into the city and his impressions of the city:

'[*Sept.*] *26th.* This morning at eight oclock, the British and Hessian grenadiers under the command of Lord Cornwallis, preceeded by six medium twelve pounders, and four royal howitzers; marched in a kind of procession (with bands of music playing before them), and took possession of the city of Philadelphia. The rebels had not erected any kind of fortifications here. —We found between twenty and thirty iron guns disposed about, but their military stores had been conveyed away, probably to the Jersies, and on board their vessels in the river.

This city is large, the streets spacious and regularly laid out, at right angles, and parallel to each other which together with the houses being

183

built of good coloured bricks, gives it a very neat appearance in general. Its situation, however, so closely pent up as it is between the two fresh water rivers (the Delaware and Schuylkill) makes it unhealthy. The usual number of inhabitants are estimated at thirty thousand, one third of which are said to have evacuated the city on various accounts, some engaged in rebellion, some carried away by force, and others retired from the persecutions of the rebels; which has by all reports been very grievous to those not inclined to their infamous cause.

The rebels have endeavoured with vast labour and expence, to stop of the navigation of the Delaware river; by sinking several ranges of chevaux de frise across the channel: to prevent our fleet from geting up to the city. A number of small islands that could extend from the mouth of the Schuylkill, favoured this design very much. The first range runs from little Tennicomb Island (about ten miles below the city) across to the Jersey shore; where there is a large battery to protect it, called Billens fort. The second range is about two miles higher up—nine hundred yards below Mud Island where the rebels have a considerable work called Mifflens fort—but afterwards thinking this as to great a distance, they sunk a couple of piers nearer to the fort including that part of the channel and fixed a boom across—besides having another range of Chevaux de frise ready to sink occasionally.

This kind of Chevaux de frise consists of a large timber, like the main mast of a ship at the top of which, are three branches armed and pointed with iron, spreading out fanwise in this manner fifteen foot asunder. The main boom is fixt at an elevation to the frame of a float or stage, composed of vast logs, bound together as fast as possible; then covered with plank to top and caulked. When this machine is towed to its place; it is loaded with about thirty tuns of stones, secured in cases, which by taking the plugs out of the deck, to admit the water into the float, sinks it down, and keeps it firm and steady. It then makes this appearance in profile—the points of the branches about six or seven feet under the surface of the water; and they spread in front thirty feet. A row of these chevaux de frise are sunk sixty feet asunder from each other and another row behind to form a range.'[12]

Congress before they fled Philadelphia had, for the second time during the war, conferred almost dictatorial powers upon Washington. He began a series of light marches, working his way towards the British garrison at Germantown. Although Cornwallis had entered Philadelphia with the air of a conqueror, the major portion of the British army lay at Germantown, a post that Howe refused permission to fortify lest it be interpreted as a sign of weakness. Because of the forts on the Delaware, detachments of troops were escorting supplies into the city while others had been ordered to prepare for an attack upon the river defences.

Reinforcement had begun to trickle into Washington's army. It now numbered almost 11,000 men. On 2 October, his army was within sixteen miles of Germantown. Reports suggested that Howe had no more than 9,000 men with him at that place. Washington called his inevitable council of war; it was decided that conditions for an assault upon Germantown were favourable.

Germantown, despite pretensions to the contrary, was little more than a village, strung out for two miles along the Skippack road running from Reading to Philadelphia.

Scouting parties from the two armies were almost constantly in sight of each other. The American Lieutenant James McMichael, who had a penchant for enlivening his diary with bits of doggerel, wrote:

'Just when we came into our camp, an army did appear,
They were on an adjacent hill, which was to us quite near,
They traver'd all the hill about, as tho' we were their foes,
And seem'd uneasy the secret to disclose.
And we with mirth and jollity did seat ourselves to rest
Upon the hill right opposite, tho' they seem'd quite distress'd.
Then taking Carnaghan's canteen, which in it had some rum,
We took to us a little draught, my rhyme to end did come.'[13]

Harassing actions kept the British off guard. At midnight on 2 October, a British officer sat in his tent writing with a nervous hand:

'There has been much firing this night all round the Countrys, which seems as if they endeavour to feel our situation. I am fatigued & must sleep. Could'st *Thou* sleep thus? No more could'st act Sir Wildair in a ship on fire—Nor I at first (entre nous) but Tyrant Custom &c., yet my rest is interrupted—I wake once or twice, my Ear is susceptible of the least noise.'[14]

Washington's plan of attack suggested that he had learned the value of a flanking movement from his battles with Howe. The attack on Germantown was to be made by four thrusts; John Sullivan was to lead one column into town by the Skippack road; the second under Nathanael Greene was to swing out to the left and hit the British right flank by way of the Lime Kiln road; flanking Greene were the Maryland and New Jersey militia who were to march along the Old York road and hit the rear of the British right flank; the fourth, of John Armstrong's Pennsylvania militia, were to slip around by the Manataway road and come in the rear of the enemy's left flank. All were to be in position by two o'clock on the morning of 4 October, and at five were to launch a bayonet charge upon the unsuspecting enemy. Pieces of white paper attached to hats were identification. It was a good plan, on paper, but battles are not fought on paper, and there was too much involve-

148. View from Bushongo Tavern 5 miles from York Town on the Baltimore Road

The rutted dirt road stretching west of Philadelphia was probably one of the better thoroughfares used in the Revolution by riders such as the one shown here, or by weary marchers. The difficulty and slowness of overland travel on the huge continent was a potent force in the conduct of the war.

ment of militia. The American Private Joseph Plumb Martin was not aware of his destination during his march through the night, although he 'naturally concluded there was something serious in the wind'. In the grey light of dawn,

'There was a low vapour lying on the land which made it very difficult to distinguish objects at any considerable distance. About daybreak our advanced guard and the British outpost came in contact. The curs began to bark first and then the bull-dogs.

Our brigade moved off to the right into the fields. We saw a body of the enemy drawn up behind a rail fence; we immediately formed in line and advanced upon them,—our orders were, not to fire until we could see the

TEUCRO DUCE NIL DESPERANDUM.

First Battalion of Pennsylvania Loyalists, commanded by His Excellency Sir WILLIAM HOWE, K. B.

ALL intrepid, able-bodied HEROES, who are willing to serve His Majesty King GEORGE the Third, in Defence of their Country, Laws, and Constitution, against the arbitrary Usurpations of a tyrannical Congress, have now not only an Opportunity of manifesting their Spirit, by assisting in reducing their too-long deluded Countrymen, but also of acquiring the polite Accomplishments of a Soldier, by serving only two Years, or during the present Rebellion in America.

Such spirited Fellows, who are willing to engage, will be rewarded at the End of the War, besides their Laurels, with Fifty Acres of Land in any County they shall chuse, where every gallant Hero may retire, and enjoy his Bottle and Lass. [every non Com' officer want to receive 200 Acres of land]

Each Volunteer will receive, as a Bounty, FIVE DOLLARS, besides Arms, Cloathing and Accoutrements, and every other Requisite proper to accommodate a Gentleman Soldier, by applying to Lieutenant-Colonel ALLEN, or at Captain STEVENS's Rendezvous, in Front-street.

PRINTED by JAMES HUMPHREYS, JUNR. in Market-street, between Front and Second-streets.

200

149. All intrepid able-bodied HEROES...
This recruiting poster for the First Battalion of Pennsylvania Loyalists was put out by Sir William Howe. Having taken Philadelphia he sought to augment his forces by enlisting Tories, but was disappointed at the small response received. The rewards he offers are varied and interesting: the chance to 'reduce to Obedience their too-long deluded Countrymen', to acquire 'the polite Accomplishments of a Soldier', and eventually to retire with '50 Acres of Land, where every gallant Hero may... enjoy his Bottle and Lass'. During the gay social season of 1777–8 in Philadelphia, the General himself was not without his pleasures.

150. Battle of Germantown, 4 October 1777

Germantown was a one-street Pennsylvania village, two miles long and five miles from Philadelphia. Here, and stretching on either side to its south, was encamped the main body of Howe's army. Sullivan's force drove back all British reinforcements until they reached the Chew House (left centre of map). Meanwhile the divisions under Greene attacked the main British camp from the direction of Luken's Mill ('Lewis's Mill' at the right centre of the map). Cornwallis later arrived with 3,000 grenadiers (bottom of map; Philadelphia Road). The rebels retreated; but the battle was so close that both commanders avoided a full-scale engagement during the remainder of Howe's command.

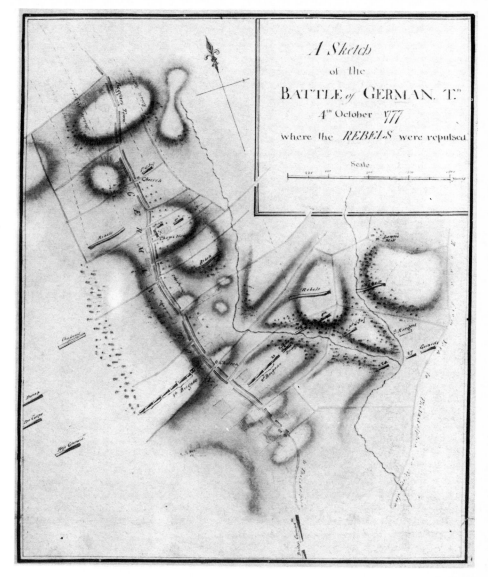

buttons on their clothes; but they were so coy that they would not give us an opportunity to be so curious, for they hid their clothes in fire and smoke before we had either time or leisure to examine their buttons. They soon fell back and we advanced, when the action became general. The enemy were driven quite through their camp. They left their kettles, in which they were cooking their breakfast, on the fires, and some of their garments on the ground, which the owners had not time to put on. Affairs went on well for some time.'[15]

A young British lieutenant, Martin Hunter, was on outpost duty at Biggentown:

'General Wayne commanded the advance and fully expected to be revenged for the surprise we had given him. When the first shots were fired at our pickets, so much had we all Wayne's affair in remembrance, that the battalion was out under arms in a minute. At this time the day was just broke; but it was a very foggy morning, and so dark that we could not see a hundred yards before us. Just as the battalion had formed, the pickets came in and said the enemy was advancing in force.

They had hardly joined the battalion, when we heard the loud cry of "Have at the bloodhounds; revenge Wayne's affair!" and they immediately fired a volley; we gave them one in return, cheered. and charged.... On our charging they gave way on all sides, but again and again renewed the attack with fresh troops and greater force. We charged them twice, till the battalion was so reduced, by killed and wounded, that the bugle was sounded to retreat;... this was the first time we had retreated before the Americans, and it was with great difficulty to get our men to obey our orders.

The enemy were kept so long in check that the two brigades had advanced to the entrance of Biggenstown, when they met our battalion retreating. By this time General Howe had come up, and seeing the battalion retreating, all broken, he got into a passion and exclaimed—"For shame, light infantry! I never saw you retreat before; form! form! it's only a scouting party." However, he was soon convinced it was more than a scouting party, as the heads of the enemy's columns soon appeared. One coming through Biggenstown, with three pieces of cannon in their front, immediately fired at the crowd that was standing with General Howe under a large chestnut-tree. I think I never saw people enjoy a charge of grape before, but we really all felt pleased to see the enemy make such an appearance, and to hear the grape rattle about the commander-in-chief's ears, after he had accused us of having run away from a scouting party. He rode off immediately full speed, and we joined the two brigades that were now formed a little way in our rear; but it was not possible for them to make any stand against Washington's army, and they all retreated to Germantown, except Col. Musgrave....'[16]

Colonel Thomas Musgrave, commanding the 40th Regiment, had come to the support of the light infantry, but had seen them driven on through back to the British encampment. 'Cliveden', the massive stone house of Benjamin Chew, offered sanctuary and because of the thickness of its walls became a veritable fortress. Musgrave threw his men into the building, barricading the doors and windows. Timothy Pickering was riding with Washington:

'In the march of the army, General Washington, following Sullivan's column, kept in the road leading to and through Germantown to Philadelphia. When we entered the northern part of the village, we heard in advance of us (I was riding by the General's side), a very heavy fire of musketry. General Sullivan's divisions, it was evident, were warmly engaged with the enemy; but neither was in sight. This fire, brisk and heavy, continuing, General Washington said to me; "I am afraid General Sullivan is throwing away his ammunition; ride forward and tell him to preserve it."... the instant I received the General's orders, I rode forward; and in the road, three or four hundred yards beyond Chew's house, met Sullivan, and delivered to him the General's orders.

At this time I had never heard of Chew's house; and had no idea that an enemy was in my rear. The first notice I received of it was from the whizzing of musket balls, across the road, before, behind, and above me, as I was returning, after delivering the orders to Sullivan. Instantly turning my eyes to the right, I saw the blaze of the muskets, whose shot was still aimed at me, as I was returning, from the windows of a large stone house, standing back about a hundred yards from the road. This was Chew's house. . . .'[17]

Cannon and musket balls ricocheted harmlessly off the thick walls of the improvised fortress. By the time it was decided to by-pass the Chew House, matters had taken a turn for the worse. Greene had not arrived on the right flank until half an hour after the battle began, but when he entered the action he was successful in turning the enemy. Fog added to the general confusion. Wayne, driving up the opposite side of the road from Sullivan, heard the artillery blasting away at the Chew House, and turned to help Sullivan who he supposed had run into unexpected resistance. Instead, he ran into a detachment of Greene's men under the command of Adam Stephen who had reinforced his courage that day with a bottle, and who saw the dim figures of soldiers through the mist. His men fired on those of Wayne, who returned a volley. Both groups turned and fled.

Joseph Plumb Martin had his explanation why Washington's army ran from possible victory:

'The enemy were retreating before us, until the first division that was engaged had expended their ammunition; some of the men inadvisedly calling out that their ammunition was spent, the enemy was so near that they overheard them, upon which they made a stand, and then returned upon our people, who, for want of ammunition and reinforcements, were obliged to retreat, which ultimately resulted in the rout of the whole army. . . .

There was one thing in such cases as I have just mentioned, (I mean, in retreating from an enemy,) that always galled my feelings, and that was, whenever I was forced to a quick retreat to be obliged to run until I was worried down. The Yankees are generally very nimble of foot and in these cases are very apt to practice what they have the ability of performing. Some of our men at this time seemed to think that they could never run fast or far enough. I never wanted to run, if I was forced to run, further than to be beyond the enemy's shot, after which I had no fear of their overtaking me than I should have of an army of lobsters doing it, unless it were their horsemen, and they *dared* not do it.'[18]

Thomas Paine 'breakfasted next morning at Gen Washington's quarters, who was at some loss, with every other, to account for the accidents of the day. I remember his expressing his surprise that at the time he supposed everything secure, and was about giving orders for the army to proceed down to Philadelphia, that he saw most unexpectedly a part (I think) of the artillery hastily retreating. This partial retreat was I believe misunderstood, and soon followed by others. The fog was frequently very thick, the troops young, and unused to breaking and rallying, and our men rendered suspicious to each other, many of them being [dressed] in red. A new army, once disordered, is difficult to manage. and the attempt dangerous. To this may be added prudence in not putting matters to too hazardous a trial. The first time the men must be taught regular fighting by practice and degrees, and though the expedition failed, it had this good effect that they seemed to feel themselves more important after, than before, as it was the first general attack they had ever made.'[19]

Although Howe could claim a victory at Germantown, he was still faced with the problem of opening the Delaware to river traffic so that his army might be supplied more easily than by the dangerous overland pattern then in force. As early as 2 October, he had dispatched a regiment and a half against the rebel works at Billingsport. The resultant action cannot be dignified by terming it a skirmish. As the British landed below the fort and came up from the rear, the small garrison immediately spiked its guns, fired the half completed barracks, and fled. A passage through the chevaux de frise was immediately opened, allowing some ships to proceed cautiously up the stream.

Not until two weeks later did Howe follow up the advantage thus gained. The line of chevaux de frise blocking the river was protected on the Jersey shore by Fort Mercer at Red Bank. The opposite end was under the protective fire of Fort Mifflin, situated on Mud Island. The first attack was launched against the 400-man garrison of Fort Mercer by 2,000 Hessians under Colonel von Donop. Colonel Christopher Green, commanding the fort, refused the summons presented by an arrogant German officer:

'The answer was, that they accepted the challenge, and that there should be no quarters on either side. About four o'clock in the afternoon, the Hessians made a very brisk fire from a battery of cannon, and soon after they opened, and marched to the first entrenchment, from which, finding it abandoned, but not destroyed, they *imagined* they had driven the Americans. They then shouted *victoria*, waved their hats in the air, and advanced towards the redoubt. The same drummer, who a few hours before had come to summon the garrison, and had appeared as insolent as his officer, was at their head beating the march; both he and that officer were knocked on the head by the first fire. . . .

The Hessians, repulsed by the fire of the redoubt, attempted to secure themselves from it by attacking on the side of the escarpment, but the fire from the gallies sent them back with great loss of men. At length they relinquished the attack, and regained the wood in disorder.'[20]

A few more faint-hearted attacks were thrown back; the Hessians withdrew. In addition to Donop, the Hessians had lost 371 men, including twenty-two officers. The Americans had suffered only fourteen dead and twenty-three wounded. One reason for the failure of the attack was that British naval vessels had been prevented from supporting the Hessians by the fort on Mud Island. Fort Mifflin, termed by Surgeon Albigence Waldo as 'a Burlesque upon the art of Fortification', had been reinforced and was under the command of Major Simeon Thayer of Rhode Island. Among those reinforcements sent over into the fort was that ebullient private with the grand sense of humour, Joseph Plumb Martin:

'The first attempt the British made against the place after I entered it was by the *Augusta*, a sixty-four gun ship. While manoeuvering one dark night she got on the chevaux-de-frise which had been sunk in the channel of the river. As soon as she was discovered in the morning we plied her so well with hot shot, that she was soon in flames. Boats were sent from the shipping below to her to her assistance, but our shot proving too hot for them, they were obliged to leave her to her fate; in an hour or two she blew up with an explosion which seemed to shake the earth to its centre, leaving a volume of smoke like a thunder cloud, which, as the air was calm, remained for an hour or two. A twenty gun ship which had come to the assistance of the *Augusta* in her distress, shared her fate soon after.

Our batteries were nothing more than old spars and timber laid up in parallel lines and filled between with mud and dirt; the British batteries in the course of the day would nearly level our works; and we were, like the beaver, obliged to repair our dams in the night. During the whole night, at intervals of a quarter or half an hour, the enemy would let off all their pieces, and although we had sentinels to watch them and every flash of their guns to cry, "a shot," upon hearing which every one endeavoured to take care of himself, yet they would ever and anon, in spite of all our precautions, cut up some of us. . . .

It was utterly impossible to lie down to get any rest or sleep on account of the mud, if the enemy's shot would have suffered any of us to do so. Sometimes some of the men, when overcome with fatigue and want of sleep, would slip away into the barracks to catch a nap of sleep, but it seldom happened that they all came out again alive. I was in this place a fortnight, and can say in sincerity that I never lay down to sleep a minute in all that time. . . .

We had . . . a thirty-two pound cannon in the fort, but not a single shot for it; the British also had one in their battery upon the Hospital point, which . . . was so fixed as to rake the parade in front of the barracks. . . . The Artillery officers offered a gill of rum for each shot, fired from that piece, which the soldiers would procure, I have seen from twenty to fifty men standing on the parade waiting with impatience the coming of the shot, which would often be siezed before its motion had fully ceased and conveyed off to our gun to be sent back again to its former owners. When the lucky fellow who had caught it had swallowed his rum, he would return to wait for another, exulting that he had been more lucky or more dexturous than his fellows. . . .

We continued here suffering cold, hunger and other miseries, till the fourteenth day of November; on that day, at the dawn, we discovered six ships of the line, all sixty-fours, a frigate of thirty-six guns and a galley in a line just below the Chevaux-de-frise; a twenty-four gun ship, (being an old ship cut down,) . . . within pistol shot of the fort, on the western side. We immediately opened our batteries upon them, but they appeared to take very little notice of us; we heated some shot, but by mistake twenty-four-pound shot were heated instead of eighteen, which was the calibre of our guns in that part of the fort. The enemy soon began their firing upon us, and there was music indeed. The soldiers were all ordered to take their posts at the palisadoes, which they were ordered to defend to the last extremity, as it was expected the British would land under the fire of their cannon and attempt to storm the fort. The cannonade was severe . . . playing at once upon our poor little fort, if fort it might be called. . . .

The cannonade continued, directed mostly at the fort, till the dusk of the evening. As soon as it was dark we began preparations for evacuating the fort and endeavouring to escape to the Jersey shore. When the firing had in some measure subsided and I could look about me, I found the fort exhibited a picture of desolation; the whole area of the fort was as completely ploughed as a field. The buildings of every kind hanging in broken fragments, and the guns all dismounted, and how many of the garrison sent to the world of spirits, I knew not. If ever destruction was complete, it was here. The surviving part of the garrison were now drawn off and such of the stores as could conveniently be taken away carried to the Jersey shore. I happened to be left with a party of seventy or eighty men to destroy all that was left in the place. . . .

I returned directly back into the fort to my party and proceeded to set fire to everything that would burn, and then repaired immediately to the wharf where three batteaux were waiting to convey us across the river. And now came on another trial. Before we could embark the buildings in the fort were completely in flames, and they threw such a light upon the water that we were plainly seen by the British as though it was broad day. Almost their whole fire was directed at us; and sometimes our boat seemed to be almost thrown out of the water, and at length a shot took the sternpost out of the rear boat. We had then to stop and take the men from the crippled boat into the other two; and now the shot and water flew merrily; but by the assistance of a kind Providence we escaped without any further injury and landed, a little after midnight, on the Jersey shore.'[21]

With Fort Mifflin now a heap of charred ruins, Fort Mercer was useless and was evacuated. The Delaware became a British river. Washington marched and countermarched, his excursions at times almost like aimless wanderings. On 19 October, Howe had marched the Germantown garrison into Philadelphia after the city had been properly fortified. Howe settled down for a snug winter in company with Mrs Loring. The British general did make several forays into the countryside, but Washington refused to be drawn into a decisive battle.

The days had begun to grow cool and nights held a nip of frost. Washington decided to move into winter quarters. His prime requirement for a site was one that would allow him to watch the British in Philadelphia and to 'cover this Country against the Horrid rapine and Devastation of a Wanton Enemy'. To meet these requirements, the General chose a location that bore the name that was to become a synonym for hardship and suffering— Valley Forge.

151. Philadelphia; Second Street North from Market Street. *W. Birch*

Revolutionary Philadelphia was a city of soft red brick. Here the view is looking up Second Street from its intersection with Market, or High Street. The building at the left is the Court House, seat of the Pennsylvania Legislature before the State House was built. The tall white spire is that of the Episcopal Church, Christ Church. The delegates to the Continental Congress were impressed by the wealth, the gracious living, and the elegant food and drink to be found in this city of Quaker foundation. When the British occupied it, they did not fail to profit from all these amenities.

This picture was drawn and engraved by W. Birch, and published in 1799; the next year he included it in the first edition of his 29 coloured views of Philadelphia, on which he and his son had been working for two years.

9. Valley Forge: The Making of an Army

IN PHILADELPHIA, the troops looked forward to a comfortable winter. Yet some, like Captain Johann Heinrichs of the Jaeger corps, were not entirely content; his desire to fascinate his audience in his native Hesse may have led him to exaggerate what he observed:

'Among 100 persons, not merely in Philadelphia, but also throughout the whole neighborhood, not one has a healthy color, the cause of which is the unhealthy air and the bad water. Assuredly this is not a consequence of this latitude, for Pennsylvania lies in one of the healthiest degrees, but for woods, morasses, and mountains, which partly confine the air, and partly poison it, make the country unhealthy. Nothing is more common here than a fever once a year, than eruptions, the itch, etc. . Nowhere have I seen so many *mad* people as here. Only yesterday, as I was dining with a Gentlemen, a third person came into the room, and he whispered into my ear: *Take care, this gentleman is a madman.* Frequently the people are cured, but almost all have a quiet madness, a derangement of mind which proceeds from sluggish, not active blood. One cause, perhaps, is that no food here has as much nourishment as with us. The milk is not half so rich, the bread has little nourishment. There is a noticeable difference in the quality of the produce that is brought to market in Philadelphia, from the Jerseys and from Pennsylvania. . . .

Like the products of the earth, animals too are only half developed. A hare, a partridge, a peacock, etc., is only half-grown. Wild game tastes like ordinary meat. One of the good consequences of this war is, that more forests will be destroyed, and the air will become purer. A man from this city, by the name of Hamilton, alone lost 1500 [probably 150 acres] of woodlands, which was cut down for the hospital, and he had sufficient patriotism to remark recently in company, that it was good for the country. . . .

There is no scarcity of *snakes*. The *great blacksnake* has been near the Schuylkill lately, quite near our quarters. A countryman, cutting wood, was chased by one quite recently, but a neighbor killed it with a big stick.

152. George Washington. *Gilbert Stuart*

To understand Washington, the best known of the famous figures of this period, a record of his leadership in the American War of Independence, such as that contained in this book, is needed: his triumphs and his failures, his long patience and occasional anger, and all the varied reactions to him of his contemporaries, from disaffection to the growing love and loyalty which recalled him to service after the war as the first president of the United States. Perhaps Abigail Adams, that astute observer of men and events, may be allowed to introduce him. She met General Washington first in 1776 during the Siege of Boston, and wrote to her husband John in Philadelphia: 'You had prepared me to entertain a favorable opinion of him, but I thought the one half was not told me. Dignity with ease & complacency, the Gentleman & Soldier look agreeably blended in him. Modesty marks every line & fiture of his face. Those lines of Dryden instantly accu'rd to me
  "Mark his Majestick fabrick; he's a temple
    Sacred by birth, and built by hands divine . . ."'
Twenty years later, Gilbert Stuart painted this portrait of Washington, known as the Athenaeum Head.

There is nothing, however, more terrible than the big *rattlesnake*, which is from twelve to fifteen feet long, and which, it is believed here, kills by its glands. A countryman in my quarters lost a relative of his in this way, some years ago. He had gone hunting, and seeing a bear standing still, aimed at and shot it; scarcely had he reached the bear, when he too was obliged to stand motionless, remained thus awhile, fell and died; all of this was caused by a rattlesnake, which was perched in a high tree. The nearest ones to Philadelphia are in Tolpahaky [Tulpehocken]. and there are some also between Elk Ferry and Head of Elk, where we encamped three days.'[1]

153. 'Plan Du Camp De Vallée forge'. *Duportail*

The best contemporary sketch of the encampment and early fortification of Valley Forge is this rough manuscript plan by the French engineer officer Louis Lebeque Duportail, who, as recently appointed Brigadier-General of the Corps of Engineers, laid out the camp's defences. The plan was not drawn before early 1778, when the bridge across the Schuylkill, delayed because of freezing weather, was completed by General Sullivan.

On the plan north is at the bottom, towards the river. To the left, towards Philadelphia, B and F are the ramparts overlooking steep declivities and the first log huts built by the soldiers. At the bottom, near the bridge, is a star redoubt. Just above the centre of the map the four heavy parallel lines represent General Knox's artillery park; across the road above them the parallel lines are rows of soldiers' huts. Running diagonally across the right half is Valley Creek, after which the forge was named. At the creek's mouth and to its left is the Isaac Potts house, Washington's headquarters, with its outlying buildings. To the extreme right, across the creek, are the long sheds under General Stirling's command, where rifles, wagons, and other military equipment were repaired and made.

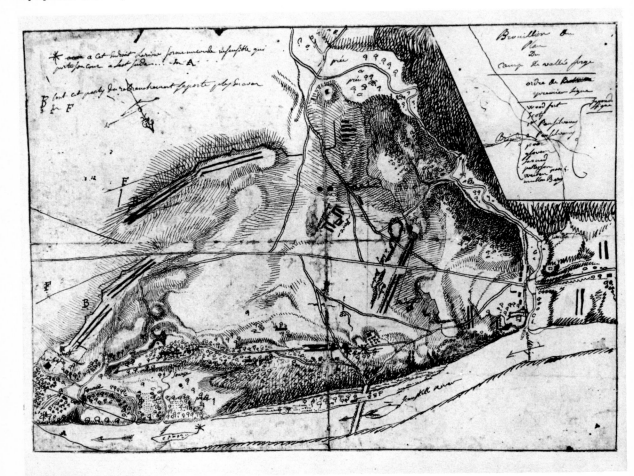

154. A Chorographical Map of the Country round Philadelphia *(detail)*.
Bernard Romans

This detail shows the location of the American camp at Valley Forge, 'Genl Howes Track', Philadelphia and its defences, and the relation of Chew's house to Germantown.

Romans, a Dutchman by birth, made a number of important maps before and during the war.

The American army, hungry, cold, and miserable, marched along country roads, perhaps feeling that even rattlesnakes would provide a welcome change in diet. The week before Christmas, Washington, contrary to the advice of most of his generals, moved his troops to a barren site called Valley Forge, some twenty miles above Philadelphia. It was not a place calculated for rest and relaxation. The British had swept through in September and gleaned all provisions from the area. On 17 December, the General felt compelled to explain to his troops in general orders why he had selected such a dismal bivouac:

'The General ardently wishes it were within his power, to conduct the troops into the best winter quarters. But where are these to be found? Should we retire to the interior parts of the State, we should find them crowded with virtuous citizens, who, sacrificing their all, have left Philadelphia, and fled thither for protection. To their distresses humanity forbids us to add. That is not all, we should leave a vast extent of fertile country to be despoiled and ravaged by the enemy, from which they could draw vast supplies, and where many of our firm friends would be exposed to all the miseries of the most insulting and wanton depredations. A train of evils might be enumerated, but these will suffice. These considerations make it indispensably necessary for the army to take such a position, as will enable it most effectually to prevent distress and give the most extensive security; and in that position we must make ourselves the best shelter in our power. With activity and diligence Huts may be erected that will be warm and dry. In these the troops will be compact, more secure against surprises than if in divided state and at hand to protect the country. These cogent reasons have determined the General to take post in the neighbourhood of this camp; and influenced by them, he persuaded himself, that the officers and the soldiers, with one heart, and one mind, will resolve to surmount every difficulty, with a fortitude and patience, becoming their

195

profession, and the sacred cause in which they are engaged. He himself will share in the hardship, and partake of every inconvenience.'[2]

Valley Forge was surrounded by a series of rambling hills, and was about four and one half miles long, bisected by Valley Creek which crawled its way between the hills. The Bavarian giant and veteran military man, Johann Kalb, who had just joined the American forces, was disgusted with the choice of the site. And he was just as unhappy with the military amateurs he found around Washington. On Christmas Day he wrote to a friend:

'On the 19th instant, the army reached this wooded wilderness, certainly one of the poorest districts of Pennsylvania; the soil thin, uncultivated and almost uninhabited, without forage and without provisions! Here we are to go into winter-quarters, i.e., to lie in shanties, generals and privates, to enable the army, it is said, to recover from its privations, to recruit, to re-equip, and to prepare for the opening of the coming campaign, while protecting the country from hostile inroads. The matter has been the subject of long debates in the council of war. It was discussed in all its length and breadth—a bad practice to which they are addicted here—and good advice was not taken. The idea of wintering in this desert can only have been put into the head of the commanding general by an interested speculator or a disaffected man. Means were found of implicating Congress, which body has the foible of interfering with matters which it neither understands nor can understand, being entirely ignorant of the locality. It is unfortunate that Washington is so easily led. He is the bravest and truest of men, has the best intentions and a sound judgment. I am convinced that he would accomplish substantial results if he would only act more on his own responsibility; but it is a pity that he is so weak, and has the worst of advisers in the men who enjoy his confidence. If they are not traitors, they are certainly gross ignoramuses. . . .

I do not know what is done in the clothing departments; but it is certain that half the army are half naked, and almost the whole army go barefoot. . . . Our men are also infected with the itch, a matter which attracts very little attention either at the hospitals or in camp. I have seen the poor fellows covered over and over with scab. I have caused my seven regiments to put up barracks large enough to hold all these unfortunates, so that they can be subjected to medical treatment away from the others. . . .

Now we have hardly been here more than six days, and are already suffering from want of everything. The men have had neither meat nor bread for four days, and our horses are often left for days without any fodder. What will be done when the roads grow worse, and the season more severe? Strong detachments ought to be sent out at once, to get in provisions. . . .

My blacksmith is a captain! The very numerous assistant-quartermasters are for the most part men of no military education whatever, in many cases ordinary hucksters, but always colonels. The same rank is held by the contractors-general and their agents (*fournisseur général et facteur général*). It is safe to accost every man as a colonel who talks to me with familiarity; the officers of the lower grade are invariably more modest. In a word, the army teems with colonels.

The quartermasters-general provide quarters for the commander-in-chief and for themselves, but for nobody else. The other generals, even some of

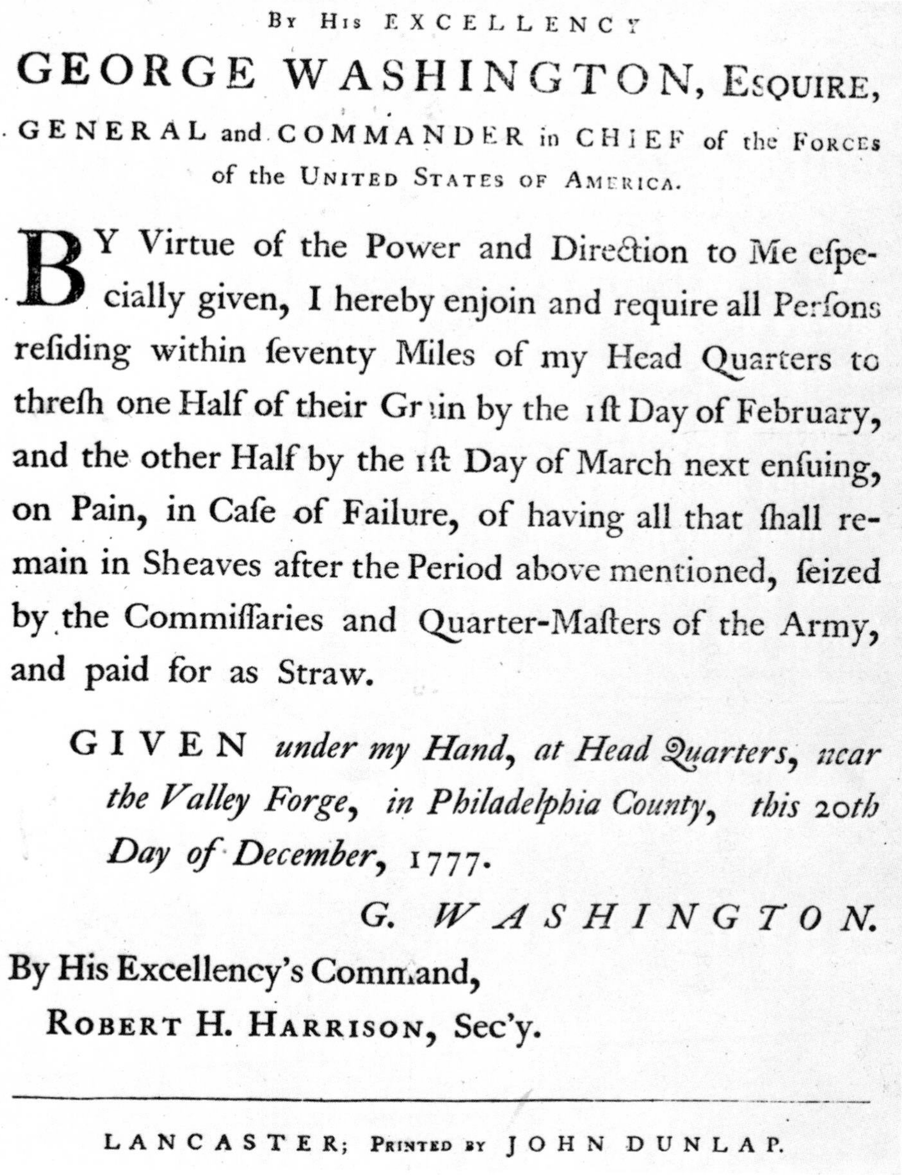

By His EXCELLENCY

GEORGE WASHINGTON, Esquire,

GENERAL and COMMANDER in CHIEF of the Forces
of the UNITED STATES OF AMERICA.

BY Virtue of the Power and Direction to Me efpe-
cially given, I hereby enjoin and require all Perfons
refiding within feventy Miles of my Head Quarters to
threfh one Half of their Grain by the 1ft Day of February,
and the other Half by the 1ft Day of March next enfuing,
on Pain, in Cafe of Failure, of having all that fhall remain in Sheaves after the Period above mentioned, feized
by the Commiffaries and Quarter-Mafters of the Army,
and paid for as Straw.

GIVEN *under my Hand, at Head Quarters, near
the Valley Forge, in Philadelphia County, this 20th
Day of December,* 1777.

G. *WASHINGTON.*

By His Excellency's Command,
ROBERT H. HARRISON, Sec'y.

LANCASTER; Printed by JOHN DUNLAP.

155. Proclamation by General Washington, dated Valley Forge, 20 December 1777

the officers, take their quarters where and as they please and can. For this purpose thousands are often to be seen hastening on in advance of the army. . . . Luckily we have an enemy to deal with as clumsy as ourselves.'[3]

Christopher Marshall, a Philadelphia exile living in Lancaster, made a bitter entry in his diary that could be repeated almost daily as the cold, hard winter wore on:

'Our affairs wear a very gloomy aspect. Great part of our army gone into winter quarters; those in camp wanting breeches, shoes, stockings, blankets, and by accounts brought yesterday, were in want of flour, yet being in the land of plenty; our farmers having their barns and barracks full of grain; hundreds of barrels of flour lying on the banks of the Susquehannah perishing for want of care in securing it from weather, and from danger of

197

being carried away, if a freshet should happen in the river; fifty wagon loads of cloths and ready made clothes for the soldiery in the Clothier General's store in Lancaster; (this I say from the demand made by John Mease to the President a few days past, when the enemy was expected to be coming this way, for this number of wagons to take away the stores,) our enemies revelling in balls, attended with every degree of luxury and excess in the City; rioting and wantonly using our houses, utensils and furniture; all this [and] a numberless number of other abuses we endure from that handful of banditti, to the amount of six or seven thousand men, headed by that monster of rapine, Gen. Howe.

Add to this their frequent excursions round about for twenty miles together, destroying and burning what they please, pillaging, plundering men and women, stealing boys above ten years old, deflowering virgins, driving into the City for their use; droves of cattle, sheep, hogs, poultry, butter, meal, meat, cider, furniture and clothing of all kinds, loaded upon our own horses. All this is done in view of our Generals and our army, who are careless of us, but carefully consulting where they shall spend the winter in jollity, gaming and carousing, O tell not this in France or Spain! Publish it not in the streets of London, Liverpool or Bristol, lest the uncircumcised there should rejoice, and shouting for joy say "America is ours, for the rebels are afraid to fight us any longer! O Americans, where is now your virtue? O Washington, where is your courage?"'[4]

And now the dissensions and factions of the army, which had lain seemingly dormant during the months of fighting, began to flare into the open. Back in May, John Adams had noted the vicious in-fighting among the military:

'I am wearied to death with the wrangles between military officers, high and low. They quarrel like dogs and cats. They worry one another like mastiffs, scrambling for rank and pay like apes for food. I believe there is no one principle which predominates in human nature so much, in every stage of life from the cradle to the grave, in males and females, old and young, black and white, rich and poor, high and low, as this passion for superiority. Every human being compares itself with every other round about it, and will find some superiority over every other, real or imaginary, or it will die of grief and vexation. I have seen it among boys and girls at school, among lads at college, among practicioners at the bar, among the clergy in their associations, among clubs of friends, among people in town-meetings, among the members of a House of Representatives, among the grave councillors on the more solemn bench of Justice, and in that awfully august body, the Congress, and on many of its committees, and among ladies everywhere; but I never saw it to operate with such keenness, ferocity and fury as among military officers. They will go terrible lengths in their emulation, their envy, and revenge in consequence of it.'[5]

One reason for the petty quarrels among officers was the large number of foreigners who held positions of authority in the Continental Army, most of whom had been recruited in Europe by Silas Deane and Benjamin Franklin. Among those who caused trouble was the quarrelsome Polish nobleman, Count Casimir Pulaski, who not only refused to take orders from Washington, but insisted upon making his reports directly to the Continental Congress, traits that added to his unpopularity among the American officers, and whose future activities were to lead to military frictions and personality clashes. And it was one of these foreign officers who lighted the fuse that sputtered into the uproar within the military that was to become known as the 'Conway Cabal'.

George Washington, whose victories had been thin, was no longer the great man to many Americans. Horatio Gates, because of his smashing victory over Burgoyne, was the new idol. Peter du Ponceau noted the change in attitude:

'The only ray of light, which appeared amidst this darkness, was the defeat of Burgoyne, which cheered the spirit of those who otherwise might have despaired of the Commonwealth. But that brilliant victory, had liked to have produced the most fatal consequences. Genl. Gates became the hero of the day: Saratoga was then . . . the watchword of the discontented. A party was formed even in Congress, to raise the conqueror of Burgoyne to the Supreme command of our armies. But the great figure of Washington, stood calm, and serene at his Camp at Valley Forge; and struck the conspirators with awe. With the exception of a few factious chiefs he was idolized by the army, and by the nation at large. The plot was discovered and the plan was frustrated without a struggle. Without any effort, or management on his part, and by the mere force of his character, Washington stood firm, and undaunted in the midst of his enemies; and I might almost say, looked them into silence.'[6]

But Washington held little inclination to look his critics into silence. He was a vain and proud man, a born aristocrat, and sensitive to criticism. His pride was easily bruised and indeed had been in the recent past. The messy business had begun with Thomas Conway, an Irishman who had served in the French army, and James Wilkinson, a young aide with a fondness for gossip, who had mentioned to a drinking companion a letter from Conway to Gates heavily critical of Washington, a copy of which eventually came into the hands of Washington. In this letter there was the suggestion that Gates should replace him as the commanding general of the army, a suggestion that seemed to reinforce the rumours then going around that there was a 'cabal' planning to remove the commander-in-chief. On 9 November, Washington sent Conway a curt note:

'*Sir:* A Letter which I received last Night, contained the following paragraph

In a Letter from Genl. Conway to Genl. Gates he says:

"Heaven has been determined to save your Country; or a weak General and bad Councellors would have ruind it."

I am Sir Yr. Hmble Servt.'[7]

This short note set off a flurry of charges and countercharges, with Gates demanding to know who had been spying on his correspondence, and Washington answering that he did not 'suspect that I was the subject for your confidential Letters'. Others seized the opportunity to make critical evaluations. The affair boiled, then settled down to a simmer, although there were several challenges to duels among those involved, including one issued by Wilkinson to Gates which Gates avoided. Conway had irritated so many with his free-wheeling tongue that on 4 July 1778 he was challenged by and fought a duel with Brigadier-General John Cadwalader. Conway was wounded in what seemed a most appropriate spot—his mouth. And passions eventually began to cool when he, thinking himself on his death-bed, wrote to the commander-in-chief:

'I find myself just able to hold the pen during a few minutes, and take this opportunity of expressing my sincere grief to you for having done, written, or said any thing disagreeable to your Excellency. My career will soon be over; therefore justice and truth prompt me to declare my last sentiments. You are in my eyes the great and good man. May you long enjoy the love, veneration, and esteem of these States, whose liberties you have asserted by your virtues.'[8]

Despite his fears, Conway survived, returned to France and pursued an honourable career in the French army. The question of whether there was a 'Conway Cabal' led to years of debate. Although there is no concrete evidence that there was a concerted movement to replace Washington, the General thought there was, which was in itself a disturbing and disrupting influence.

But this was almost a sideline, an exercise in trivia when placed in perspective, for the winter at Valley Forge became the low-water mark for the American army. In early February one officer was writing that 'In all human probability the army must dissolve. Many of the troops are destitute of meat and are several days in arrears. The horses are dying for want of forage. The country in the vicinity of the camp is exhausted.' Surgeon James Thacher wrote:

'It was on this occasion that a foreign officer of distinction, said to a friend of mine, that he despaired of our Independence, for while walking with General Washington, along the soldiers' huts, he heard from many voices echoing through open crevices between the logs, *"no pay, no clothes, no provisions, no rum,"* and when a miserable being was seen flitting from one hut to another, his nakedness was only covered by a dirty blanket. It will be difficult to form a just conception of the emotions of grief and sorrow which must have harrowed up the soul of our illustrious patriot and philanthropist. In this darkening hour of adversity, any man who possesses less firmness than Washington, would despair of our Independence.'[9]

On 23 February, two riders dressed in red coats, faced in blue, came riding down the Lancaster road. One was a young Frenchman, Peter Stephen du Ponceau, who had come to America as an aide to his companion, a man who called himself Friedrich Wilhelm Ludorf Gerhard Augustin, Baron von Steuben. He spoke of his great military exploits in Europe. He had been a soldier of considerable merit, and had obtained letters from Silas Deane and Benjamin Franklin in Europe and presented himself to Congress as a volunteer. Possibly attempting to mellow some of the recent antagonism against foreign officers, the Baron told Washington that he felt that he should not be given the command of a division, although he would be happy to receive the rank and pay of a major-general. He was placed in charge of troop training, with 100 men assigned to him who, in turn, were to drill the remainder of the army. Steuben was appointed temporary Inspector-General and, within two months, Congress was to confirm his rank of major-general. No other foreigner other than the young Lafayette had so readily won the affection of the men, and soon the muddy parade grounds of Valley Forge presented a scene of marching men, in time to the guttural curses of Steuben,

'*Viens*, Walker, *mon ami, mon bon ami! sacre! Goddam de gaucheries of* dese *badnauts, Je ne puis plus*. I can curse them no more.'

Within a month the Baron had established a regular drill routine, a routine described by William Fleury of the Maryland brigade:

'At six o'clock in the morning the division is ordered to general parade and the soldiers in the squads of always eight, are drilled in ordinary marching. A non-commissioned officer marches at their right, a little in advance, to give the time and the step, and he drills them in marching with and without music or drums. This drill lasted two hours. At nine o'clock is the parade; the soldiers are then taught the few movements in which they are instructed after the use of arms. At noon particular instruction is given to the non-commissioned officers. At three o'clock P.M., a meeting of the adjutants in my quarters for instructions in theoretic maneuvering and the emphasis to be used in giving the word of command.'[10]

As spring came on, men who had left during the winter began to drift back into camp. As time went on, it became more evident that Steuben had performed a minor miracle—the army was beginning to take on something of the appearance of a fighting machine. Troops were being trained as a unit and were sent out on manoeuvres. There were occasional moments of humour, and nearsighted Peter du Ponceau was able to laugh at himself:

'In the spring of 1778 . . . the commander-in-chief ordered a sham fight to be executed by two divisions of troops, one of which was under the command of Baron Steuben. In the capacity of his aid-de-camp I was sent to reconnoitre with orders to return immediately at full gallop, as soon as the enemy should be in sight. I rode on to the distance of about a quarter of a mile when I was struck with the sight of what I was since informed to be some red petticoats hanging on a fence to dry which I took for a body of British soldiers. I had forgotten it seems the contending parties were all Americans, and none of them clothed in scarlet regimentals. Full of my hallucination, I returned in haste to camp, with the news that the enemy were marching upon us. Our division took the road I indicated, and, behold! the sight of the red petticoats was all the result of their movement. It excited of course, a great deal of merriment, to my utter confusion and dismay.

The adventure was related the same day at Head quarters to General Washington in my presence, but such was the conduct of that excellent man, that I retired comforted . . . a huge bowl of punch was handed round to the company, and of which I took my share. . . . This true incident gave rise amongst my fellow soldiers to many tales in which there was not the shadow of truth. It was said for instance, that I once rode out to the Adjutant-General's office on a black horse and returned on a white one without perceiving the difference.'[11]

Now that his army was in better shape to fight, Washington made a move to strengthen its leadership. Ever since Charles Lee had been taken prisoner he had felt a loss. Elias Boudinot, Commissary of Prisoners, reported the return of the eccentric general:

'In the spring of 1778, a proposition was made by both parties for a partial Exchange of Prisoners, and I was ordered to Germantown to meet the British Commissary, to attempt the business. When I was setting out from Camp, Genl. Washington called me into his Room and in the most earnest manner intreated of me, if I wished to gratify him, that I would obtain the exchange of Genl. Lee, for he was never more wanted by him, than at the present moment, and desired I would not suffer trifles to prevent it. . . .

When the day arrived the greatest preparations were made for his [Lee's] reception; all the principal officers of the Army were drawn up in two lines, advanced of the Camp about 2 miles towards the Enemy.—Then the troops with their inferior officers formed a line quite to head Quarters. All the music of the Army attended. The General, with a great number of the principal officers, and their Suites, rode about four miles on the road towards Philadelphia and waited till Genl. Lee appeared.—Genl. Washington dismounted & recd Gen. Lee as if he had been his brother.—he passed thro' the lines of Officers & the Army, who all paid him the highest military honors to Head quarters, where Mrs. Washington was, and there he was entertained with an Elegant Dinner, and the Music playing the whole time.

A Room was assigned him, Back of Mrs. Washington's Sitting Room, and all his Baggage was stowed in it. The next morning he lay very late, and Breakfast was detained for him. When he came out, he looked as dirty as if he had been in the street all night. Soon after I discovered that he had brought a miserable dirty hussy with him from Philadelphia (a British Sergeant's Wife) and had actually taken her into his Room by a Back Door and she had slept with him that night.'[12]

Lee was granted command of the right wing of the army, but before he assumed command he requested permission to visit Congress. Before he set out he saw Boudinot and told him that Washington 'was not fit to command a Sergeant's Guard'. The man, as Richard Peters later observed, 'exhibited human nature in whimsical, sarcastical and sombre caricature'.

But as happy as Washington was to have Lee back with the army, there was even greater reason for rejoicing in the American camp. There was the news that France had finally signed a treaty of alliance with the United States. This first accomplishment of American diplomacy was the work of Benjamin Franklin, Silas Deane, and Arthur Lee, envoys to Paris; it was Franklin, however, who was responsible for its success. 'Le bon-homme Richard' had won French goodwill to a surprising degree: his shrewd common sense in terms offered, his scientific eminence, his Rousseau-esque simplicity of dress and manner, coupled with wit and charm, all had told in favour of the new country. The French government had long been impressed with the staying power of the Americans, and the victory of Saratoga had demonstrated that they could win important battles. The date selected by Washington to celebrate the occasion was 6 May 1778:

'At nine o'clock the several brigades of the army were assembled on their own parade, where divine service was performed and discourses suited to the occasion delivered by their respective chaplains.

At half-past ten a cannon was fired at the artillery-park, as a sign for the troops to be under arms; and at eleven, a second signal being given, each brigade marched by the right to its post, and formed in line of battle. . . .

A third signal being given, there was a discharge of 13 pieces of cannon, which was immediately followed by a running fire of musquetry, commenced by his Excellency's guards, which were posted at some distance in front of the first line, and continued by the corps posted in the grand

156. 'D. Beniamin Fraencklin, Grand Comissaire plenipotentiaire du Congres d'Amérique en France'

The French alliance, crucial to the success of the American cause, was a culminating achievement in the long career of one of the most versatile and most individual of Americans. In 1776, with American fortunes of war at low ebb, Franklin undertook the difficult mission to France, where he played skilfully on the French desire for revenge on the British. He seems to have used every resource of charm, tact, and a mild cunning, even posing a bit under his fur cap and behind his steel-rimmed spectacles as a more simple, natural man than he was, to build up the powerful 'culte Franklin' which helped to bring the sophisticated French nation in on the side of America.

de̊s̊ine par C. N. Cochin Chev. de l'Ordre du Roi à Paris 1777.

D. BENIAMIN FRÆNCKLIN.

Grand Comissaire plenipotentiaire du Congres d'Amerique en France né à Boston 1706. en 17. Janvier.

Se vend a Londres chez Thom. Hart.

redoubt on the right, and from thence thro' the two lines. A fourth signal gun was fired, when an universal Huzza and *long live the King of France* resounded, at the same instant, thro' the whole army.

To this succeeded a second discharge of the thirteen cannon, and another general fire of musquetry—and upon a signal, loud Huzzas to the *Friendly European Powers*—This was immediately followed by a third discharge of the artillery and musquetry, and Huzza to *The United States*.

The whole army returned to its encampment, and the officers of the several brigades were invited by his Excellency to a collation, which was enlivened by a brilliant company of Ladies.

The exact order in which the columns marched to their ground—the celerity and precision with which the lines were formed—the regularity of the fire—the pillars of fleecy smoke ascending in rapid succession—the continued sound of musquetry, not unlike the rolling of distant thunder—the martial appearance of the troops—conspired to exhibit a magnificent scene of joy, worthy of great occasion.

The Feu de Joye being over, the rest of the day was devoted to convivial pleasures. . . . Mutual congratulations and the most unaffected hilarity crowned the feast.—and the following toasts, among the many others, were given, and received the loudest acclamations:

> The KING OF FRANCE
> The FRIENDLY EUROPEAN POWERS
> The HON. CONGRESS AND UNITED STATES.
> The immortal Memory of those HEROES who
>   have died in defence of AMERICAN LIBERTY.

The spontaneous marks of attachment and respect, which were heaped on our illustrous Commander in Chief, when the restraint and formality and etiquette were laid aside, must have given him the most enviable feelings.

We were favored with a day as serene and delightful as if it had been commissioned for the purpose, in a word, Heaven seemed to smile, and grant every auspicious omen to the League which we were celebrating.—For the military part of our entertainment, we are much indebted to the Baron de Steuben, Inspector-General of the American Army.'[13]

The soughing winds of spring brought a new ally, a new spirit of discipline to the army, and a renewed joy in living. The men began to look around for entertainment other than attempting to edge in nearer a smoky fire. William Bradford discovered the officers to be resourceful in amusing themselves:

'The Camp could now afford you some entertainment. The manoeuvring of the Army is in itself a sight that would Charm you.—Besides these, the Theatre is opened—Last Monday Cato was performed before a very numerous and splendid audience. His Excellency & Lady, Lord Stirling & Lady Kitty, & Mr Green were part of the Assembly. The Scenery was in Taste—& the performance admirable—Col. George did his part to admiration—he made an excellent *die* (as they say)—pray heaven, he dont *die* in earnest—for yesterday he was seized with the pleurisy & lies extremely ill—If the Enemy does not retire from Philad*a* soon, our Theatrical amusements will continue—the fair Penitent and Padlock will soon be acted. The "recruiting officer" is also on foot.

I hope however we shall be disappointed in all these by the more agreeable Entertainment of taking possession of Philad*a*—There are strong rumors that the English are meditating a retreat—Heaven send it—for I fear we shall not be able to force them to go these two months.'[14]

So strong were the rumours that the British were evacuating Philadelphia that Lafayette was sent out with a force of several thousand men. An enemy detachment sallied forth, but after little more than a staring match at Barren Hill both armies drew back. But there was truth to the rumour.

The British had spent a comfortable winter in Philadelphia, indulging themselves in theatricals, balls, and frolicking in general. Occasionally there had been harassment of the outposts, but these were but minor irritants. Their greatest fright had come in January, leading one rebel

157. Lafayette. *F. G. Casanova*

Among all the pictured faces of the leaders of the American Revolution, that of Lafayette looks out with a youth and purity which sets it apart. He was indeed remarkable, this youth of nineteen who wrote from France, 'It is especially in the hour of danger that I wish to share your fortune'; and he won, both from the emerging nation and from her hard-driven commander-in-chief, a remarkable affection.

He arrived in America in 1777 and joined Washington near Philadelphia. Washington was ashamed of the ragged condition of his troops, but Lafayette saluted them, saying, 'It is to learn, and not to teach, that I come hither.' Congress received him coldly, having had a glut of foreigners wanting commissions; but Lafayette disarmed them completely saying, 'After the sacrifices I have made, I have the right to exact two favours; one is, to serve at my own expense,—the other is, to serve at first as volunteer'. They made him a major-general. Soon he was in action, and wounded at Brandywine. At Valley Forge, he imposed upon himself an extra austerity and was constantly at Washington's side, supporting him in adverse fortune and internal disaffections with a warmth of feeling that was almost filial.

newspaper to comment, 'The British heroes in Philadelphia, have lately furnished us with laughing matter for a month, and will be a standing jest forever.' This had resulted from the fertile brain of a young Yale graduate, Captain David Bushnell, who had earlier thrown a scare into the enemy fleet with his one-man submarine, the *American Turtle*, in New York in 1776. This time the diversion consisted of a number of kegs filled with powder, triggered by a match lock and set afloat above the city to drift down the tide amongst the British fleet anchored in the Delaware. A Boston newspaper carried an account of the resultant terror and hysteria matched only by that resulting from Indian raids on the frontier:

'This city has lately been entertained with a most astonishing instance of the activity, bravery, and military skill of the royal navy of Great Britain. The affair is somewhat particular and deserves your notice. Some time last week two boys observed a keg of singular construction, floating in the river opposite to the city. They got into a small boat, and attempting to take up the keg, it burst with a great explosion and blew up the unfortunate boys. On Monday last several kegs of a like construction made their appearance—an alarm was immediately spread thro' the city.

Various reports prevailed; filling the city and the royal troops with unspeakable consternation. Some reported that the kegs were filled with armed rebels; who were to issue forth in the dead of night, as the Grecians did of old from their wooden horse at the siege of Troy, and take the city by surprise; asserting that they had seen the points of their bayonets through the bung holes in the kegs. Others said they were charged with the most inveterate combustibles, to be kindled by secret machinery, and setting the whole Delaware in flames, were to consume all the shipping in the harbour; whilst others asserted that they were constructed by art magic, would of themselves ascend the wharfs in the night time and roll all flaming through the streets of the city, destroying every thing in their way.

Be this as it may—Certain it is that the shipping in the harbour, and all the wharfs in the city were fully manned—The battle began, and it was surprizing to behold the incessant blaze that was kept up against the enemy, the kegs. Both officers and men exhibited the most unparalleled skill and bravery on the occasion; whilst the citizens stood gazing, as solemn witnesses of their prowess. From the Roebuck and other ships of war, whole broadsides were poured into the Delaware. In short, not a wandering ship, stick, or drift-log but felt the vigour of British arms.

The action began about sun-rise, and would have been compleated with great success by noon, had not an old market woman coming down the river with provisions unfortunately let a small keg of butter fall over-board, which (as it was then ebb) floated down to the scene of action. At sight of this unexpected reinforcement of the enemy, the battle was renewed with fresh fury—the firing was incessant till the evening closed the affair. The kegs were either totally demolished or obliged to fly, as none have shown their heads since.

It is said his Excellency Lord Howe has dispatched a swift sailing packet with an account of this victory, to the court of London. In a word, Monday the 5th of January 1778, must ever be distinguished in history for the memorable BATTLE OF THE KEGS.'[15]

Most of the British shrugged off their mortification as a dirty rebel trick

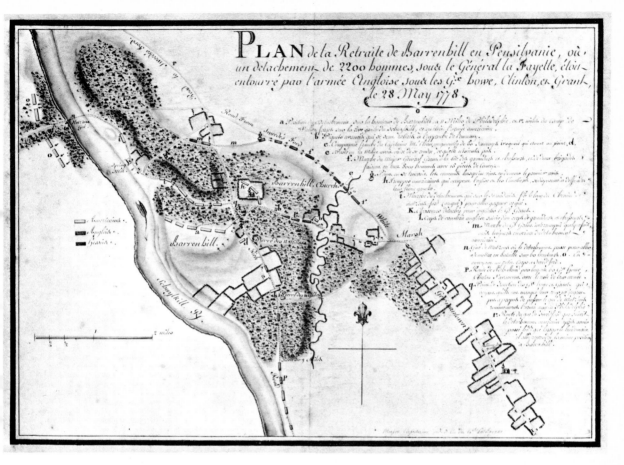

158. Brouillion ou Plan de la Retraite de Barrenhill en Pensilvanie. *Michel Capitaine du Chesnoy*

On 15 May, while British officers were enjoying the Meschianza, Lafayette received orders from Washington for his first major independent command; with a force of over 2,000 men he was to approach the enemy's lines and find whether and when the British intended to evacuate the city. Early on the morning of 19 May Lafayette crossed the Schuylkill below Valley Forge and bivouacked that night on Barren Hill, between Germantown and the river. Howe thereupon planned a flanking movement to encircle the entire American detachment. So certain was he of success that he also planned a dinner the following night at which he could present the captured young marquis.

By the morning of 20 May one prong under Major-General Grant reached a position on the main Barren Hill–Valley Forge road; Major-General Grey was approaching by Germantown; and Howe, accompanied by Lord Howe and Clinton, moved along the main ridge road. But Lafayette was alerted; quickly and calmly he ordered a retreat across Matson's Ford, three miles away, and there waited. He sent out small delaying forces that confused the British. The river posed an obstacle too formidable for Howe to attempt. Lafayette returned to Valley Forge, where he was commended by Washington.

and continued their gay social whirl. Many older officers cursed Howe for his inactivity, but few realized that the commander-in-chief was spending his last few months on American soil. Even before the fall of Philadelphia he had requested that he be relieved of 'this very painful service, wherein I have not the good fortune to enjoy the necessary confidence of my superiors'.

Not until 8 May did a ship arrive carrying the news that Howe had been granted his request and was to be replaced by the portly, yet sensitive and thin-skinned Major-General Sir Henry Clinton. No sooner was the word out that Howe was returning to England than twenty young officers, under

207

Ticket for the Meschianza.

Drawn by Major André

PL.XXVII.

the guidance of Captain John André, prepared an elaborate farewell party for their departing general. Once more knighthood flowered, with a colourful water parade, balls, and a tournament between two sets of 'knights'; the 'Knights of the Blended Rose' rode in the lists against the 'Knights of the Burning Mountain' to gain the favour of their ladies. In this so-called Mischianza, or Medley, a number of the young ladies of the city made an appearance in Turkish trousers, scandalizing many of the pious Quakers who had remained in the city. Other than the young ladies of the city who did not receive an invitation, the most caustic critics of the extravaganza were veteran military men such as one grizzled artillery officer who made the wry comment, 'The "Knights of the Burning Mountain" are tom-fools, and the "Knights of the Blended Rose" are damned fools! I know of no other distinction between them.' Ambrose Serle, whose employer, the Admiral Lord Howe, was honoured along with his brother, Sir William, was appalled at the expense:

'This afternoon was exhibited a strange kind of entertainment, which the Projectors styled a Meschianza or Medley, consisting of Tilts and Tournaments in Honor of the General upon his Departure. It cost a great Sum of money. Our Enemies will dwell upon the Folly & Extravagance of it with Pleasure. Every man of Sense among ourselves, tho' not unwilling to pay a due Respect, was ashamed of this mode of doing it.'[16]

With the conclusion of this fandango, Howe sailed for England, there to receive criticism such as that by Horace Walpole who commented that 'the only bays he possessed were those who drew his carriage'. Sir Henry Clinton was faced with the task of the evacuation of Philadelphia.

With the entry of France into the conflict, the British Ministry had been forced to re-evaluate the American situation. The land campaign in the north was to be henceforth conducted only as a holding action. With the prospect of a naval war, St Lucia in the French West Indies became a prime objective. The army was henceforth to be used, in a large measure, to guard naval bases and provide support for coastal raids. Clinton had been ordered to detach 5,000 troops to St Lucia and another 3,000 to Florida to protect the British flank. Philadelphia was to be evacuated and New York held as long as possible. If they were driven out of New York, the army was to protect the naval base at Newport, and if that proved impracticable, were to establish a base at Halifax. In the fall, when the French fleet would be occupied in protecting their West Indian possessions, British military efforts would be transferred to the southern states.

As a result of these developments, Parliament, after repealing a number of the obnoxious acts and offering concessions to the rebels, provided for a peace commission to be headed by the Earl of Carlisle. This commission was not only ineffective, it became something of an exercise in futility. In June, when their transport dropped anchor in the Delaware off Philadelphia, Carlisle discovered the army making preparations to evacuate the city under orders that had been issued before the peace commission had sailed from England, but of which they had not been informed. The Continental Congress offered little hope, and on 13 June that body had passed a resolution declaring that no considerations should be given peace overtures until the 'King of Great Britain shall demonstrate a sincere disposition for that purpose. The only solid proof of this disposition will be, an explicit acknowledgement of the independence of these states, or the withdrawing his fleet and armies.' The following day Carlisle sadly admitted to his wife, 'at present we depend upon Fortune as anything else for success. We all look very grave, and perhaps we think we look wise. I fear nobody will think so when we return. As I begin to think our business nearly over, I don't see what we have to do here. . . .'

Even as Carlisle wrote, the military was moving out of Philadelphia and had been since 8 June. The most pitiful group was that of the loyalists who now found themselves to be refugees and were leaving with only the possessions they could carry—the price for supporting the established government. No sooner had the last redcoat left than the Americans marched in. A form of martial law was initiated, and the light-horse troops were among the first to enter with 'drawn swords in their hands, [and] galloped about the streets, and frightened many by their appearance'. They were soon followed by other troops, some of whom described the city as 'filthy', while Henry Knox was to write that 'Lucy and I went in, but it stunk so abominably that it was impossible to stay there. . . .' Yet among the civilian observers it was perceived that the city itself was in better shape than they had dared hope.

With the transports filled with loyalists and some of the more unreliable Hessian units, Clinton led his army across New Jersey towards New York. The main road from Philadelphia to New York ran through Trenton, Princeton, and Brunswick to South Amboy. But Clinton confused Washington when he turned off to take the road to Sandy Hook, where he expected to ferry his troops across to New York. The march across Jersey was almost lazy in its execution. Following the marching columns was a long baggage train, trailing back for seven miles. So leisurely was the march that in the first six days the long red column travelled only thirty miles.

Washington set out in pursuit, departing from Valley Forge on 19 June and crossing Corywell's Ferry north of Trenton; by 24 June his scouting parties had made contact with the enemy. The New Jersey militia were out, annoying the British rear and flanks, destroying bridges and felling trees across the roads. The heat lay like a great blanket over the countryside, often reaching 100 degrees, wilting weary British soldiers staggering along in heavy winter clothing and weighted down by field packs. By 25 June, over 300 had come into the American camp and surrendered themselves as prisoners-of-war.

The young American Lieutenant-Colonel Alexander Hamilton was unhappy with the confusion and indecision prior to the initial contact with the enemy:

'When we came to Hopewell Township, the General unluckily called a council of war, the result of which would have done honor to the most honorable body of midwives, and to them only. The purport was, that we should keep a comfortable distance from the enemy, and keep up a vain parade of annoying them by detachment. In persuance of this idea, a detachment of 1500 men was sent off under General Scott to join the troops near the enemy's lines. General Lee was *primum mobile* of this sage plan; and was even opposed to sending so considerable a force. The General, on mature consideration of what had been resolved on, determined to persue a different line of conduct at all hazards. With this in view, he marched the army next morning towards Kingston, and there made another detachment of 1000 men under General Wayne, and formed all the detached troops into the command of the Marquis de la Fayette. The project was, that this advanced corps should take the first opportunity to attack the enemy's rear on the march, to be supported or covered as circumstances should require by the whole army.

General Lee's conduct with respect to the command of this corps was truly childish. According to the incorrect notions of our army, his seniority would entitle him to a command of the advanced corps; but he in the first instance declined it, in favour of the Marquis. Some of his friends having blamed him for doing it, and Lord Stirling having shown a disposition to interpose his claims, General Lee very inconsistently reasserted his pretensions. The matter was a second time accomodated; General Lee and Lord Stirling agreed to let the Marquis command. General Lee, a little time after recanted again, and became very importunate. The General, who all along had observed the greatest candor in this matter, grew tired of such fickle behaviour, and ordered the Marquis to proceed.

The enemy in marching from Allen Town had changed their disposition, and thrown all the best troops in the rear; this made it necessary, to strike a stroke with propriety, to reinforce the advanced corps. Two brigades were detached for this purpose, and the General willing to accomodate General Lee, sent him with them to take command of the whole advanced corps, which rendezvoused the forenoon of the 27th at English Town, consisting of at least 5000 rank and file, most of them select troops. General Lee's orders were, the moment he received intelligence of the enemy's march to pursue them and to attack their rear.

This intelligence was received about five o'clock in the morning of the 28th, and General Lee put his troops in motion accordingly. The main body

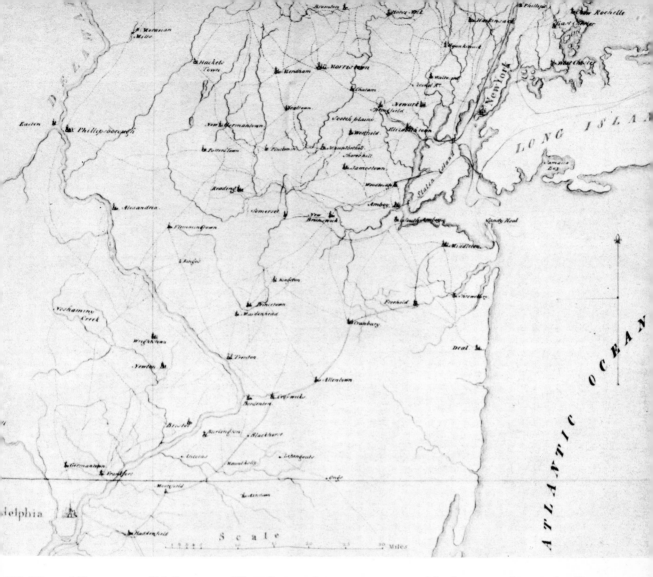

160. Plan of the Country between New York and Philadelphia, copied from one taken in the baggage of M. De la Fayette. The retreat of the British Army from Philadelphia to New York is marked . . . (detail)

This manuscript map is inserted at the end of a copy of Lieutenant-Colonel John Simcoe's *Journal of the Operations of the Queen's Rangers* (1787) which he presented to the King.

did the same. The advanced corps came up with the enemy's rear a mile or two beyond the [Monmouth] Court House; I saw the enemy drawn up, and persuaded there was not a thousand men—their front from different accounts was then ten miles off. However favourable this situation may seem for an attack, it was not made; but after changing their position two or three times by retrograde movements, our advanced corps got into a confused general retreat, and even rout would hardly be too strong an expression. Not a word of all this was officially communicated to the General; as we approached the supposed place of action, we heard some flying rumors of what had happened, in consequence of which the General rode forward, and found the troops returning in the greatest disorder, and the enemy pressing upon their rear. I never saw the General to so much advantage.'[17]

Washington had known little about the retreat. When he sent messengers forward, all General Lee would say was: 'Tell the General I am doing well enough.' The commander-in-chief had spurred towards the firing and ran into Lee and the retiring troops. Captain Thomas Washington later reported the story told him by Colonel William Grayson:

'He and Col Grayson were, therefore, both at the head of the column, when General Washington rode up and upbraided General Lee for his dastardly conduct. . . . General Washington demanded of General Lee the reason for the retreat, to which General Lee replied: "Sir, these troops are not able to meet British Grenadiers." "Sir," said General Washington, much excited, "they are able, and by G–d they shall do it," and immediately gave the order to countermarch the column.'[18]

General Charles Scott of Virginia once said of Washington's behaviour at Monmouth, 'Yes, Sir, he swore on that day till the leaves shook on the trees, charming, delightful. Never have I enjoyed such swearing before, or

161. Battle of Monmouth 28*th* June 1778. *G. Spencer*

The battle around Monmouth County courthouse is difficult to portray because of the back-and-forth surges of fighting and scattered encounters of small forces. Although the topography of this plan is not entirely accurate, it shows the main field of action. In the lower centre is the Monmouth county courthouse in the little village of Freehold. To its right, bordering either side of the headwaters of Weamacock Creek, is the East Morass. Lee's main army, following on the heels of Clinton's retreat, approached the courthouse; Lee sent out detachments which skirted the East Morass to its south and north. They met strong British rearguard action, including that of the Queen's Rangers (at H, with details in the inset). Increased British pressure and confusion of Lee's orders caused a rapid retreat of Lee's forces along the road leading back from Freehold across another swamp, the West Morass. There (at Y-Y) Washington, with his advancing troops (Z), met Lee and took over command after a reprimand. While the British made their farthest advance (U,M,N,O), Washington sent the troops back over the West Morass (W); he sent General Nathanael Greene with fresh troops around the swamp to Combs Hill (Y, bottom left), where Greene's artillery poured a devastating fire on the British advance. General Clinton ordered his troops to withdraw to their bivouac area of the previous night, east of the East Morass. At midnight Clinton ordered his troops to resume their march towards Sandy Hook, in north-east Monmouth county.

This manuscript copy of Lieutenant George Spencer's map is found in the copy of Simcoe's *Journal* presented to George III.

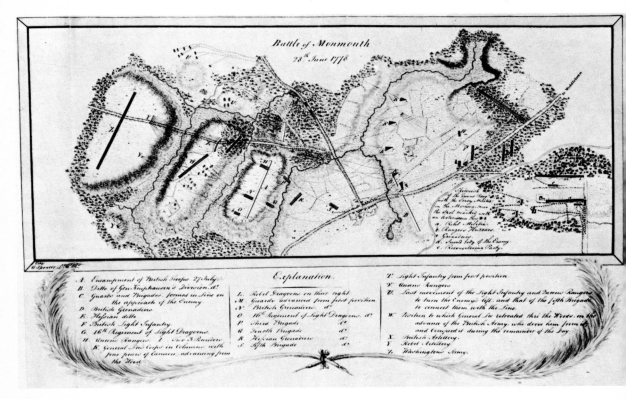

162. Major General Charles Lee with his black poodle.
Rushbrooke

Charles Lee was born in Cheshire in 1731 and schooled at Bury St Edmunds. Bitterly anti-Tory in England, he settled in Berkeley County, Virginia, in 1773. He was the second major-general appointed by Congress. Dr Thomas Girdlestone, whose book proposing the untenable theory that Lee was the author of the Junius Letters has this engraving by J. Neagle as a frontispiece, notes that the portrait was 'Taken from a caricature drawing by Barham Rushbrooke Esq. of West Stowe near Bury . . . allowed, by all who knew General Lee, to be the only successful delineation either of his countenance or person.'

since. Sir, on that ever-memorable day he swore like an angel from Heaven.' James McHenry reported:

'He gave a new turn to the action. He retrieved what had been lost. He was always in danger—examining the enemy's manoeuvres—exhorting the troops—and directing the operation of his plans. He unfolded surprising abilities, which produced uncommon results. Gen. Greene, also, who commanded on the right, and Lord Stirling, on the left, distinguished themselves also by great address, coolness and courage.'[19]

Washington had stationed one group behind a fence, and it was this group who bore the brunt of the attack when the British came up. Joseph Plumb Martin took it in his stride; he was fast becoming a veteran soldier, and the training at Valley Forge was now beginning to pay off in the coin of military success:

'By this time the British had come in contact with the New-England forces at the fence, when a sharp conflict ensued; these troops maintained their ground, till the whole force of the enemy could be brought to bear, had charged upon them through the fence, and after being overpowered by numbers, and the platoon officers had given orders for their several platoons to leave the fence, so eager were they to be revenged on the invaders of their country and rights. . . .

The British immediately formed and began to retreat to the main body of their army. Col. Cilly, finding that we were not likely to overtake the enemy before they reached the main body of the army, on account of fences and other obstructions, ordered three or four platoons from the right of our corps to pursue and attack them and thus keep them in play till the rest of the detachment would come up.

I was in this party, we pursued without order; as I passed through the orchard I saw a number of the enemy lying under the trees, killed by our fieldpieces, mentioned before. We overtook the enemy just as they were entering the meadow, which was rather bushy. When within about five rods of the rear of the retreating foe, I could distinguish every thing about them they were retreating in line, though in some disorder; I singled out a man and took my aim directly between his shoulders (they were divested of their packs,) he was a good mark, being a broad shouldered fellow; what became of him I know not, the fire and smoke hid him from my sight; one thing I know, that is, I took as deliberate aim at him as ever I did in my life. But after all, I hope I did not kill him, although I intended to at the time.

By this time our whole party had arrived, and the British had obtained a position that suited them, as I suppose, for they returned our fire in good earnest, and we played the second part of the same tune. They occupied a much higher piece of ground than we did, and had a small piece of Artillery, which the soldiers called a grasshopper; we had no Artillery with us. The first shot they gave us from this piece, cut off the thigh bone of a captain, just above the knee, and the whole heel of a private in the rear of him. We gave it to poor Sawney (for they were Scotch troops) so hot, that he was forced to fall back and leave the ground they occupied. When our Commander saw them retreating, and nearly joined with their main body, he shouted, "come, my boys, reload your pieces, and we will give them a set-off." We did so, and gave them a parting salute, and the firing on both sides ceased. We then laid ourselves under the fences and bushes to take breath, for we had need of it; I presume every one has heard of the heat of that day, but none can realize it that did not feel it. Fighting is hot work in cool weather, how much so in such weather as it was on the 28th of June, 1778.

After the action in our part of the army had ceased, I went to a well, a few rods off, to get some water; here I found the wounded captain, mentioned before, lying on the ground, and begging his sergeant, who pretended to have the care of him, to help him off the field, or he should bleed to death; the sergeant, and a man or two he had with him, were taken up in hunting after plunder. It grieved me to see the poor man in such distress, and I asked the sergeant why he did not carry his officer to the surgeons, and he said he would directly; directly! said I, why he will die directly. I then offered to assist them in carrying him to a meeting-house, a short distance off, where the rest of the wounded men and the surgeons were; at length he condescended to be persuaded to carry him off, I helped him to the place, and tarried a few minutes, to see the wounded and two or three limbs amputated, and then returned to my party again, where we remained the rest of the day and the following night, expecting to have another hack at them in the morning, but they gave us the slip.'[20]

Washington had fully expected a renewal of hostilities the following morning and had lain wrapped in his coat under a tree on the battlefield that night. But Clinton had slipped off under the cover of darkness and two days later was reported at Sandy Hook, and by 5 July the battered British army was in New York. Washington rested his army at English Town for two days before beginning a rather leisurely northward movement on 1 July.

Legends were built that sultry June day. Sir Henry Clinton had displayed great personal courage, but little generalship, according to one of his officers who noted that he 'showed himself the Soldier, but not the wise General, on the occasion, exposing himself and charging at the head of a few Dragoons'. There were many words of praise for Washington, who in an almost reckless fashion had turned an American rout into a drawn contest, if not actually a victory of sorts.

There was even a heroine who became a legend; Mary Ludwig Hays, wife of a barber turned artillery sergeant. This woman had earned for herself the nickname of 'Molly Pitcher', by carrying water to the cannoneers as they worked their pieces during the heat of battle. When her husband had been struck down, she had taken his place at the gun. Private Martin saw her in action that day:

'One little incident happened, during the heat of the cannonade, which I was an eye-witness to, and I think would be unpardonable not to mention. A woman whose husband belonged to the Artillery, and who was then attached to a piece in the engagement, attended with her husband at the piece the whole time; while in the act of reaching a cartridge and having one of her feet as far from the other as she could step, a cannon shot from the enemy pased directly between her legs without doing any damage than carrying away all the lower part of her petticoat,—looking at it with apparent unconcern, she observed, that it was lucky that it did not pass higher, for in that case it might have carried away something else, and she continued her occupation.'[21]

Charles Lee was not listed among the heroes of the battle of Monmouth. Although there had been talk of treason, a court-martial convicted him on three accounts: disobedience of orders; misbehaviour before the enemy; and disrespect to the commander-in-chief. The last conviction resulted from the heated letters Lee had written Washington the day after the battle and on 1 July. Gathering his dogs, the colourful general wandered off into obscurity and an early grave.

The Americans hailed the battle of Monmouth as a victory, chiefly because they were in possession of the field at the end of the battle. But at best, it must be declared a drawn contest. The greatest result of the battle was the vindication of the long hours Steuben had spent in the snow and mud of the drill fields of Valley Forge. At Monmouth the Americans performed more like an army than an armed mob. But little did either commander realize that this would be the last battle fought by Washington or Clinton in the northern theatre.

10. Treason!

By 6 JULY, Sir Henry Clinton had all of his weary troops back in New York. Three days later another threat presented itself; the white flag of the French Admiralty was seen in American waters for the first time since the shooting began. After an incredibly slow crossing of eighty-seven days from Toulon, the French fleet under the command of Comte d'Estaing made its appearance in Delaware Bay, only to discover that the British had sailed from Philadelphia. The admiral straight away hoisted sail for Sandy Hook, hoping to surprise the British during the confusion of ferrying operations, but was disappointed to discover this movement was complete by the time of his arrival. Lord Howe's ships lay secure behind the long sand bar that ran from Staten Island to Sandy Hook. The ponderous French vessels, heavily armed and standing against the horizon like so many sea-going

163. John Paul Jones. *Moreau*

This portrait of Jones was painted by Jean-Michel Moreau le Jeune in 1781 and engraved by Jean-Michel Moreau le Père in 1789.

castles, drew too much water to slide across the bar. Washington dispatched pilots to the area and d'Estaing offered a reward of 50,000 Crowns to anyone who would pilot him safely across the obstruction, notwithstanding the obvious fact that if the battle went against him, he would be bottled up within the harbour with no avenue of escape. After eleven days of swaying at anchor, d'Estaing gave up.

The Americans had been too long without a fleet not to recognize the value of d'Estaing's warships, although John Paul Jones was writing his name in bold-face type across the pages of history, and American privateers were not only irritating British shipping but gathering profits for themselves. Washington planned the initial Franco-American effort by a land-sea manoeuvre against Newport in Rhode Island.

Newport had fallen to Sir Henry Clinton in 1776, and the area had since been maintained as something of a secondary British naval base. At this time, the American Major-General John Sullivan was occupying Providence with a small army of observation. With naval support, it seemed possible that an impressive defeat could be inflicted upon the enemy. The Marquis de Lafayette was dispatched to Rhode Island with two crack brigades under his command, while Nathanael Greene, hungry for the glory he felt had been denied him while serving as quartermaster general, volunteered to serve under Sullivan. Six thousand New England militia marched under their general, John Hancock, who was making his first and only appearance as a

164. The French fleet blocking the British fleet before New York harbour. *Pierre Ozanne*

The first fruit of the French alliance was the entry into American waters of a French fleet in support of the Patriot cause, under the command of the Comte d'Estaing. In July 1778 Howe awaited the French on the inside of Sandy Hook, that narrow but effective bar across part of lower New York harbour, with his boats drawn up in a brilliantly conceived defensive formation. On 11 July, d'Estaing, who had Ozanne with him on board, approached and anchored outside the Hook, as shown in this picture. His fleet outweighed Howe's; he had a 90-gun ship, one 80, six 74s and one 50, to the British six 64s, three 50s, and six frigates. But d'Estaing, to quote Admiral Mahan, was 'timid in his profession'. When the New York pilots, sent to him by Washington, told him that there were not more than 23 feet of water over the sand bar across the entrance, and that his ships were too heavy to cross, he was easily convinced. On 22 July, a spring tide and a north-east wind combined to give 30 feet of water over the bar, and the French squadron appeared under way. The British braced for crucial action; but instead of making the attempt, d'Estaing bore off to the south, and was soon out of sight. Reported Lord Howe, 'I conclude the French commander has desisted.'

military man. One Frenchman was more than amused when the New Englanders straggled in:

'I have never seen a more laughable spectacle. All the tailors and apothecaries in the country must have been called out. . . . One could recognize them by their round wigs. They were mounted on bad nags and looked like a flock of ducks in cross-belts. The infantry was no better than the cavalry and appeared to be cut after the same pattern. I guessed that these warriors

CHARLES HENRI
Chevalier des Ordres
général de ses Armées
Né le 24 Novembre
1729.

COMTE D'ESTAING
du Roi Lieutenant
Vice Amiral de France
Presenté
Par son très Humble Serviteur Bligny Père.

165. Charles Henri, Comte d'Estaing.
F. Sablet
The Comte d'Estaing was a nobleman, well-connected and charming; he was entrusted with responsibilities greater than his ability, and was pursued by misfortunes not of his own making. Given command of the French fleet sent to assist the Americans in 1778, he arrived just too late to intercept Howe's passage to New York. His chance of beating him off Newport was foiled by a storm; he encountered hostility instead of the expected welcome in Boston; and he reached Santa Lucia just too late to prevent Barrington's taking it. His attack on Savannah did not succeed. He returned to France in 1780, and was executed in the Reign of Terror in 1794.

166. Great Encouragement for SEAMEN

This Congressional broadside of 29 March 1777 offers the opportunity to enlist under John Paul Jones on the *Ranger* of Portsmouth, New Hampshire, carrying 140 men. She was a sloop-of-war of the new American Navy, and the first to carry the Stars and Stripes.

Jones's raids had great propaganda value, causing consternation along the coasts and in the press of Britain. In April 1778 he raided Kirkcudbright Bay in Scotland, and then took fourteen men with him to St Mary's Isle, the seat of the Earl of Selkirk, intending to take the Earl hostage. Finding him away he allowed his men to demand, very politely, the family silver. This being as politely supplied by the Countess, Jones sailed away with it, only to buy it back from his prize-hungry men and return it to her, with an elegantly phrased letter.

GREAT ENCOURAGEMENT FOR SEAMEN.

 ALL GENTLEMEN SEAMEN and able-bodied LANDSMEN who have a Mind to diftinguifh themfelves in the GLORIOUS CAUSE of their COUNTRY, and make their Fortunes, an Opportunity now offers on board the Ship RANGER, of Twenty Guns, (for FRANCE) now laying in PORTSMOUTH, in the State of NEW-HAMP-SHIRE, commanded by JOHN PAUL JONES Efq; let them repair to the Ship's Rendez-vous in PORTSMOUTH, or at the Sign of Commodore MANLEY, in SALEM, where they will be kindly entertained, and receive the greateft Encouragement.—The Ship RANGER, in the Opinion of every Perfon who has feen her is looked upon to be one of the beft Cruizers in AMERICA,—She will be always able to Fight her Guns under a moft excellent Cover ; and no Veffel yet built was ever calculated for failing fafter, and making good Weather.

Any GENTLEMEN VOLUNTEERS who have a Mind to take an agreable Voyage in this pleafant Seafon of the Year, may, by entering on board the above Ship RANGER, meet with every Civility they can poffibly expect, and for a further Encouragement depend on the firft Opportunity being embraced to reward each one agreable to his Merit.

All reafonable Travelling Expences will be allowed, and the Advance-Money be paid on their Appearance on Board.

IN CONGRESS, MARCH 29, 1777.

RESOLVED,

THAT the MARINE COMMITTEE be authorifed to advance to every able Seaman, that enters into the CONTINENTAL SERVICE, any Sum not exceeding FORTY DOL-LARS, and to every ordinary Seaman or Landfman, any Sum not exceeding TWEN-TY DOLLARS, to be deducted from their future Prize-Money.

By Order of CONGRESS,

JOHN-HANCOCK, PRESIDENT.

DANVERS; Printed by E. RUSSELL, at the Houfe late the Bell-Tavern.

---

were more anxious to eat up our supplies than to make a close acquaintance with the enemy, and I was not mistaken; they soon disappeared.'[1]

In the midst of disembarking troops, d'Estaing received intelligence that Admiral Howe had received reinforcements and had ventured forth to seek battle with the French. The French admiral immediately recalled his troops and put out to sea. The two fleets parried for two days, each seeking to gain the advantage of the wind, with only token shots sent across wide expanses of sea. A sudden gale scattered the fleets; Howe put back into New York for repairs while d'Estaing returned to Newport. To the consternation of the Americans, he announced that he was steering for Boston for repairs to his storm-damaged vessels. Greene and Lafayette went aboard the flagship in an attempt to persuade him to change his mind, but he was adamant, and set his sails for Massachusetts, leaving Greene to comment, 'To evacuate the [Rhode] Island is death; to stay may be ruin.'

Sullivan moved up to attack the British in Newport, but the enemy, commanded by Sir Robert Pigot, merely evacuated their outer lines and pulled into Newport, prepared to wait out a siege. Sullivan soon discovered that without naval support, he could not prevent enemy supplies and provisions from coming in by water. He was also mortified to learn that a number of volunteers had developed a case of cannon fever and skulked home. He reported the following developments to the Continental Congress:

'On the evening of the 28th we moved with our stores and baggage, which had not been previously sent forward, and about two in the morning encamped on Butt's Hill, with our right extending to the West road, and left to East road; the flanking and covering parties still farther toward the water on right and left. . . .

The Hessian column formed on a chain of hills running northward from Quaker Hill. Our army was drawn up, the first line in front of the works on Butt's Hill, the second in rear of the hill, and the reserve near a creek, and near half a mile in rear of the first line. The distance between these two hills is about one mile. The ground between is meadowland, interspersed with trees and a small copse of wood.

167. The Memorable Engagement of Capt*n* Pearson of the Serapis with Paul Jones of the Bon Homme Richard & his Squadron, Sep. 23, 1779. *Richard Paton*

The historic victory of the *Bon Homme Richard*, a worn-out French East Indiaman with a motley crew, over the *Serapis*, a new ship of the line with an experienced British crew, was a fight to the finish and displayed the indomitable courage, the naval skill, and the leadership of a captain fighting against overwhelming odds.

168. Capt. Paul Jones shooting a Sailor who had attempted to strike his Colours in an Engagement

At the height of the conflict with the *Serapis*, the *Bon Homme Richard*, holed beneath the waterline and with one of the four pumps shot away, was rumoured to be sinking. Hearing that Jones and the chief officers were all dead, the gunner, master at arms, and ship's carpenter climbed the quarter-deck to haul down the pennant. When Jones realized what had happened he 'threw both of his pistols at his [the gunner's] head, one of which struck him in the head, fractured his skull and knocked him down at the foot of the gang-way ladder, where he lay till the battle was over.'

The enemy began a cannonade upon us about nine in the morning, which was returned with double force. Skirmishing continued between the advanced parties till near ten o'clock, when the enemy's two ships-of-war and some small armed vessels having gained our right flank and began a fire, the enemy bent their whole force that way and endeavoured to turn our right and under cover of the ship's fire, and to take the advanced redoubt on the right. They were twice driven back in the greatest confusion, but a third trial was made with greater numbers and with more resolution, which, had not been for the timely aid sent forward, would have succeeded.

A sharp contest of near an hour ensued, in which the cannon from both armies, placed on the hills, played briskly in support of their own party. The enemy were at length routed, and fled in great confusion to the hill where they first formed, and where they had artillery and some works to cover them, leaving their dead and wounded behind them. It was impossible to ascertain the number of dead on the field as it could not be approached by either party without being exposed to the cannon of the other army. . . . Colonel Campbell came out the next day to gain permission to view the field of action, to search for his nephew, whose body he could not get off, as they were closely pursued.

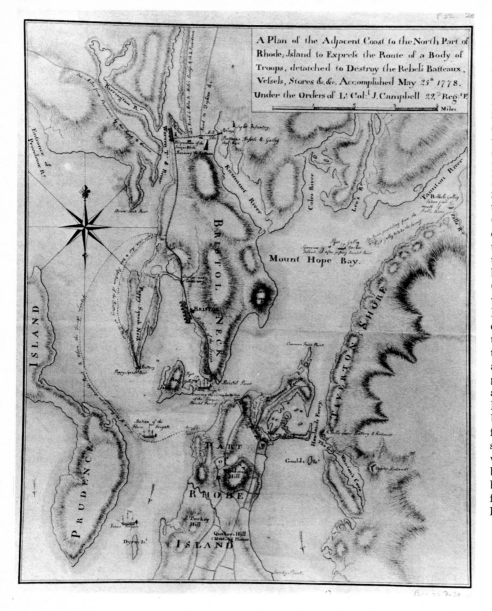

A Plan of the Adjacent Coast to the North Part of Rhode, Island to Express the Route of a Body of Troops, detached to Destroy the Rebels Batteaux, Vessels, Stores &c.&c. Accomplished May 25th 1778. Under the Orders of Lt. Col.l J. Campbell 22.d Reg.t F.

169. British preventive action before the invasion of Rhode Island by General Sullivan.
Seix(?)

As the American forces were gathering on the mainland for their assault against General Sir Robert Pigot's command at Newport, he sent a multi-pronged expedition under Lieutenant-Colonel Campbell to destroy their transports. At Warren the British burned the batteaux and galleys; Captain Seix marched with 30 men down to Bristol Point to destroy the battery at the ferry landing there; six boats, accompanied by the galley Pigot, captured a 'rebel galley' at the Battle of Fall River. Up the Fall River they found and destroyed a sawmill, the loss of which seriously set back plans for the building of transports for the invasion of the Island.

The firing of artillery continued through the day, the musketry with intermission of six hours. The heat of the action continued near an hour, which must have ended in the ruin of the British army, had not their redoubts on the hill covered them from farther pursuit. We were about to attack them in their lines, but the men having had no rest the night before, and nothing to eat either that night or the day of the action, and having been in constant action through most of the day, it was not thought advisable, especially as their position was exceedingly strong, and their numbers fully equal, if not superior to ours. . . . Our army retired to camp after the action; the enemy employed themselves in fortifying their camp through the night.

In the morning of the 30th I received a letter from his Excellency General Washington, giving me notice that Lord Howe had again sailed with the fleet; and receiving intelligence at the same time that a fleet was off Block

170. The French and British fleets at Newport, Rhode Island. *Pierre Ozanne*

After failing to enter New York harbour, d'Estaing made for Newport, held by the British under General Pigot. He entered Narragansett Bay, disembarked troops on neighbouring Conanicut Island, and prepared to co-ordinate an attack with the American General Sullivan, advancing from the north. Lord Howe, reinforced by several ships but still inferior to the French squadron, lost no time in following him and anchored off Point Judith, outside the bay, on 9 August 1778. The apparent assurance of a decisive victory against the British on land was not sufficient for d'Estaing, who also wished to overcome the British fleet at sea. At once he re-embarked his men, and sailed. Howe withdrew southward, and then made a great circle, seeking the most favourable conditions to meet the attack of the French, who were rapidly gaining upon him. The wind increased; the sea became rougher and rougher; and Captain Henry Duncan of the British flagship *Eagle*, watching anxiously, observed that the French 'bore away to the southward, apparently from the state of the weather, which, by the wind freshening much, with frequent rain, was now rendered very unfavourable for engaging'. This was British understatement for a storm of extreme violence.

Ozanne, with his skilful and delicate brush, has here caught the approach of the storm, with ships and men at its mercy.

171. The *Languedoc* demasted; attacked by the *Renown*. *Pierre Ozanne*

The great storm caused much damage, especially to the French ships. The *Languedoc*, their great 90-gun flagship, lost her bowsprit and all her lower masts, and had her tiller broken. Alone and in this enfeebled condition, she was attacked on the evening of 13 August 1778, by the *Renown*, a smaller British ship of 50 guns, which had recently been sent from Halifax to reinforce Howe. The *Renown* drew off, however, when night fell, and in the morning with the approach of other French ships, lost her prize.

Island, and also a letter from Boston, informing me that the Count d'Estaing could not come round so soon as I expected, a council of war was called, and, as we could have no prospect of operating against Newport with success without the assistance of a fleet, it was unanimously agreed to quit the island until the return of the French squadron.'[2]

In many respects, the battle of Newport was little more than a rearguard action. Casualties were surprisingly light in view of the vicious fire from both sides.

The most critical result of the business was that it came near to creating a breach in the alliance with France. So great was the indignation at the French abandonment of Newport that anyone in a French uniform became almost an enemy. It was not difficult for New Englanders to remember their long years of war with France. In Boston, on 15 September, a French officer was killed while trying to calm a riot brought on by a Boston mob

172. The Siege of Rhode Island, taken from Mr. Brindley's House, on the 25*th* of August, 1778

The heavy cannonading and bombardment by the Americans at the height of their attack is seen from behind the British defences north of Newport; the American general, John Sullivan, began his retrograde movement the next day, 26 August. He had expected the support of Admiral d'Estaing, who had disembarked 4,000 troops on neighbouring Conanicut Island but re-embarked them before sailing out to meet Lord Howe. Sullivan had about 10,000 troops, mainly militia, with divisions under Lafayette and Greene. The British general, Pigot, had 6,860 men; but Sullivan, faced with desertions and the fear of annihilation, withdrew his forces to the mainland without much loss on 30 August. The British remained in possession of Rhode Island.

The SIEGE OF RHODE ISLAND, taken from Mr. Brindley's House, on the 25th of August, 1778.

173. Richard Viscount Howe.
James Watson

Lord Howe was the head of a distinguished family, an intimate of the King; honour was very important to him. He was an admiral of the Royal Navy with a fine record of courage and skill, and the admiration of his men, who called him 'Black Dick'. Deeply disappointed by his failure as a peace commissioner to reconcile Britain and America, he felt the more keenly his shared responsibility with his brother Sir William, his joint commander-in-chief, to end the rebellion by force. Having failed to do this also, and Lord Howe having lost his last great opportunity to destroy the French fleet, both brothers requested and were allowed to return to England in 1778.

assaulting sailors from d'Estaing's squadron. The Massachusetts Assembly acted quickly, and the following morning appropriated money to erect a statue to the memory of the slain officer. French officers were wined and dined in an effort to heal the breach. Local politicians made every effort to conceal the smouldering resentment of the townspeople from their allies. Nathanael Greene, returning to Washington's army, wrote to the commander-in-chief:

'The late affray that happened in this place between the people of the town and those of the fleet had been found to originate from a parcel of soldiers belonging to the convention troops, and a party of British sailors which were engaged on board a privateer. The secret enemies of our cause, and the British officers in the neighborhood of this place, are endeavouring to sow the seeds of discord as much as possible between the inhabitants of this place and the French belonging to the fleet. The French officers are well

225

satisfied this is the state of the case, and it fills them with double resentment against the British. The Admiral and all French officers are now on exceedingly good footing with the gentlemen of the town. General Hancock takes unwearied pains to promote a good understanding with the French officers. His house is full from morning to night. . . .

General Hancock made the Admiral a present of your picture. He was going to receive it on board the fleet by firing a royal salute, but General Hancock thought it might furnish a handle for some of the speculative politicians to remark the danger of characters becoming too important. He therefore dissuaded the Admiral from carrying the matter into execution.'[3]

Frictions were dissipated and forgotten by 3 November, when the French fleet weighed anchor and sailed off to Martinique in the West Indies. The French were once again cherished allies. In the meantime, Washington crossed the Hudson and pitched camp at White Plains, but showed little inclination to move against the British in New York. The summer months droned away, but in October there was additional evidence that the French Alliance was beginning to pay off when a large shipment of shoes and clothing arrived.

Not until October was there a prospect of action, when Clinton made a show of force. One column under Lord Cornwallis marched out of New York along the east side of the river, another under Knyphausen on the west side of the Hudson, on foraging expeditions. Washington refused to be drawn out, and sent out small harassing parties. Among them was the Third Continental Dragoons under Lieutenant-Colonel George Baylor, a group often referred to as 'Mrs. Washington's Guards'. When other units in the area pulled back, no one took the trouble to inform Baylor. He was bedded down in a barn at New Tappan when a British detachment under 'No Flint' Grey repeated the surprise at Paoli. Surgeon Thacher recorded this instance of 'savage cruelty':

'Colonel Baylor's detachment consisted of four hundred horsemen, the attack was so sudden, that they were entirely defenceless, and the enemy immediately commenced the horrid work of slaughter; their entreaties and cries for mercy were totally disregarded by their savage foes. It has been well ascertained that the British soldiers were ordered by their inhuman officers to bayonet every man they could find, and to give no quarter. . . . Thomas Hutchinson, sergeant of the third troop, escaped unhurt; but heard the British soldiers cry out "Sliver him," repeatedly. Cullency, of the first troop, who received twelve wounds, says, "that when the enemy entered the barn where his troops lay, he and the men asked for quarter, and were refused; that the British Captain Bull, after inquiring how many of the rebels were dead, on being told the number, ordered all the rest knocked on the head, and that his orders were executed on five or six of the wounded." '[4]

About thirty of Baylor's one hundred men were killed and another fifty wounded, including Baylor who was bayoneted through the lungs and captured. Anthony Wayne, who had been in overall command of the harassing parties, was furious that a second massacre had been perpetrated on men under his command.

But now the breezes of autumn were beginning to send gold and brown

174. Detail from drill and manoeuvre. *Diderot*

Ready; Aim; Fire. Drill in the eighteenth century was both a training for combat and a method of instilling discipline.

175. A Prospective View of old Newgate, Connecticut's State Prison. *Brunton(?)*

Prison conditions on both sides were bad, made worse by the British regarding the Americans as rebels and traitors, and the Americans regarding the Loyalists as traitors rather than prisoners of war. The worst of the British prisons were the prison ships like the *Jersey*, anchored off New York, with terrible conditions of overcrowding, filth, and disease in her sweltering hold. The worst of the American prisons was that in the old copper mines at Simsbury, Connecticut.

leaves swirling to the ground and it was time to go into winter quarters. Washington established his headquarters at Middlebrook, New Jersey. In general, it was a pleasant winter, with one officer writing:

'We spend our time very sociably here; we are never disturbed by the enemy, have plenty of provisions, and no want of Whiskey Grogg. We sometimes get good Spirits, Punch, etc., and have Maderia sometimes. We have a variety of amusements. Last evening the Tragedy of Cato was performed at Brunswick by officers of the army.'[5]

And Nathanael Greene was to report to a friend, 'We had a little dance at my quarters a few evenings past. His Excellency and Mrs.Greene danced upwards of three hours without sitting down. Upon the whole, we had a pretty little frisk.' Despite this surface gaiety among the officer corps, the troops were suffering most of the old shortages. The question of supply remained critical, with Major Ebenezer Huntington writing letters brimming with angry complaints:

'This whole part of the Country are Starving for want of bread, they had been drove to the necessity of Grinding Flaxseed & oats together for bread— It is not Possible for the State to do something else besides Promises, Promises cannot feed or Clothe a Man always—Performance is sometimes necessary to make a man believe you intend to Perform—Let us wait if Possible the Event of the next Session, & Possibly Hatters and Wine drawers can Effect what wise men Can not.'[6]

Nathanael Greene, Quartermaster General, blamed shortages on the procrastinations of those of the legal profession who had found politics to their liking, and had found in that endeavour a way of overcoming the low esteem in which they had been held in the past. Some used legislative positions to feather their own nests:

'This State [New Jersey] grows more and more litigious. The pettifogging lawyers, like frogs in the spring, begin to peep, in great plenty. Besides this pest of creatures not less pernicious to the peace and welfare of a State than the locusts was to the growth of herbage in Egypt, there is a great multitude of Justices of the Peace who parade with Constables at their heels, and are as formidable in numbers as a Roman legion. This class of men, to show their learning and improve their genius, swarm about us like birds of prey, seeking whom they may devour. You may remember I made an

176. American dollars, 1776. *Anburey*

In 1779 Anburey, an officer of Burgoyne's army on parole in Virginia, wrote of 'the great depreciation of Congress money, as the exchange at present is after the rate of five hundred paper dollars for one guinea. The depreciation of Congress money arises from the vast quantity of the counterfeit, which any person who hazards the risk, may have gratis at New York, to circulate throughout the province. . . . There are many persons now in actual possession of plantations, which they purchased with the counterfeit money they brought from New York.'

Anburey enclosed several paper currency notes in his letters, which were reproduced in his *Travels* in 1789.

armor-bearer of one, upon my first coming to this ground, and I intend to keep them running upon every occasion. If they want business they shall have it.'[7]

A major difficulty in the purchasing of military supplies and provisions was the paper currency issued by the Continental Congress, money that purchased little more than its own bulk. Yet there were those who copied the stuff. Newspapers warned:

'The public are desired to beware of counterfeit *Thirty Dollar Bills*. They are dated May 10, 1775, done on copper plate, and easily discovered. On the back of the genuine bill the word Philadelphia is spelled *Philadelpkia*, and that of the counterfeit properly. The figure of the lower ship in the true bill, especially its bottom is much blacker and less discernable than in the counterfeit; and the paper of the latter is much thinner and smoother and in that of the counterfeit in the upper *ship* a ray of light appears between it and the representation of the sea, which is not so in the genuine bill.'[8]

Surgeon James Thacher especially enjoyed the early spring:

'We have passed a winter remarkably mild and moderate; since the 10th of January, we have scarcely had a fall of snow, or a frost, and no severe weather. At the beginning of this month [April] the weather was so mild that vegetation began to appear; the fruit trees were budded on the first, and in full blossom on the 10th. In Virginia the peach trees were in blossom on the 14th of February, but a small frost since, has, it is feared, proved fatal to the fruit.'[9]

Still, soft spring breezes called men home to their families now that it was time for the early planting. Frequent desertions called for stern measures. Peter Ten Broeck, his fat Dutch face unmoved by emotion, looked on as discipline was tightened:

'We hear there is a great Number of Men Deserts Dayly both to and from the enemy [the Americans]; yesterday three men belonging to the Maryland line were found going in to the enemy, they were brought to their camp. The one was shot and his head cut off and this morning was brought to the Virginia Camp and put on top of the gallows of a man who was executed and hung; the man who was hung it is said to have deserted and repreaved twice before and expected to be repreaved the third time.'[10]

Sir Henry Clinton made his move in late May. Washington earlier had set men to work fortifying positions on Verplanck's Point, which he named Fort Lafayette, and Stony Point which lay directly across the river, both strong points designed to protect King's Ferry. Of the two, Stony Point was considered to be the more important. Located on a jagged precipice one hundred and fifty feet high, the peninsula thrust its rugged face for a half mile towards the middle of the Hudson River. On the land side the slope gradually fell away until it lost itself in a marsh, which at high tide practically made the point an island. On 28 May 1779 the British had descended upon Stony Point; not a shot was fired as its forty defenders took to their heels. On the far side of the river, and in the face of overwhelming odds, the slender garrison at Fort Lafayette meekly surrendered.

Anthony Wayne, still seething over the massacre of Baylor's troops, had been given the command of an elite corps of light infantry, and begged for an opportunity to storm Stony Point. On the morning of 15 July, Wayne marched thirteen miles to within a mile and a half of their objective. At eight that evening they were ordered to draw the charges from their muskets, fix bayonets and attach white pieces of paper to their hats for identification. A New York paper carried the story:

'July 16, This morning General Wayne, with the light infantry, consisting of about twelve hundred men, . . . surprised the British garrison, consisting of five hundred men, commanded by a Colonel Johnson, in their works at Stony Point, . . . and made the whole prisoners, . . .

The detachment marched in two divisions, and about one o'clock came up to the enemy's pickets, who, by firing their pieces, gave the alarm, and with all possible speed ran to the fort, from every quarter of which, in a short time, they made an incessant fire upon our people. They, with fixed bayonets and uncharged pieces, advanced with quick but silent motion, through a heavy fire of cannon and musketry, till getting over the abbatis, and scrambling up the precipice, the enemy called out, "Come on, ye damn'd rebels; come on!" Some of our people softly answered, "Don't be in such a hurry, my lads; we will be with you presently." And accordingly in a little more than twenty minutes from the time the enemy first began to fire, our troops, overcoming all obstructions and resistance, entered the fort.

Spurred on by their resentment of the former cruel bayoneting, which many of them and others of our people had experienced, and the more recent and savage barbarity of plundering and burning unguarded towns, murdering old and unarmed men, abusing and forcing women, and reducing multitudes of innocent people from comfortable livings to the most distressful want of the means of subsistence; . . . our men entered the fort with the resolution of putting every man to the sword; but the cry "Mercy! Mercy! dear Americans! mercy! quarter! brave Americans! quarter! quarter!" disarmed their resentment in an instant . . . O Britain! turn thy eye inwards, —behold, and tremble at thyself. . . .

Among the prisoners are two sons of Beverley Robinson (of New York, now a Colonel in the service of the enemy against his country!) and a son of the late Dr. Auchmuty, late rector of Trinity Church. It was with great difficulty these three were saved by our officers from being sacrificed to the resentment of the soldiery, who were about to retaliate upon them with bayonets, (the usage our people have repeatedly received from British troops,) they begged for mercy, and to excite pity, said they were Americans. This plea proving them to be traitors as well as enemies, naturally increased the fury of the soldiers, who were on the point of plunging bayonets into their breasts, when they were restrained by their officers.'[11]

Baron von Steuben, an expert in the ways of exaggeration, coached the messenger carrying the news to Congress. Captain Henry Archer, a volunteer aide under Wayne, reported his entry into Philadelphia to his general:

'I came into the city with Colours flying, Trumpet sounding, and heart elated, drew crowds to the doors and windows, and made a little parade I assure you—these were Baron Stubens instructions and I pursued them literally, tho' I could not help thinking it had a little of the appearance of a puppet show.'[12]

Militarily, Stony Point was of little value to the Americans. The post was

230

abandoned after its armament was removed and its walls levelled. Clinton immediately reoccupied the position, rebuilt the works and installed a stronger garrison. But its capture had been a great boost to American morale.

Wayne basked in glory, receiving a gold medal from Congress; his exploit was hailed throughout the country as a great victory. This, in turn, excited the ambitions of a young Virginia major who strutted about camp in the green tunic of the elite cavalry corps under his command. Henry Lee selected as his stepping stone to fame the British outpost at Paulus Hook, on the Jersey side of the Hudson directly across from New York. By contrast with Stony Point, Paulus Hook was a low-lying sand spit, with something of the characteristics of an island in that a creek separated it from the mainland. Washington allowed himself to be talked into approving the scheme, yet was fearful that 'We should lose more in case of failure, than we would gain in case of success. . . .' Although the commanding general

177. A Plan of the Surprise of Stoney Point . . . 15th July 1779. Also of the Works erected on Verplanks Point, for the Defence of King's Ferry . . . Printed for Wm Faden. *John Hills*

Stony Point is across the Hudson River from Verplanck's Point at the northern end of Tappan Zee; these two 'Pillars of Hercules', Washington thought, were 'the key to the continent'.

John Hills, draftsman and surveyor through the war for the British, became a lieutenant of Engineers during the conflict and is entered in the British army lists as second lieutenant of the 23rd Regiment of Foot from October 1781 to 1784. His series of manuscript maps of New Jersey, finely drawn and executed, was gathered into an atlas for General Clinton. Now in the Library of Congress, it is the only atlas of a province made during the Revolution.

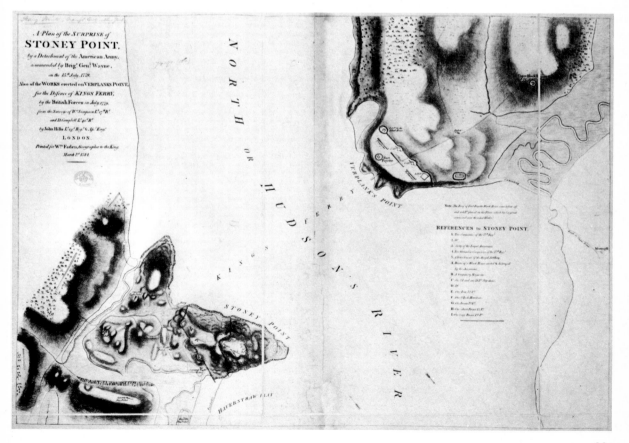

was later to term the 'success brilliant', his opinion was not shared by Captain W. Crogham, whose report was more of a critical review than a narrative:

'I suppose you have a variety of accounts of the sacking of the Garrison at Powel's Hook, which was taken by surprise about 3 o'clock on the morning of the 19th inst. [August], and instantly evacuated by us after doing no greater damage than taking 7 officers and about 160 Rank & File prisoners and killing about 20 in the Garrison. We have about 7 privates missing.

Had not the officer who Commanded—Major Lee—been in so great a hurry from the Garrison, much more execution might have been done, as they did not take time to carry off all the prisoners, or even to take a Major & party of men who were then in their power. Not the least damage whatever was done to the Garrison. The Magazine was not blown up, the Barracks not sett on fire, the Cannon not spiked, no article of Stores, Clothing, &c., &c., of which a great plenty were there, was the least damaged; in fact, nothing further was done than rushing into the Garrison in confusion & driving out the prisoners, mostly without their cloths.

Perhaps there still will be an enquiry into the reason of the confusion and great haste the party made to get out of the fort, without destroying so many valuable stores in their possession. Several officers have been much injured in the Virginia line, on account of giving Major Lee the command of 300 of our men to reduce Powel's Hook, and unjust methods taken by him to have the command, by telling one of our Majors, who marched with the 300 men, that his commission was older than it really is—otherwise he would not have had the command over him. I believe Major Lee will be arrested.'[13]

Lee knew he would be criticized for his sloppy operation, and in his initial report tried to explain away his shortcomings; he did not mention that the enemy garrison was made up of convalescent invalids. He defended his actions thus:

'I intended to have burnt the barracks; but on finding a number of sick soldiers and women with young children in them, humanity forbade the execution of my intention. The key to the magazine could not be found, nor could it be broken open in the little time we had to spare, many attempts having been made to that purpose by the Lieutenants M'Callister and Reed. It was completely impracticable to bring off any pieces of artillery. I consulted with Captain Bradford on this point, who confirms me in my opinion. The circumstance of spiking being trivial, it was omitted altogether.'[14]

In retrospect, the taking of Paulus Hook seems little more than an exercise in bluster, but even tarnished victories were needed in the summer of 1779. Skirmishes were blown up into battles, and laurels placed upon the brows of Wayne and Lee. War often includes, and needs, such trivia. Some of the British blamed Clinton, for many considered him no military man but merely Sir William Howe's successor. In his first letter home, J. Mervin North was to castigate the commander-in-chief:

'Since our arrival nothing has happened sufficiently important to deserve your attention, and (entre nous) we expect nothing greater under our present commander. Nothing, surely can be more shameful than our perfect inactivity through the whole summer and autumn. Not a single attempt has been made to annoy the enemy, although, exclusive of our sick, we have had a full twenty thousand men in arms in the environs of this city ever since the arrival of the fleet from Europe. But it is unfortunately our fate to be commanded by a person that has no abilities to plan, nor firmness to execute, the most trivial military operation.

I don't by any means pretend to have the second sight, but I believe you must recollect that last spring I foretold the inglorious campaign we ought to expect under our *adventurous* knight. The campaign before Charles Town, some years since, was such a series of misconduct that it was not to be expected administration of this army would be better conducted by the same commander. For God's sake let us have a man of resolution or abilities! It would, without doubt, be better to have those qualities united in the same person; but to have an ignorant, irresolute commander is the excess of madness in administration, and will prove, I am much afraid, the ruin of our cause on this side of the Atlantic.'[15]

But discontent was not limited to the British. There were many former colonists who now felt that the seeds of democracy sown in the Declaration of Independence were bearing a bitter fruit. Thomas Hughes, a British officer and prisoner of war in Lancaster, Pa., witnessed the rumblings of the democratic spirit during a local celebration:

'*July 4th.* This day being the anniversary of American independence, the militia paraded in great pomp and fired; but in the afternoon these sons of liberty being a little elated took it into their heads to attack a set of the chief people in the town who were making merry at a tavern on this joyous occasion. The only reason for this assault was the militia being affronted at the gentlemen drinking by themselves—they were thinking that there ought to be no distinction but all get drunk together. The affair ended in breaking some windows—for on this salutation the gentlemen (as they call themselves) sallied forth sword in hand and routed the mobile. I am in hopes it will not end so quietly as the vanquish'd denounce vengeance.
July 16th. The mob rose this even—and paraded through the streets to beat the gentleman party. One unfortunate hero fell into their hands and they thrash'd him very soundly.'[16]

Politics annoyed many. Thomas Paine, now serving as a clerk for the Pennsylvania Assembly, noted:

'As to Politics, they are at all at a stand. The world, I believe, are looking at one another. A quick Peace, or a long War, will, I think, shortly Commence. . . . A Drawn Battle, or no battle, is my wish at the present. . . . We are making laws here like fury—twice as many as any country wants:— however we have a bill for a monthly Tax of 2,500,000 dollars pr. month for eight months. God knows where the money is to come from, if nobody has got more than myself. But 'tis a Tax of quick digestion, and as the money will be out again almost as soon as it is in, perhaps we shall rub thro'.'[17]

And with inactivity it became necessary for the commander-in-chief to engage in diplomatic niceties:

'*Sept. 15, 1779*—His Excellency Gen. Washington and Gen. Green with there Addecamps went to New Winsor the honourable Chevalier Le De Luzerne and Emobasender from the Court of France and accompanied him to Head Quarters at West Point and when they arrived they was Receeved and wellcomed with the selute of Drums and fifes and the gard present there arms. They arrived at three in the afternoon and at five there was thirteen Cannon fired from the fourt on account of his arrival.'[18]

It was late November before Washington made up his mind to go into winter quarters. He selected Morristown, New Jersey, as a place that could be easily defended and one from which British activities could be watched. It was the time to move, for the winter of 1779–80 was to become one of the coldest on record, with the Hudson freezing over between New York and Paulus Hook with ice so thick it was 'practicable for the heaviest Cannon, an Event unknown in the Memory of Man'. Although usually billeted in comfortable quarters, many general officers were concerned as to the comfort of their men. Hot-headed Anthony Wayne was not

'much pleased at the prospect of once more Clothing our Officers & Soldiers. I must confess that the latter would make a better appearance had they a sufficiency of *hatts*—but as Congress don't seem to think *that* an essential or necessary part of Uniform—they mean to leave us uniformly bare headed —as well as bare footed—& if they find we can *bare* it tolerably well in the two extremes—perhaps they may try it in the *Center*.'[19]

The men needed clothing. Soon after the first of the year, Private Martin huddled close to the fire as

'there came on several severe snow-storms. At one time it snowed the greater part of four days successively, and there fell nearly as many feet of snow and here was the keystone of the arch of starvation. We were absolutely, literally starved;—I do solemnly declare that I did not put a single morsel of Victuals into my mouth for four days and as many nights, except a little black birch bark which I knawed off a stick of wood, if that can be called victuals.

I saw several of the men roast their old shoes and eat them, and I was afterwards informed by one of the officers' waiters, that some of the officers killed and ate a favourite little dog that belonged to one of them.—If this was not "suffering" I request to be informed what can pass under that name; if "suffering" like this did not "try men's souls," I confess that I do not know what could.

The fourth day, just at dark, we obtained a half pound of lean fresh beef and a gill of wheat for each man, whether we had any salt to season so delicious a morsel, I have forgotten, but I am sure we had no bread, (except the wheat,) but . . . we had the best of sauce; that is, we had keen appetites. When the wheat was so swelled by boiling as to be beyond the danger of swelling in the stomach, it was deposited there without ceremony.

After this, we sometimes got a little beef, but no bread; we, however, once in a while got a little rice, but as for flour or bread, I do not recollect that I saw a morsel of either (I mean wheaten) during the winter, all the bread kind we had was Indian meal.'[20]

Many of the British soldiers stationed in New York escaped the cold for Clinton held little fear of the American army. He and Lord Cornwallis sailed off on an expedition against Charleston in South Carolina. General Knyphausen was left in command. With their officers away British troops became a bit more boisterous. Sergeant von Kraft, of the Hessian forces, was disgusted with the behaviour of one British trooper:

'An amusing incident, which seemed, however, to us Germans to be a repulsive occurrence must be related here. I met a soldier of the 38*th* English regiment who asked me to tell him where our clergyman [chaplain] lived. He said they had none in their regiment and the one in Donop's regiment had refused, when he desired to be married to a woman whose acquaintance he had made in the street a few hours before. He said he had received permission from the commander of his regiment to marry. I gave him a short answer, but could not help laughing and proceeded on my way. Such things and a thousand others of like or worse character were not rare here. A certain Sergeant of the above named English regiment, a handsome young fellow, had been married sixteen times to loose women of the town by different English and German chaplains, through shrewd contrivances, without the consent of his officers and told me he hoped to do so often again, before making up his mind in real earnest.'[21]

Not until June did the British move out of New York. The American Lieutenant John Shreve had been stationed in the Amboy area and reported the British thrust into Jersey:

'After the British Gen. Clinton arrived at New York from Charlestown in South Carolina with troops, Gen. Knyphausen, being reinforced, came out with nine or ten thousand men to destroy our stores at Morristown. Maxwell had but about fifteen hundred men, but the militia and Gen. Green with troops came to our assistance. My father's regiment, with Col. Angel's regiment of Rhode Island troops, contended with the enemy at the bridge east of the town of Springfield; after their pioneers had relaid the bridge and crossed over, we were forced to retire to the bridge west a quarter of a mile, of the town and in a fair view of it, where we met Gen Greene and several thousand militia. The enemy burnt all the town, but two or three houses belonging to Tories, and retreated rapidly to Elizabethtown and crossed over to Staten Island. We followed them, but no engagement was brought on. The inhabitants residing on the road said they had thirty wagons on their retreat, all filled with their dead and wounded.'[22]

One reason for the British withdrawal was that Benedict Arnold had sent Clinton treasonable information that the French expeditionary force of General Rochambeau was expected soon at Newport. Rather than be caught between the two armies, with a part of his command dispersed, Clinton recalled them. But for the rebels it was a victory, and many tales circulated of a frightened beaten enemy.

Thomas Hughes called it only 'A very pretty expedition: six thousand men having penetrated 12 miles into the country—burnt a village and returned.' But soldiers boasted of their prowess, as did Simon Bogart to a friend of his college days:

'Should the enemy have presumption enough to lead them to an Attack upon our Works in the Highlands, You will hear of Bloody Noses. They have last Friday experienced the resoluteness of our Troops the' only a small detachment to give them a sample of what they might expect.'[23]

No one realized it at the time, but Springfield marked the end of the longest phase of the war in the northern theatre. Few Americans realized that the war could be winding down. Spain, in anticipation of regaining Gibraltar, had allied herself with France against England and in February 1780 Russia, Denmark and Sweden, with other nations to join later, formed the League of Armed Neutrality for the protection of their shipping against arbitrary seizure by the British. Troops were needed more in England, especially with the unhappy situation in Ireland and with the civilian population restless. From Paris, John Adams wrote to Nathanael Greene:

'Every operation of your Army has its influence upon all the powers of Europe—in France, Spain, England, Ireland, Holland, Sweden, Denmark, Russia, Prussia, Portugal, and even in the German empire.

America is the City, set upon a Hill, I do not think myself guilty of exaggeration, vanity or Presumption, when I say, that the proceedings of Congress are more attended to, than those of any Court in Europe, & the motion of our Armies than any of theirs—and there are more political Lies made and circulated about both, than all the rest: which renders genuine Intelligence, from good Authority, the more interesting & important.

There is a great Variety of Policy on foot in England, Ireland, Holland, and among the northern Powers, all tending to favour the Cause of America, which is promoted by nothing more than by prompt and accurate intelligence.'[24]

And French aid had now become more than a promise. In October 1779, Clinton pulled the British garrison from Newport. On 10 July 1780 a French fleet had stood in for the harbour and disembarked 6,000 troops under the Comte de Rochambeau, who was quick to reassure the Rhode Islanders that his was merely the vanguard of a much larger force. This, however, proved but a well-intentioned promise, for no sooner had the French settled in Newport than a British fleet blockaded the port, while a similar squadron blocked Brest on the French coast. Not until 20 September did Washington and the French general meet in Hartford. The young Swedish count serving as aide to Rochambeau, Jean Axel de Fersen, described the meeting for his father:

'An interview was arranged between the generals, Washington and Rochambeau. I was sent on slightly in advance to announce Rochambeau's approach, and thus had an opportunity of studying this most illustrious man of our century (not to say the *only one*). His majestic, handsome countenance is stamped with an honesty and a gentleness which corresponds well with his moral qualities. He looks like a hero; he is very cold, speaks little, but is frank and courteous in manner; a tinge of melancholy affects his whole bearing, which is not unbecoming; on the contrary it renders him, if possible, more interesting . . .

During our stay in Hartford, the two generals and the Admiral were closeted together all day. The Marquis de Lafayette acted as interpreter, as General Washington does not speak French nor understand it. They separated, quite charmed with one another; at least they said so.'[25]

It was after Washington rode out of Hartford, on his way for a visit to West Point, that the world suddenly seemed to explode; Benedict Arnold had turned traitor! Arnold was a man of complex psychology. He had been indomitable in courage and initiative on the Patriot side in the first

178. Count de Rochambeau, French General of the Land Forces in America Reviewing the French Troops. *T. Colley*

When Rochambeau and his army of 5,500 arrived off Rhode Island, British rage was soon expressed in caricature. Rochambeau, holding a large spear with a fleur-de-lys head, stands on the right. He faces three soldiers and an officer with large shirt frills; three privates stand behind. The French have exaggeratedly long noses and chins; this feature, their effeminacy, and their gauntness because of their diet were stock fare for British cartoonists.

236

years of the war. In 1779 he claimed that he had been unable to take the field in an active command because of his wounded leg and asked for, and received, the position of military commandant of Philadelphia. He had met, wooed and married eighteen-year-old Peggy Shippen, daughter of a well-to-do loyalist, as his second wife. She was both beautiful and demanding. After the council of Pennsylvania accused him of mismanagement of army funds and materials, a court martial found him guilty of misconduct in office, and Arnold received a reprimand from Washington. The high military rank which he craved still eluded him. Shortly thereafter the commanding general had granted his request that he be given the command of the strategic post at West Point on the Hudson. Sulking, Arnold had earlier opened correspondence with Clinton, offering to turn over West Point if he could but gain the command.

For the Governor of Maryland, Henry Lee reconstructed the first stages of treason:

'The object in view was the betraying West Point into the hands of the enemy. Appearances were to be kept up, the place was to have been surrendered on terms of capitulation, and Mr. Arnold, a general in our service, on parole. In other words, the object was the subjugation of America.

Sir Henry Clinton committed the management of this important business to Major André, a young gentleman equal in eminence to any the world

COUNT DE ROCHAMBEAU   25 Nov. 1780
French General of the Land Forces in America Reviewing the French Troops

237

179. Cypher letter from Arnold to André, 12 July 1780

The treasonous correspondence of Benedict Arnold with General Clinton covered more than a year (1779–80). Arnold used the name 'John Moore'; for most of the time his correspondent was Major André, Clinton's adjutant-general in charge of intelligence, signing himself 'John Anderson'. Nearly broken off at one time, the correspondence quickened in importance for the British as Arnold's identity was revealed, and he began to suggest his ability to hand over West Point and the control of the Hudson; Washington gave him that command on 4 August 1779. This cypher letter of the month before refers to the expected arrival of the French fleet.

ever produced. Major André came up the North river in an armed sloop, & lay near King's ferry, at which place we have two small posts. King's ferry is distant from West Point between 12 and 16 miles.

Gen. Arnold, by means of a Mr. Joshua Smith, held a conference with Major André in the night on the shore of the river. From the shore they adjourned to this Mr. Smith's house, one mile into the country. Here matters were completely signed. The American Gibraltar betrayed, & the traitor secured, as to the reception of the bribe.

They prepared to return, Arnold to W. Point, André to Vulture. Some embarrassment arose as to getting on board again, the two peasants who had landed Major André having been up the night before, & most of that night, were loth to assist when called upon. It was then proposed to spend the day in secret at Smith's house. André consented. Arnold left him. In the evening, André & his guide, Smith, set out, and by virtue of Gen. Arnold's pass they uninterruptedly crossed King's ferry. André left his regimental coat in Mr. Smith's house, & wore one borrowed from Mr. Smith.

Mr. Smith conveyed his charge safe to a solitude without the line of our usual patrols, & left him pushing for New York. Fortunately, when very near the enemy's advance post, he met with three young militia men, whom quest for plunder had carried thus far. Major André accosted them, asking them from whence—replied from below. Above & below are country terms on the lines for the American & B[ritish] armies. André in his transport of joy, discovered to them that he was a B[ritish] officer. The lads instantly seized him. He made every attempt on the virtue of his captors. Ten thousand guineas were assured to them, & every necessary of life was lavishly proffered—all in vain.

André was brought a prisoner to our advanced horse guards. Papers announcing the object of his mission were found about him. Arnold's villainy was also discovered. Yet, so blundering was the officer in his measures, that he contrived to give the first notice of the capture of the spy to Mr. Arnold, & consequently furnished Arnold with time to escape. This was erroneous, not intentional. Arnold made the best use of this notice, & got to the Vulture under sanctity of a flag. The poor bargemen whom he made use of on this occasion were, at his instance, retained as prisoners of war. André and Smith were brought to camp for trial.'[26]

Count de Fersen heard of Arnold's action before he fled to the Vulture:

'At the same time Washington arrived at West Point; he sends two of his aids-de-camp to General Arnold to invite him to dine with him, and goes in person to visit the forts. The aids-de-camp find him at breakfast with his wife. A moment after they had seated themselves a person comes in who whispers a word into the ear of the General [Arnold], who rises and says a word in an undertone to his wife; this word was: *"Good bye forever"*—and goes out.

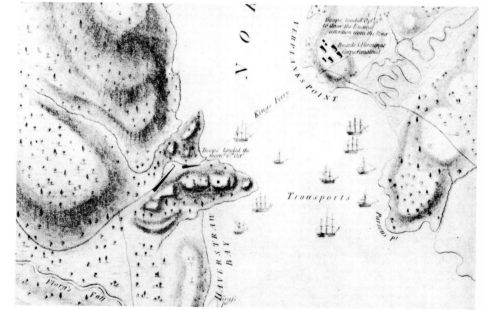

180. King's Ferry at Stony Point (detail). *Stedman*

Major André crossed the Hudson at King's Ferry on 22 September; he was captured near Tarrytown. The forts on either side of the river were still in Patriot hands after General Wayne's exploit of 15 July. They were retaken by Clinton on 6 October in the action shown on this map.

THE *Taking of* MAJOR ANDRE.
By the Incorruptible PAULDING, WILLIAMS and VANVERT.

181. The Taking of Major André by the Incorruptible Paulding, Williams and Vanvert. *T. W. Freeman*

André, persuaded by Arnold and Smith that it was impossible to return to the *Vulture*, assumed a disguise for the overland journey to New York. This disguise, and the incriminating papers found in his shoes, led to his designation as a spy and to his ultimate execution. Here he is captured at Tarrytown by three men, variously described as 'militiamen', 'bushmen', 'volunteers', and 'American prowlers, or skinners'. He thought they were British, and made the mistake of admitting that he was a British officer. After that, neither Arnold's pass nor his offer of money availed him. He said to them, ' "If you will not trust my honor two of you may stay with me, and one shall go with a letter I shall write [to the British]. Name your sum" . . . They held a consultation a considerable time, and finally they told him, if he wrote a party would be sent out to take them, and they would all be prisoners.' For this reason, Paulding, Williams and Vanvert remained 'incorruptible'.

Freeman was listed as a carver and gilder in Philadelphia in 1813.

The wife falls into a swoon. The aids-de-camp assist her without understanding the meaning of the scene; and some minutes after arrives the courier who brings the news to General Washington. The traitor is pursued, but it is too late.'[27]

In the old Dutch church in Sleepy Hollow at Tappan (often called Orangeburg), a court martial, presided over by Nathanael Greene, on Sunday 1 October 1780, found 'that Major André, Adj*t*-general to the British Army, ought to be considered as a Spy from the Enemy, and that agreeable to the Law and Usage of Nations, it is their opinion he ought to Suffer death'. André had entered enemy territory, forsaken his uniform for a civilian disguise, and been caught with incriminating papers; he was legally a spy, as had been young Nathan Hale, the Connecticut schoolteacher executed by the British in 1776. Washington ordered the sentence to be carried out on 2 October.

Although André had written to Clinton, 'I am perfectly tranquil in mind and prepared for any Fate to which an honest Zeal for my Kings Service may have devoted me', the British general made every effort to save him,

182. General Anthony Wayne. *Edward Savage*

General Wayne was one of Washington's officers who served throughout the war, from his first hot fight with a superior British force at Three Rivers in the Canadian campaign of 1776 to his victory over hostile Creek Indians in Georgia after Yorktown.

240

184. Self-portrait.
Major John André

André sketched himself in captivity, on 1 October 1780, the day before his execution, at ease beside his writing table, relaxed, handsome, and debonair. The quill pen with which he has written his famous request to Washington, asking no clemency but a gentlemanly manner of death, is on the table beside him. He had extraordinary style, and would well have understood the dictum, 'The style is the man.'

183. Colonel Guy Johnson and Joseph Brant. *Benjamin West*

This famous and effective portrait of Sir Guy Johnson, British Superintendent of Indian Affairs in the north, with his Indian ally Joseph Brant looming menacingly behind him, seems to express better than words the dichotomy of feeling which both British and Americans had about the enlistment of Indians in the Revolutionary War, practised by both sides.

short of returning Arnold to the Americans. A newspaper reported the proceedings:

'General Robertson came up yesterday to Dobb's Ferry with a flag, which was soon dismissed, it being of so trite a nature, viz. to entreat his Excellency General Washington, at the request of Sir Henry Clinton, to use lenity on Major André. It had the effect to respite him for a few hours, as the flag did not return until after five o'clock, which was the hour fixed in general orders for his execution. . . .

The flag mentioned to have come out with General Robertson was received by General Green and Colonel Hamilton; and what is curious, Arnold sent his resignation by desire that General Washington should forward it to Congress, with an insolent letter intimating he never would serve Congress any more, *nor need they expect it*; and, moreover, if Major André should be executed by order of General Washington, that he would strike a blow at some of his friends on the continent that should sufficiently retaliate for the loss to his Prince. General Green, when he had read the letter, treated it with contempt and threw it on the ground before General Robertson, which he might return to the traitor if he thought proper.'[28]

Years later, Benjamin Russell recorded his memories of the execution for Surgeon James Thacher:

'Major André was executed on the 2d of October, 1780, in the Dutch village of Tappan (Orangetown). He was dressed in the rich uniform of a British staff officer, with the exception, of course, of sash, gorget, sword and spurs. The place of execution was near the centre of the encampment of the American Grand Army, and in full view of many of its regiments. The lofty gibbet was surrounded by an exterior guard of nearly five hundred infantry, with an inner guard of a captain's command. None were admitted inside the square but the officers on duty and the Assistants of the Provost Marshal. The spectators outside the square were very numerous. Proceeding to the place of execution, under the above guard, André was accompanied by two officers of the inner guard, which he at first thought had been detailed as his executioners. He had previously requested of General Washington the favor of dying the death of a soldier. The mode of death the high sense of duty of the Commander-in-Chief could not grant, and his delicacy forbade him to announce his determination in an answer. The officers of the American Army performing duty on horseback, with General Green at their head, were formed in a line on the road. To those, whom Major André knew, particularly those who made part of the Board of General Officers who pronounced his fate, he paid the salute of the hat, and received the ADIEUS of all with ease and complacency. The Commander-in-Chief and Staff were not present at the execution; and this mark of decorum, I was told, was feelingly appreciated by the sufferer. . . .

When the procession on the main road, the gallows was not visible; but when it wheeled at an angle, the place of execution was seen directly in front. On viewing it, the sufferer made a halt, and exhibited emotion. To an inquiry made by the captain of the guard, Major André gave the answer . . . , *"I am reconciled to my death, but detest the mode of it."* The captain rejoined—*"It is unavoidable, sir."* Arrived at the scaffold, André after a short conversation with his servant, (who arrested much attention by the vehemence of his grief and loud lamentation) ascended with gaiety the baggage-wagon. The General Order of execution was then read. . . . The reading was very impressive, and at the conclusion Major André uncovered, bowed to the General and other Officers and said with dignity and firmness, *"All I request of you, gentlemen, is that you will bear witness to the world that I die like a brave man."* He added nothing more aloud, but while the preparations for immediate execution were being made, he said, in an under tone, *"it will be but a momentary pang."*

Thus died Major John André, Adjutant-General to the British Army. The sympathy of the American Officers was universally expressed, and the Father of our country, in announcing his death to Congress, pronounced that he met his fate like a brave man. . . . I saw the servant of André receive the military hat and stock of his master, immediately before the execution. I did not see the body placed in the coffin, but I did see, as I marched by the grave, that servant standing near it, and evidently overseeing the interment.'[29]

One British soldier described the reaction of the British in New York:

'Genl. Arnold is made a Brig*dr* in our service. He has published a Memorial to his Countrymen in behalf of the step he has taken. . . . We are going on a expedition, I believe, to the Southward. The Troops are embarked *who* vow Revenge with Vengeance on those who fall into their Hands for Andrie's Death. The first news you hear of the expedition expect a great Carnage. When the account arrived at York the Soldiers lips vibrated Andrie Andrie & the streets reechoed Vengeance with the bayonet to the sons of Rebillion.'[30]

185. The Allies—Par nobile Fratrum!
There was no more savage subject of controversy during the American Revolution than the British policy of using the Indians as allies. In this cartoon made by one signing himself 'Indignatio', published in February 1780, King George, under the tattered royal standard, is sharing the cannibalistic meal of the Indians. The Bible is upside down. The large, approving clergyman is probably Markham, the belligerent Archbishop of York, who appears in several Whig cartoons. The dog alone vomits.

242

11. War in the West

To the west, along the fringes of and beyond the frontier, there was a different war being fought. On the eastern seaboard, battles were conducted in formal fashion, in which men in formation met other men in formation, fired their cannon, muskets and rifles, accompanied by dashing dragoons and bloody bayonet charges, then withdrew to lick their wounds and prepare for another battle. Beyond the edge of civilization, war often came without warning on quiet feet and bringing sudden and violent death. It was the silent warfare of the tomahawk and the scalping knife as opposed to the controlled thunder of artillery and the crackle of musketry.

The Indians had been of great concern to both rebels and redcoats, each seeking the red men as allies. The rebels, wishing to avoid a two-front war, urged the Indians to remain neutral if they did not choose to aid the Americans. One address to the Iroquois ran, 'Brothers and friends! . . . This is a family quarrel between us and Old England. You Indians are not concerned in it.' And a treaty drawn up with the Indians at Fort Pitt made the promise that good relations were to last between the two parties 'until the sun shall shine no more, or the waters fail to run in the Ohio'. Although

THE ALLIES._ *Par nobile fratrum!*

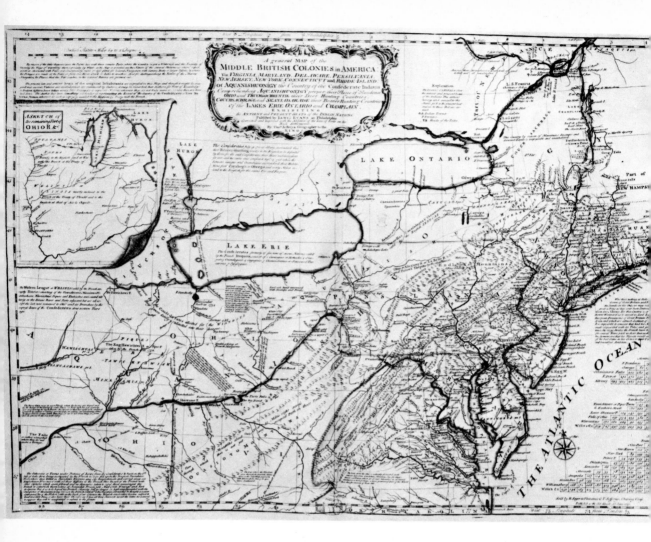

186. Middle British Colonies in America. *Lewis Evans*

One of the few great maps of the colonial period, this work by Evans, of which over twenty-seven issues and editions have been identified, was extensively used during the Revolution. It was one of six maps included in Sayer and Bennett's *American Military Pocket Atlas* (1776), known as the 'Holster Atlas' because it was made for mounted British officers. From the North Carolina–Virginia boundary line the map extends north to Montreal and from Rhode Island west to the falls of the Ohio. West of the Allegheny mountains the increasing inaccuracy and sparseness of information is obvious; little was then known of that area. Evans was a Philadelphian; his chief contribution was to the province of Pennsylvania.

Evans's work was the product of extensive geographical, scientific, and political study and insight. From his own observation and travel as well as from the reports of the best qualified surveyors and Indian traders, Evans accumulated information which he incorporated in a series of manuscript and printed maps of increasing accuracy and detail. Despite their inaccuracies, his delineation of territories west of the established settlements was of especial importance. An earlier manuscript version of this map was used by General Braddock in planning his campaign against the French in 1755.

244

there were no perceptible changes in either sun or river, both sides broke their pledges and the raw frontier ran red with blood.

The rebels had first utilized the services of Indians during the siege of Boston by the employment of the tame Stockbridge tribe, the use of whom gave Thomas Gage the opportunity to write to Lord Dartmouth in June 1775: 'We need not be tender of calling on the Savages, as the rebels have shown us the example, by bringing as many Indians down against us here as they could collect.' And six weeks later Lord George Germain was answering that 'It is therefore His Majesty's pleasure, that you lose no time in taking such steps as may induce them to take up the hatchet against his Majesty's rebellious subjects in America. . . .'

Fort Niagara became the home base for the Indian and Tory raiders operating under the commands of John Butler, his son Walter and the Mohawk war-chief who bore the Indian name of Thayendanegea, but was more commonly known as Joseph Brant. In the west, Fort Niagara's counterpart was Fort Detroit under Lieutenant-Colonel Henry Hamilton, lieutenant-governor of Canada. Although many raids went unnoticed in the east, it was the defeat and massacre of early July 1778 that excited the anger of the seaboard states. At that time a tale of carnage came out of the Wyoming Valley in Pennsylvania, its name coming from the Delaware Indian word meaning 'upon the great plain'. The Valley stretched for twenty-five miles along the Susquehanna River below the mouth of the Lackawanna. Its primary protection was two blockhouses called Fort Jenkins and Forty Fort, the latter named for the first forty Connecticut settlers in the area. The Butlers had swooped down from Niagara in July to attack the fort commanded by John Butler's cousin, Colonel Zebulon Butler. A year later, when the Reverend William Rogers visited the scene, he received a first-hand account of the massacre and rode out to

'take a view of the noted place where the battle was fought July 3, 1778,

187. A log cabin.
Collot
The frontiersman cleared the land around his house, building it of logs that he had felled. The house was usually near a spring or stream. This cabin can be considered characteristic of many eighteenth-century pioneer homes.

George Collot, who fought under Rochambeau during the Revolution and became governor of Guadaloupe, returned to America for a visit in 1796. This drawing was not published until 1826.

between Colonel [John] Butler, with his Tories and savages on one side, five hundred in number, and our Colonel [Zebulon] Butler, on the other with three hundred of the inhabitants, who had formed themselves into militia companies, having nothing but bad muskets without bayonets.

Our people, sallying out of Forty Fort, proceeded to Wintermute's Fort [a loyalist stronghold near the head of the valley], where the enemy, forming their left and extending their right quite to a swamp, were prepared to receive the defenders of their country. Our Colonel Butler, having judiciously drawn up his men in line of battle to oppose the barbarians, a severe firing ensued; six or seven rounds were in a few moments discharged on both sides, when the enemy's centre, fallen a few paces back and a part of their right filing off, our people supposing that they had intentions of surrounding them, instantly got confused and notwithstanding the spirited exertions of their Colonel, a retreat took place and ended in a general rout, which gave rise to the most horrid scene of butchery. Out of our party only one hundred escaped; among these was Colonel Butler.

From many circumstances it appeared Wintermute's fort proved treacherous, old Mr. Wintermute with all his sons and about twenty-five others who composed the garrison, having on the enemy's approach delivered up the fort, without the least opposition, the major part of whom immediately joined the enemy and took up arms against their friends. Moreover it was alleged that they corresponded with the enemy many months before.

The place where the battle was fought may with propriety be called "a place of skulls," as the bodies of the slain were not buried, their bones were scattered in every direction all around; a great number of which for a few days past having been picked up, were decently interred by our people. We passed a grave where seventy-five skeletons were buried; also a spot where fourteen wretched creatures, who having surrendered upon being promised mercy, were nevertheless made immediately to sit down in a ring, and after the savages had worked themselves up to the extreme of fury in their usual manner, by dancing, singing, halloaing, etc., they proceeded deliberately to tomahawk the poor fellows one after another. Fifteen surrendered and composed the ring. Upon the Indians beginning their mark of cruelty, one of them providentially escaped, who reported the matter to Colonel Butler, who upon his return to Wyoming, went to the spot and found the bones of the fourteen lying as human bodies in an exact circle. It is remarkable, that on this spot grows a kind of grass different from all other grass around it. The bones of seven or eight other persons were found nearly consumed, they having been burned to death.

[The American] Colonel Butler related the following occurrence. On a small island in the Susquehannah below the field of action, Giles Slocum, having reached thus far in safety, concealed himself in the bushes, where he was a witness to the meeting of John and Henry Pensell, brothers. John was a Tory and Henry was a whig. Henry, having lost his gun, upon seeing his brother John, fell upon his knees and begged him to spare his life; upon which John called him a damned rebel. John then went deliberately to a log, got on the same, and began to load his piece, while Henry was upon his knees imploring him as a brother not to kill him. "I will," said he, "go with you and serve you as long as I live, if you will spare my life." John loaded his gun. Henry continued, "You won't kill your brother, will you?" "Yes," replied the monster, "I will as soon as look at you, you

188. Blockhouse.
Anburey

Blockhouses were a type of fortification developed on the American frontier; they proved valuable both in preserving peace with the Indians and in giving refuge to settlers during Indian attacks.

'Blockhouses', wrote Anburey, 'are constructed of timbers, placed one on the other, of a sufficient thickness to resist a musket shot, and large enough to contain from 100 to 120 men. . . . In case an enemy should in the night endeavor to set fire to the house, there are loop-holes, through which the troops on the inside can level their pieces and fire upon the assailants. They are reckoned to be a very strong defence, as it has been known that a small body of men, in one of these block-houses, have repulsed treble their number.'

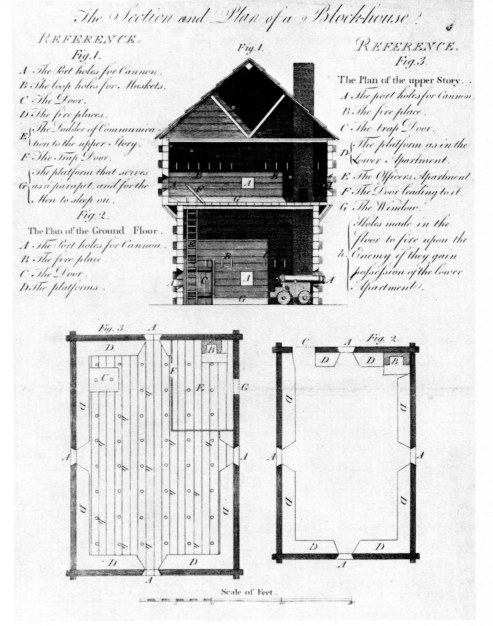

are a damned rebel." He then shot him and afterwards went up and struck him four or five times with a tomahawk and scalped him. Immediately after one of the enemy coming to him said, "What have you been doing, have you killed your brother?" "Yes," said he, "for he was a damned rebel." The other replied, "I have a great mind to serve you in the same manner." They went off together. In the evening, Slocum made his escape. . . .

Colonel Denison, retreated to Forty Fort that night, next day capitulated. The savages, notwithstanding the capitulation, plundered the inhabitants of everything that came in their way; sparing neither woman or child. Good God! who, after such repeated instances of cruelty, can ever be totally reconciled to that government which divesting itself of the feelings of humanity, has influenced the savage tribes and wretchedly to torture to death, persons of each sex and every age—the prattling infant, the blooming maid and persons of venerable years, have alike fallen victim to its vindictive rage.'[1]

This entire summer of 1778 the Indians bore down on frontier settlements. After Colonel William Butler led his Fourth Pennsylvania Continental Regiment and a small detachment of Morgan's riflemen against the Indian town of Unadilla and destroyed it, back came the savages, led by Walter Butler (son of the Tory Colonel John Butler) and Joseph Brant. This time their objective was Cherry Valley, just a few miles from Fort Stanwix.

Colonel Ichabod Alden, commanding a small detachment of Continental troops, had been ordered into the community and had occupied the small village meeting-house which had been surrounded by a stockade. An American officer wrote an account of the events, later published by a New Jersey newspaper:

'On Saturday night, 8th November, an express arrived from Fort Stanwix, informing an Oneida Indian had acquainted them that he sat in Council in the Seneca country with the Six Nations, and other tribes, and that they had concluded to attack Fort Alden, in Cherry Valley.

On Sunday morning a sergeant and twelve men were sent on the road by Beaver Dam, towards the enemy, to continue five days; another scout, with a non-commissioned officer and five men, were sent on the road to Springfield, to continue four days. These two roads being the only avenues from the enemy's country to this place, except an old Indian path, which had been neglected by us; at the same time we sent by the same roads scouts, in the morning, which returned at night.

On Wednesday, the 11th, it rained very hard, the enemy came by the abovementioned path, passed by two houses, and lodged themselves in a swamp a small distance back of Mr. Wells's house, headquarters; half-past eleven A.M. Mr. Hamlin came by and discovered two Indians, who fired upon him and shot him thro' the arm. He rode to Mr. Wells's and acquainted the Colonel, the Lieut. Colonel, Major, and Adjutant being present, the two last (the house at this time being surrounded by the Indians) got to the Fort through their fire, the Colonel was shot near the fort.

The enemy, 800 in number, consisting of 500 Indians commanded by Brant, 50 regulars under Capt. Colvill, and another Captain with some of Johnson's Rangers and above 200 tories, the whole under Col. Butler's command, immediately surrounded the fort, excluding several officers who were quartered out of the garrison and had gone to dinner. They commenced a very heavy fire on the fort, which held three and a half hours, and was as briskly returned. They were answered with three cheers and a discharge of cannon and musketry. At four P.M. the enemy withdrew, Capt. Ballard sallied out with a party, which the enemy endeavoured to cut off, but were prevented by a reinforcement.

The next day they made it their whole business to collect horses, cattle and sheep, which they effected, and at sunset left the place. On Friday morning the fort was reinforced by 800 militia. The enemy killed, scalped, and most barbarously murdered 32 inhabitants, chiefly women and children, also Colonel Alden . . . burned 24 houses with all the grain &c., took above 60 inhabitants prisoners, part of whom they released on going off.

They committed the most inhuman barbarities on most of the dead. Robert Henderson's head was cut off, his scull-bone was cut out with the scalp. Mr. Willis's sister was ripped up; a child of Mr. Willis's, two months old, scalped, and arm cut off; the clergyman's wife, leg and arm cut off; and many others as cruelly treated.

Many of the inhabitants and soldiers, shut out from the fort, lay all night in the rain, with children, which suffered very much. The cattle that were not easy to drive they shot. We were informed by the prisoners that they sent back, that the Lieutenant-Colonel, all the officers and continental soldiers, were stripped and drove naked before them.'[2]

Many of those in the wilderness further west blamed Lieutenant-Colonel Henry Hamilton (British commander of Fort Detroit) for their miseries. It was reported that he, joining the war chant of the Mingo tribe, had told them:

'That he wonder'd to see them so foolish as not to observe that the Big Knife [white man] was come up very near to them, & claimed one half of the water in the Ohio, & that if any of the Indians cross'd over to their side of the River they immediately took him, laid his head on a big Log & chopp'd it off—that he had now put them in a way to prevent such Usage, & that if they met any of them they should strike their Tomahawks into their heads, cutt off some of the hair and bring it to him.'[3]

Such reports and allegations led to Hamilton's acquiring the epithet of 'Hair Buyer'. It has never been proved that he actually bought scalps, but upon one occasion he reported that 129 scalps had been brought in to him, while an inventory of Indian goods at Fort Detroit, dated 5 September 1778, included '150 doz. scalping knives'. And if true, paying a bounty for scalps was not confined to the British. In 1776, New Hampshire had offered £70 for each scalp of a hostile male Indian and £37 10s for each scalp of a woman or of a child twelve years of age.

But a champion for the frontier was beginning to make himself known. Only twenty-six years old, George Rogers Clark was a hard-drinking six-footer whose shock of red hair shaded a sharp nose and 'black, penetrating sparkling eyes'. He had crossed the mountain from Kentucky County down to Williamsburg where he had argued eloquently that 'If a Cuntrey was not worth protecting, it was not worth Claiming.' So impressed were Governor Patrick Henry and the Council of State that he was given a commission as lieutenant-colonel, £1,200 in inflated currency and authorization to raise 350 men for a drive against Detroit on Lake Erie, the post that Clark argued was the root of all frontier evils.

Clark's plan was to float down the Ohio River towards the Mississippi as far as practicable, march through the Illinois country and seize the French settlements of Kaskaskia, Cahokia and Vincennes as stepping-stones towards his primary objective. This was the Illinois territory settled and long held by the French, and only ceded to the British in the Peace of Paris in 1763. By 24 June Clark had gathered 175 men on an island at the Falls of the Ohio. Loaded aboard flatboats, they pushed out into the stream to 'run about a mile up the River in order to gain the main Channel, and shot the Fall at the very moment of the suns being in a great Eclipse which caused Various conjectures among the superstitious'. He came ashore some ten miles below the mouth of the Tennessee River to begin the 120-mile march

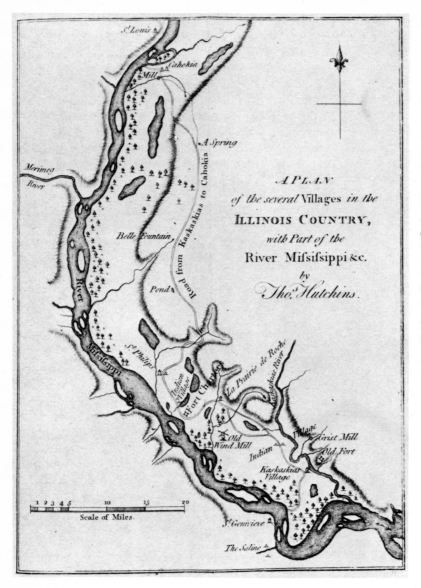

189. A Plan of the several Villages
the Illinois Country. *Hutchin.*

This map was published in London
the year that George Rogers Clar
expedition captured Kaskaskia a
Cahokia. Both places were settled a
inhabited by the French, as was V
cennes, on the Wabash River direc
east of Cahokia. Between these was
Illinois country, which Major Rob
Farmar of the 34th Regiment took o
from the French in 1765.

Thomas Hutchins, a New Jer
surveyor and map-maker, began s
veying the land on both sides of
Ohio in 1764 on an expedition w
Colonel Bouquet. He was a captain
the 60th or Royal American Regime
composed largely of colonial loyalis
when he published this map, w
several others, in his *A Topographi*
History of Virginia. He was suspec
of Patriot sympathies by the Brit
because of his friendship with Ben
min Franklin and other Philadelphia
After the war Washington appoin
him the first geographer of the Uni
States.

overland to Kaskaskia, close to the Mississippi. Even Clark was surprised
at the ease with which the town fell:

'On the evening of the 4th of July, we got within three miles of the town,
Kaskaskias, having a river of the same name to cross to the town . . . we
marched after night to a farm that was on the same side of the river, about
a mile above the town, took the family prisoners, and found plenty of boats
to cross in; and in two hours transported ourselves to the other shore with
the greatest silence.

I learned they had some suspicion of being attacked and had made some
preparations, keeping out spies, but they, making no discoveries, had got
off their guard. I immediately divided my little army into divisions, ordered
one to surround the town, with the other I broke into the fort, secured the
Governor Mr. Rochblave, in 15 minutes had every street secured, sent
runners through the town ordering the people on the pane of death to keep

close to their houses, which they observed and before daylight had the whole disarmed; nothing could excell the confusion these people seemed to be in, being taught to expect nothing but savage treatment from the Americans. Giving all for lost, their lives were all they could dare beg for, which they did with the greatest fervency; they were willing to be slaves to save their families. I told them it did not suit me to give an answer at that time. They repaired to their houses, trembling as if they were led to execution; my principal would not suffer me to distress such a number of people, except, through policy it was necessary; A little reflection convinced me that it was to my Interest to Attach them to me. . . .

I sent for all the Principal Men of the Town who came in as if to a Tribunal that was to determine their fate forever, Cursing their fortune that they were not apprised of us to have defended themselves. I told them that I Was sorry to find that they had been taught to harbour so base an opinion of the Americans and their Cause: Explain'd the nature of the dispute to them in as clear a light as I was capable of, it was certain that they were a Conquered People and by the fate of War was at my mercy, and that our Principal was to make those we Reduced free instead of enslaving them as they imagined, that if I could have surety of their Zeal and attachment to the American Cause, they should immediately enjoy all the privileges of our Government and their property secured to them; that it was only to stop further effusion of Innocent Blood by the Savages under the influence of their Governour, that made them an object of our attention, &c.

No sooner had they heard this than Joy sparkled in their Eyes and [they] fell into Transports of Joy that really surprised me. . . . The Priest . . . was rather prejudiced in favour of us. He asked if I would give him liberty to perform his duty in his Church. I told him I had nothing to do with Churches more than to defend them from Insult. That by the laws of the state his Religion had as great Previledges as any other: This seem'd to compleat their happiness.'[4]

Next in Clark's scheme of conquest was the village of Cahokia, situated across the Mississippi from the Spanish post of St Louis. Captain James Bowman and thirty mounted men sped across the sixty intervening miles and

'Attended by a considerable number of the Inhabitants . . . got into the middle of the Town before they were discovered; the French Gentlemen Calling aloud to the People to submit to their happier fate, which they did with very little hesitation. A number of Indians, being in Town, on hearing of the Big knives, immediately made their escape; in a few days the inhabitants of the Country took the Oath Subscribed by Law, and every Person appeared to be happy. Our friends, the Spanyards, doing everything in their power to convince me of their friendship.'[5]

The villages of Prairie du Rocher and St Phillipe submitted just as quietly, with their inhabitants taking an oath of allegiance to the 'Republic of Virginia'. Vincennes, on the Wabash, came into the fold with even less effort. The priest, Father Gibault, offered to go to that town and persuade the people to submit. By 1 August, Gibault had returned with the information that the American flag was now floating over Fort Sackville in that village. Captain Leonard Helm was sent to take command of the French militia while Clark busied himself with the pacification of the local tribes. All but a hundred of his men went home.

On 6 August 1778 Francis Maisonville trudged into Detroit, reporting to Henry Hamilton the fall of Kaskaskia and 'the shamefull treatment of Monsieur de Rocheblave, who was laid in irons, and put in a place where hogs had been kept, ankle deep in filth, the indignities offered the Madame de Rocheblave, the destruction of his property, &c'. After a journey of 600 miles and seventy-one days, Hamilton arrived before Vincennes with a mixed group of 500 whites and Indians. On 17 December, they could see the American flag whipping wildly in the swirling snow above the fort. Captain Helm, deserted by his French militia, surrendered Fort Sackville with his entire garrison of three Virginians.

When the intelligence that Vincennes had fallen to the British reached Kaskaskia, Clark hastily recruited a force of 170 men, nearly half of whom were French volunteers. On 5 February he marched, his goal some 240 long, cold, wet miles ahead. The muddy prairies and soggy lowlands seemed almost endless, but when within twenty miles of their goal, an almost impossible obstacle stretched out in a shimmering expanse of water before them. They had reached the banks of the Little Wabash, the beginning of the 'drowned lands'. Clark stood on the bank and

'Viewed this sheet of Water for some time with Distrust, but accusing myself of Doubting, I emediately Set to work . . . ordered a Perogue Amediately built and acted as though crossing the water would only be a piece of divertion . . . in the eavening of the 14th our Vesseal was finished, maned and sent to Explore the Drownd Lands with private Instructions what Report to make, and, if possible, to find some spot of dry Land on the Bank of the opposite small River, which they did, about half a Acrae, and marked the Trees from thence to the camp and made a very favourable Report.

Fortunately the 15th happened to be a warm, moist Day for the Season, and the channel of the River whare we lay about Thirty yds wide, a scaffold was built on the opposite Shore that was about 3 feet under water, our Baggage ferroed across and put in it. Our Horse swam across and Received their Loads at the scaffold, by which time the Troops was also brought across, and we begun our march, our Vessell Loaded with those that was sickly, &c. . . .

By the eavening we found our Selves Incamped on a pretty Height in high spirits, Each laughing at the other in consequence of something that had happened in the course of this ferrying business, as they called it, and the whole at the great Exploit as they thought that they had accomplished; thus a little Antick Drummer afforded them great diversion by floating on his Drum, &c. All this was greatly Incouraged and they really began to think themselves superiour to other men, and that neither the Rivers, or seasons could stop their progress.

Their whole conversation now was what they would do when they got about the Enemy, and now began to View the main Wabash as a Creek and Made no Doubt but such men as they were could find a way to cross it. They wound themselves up to such a pitch that they soon took St Vincent, divided the spoil and before Bed time was far advanced on their Route to Detroit.'[6]

By the time they had reached the banks of the Wabash, the false courage had begun to wane into soggy fear and there were murmurings, even though

Vincennes was only six miles away. A scouting party returned with the information that the next high ground was a grove of maples that had been used as a sugar camp. Every eye was on Clark when

'I unfortunately Spoke Serious to one of the Officers—the whole was allarmed without knowing what I said. The[y] ran from one to another, bewailing their Situation. I Viewed their confution for about one minute [and] Whispered to those near to me to [do] as I did—ameliately took some water in my hand, poured on Powder, Blacked my face, gave the war hoop, and marched into the water without saying a word, like a flock of sheep . . . when getting about waist deep, one of the men Informed me that he felt a path (a path is very easyly discovered under water by the Feet). We examined and found it so, and concluded that it keep on the Highest ground which it did. . . .'[7]

Clark composed a dispatch to the inhabitants of Vincennes, suggesting that they remain in their houses or, if they felt so inclined, to hurry to the fort to fight with Hamilton. The American Captain Bowman reported the approach to the town:

'In order to publish this letter, we lay still to about Sun down when we began our March all in order, with Colors flying and drums brased. After wading to the Edge in Water breast high, we mounted the rising ground the town is built on. About 8 o clock Lieu*t* Bayley with 14 Regulars was detached to fire on the fort, while we took possession of the Town—and order'd to stay until he was reliev'd by another party which was soon done—Reconnoitred about to find out a place to throw up Entrenchment, found one and set Cap*t* Bomens comp'y to work. Soon crossed the Main street about 120 yards from the fort Gate . . . fine sport for the sons of Liberty.'[8]

190. An American New Cleared Farm.
Patrick Campbell

Patrick Campbell is in a birch-bark canoe paddled by an Indian; his own dog is in front and an Indian dog behind. The second canoe is paddled by squaws. Various kinds of fencing are shown as well as 8. the dwelling house, with wings; 9. a Dutch barn; 10. a barn roofed with shingles; 12. a shade for wintering Indian corn and an enclosed fold for cattle; 14. a log dwelling house covered with bark; and at the extreme right another barn.

Inside the fort a scout reported spotting fourteen fires. The militia was alerted. Henry Hamilton detailed his defeat:

'About five minutes after the candles were lighted we were alarmed by hearing a musket discharged; presently after, some more. I concluded that some party of Indians was returned or there was some riotous frolic in the village. Going upon the parade to enquire, I heard the balls whistle, ordered the men to the blockhouses, forbidding them to fire till they perceived the shot to be directed against the fort. We were shortly out of suspense, one of the sergeants receiving a shot in the breast. The fire was now returned, but the enemy had a great deal of advantage from their rifles, and the cover of the church, houses, barns, &c. . . .

La Mothe's volunteers now began to murmur, saying it was very hard to be obliged to fight against their countrymen and relations, who, they now perceived had joined the Americans. As they made half our number, and after such a declaration were not to be trusted, the Englishmen wounded, six in number, were a sixth of those we could depend on, and duty would fall every hour on the remaining few. Considering we were at a distance of six hundred miles from succor, that if we did not burn the village, we left the enemy most advantageous cover against us, and that if we did, we had nothing to expect after rejecting the first terms, but the extremity of revenge, I took up the determination of accepting honourable terms if they were to be procured, else to abide the worse. . . .

At ten o'clock of the morning of the 25th, we marched out with fixed bayonets, and the soldiers with their knapsacks. The colors had not been hoisted this morning that we might be spared the mortification of hauling them down. . . .

The evening of the day we capitulated, Colonel Clark ordered neck-irons, fetters, and handcuffs to be made which, in our hearing, he declared were designed for those officers who had been employed as partisans with the Indians. I took him aside and reminded him that these persons were prisoners of war, included in the capitulation which he had so lately put his hand to; he said his resolution was formed, that he had made a vow never to spare woman or child of the Indians, or those who were employed by them. I observed to him that these people having obeyed my orders, were not to be blamed for the execution of them, that I had never known that they had acted contrary to those orders by encouraging the cruelty of the savages . . . and that if he was determined to pass by the consideration of his faith and that of the public, pledged for the performance of the articles of capitulation, I desired that he might throw me into prison, or lay me in irons rather than the others. He smiled contemptously, turned away, and order'd three of these people to the guard, till the irons should be made. The scalps of the slaughter'd Indians were hung up by our tents, a young man by the name of Raimbault was brought into the fort with a halter about his neck and only for the interposition of the volunteers from the Illinois, some of whom were his relations, would infallibly [have] been hanged without any crime laid to his charge but his having been with a scouting party; he was half-strangled before he was taken from the tree.'[9]

By his conquest, and by claiming the surrounding territory for Virginia, George Rogers Clark made himself a near dictator of an area greater than half the total size of the thirteen states. He made treaties with the Indians and with the exceptions of two outbreaks in 1780 and 1782, kept them under

254

191. General John Sullivan

John Sullivan was born in New Hampshire of Irish immigrant parents and had many of the traits customarily associated with the Irish. He was brave, pugnacious, sensitive, fond of a good show, often impecunious, and a natural political organizer. Before the war he had practised law, become a major of militia, and been elected to the first and second Continental Congresses. After Valley Forge, he was given the command in Rhode Island, and was furious when d'Estaing's withdrawal forced him to give up the conquest of Newport. He remained in Providence till 1779, when Washington used his aggressive leadership in the rough campaign to lay waste the Iroquois villages in western Pennsylvania and New York. His health ruined, he resigned, but in 1780 reappeared in Congress, still fighting his opponents. In 1786, he was elected governor of New Hampshire.

control. His greatest frustration came in June 1780, when his plan to lead an expedition against Detroit was thwarted because Virginia, impoverished and threatened with possible invasion, could furnish no aid. But even as Hamilton and the other prisoners captured at Vincennes were being taken through the wilderness on the 850-mile journey to the jail in Williamsburg, an even greater expedition against the Indians was being organized under the leadership of John Sullivan and Brigadier James Clinton.

The Continental Congress had finally been prompted to act in the spring of 1779 by the flood of petitions pouring in from the west. After receiving the congressional resolution, Washington offered the command of the expedition against the Indians to Horatio Gates. Gates, then in command of the troops in the Hudson Highlands, turned down the opportunity: 'The man, who undertakes the Indian service, should enjoy youth and strength; requisites I do not possess. It therefore grieves me, that your Excellency should offer me the only command to which I am entirely unequal.' The commanding general, suspecting that Gates would refuse, had already alerted the thirty-eight-year-old John Sullivan, some twelve years younger than Gates. James Clinton with 1,400 men was to bear down from New York to make a junction with Sullivan's 2,132 troops at Tioga in northern Pennsylvania. Not until 31 July was Sullivan ready to march out of his staging area at Wyoming. It was an imposing column, accompanied by 120 boats loaded with artillery and stores. Over 1,200 pack horses were loaded with the baggage of the army, with twenty being reserved for Sullivan's personal use. There was little to prevent the enemy from knowing they were coming; they straggled through the wilderness with banners flying and drums beating, while the band of Proctor's Artillery regiment occasionally burst forth with a martial air. They marched into Tioga on 11 August, although the New York troops did not arrive until eleven days later. While awaiting James Clinton, Sullivan detached a group to destroy the Indian village of Chemung some fifteen miles from camp. Captain James Norris was along when the group marched on the night of 12 August:

'Our army marched at 8 oClock this evening in order to be ready by Day break for surprising Chemoung. Our march was attended with difficulty & fatigue, having a thick Swamp and several dangerous defiles to pass. We arrived, however, between dawning & Sun rise, but our no small mortification found the Town abandon'd & two or three Indians only to be seen sculking away.

According to the accounts of those who pretend to be acquainted with Indian Citys, this seems to have been a pretty Capital place. It consisted of about 40 Houses built chiefly with split and hewn Timber, covered with bark and some other rough materials, without Chimnies, or floors. There were two larger houses which from some extraordinary rude Decorations, we took to be public Buildings; there was little Furniture left in the Houses, except Bearskins, some painted feathers, & Knicknacks. In what we supposed to be a Chapple was found indeed an Idol, which might well enough be worshipped without a breach of the 2d Commandt. on account of its likeness to anything in either heaven or Earth.

About Sun rise, the Genl. gave orders for the Town to be illuminated, & accordingly we had a glorious Bonfire of upwards of 30 Buildings at once; a melancholy & desperate Spectacles to the Savages, many of whom must have beheld it from a Neighboring hill, near which we found a party of them had encamped last night, and from appearances had left the Town but a few hours before the Troops arrived.

Genl. Hand with some light Infantry pursued them about a mile, when they gave him a Shot from the Top of a Ridge, & ran according to their Custom, as soon as the fire was return'd; but unfortunately for us, the Savages wounded three Officers, killed Six men and wounded seven more. They were pursued, but without effect.

Our next Object was their fields of Indian Corn, about 40 Acres of which we cut down and distroyed. In doing this business, a party of Indians and Tories, fired upon three Regimts across the River, killed one and wounded five. Having compleated the Catastrophe of the Towns & Fields, we arrived at Tioga about Sun set the same day, very much fatigued, having march'd not less than 34 miles in 24 hours, without rest in the Extreamest heat.'[10]

Not until 26 August was the army ready to march in full force against the Indians on its seek and destroy mission. As the men were called out, Colonel Joseph Cilley drew up his First New Hampshire Regiment and

'walked to the right of his Regiment, and as he passed on to the left, he very pleasantly spoke to several of his soldiers, and told them whilst he applauded their courage and patriotism, he thought they were unable to endure the hardships they necessarily must, on so short an allowance.

192. Lieutenant-Colonel Banastre Tarleton. *Sir Joshua Reynolds*

Here portrayed as the prototype of a dashing cavalry officer, Tarleton was an able and audacious leader; he was also vain and brutal. He acted upon the principle that war is hell long before Sherman made that phrase famous in his raids through the South. Tarleton was feared and hated throughout the Carolina countryside. Arriving in America as a twenty-five-year-old cavalry cornet, he had raised a British legion of volunteer Tories over whom he was given command. On the voyage south from New York to Carolina most of his horses were lost; he soon replaced them by scouring the region with characteristic energy. He trained his troops to move rapidly and to fight mounted or on foot. From his surprise attack on General Huger's force, which resulted in bottling Lincoln's army in Charleston, until Morgan defeated him at Cowpens, 'Butcher' Tarleton's victories came in devastating succession.

On passing near to the left wing, he said to quite a young lad, only in his fifteenth year, by the name of Richard Drout, "Richard, you must go back; you cannot endure the march." The brave little fellow replied, "Colonel, I don't want to go back; I can stand it, I know I can." On the Colonel's telling him that he was too young to endure the march, and that he had better go back, Richard began to weep most bitterly, and exclaimed, "Colonel, I am not tired a bit, and have not been; and I know I can endure it as well as any of them; besides they will call me a coward, and I am not one." The Colonel assured him he should not be called a coward, and that he would severely flog any one who should apply such an epithet to him. Richard, however, continued weeping most bitterly, and exclaimed, "I enlisted to serve my country. Do let me go on." The Colonel, with a full heart, at length makes this reply: "Go, my lad, and God go with you." He went, and endured the march as well as any one among us.'[11]

The ungainly column blundered through brush and forest with Major John Burrowes noting, 'The sight of Carriages in this part of the world is very odd, as there is nothing but a foot path', while to Sergeant Moses Fellows the march was

'much Impeded by the Artillery and ammunition Waggons threw thick wood and Dificult Defiles. Such Cursing, cutting and Diging, over seting Wagons, Cannon and Pack Horses into the river, &c., is not to be Seen Every Day—the army obliged to Halt 7 hours at one place.'[12]

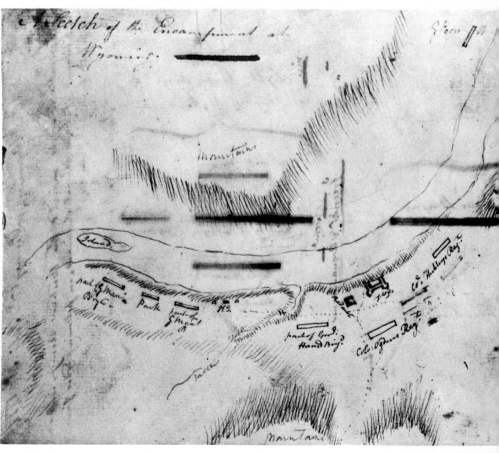

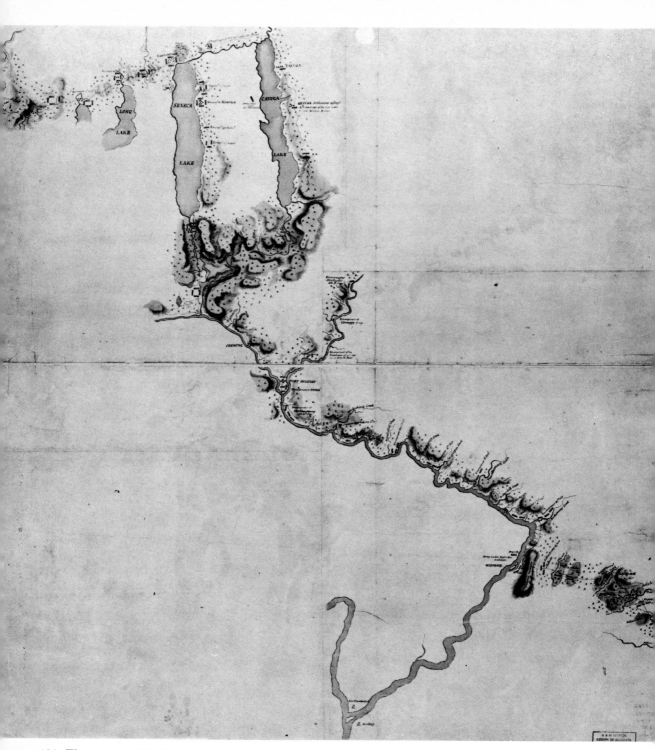

196. The route of Sullivan's expedition against the Indians of the Six Nations in Western New York

This anonymous, untitled, undated manuscript is a carefully drawn map of the entire route of the campaign made by General John Sullivan from Easton, Pennsylvania, to western New York. It presents, on a single sheet, much of the information given on two dozen large-scale rough field sketches of the same route, made during the campaign, which are among the maps of John Erskine, geographer to the army, and are now in the New-York Historical Society. General James Clinton joined Sullivan at Tioga with 1,400 additional troops.

Occasional scattered shots disrupted the march as roaming parties of Indians tried to pick off stragglers and flank guards. By nine o'clock in the morning of 29 August the column neared the Indian village known as Newtown, but proceeded with extreme caution as scouts reported an uncommon number of fires ahead. Nathan Davis seemed to enjoy the fight:

'Our riflemen discovered at a little distance in front, a sure indication of an ambush. In the direction of our march was a very deep defile, occasioned by a brook of water running through a pine plain; the banks of the brook were very steep and high, and the growth of timber small and very thick. On the opposite bank it was observed to be thicker and in greater regularity than it would have been had dame Nature herself placed it there. The conclusion was that the Indians lay concealed behind it, as finally proved to be the case. They had made a kind of breastwork of small pine timber and had that morning, cut small saplings and stuck them in the ground in front of it. . . .

197. General John Sullivan's Order of March upon leaving Wyoming

Sullivan's order was evidently intended to keep his 2,100 men, largely militia, from separating into small companies or in extended and trailing columns vulnerable to surprise attacks. It was, however, impossible to follow such a formation through the difficult frontier terrain. Equally important was his policy of sending ahead advance units of light infantry and scouring the surrounding country with far-ranging scouts. Washington, experienced in Indian tactics and warfare acquired in the Braddock expedition against Fort Duquesne in 1755, had advised Sullivan against close-order formation, suggesting a 'loose and dispersed' arrangement.

Sullivan's order of march, given to his troops upon leaving the Wyoming Valley on 31 July 1779, was a practical solution combining unity and protection against ambush. He commanded that 'the order of march . . . be adher'd to at all times when the situation of the country will possibly admit & where a deviation takes place it must be followed no further than the necessity of that time requires'.

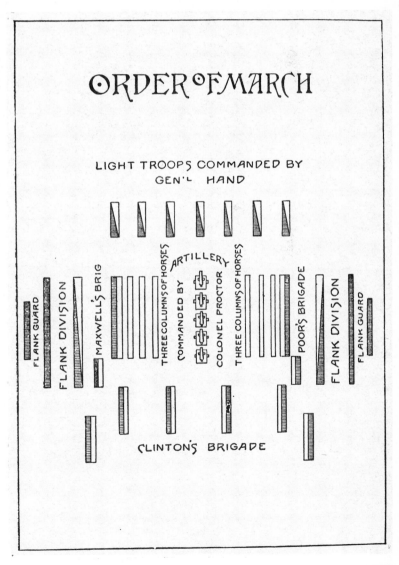

ORDER OF MARCH

LIGHT TROOPS COMMANDED BY GEN'L HAND

FLANK GUARD — FLANK DIVISION — MAXWELL'S BRIG — THREE COLUMNS OF HORSES — ARTILLERY COMMANDED BY COLONEL PROCTOR — THREE COLUMNS OF HORSES — POOR'S BRIGADE — FLANK DIVISION — FLANK GUARD

CLINTON'S BRIGADE

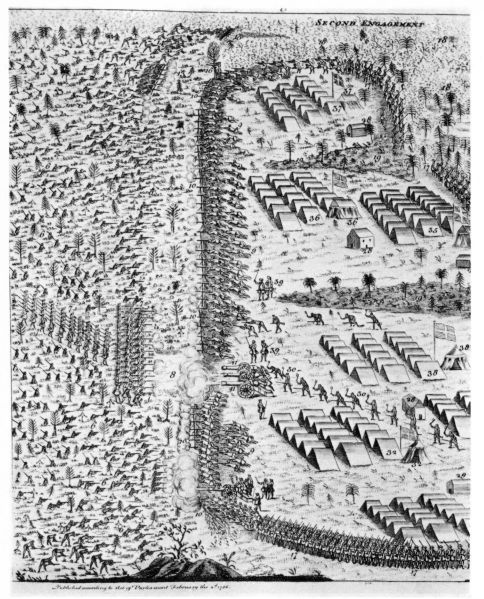

SECOND ENGAGEMENT

Published according to Act of Parliament February the 2d 1786.

198. Guerrilla warfare *(detail)*. *Jefferys*

Indian bush fighting was especially effective when attacking a body of troops marching through forested territory. American frontiersmen became as skilful as the Indians in sudden concealed onslaught; British patrols and foraging parties were continually harassed by lurking bands, even near main encampments.

This scene is from Thomas Jefferys' 'A Prospective View of the Battle fought near Lake George' (see also plate 119).

We had proceeded half a mile when General Sullivan gave orders to Colonel Proctor to open fire with his six or eight brass field guns, from three to six pounders, and also a small howitzer which hove a small bomb upon the enemy's breastwork. The object of this order was to draw the attention of the Indians off from General Poor [on the right flank].

The order was obeyed with promptness, but produced a somewhat different effect from the one anticipated. They immediately ran from their slender works as fast as their legs could carry them, and advanced directly to the hill, where they secreted themselves behind the trees, waiting our approach. When our front had advanced within a short distance of them, they commenced a fire from behind every tree, and at the same time gave a war whoop. Not all the infernals of the Prince of Darkness, could they have been let loose from the bottomless pit, would have borne any comparison to these demons of the forest. . . .

How many we killed I never could exactly ascertain, but some were killed, and one scalped to my knowledge, and much blood was seen on their track. We also took two prisoners, one negro and one white man, said to be a tory. The white man was found painted black, lying on his face, and pretending to be dead. As no blood was seen near him, after a proper discipline he was soon brought to his feelings. He was then stripped and washed, and found to be white. A rope was then tied round his neck, and he was led in front of the troops, whilst every one gave him his sentence, "You shall be hung tomorrow." This, however, was not put into execution.

We remained on the battleground till sunset, when we retreated to the plain and encamped. We had twenty-two killed and a number wounded, some mortally. The next day we buried our dead by the side of the fallen trees near our encampment, not raising their graves higher than the surface of the earth. We then burnt brush over their graves, so that the Indians might not distinguish them from the place where we built our customary fires.'[13]

One party was sent along the trail to count dead Indians: 'Towards noon they found them and skinned two of them from their hips down for boot legs; one pair for the Major the other for myself.'

Shortly after the battle of Newtown, Sullivan marched through the Indian country, tramping through forest and plain, wading streams, struggling through swamps, their trail marked by the columns of smoke struggling upward above the trees from burning villages and grain fields. Rarely did they see the inhabitants until they reached the Indian stronghold known as Seneca Castle on 7 September:

'On the first entrance of our Brigade, a young Child, I believe about 3 year old found running about the houses which one of our Officers pickt up and found it to be a White Child. But it was so much tand & smoaked that we could hardly distinguish it from an Indian Child and was Exceeding poor, scarcely able to walk. It could talk no English, noth'g but Indian, & I believe but little of that. The Officer took great care of it and Cloathed it, as it was naked when he found it, & could give no Account of itself, only said "his mamy was gone." The men got very little plunder . . . or anything [in] the town as the Indians had taken everything almost with them.'[14]

After the destruction of the town of Kanaghsaws on 13 September, the army sat down to rest while awaiting the construction of a bridge. A detachment of twenty-six men under Lieutenant Thomas Boyd was sent on to scout the next town, Gathtsegwarohare. Perhaps the ease with which they had swept through the area made them a little careless. The journal of Lieutenant Erkuries Beatty revealed the hazards of indiscretion in Indian country:

'He [Lieut. Boyd] soon after saw 4 Indians come in to town a horseback. He sent 5 or 6 men to take them or kill them. The men fired on the Indians, killed & Sculped one and wounded another and took a horse, saddle & bridle. He then sent of two more Runners to the Army, but they soon Retirnd to him & informed him they had seen five Indians on the road. He then thout proper to return with his party to the Army which he expected to meet very soon.

From Tioga Sullivan began his operations by destroying the Indian town of Chemung, twelve miles to the north at present Elmira, New York, on 13 August. The standard of living of these Iroquois was unexpectedly high: they had well furnished houses, some even of stone, beautiful orchards, cultivated gardens, and excellent fields of corn. They were all destroyed. General Frederick Haldimand of Canada had not sent aid to the Indian allies. If they were bitter because of failure of British support, the Indians made no peace with the Americans. The following year they renewed their forays with increased ferocity.

He had not gone far before he fell in with the same Indians which he fired on. They run on before him, and he pursued them Slowly & every once in a while he would come in sight of them and fire on them, & so they kept on till he came to this hill in front of camp about 3/4 of a Mile . . . when he heard our Drums and thought himself intirely safe, but to his great disappointment found a large party of Indians, found them behind trees. He Imediately formed his men for Action and began a very heavy fire which lasted some time, but the Indians whose number was so far superior to him, surrounded him and made prisoners or killed the whole, excepting a few which came in. We found 4 or 5 of our men on the ground, Dead & sculped and it is supposed that Lt. Boyd was made prisoner. The Enemy had a number killd, as the men that was hid in the bushes saw the Indians carry a number off in blankets. . . .

Tuesday 14th. The whole Army was under arms this morning an hour before Day & remained so till sunrise; about 7 oClock fatigue parties was sent out to Destroy Corn which was there in great Abundance, and beans. About 12 oClock we marched, crossed over the branch of the Jinasee River, and came upon a very beautiful flat of great extent, growing up with wild Grass higher in some places than our heads. We marched on this flat 2 Mile and Crossed they Jinesee River, which is about as big as the Tyago, but very Crooked.

Left the flats and march'd thro' the woods 3 Mile and arrived at Chenesee

Town which is the largest we have yet seen; it lies in a Crook of they River on extraordinary good land, about 70 houses, very impact and very well built, and about the same number of out houses in Cornfields, &c.

On entering the town we found the body of Lt. Boyd and another Rifle Man in a most terrible mangled condition. They was both stripped naked and their heads Cut off, and the flesh of Lt. Boyds head was intirely taken of and his eyes punched out. The other mans hed was not there. They was stabed I suppose, in 40 Diferent places in the Body with a spear, and great gashes cut in their flesh with knifes, and Lt. Boyds Privates was nearly cut of & hanging down, his finger and Toe nails was bruised of and the Dogs had eat part of their Shoulders away, likewise a knife was Sticking in Lt. Boyds body. They was imediately buried with the honour of war.'[15]

200. Bay and Harbour of Pensacola. *George Gauld*

Pensacola became the centre for the incitement and supply of the Cherokee and Upper Creek Indian attacks on the southern provincial frontier. John Stuart, the able and influential superintendent of Indian Affairs, was reluctant to persuade Indians to attack the frontier; his efforts for years had been towards peace. But Lord Germain ordered him to supply the Indians with arms and ammunition.

The Cherokee in the southern Appalachians, constantly losing their hunting grounds to encroaching settlers, were already on the warpath, attacking frontier settlements. In retaliation their villages were destroyed in 1776. A peace treaty of 1777 was soon violated and mutual destruction continued. Not until 1782, after the war, were the Cherokees forced to sign a humiliating peace with further cessions of hunting grounds.

With the surrender of Pensacola to the Spanish the British supply of arms and ammunition ceased, and the Indians were no longer a major threat.

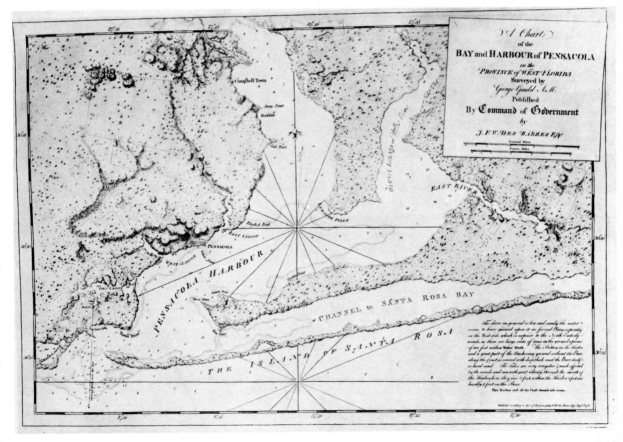

201. A North View of Pensacola, on the Island of Santa Rosa. *Serres*

Founded by the Spanish in the closing years of the seventeenth century, Pensacola was taken over by the British in 1764; they made it the capital of the province of West Florida and its chief military stronghold on the Gulf. In 1781 Bernardo de Gálvez retrieved it for Spain.

The following day, 15 September, the unexpected happened. For Major Jeremiah Fogg the day had opened on a note of happiness:

'This morning a captive woman and child at her breast came in from the woods, having escaped from the savages. Can any greater transition happen to a human being except a pardon at the gallows? She was taken at Wyoming last spring with five children, where her husband was killed, and child was scalped before her eyes. This day we spent in destroying corn which had become so ripe that we were obliged to burn it in the kilns. Some corn-stalks were seventeen feet long. The whole army was employed, but at 3 o'clock we *faced to the right about.* A most joyful day!'[16]

By 30 September, the army was back at Wyoming, its mission accomplished. In his sweep through the Indian nations Sullivan had destroyed forty-one towns, and had suffered a loss of forty-one men, not all of whom had died in combat. The general estimated that he had destroyed 1,500 fruit trees and 160,000 bushels of corn. That winter the Indians were forced to fall back on Fort Niagara for food to see them through the winter, while countless others died of starvation and disease in the forest. Still, there were to be new expeditions and the Indians still harassed the frontier with raids. When Major Jeremiah Fogg was writing the closing entries of the expedition, he allowed his pen to follow the musings of his mind:

'The question will naturally arise, what have you to show for your exploits? Where are your prisoners? To which I reply, that the rags and emaciated bodies of our soldiers must speak for our fatigue, and when the querist will point out a mode to tame a partridge, or the expediency of hunting wild turkeys, with light horse, I will show them our prisoners. The nests are destroyed, but the birds are still on the wing.'[17]

12. The South: Phase One

THE FRENCH ALLIANCE had wrought a significant change in the American war; for one thing it had led to a re-thinking of basic British military strategy. The sprawling south, with its sandy plains, red clay hills and hot, steaming swamps was much too valuable in the scheme of British mercantilism to leave undefended. Unless these states were quickly returned to their former allegiance, it was quite possible that the French would step in and replace the English as prime European distributors of southern tobacco, rice and other products of a sub-tropical nature.

With the exception of the abortive attempt against Charleston in 1776, the war had seemed remote to the South. The area promised an easy conquest; loyalists, it was said, were numerous and clamouring for an opportunity to aid the royal cause; other than Charleston, there were no great urban centres dominating the countryside; isolation of the population prevented the gathering of armies; and the warm weather suggested longer periods for action.

George III had been fascinated by, and had long busied himself with, the pursuit of military and naval matters and it was the King who had come up with a new plan of operations. The key was Charleston. Once this port was safely secured, armies could parade northward to the rich state of Virginia. North Carolina lay between, but that state was dismissed as but the 'road to Virginia'. On 8 March 1778, a little over a month after the signing of the French Alliance, a dispatch to Clinton from Lord George Germain outlined the King's views. George III had suggested that General Augustine Prevost drive up from St Augustine to take Savannah, thereby providing a base from which the attack against Charleston might be launched. Germain summed up the King's views with:

'Should the success we may reasonably hope for attend these enterprizes, it might not be too much to expect that all America to the south of the Susquehannah would return to their allegiance, and in the case of so happy an event, the northern provinces might be left to their own feelings and distress to bring them back to their duty, and the operations against them confined to the cutting off all their supplies and blocking up their ports. I have thus stated the King's wishes and intentions, but he does not mean you to look upon them as orders, desiring on the contrary, that you use your own discretion in planning as well as executing all operations which shall appear the most likely means of crushing the rebellion.'[1]

Despite the remoteness of formal warfare, the South had been the scene of a violent civil war. Families had been split, father against son, brother against brother, while armed bands of whigs and tories roamed the countryside, ambushing each other and pillaging in the name of patriotism. Although not experiencing great pitched battles as did the northern theatre, the South slept a troubled sleep.

The southern campaign was initiated on 27 November 1778 when a force of 3,500 men sailed past Sandy Hook under the command of Lieutenant-

Colonel Archibald Campbell, a striking force which was to make a junction before Savannah with an expedition marching up from East Florida under Prevost. Campbell disembarked on Tybee Island at the mouth of the Savannah River on 29 December 1778, in a semi-tropical land of moss-draped swamps and forest, surrounding a southern city of distinguished beauty.

On the American side Major-General Robert Howe of North Carolina was in active command of the Southern Department; he had recently been recalled because of South Carolina politics, although some gossiped that it was by reason of a 'little ridiculous matter . . . with regard to a female. . . .' Howe had been marking time until his successor, Major-General Benjamin Lincoln, arrived, but when the threat was posed to Savannah he rushed down to defend the town. Gathering a force of 700 Continentals and 150 militia he drew up his command half a mile east of town on Girardeau's Plantation, with each flank resting on a swamp. It was a good position, but the British commander Campbell, deciding to drive before Prevost's arrival, proved that he had learned the advantage of a flanking manoeuvre. At three o'clock in the afternoon of 29 December 1778, he was within sight of Howe's troops. His report to Germain gave the details of the battle:

'I could discover from the movements of the enemy that they wished and expected an attack upon their left, and I was desirous of cherishing that opinion.

Having accidentally fallen in with a Negro [by the name of Quamino Dolly] who knew a private path through a wooded swamp upon the enemy's right, I ordered the first battalion of the Seventy-first to form on our right of the road and move up to the rear of the light-infantry, whilst I drew off that corps to the right as if I meant to extend my front to that quarter, where a happy fall of ground favored the concealment of this manoeuvre, and increased the jealousy of the enemy with regard to their left. Sir James Baird had directions to convey the light-infantry in this hollow ground quite to the rear and penetrate the wooded swamp upon our left, with a view to get round by the new barracks into the rear of the enemy's right flank. . . .

A body of the militia of Georgia, posted . . . with some pieces of cannon to cover the road from Great Ogeeche, were at this juncture routed, with the loss of their artillery, by the light-infantry under Sir James Baird, when the scattered troops of the Carolina and Georgia brigades ran across the plain in his front. This officer with his usual gallantry dashed the light-infantry on their flank and terminated the fate of the day with brilliant success.

Thirty-eight officers of different distinctions, and four hundred and fifteen non-commissioned officers and privates, one stand of colors, forty-eight pieces of cannon, twenty-three mortars, ninety-four barrels of powder, the fort with all its stores, . . . and, in short, the capital of Georgia, the shipping in the harbor, with a large quantity of provisions, fell into our possession before it was dark, without any other loss on our side than that of Captain Peter Campbell, a gallant officer of Skinner's light-infantry, and two privates killed, one sergeant and nine privates wounded. By the accounts received from their prisoners, thirty lost their lives in the swamp, endeavoring to make their escape.'[2]

Portly, florid of face, Major-General Benjamin Lincoln of Massachusetts had been selected by the Continental Congress to succeed Robert Howe in

202. The Georgia-South Carolina Coast and Siege of Savannah

This chart of the coast between Edisto Island and St Johns River in the *Atlantic Neptune* was probably based on the surveys of William Gerard De Brahm, Surveyor General for the Southern District. De Brahm, a German surveyor-cartographer who had served as captain of engineers under Charles VII, made the first extensive professional surveys of the southern provinces.

For the inset, 'Plan of the Siege of Savannah', showing the attack on General Prevost's positions by General Lincoln and Admiral d'Estaing, Des Barres used the surveys by John Wilson, assistant engineer in the 71st Regiment, who made the plan under the supervision of the commanding engineer, James Moncrief.

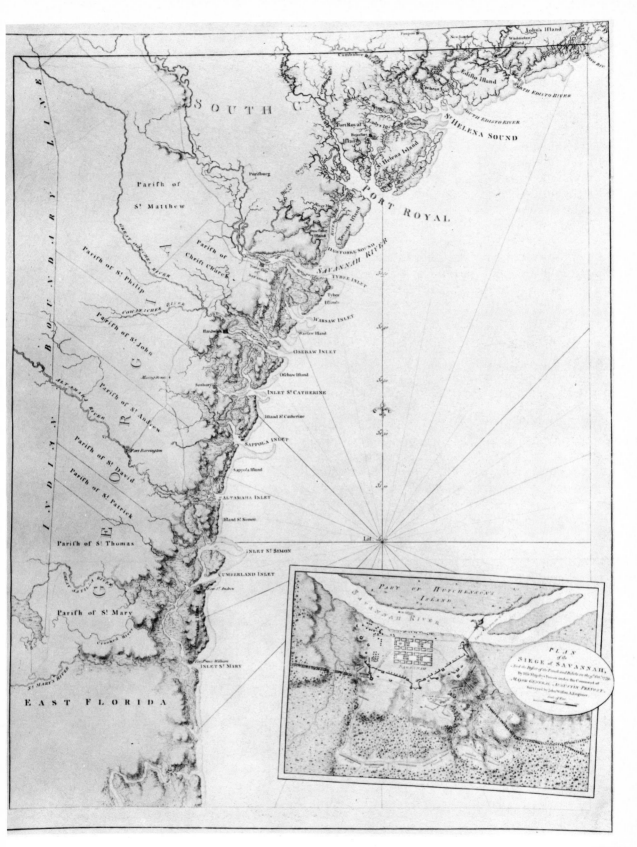

267

the Southern Department. Upon his arrival he almost immediately pushed southward from Charleston towards Savannah, pitching camp at Purysburg across from Prevost, who had by now arrived from Florida, on the far side of the river on the Georgia side. Minor battles were won by William Moultrie at Beaufort and Andrew Pickens at Kettle Creek. But disaster cost Lincoln one-third of his army when the redcoated troop under Colonel Mark Prevost whipped 1,400 North Carolina militia (plus a few Continentals) under General John Ashe at Briar Creek.

Lincoln, however, kept the initiative; crossing the river and driving towards Augusta he cut the British supply line from the west. Prevost immediately marched northward, delayed by William Moultrie's rearguard action. Charleston almost surrendered and possibly would have had it not been for Moultrie's stubbornness and Prevost's arrogance. But the British general accomplished his purpose—he lured Lincoln back out of Georgia, rushing to relieve the city. Prevost retired to the islands off the coast. On 20 June 1779 Lincoln attacked a post at Stone Ferry, but was driven back when Prevost came to their aid.

203. 'Vue de la Ville de Savannah, du Camp, des Tranchées et de L'attaque'. *Pierre Ozanne*

D'Estaing, buoyed up by a victory in the West Indies, returned to try to help the Americans retake Savannah, and with him came Pierre Ozanne, his official artist. Once more, in this great panorama of the attack, we see his delicate skill in the depiction of detail. The view is taken from the French camp, inland from Savannah, where tents and supply wagons can be seen, looking across the massed armies of a well-planned semi-circular siege to the fortified city on its elevation. Along the horizon is the river. The black, angular lines are trenches for protection in approaching the abattis. The very elaborateness of the attack proved its defeat; d'Estaing in preparing it gave the British so much time to strengthen the weak defences of Savannah that the French and Americans were repelled with dreadful loss. D'Estaing sailed back to the West Indies taking with him Ozanne, one of the most gifted painters of the Revolutionary scene.

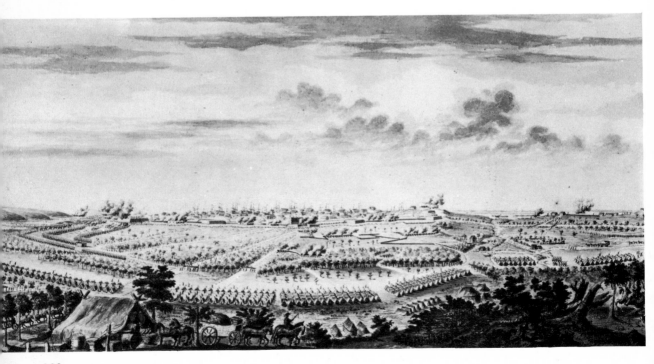

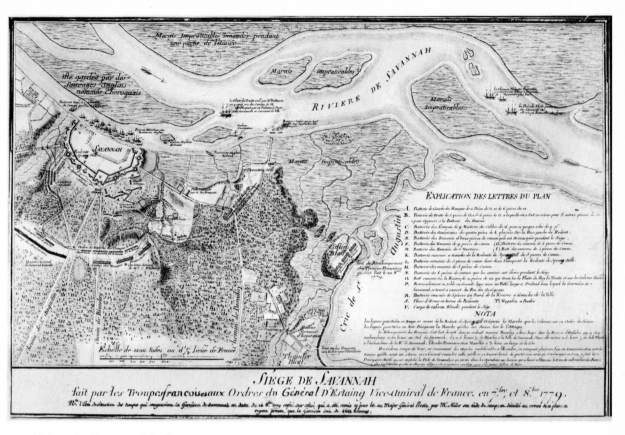

204. 'Siège de Savannah'. *Ozanne*

This plan of the unsuccessful siege shows the impassable swamps along the river, the location of the debarking of the French troops at Thunder Bluff, the encampment of the French and American troops, and the route of the attack which was repulsed. The channel to the town is blocked by British vessels; from the main channel of the river the French flute or transport 'Truile' of 18 guns cannonades Savannah.

Meanwhile, after the fall of Savannah, Congress dispatched a fast sailing vessel to the West Indies, requesting the Comte d'Estaing to return with his fleet for another combined Franco-American attempt to retake Savannah. D'Estaing, at the moment, was basking in new-won glory, having just taken the islands of St Vincent and Grenada and in a sea battle defeated Vice-Admiral John Byron, the greatest naval victory France had won over England in more than a hundred years. With temporary naval superiority, d'Estaing agreed to sail for Georgia, not only to act in support of the Americans, but to escape the hurricane season in the islands.

Without waiting for Lincoln to come up, the French admiral sent in a summons to the British in Savannah. Prevost asked for twenty-four hours to consider the terms. D'Estaing agreed. Not only were defensive works strengthened, but Lieutenant-Colonel John Maitland was able to push through the swamps from Port Royal with 900 reinforcements. At the end of the twenty-four hours Prevost notified d'Estaing that he was determined to defend the town.

The French took over the siege, with Lincoln's men mostly lying idle while d'Estaing's troops built batteries; these at last opened fire on Sunday

4 October 1779 with a thunderous roar. Among those in the town was the loyalist Chief Justice Anthony Stokes of Georgia. He described the scene for his wife:

'I heard one of the shells whistle over my quarters, and presently afterwards I got up and dressed myself; and as our neighborhood seemed to be in the line of fire, I went out with a view to go to the eastward, out of the way; but a shell that seemed to be falling near me, rather puzzled me how to keep clear of it, and I returned to the house not a little alarmed. I then proceeded to the westward, and then the shells seem to fall around. There I soon joined a number of gentlemen who had left their houses on account of the bombardment and, like me, were retiring from the line of fire to Yammacraw. Here we stayed till between one and two in the morning, when the bombardment ceased. . . .

The guns seemed to approach on each side, and about three o'clock on Wednesday morning a shell whistled close by Captain Knowles' house. Soon afterwards another came nearer and seemed to strike my quarters, and I thought I heard the cry of people in distress. We all jumped up, and before I could dress myself, my quarters were so much in flames that I could not venture further than the door, for fear of an explosion from the rum. George and Jemmy were over with me in Captain Knowles' cellar; the others were at my quarters. George ran over before me, and fortunately for me drew out of the flames the two black trunks with some of my apparel, etc., that I brought out with me, and then removed them over to Captain Knowles' passage, which was all the property I saved, . . . for I momently expected that the explosion of the rum would blow up the house and kill every one near it; and as soon as the French observed the flames, they kept up a very heavy cannonade and bombardment and pointed their fire to that object to prevent any person approaching to extinguish the flames. . . .

The appearance of the town afforded a melancholy prospect, for there was hardly a house which had not been shot through, and some of them were almost destroyed. Ambrose, Wright and Stute's, in which we lived, had upwards of fifty shot that went through each of them, as I am informed; and old Mr. Habersham's house, in which Major Prevost lived, was almost destroyed with shot and shells. In the streets and on the common there was a number of large holes made in the ground by the shells . . . and in the church and Mr. Jones' house I observed that the shells came in at the roof and went through to the ground; and a number of other houses suffered by shells. The troops in the lines were much safer than the people in town.'[3]

As the siege wore on, d'Estaing, wearied of conquest by pick, spade and artillery and despite the vigorous objections of Lincoln, decided upon an assault upon the works, a suicidal concept which made some people feel that the Count held a death wish for his men. The attack was to be made by three French columns and two American. It was foggy at four o'clock in the morning of 9 October when Major Thomas Pinckney of the South Carolina militia marched forward with his men:

'A faint attack by the South Carolina militia and the Georgians, under Brigadier-General Huger, was ordered to be made on the enemy's left; but, instead of the French troops being paraded so as to march off at 4 o'clock, it was near four before the head of that column reached our front. The whole army then marched towards the skirt of the wood in one long column and, as they approached the open space, were to break off into the different columns, as ordered for the attack. But by the time the first French column had arrived at the open space, the day had fairly broke, when Count d'Estaing, without waiting until the other columns had arrived at their position, placed himself at the head of his first column and rushed forward for the attack. But this body was so severely galled by the grape-shot and musketry when they reached the abbatis, that, in spite of the effort of the officers, the column got into confusion and broke away to their left toward the wood in that direction; the second and the third French columns shared successively the same fate, having the additional discouragement of seeing,

205. Plan of the Siege of Savannah . . . 9th October 1779. *Stedman*

The siege, here given from the British viewpoint, shows the city on its high bluff above the river, with its ordered streets and open squares as laid out by General Oglethorpe in 1733. The river is free from the French fleet, unable to pass the barriers, except for a frigate which can fire from an adjacent tidal river. Swamps on either side narrow the possible approach of the enemy.

John Wilson, assistant engineer in Campbell's 71st regiment, was present at the siege and made the original manuscript map, a copy of which is among the General Clinton Papers. William Faden, geographer to the King, made this engraving from another copy in 1784. Stedman in his *History* (1794) used Faden's engraving with slight changes on the copper plate.

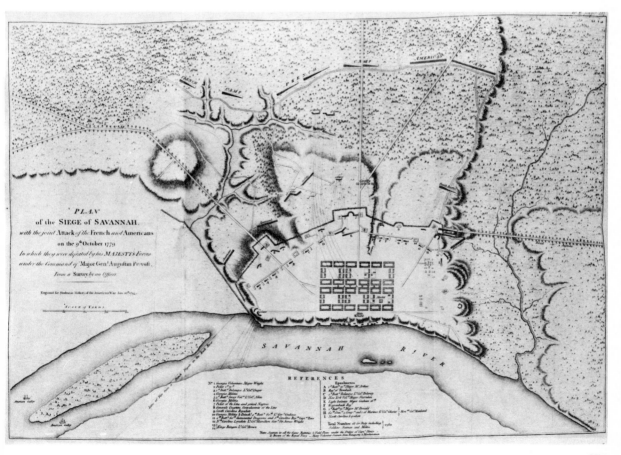

as they marched to the attack, the repulse and loss of their comrades who had preceded them.

Count Pulaski, who, with the cavalry, preceded the right column of the Americans, proceeded gallantly until stopped by the abbatis, and before he could force through it, received his mortal wound. In the mean time, Colonel Laurens at the head of the light infantry, followed by the 2d South Carolina Regiment and 1st Battalion Charlestown Militia, attacked the Spring Hill Redoubt, got into the ditch and planted the colours of the 2d Regiment on the berm, but the parapet was too high for them to scale it under so heavy a fire, and after much slaughter they were driven out of the ditch. When General Pulaski was about to be removed from the field, Colonel D. Horry, to whom the command of the cavalry devolved, asked what were his directions. He answered, "Follow my lancers to whom I have given my order to attack." But the lancers were so severely galled by the enemy's fire that they also inclined off to the left, and were followed by all the cavalry breaking through the American column, who were attacking the Spring Hill Redoubt.

By this time the 2d American column headed by Gen. M'Intosh, to which I was attached, arrived at the foot of the Spring Hill Redoubt, and such a scene of confusion as there appeared is not often equalled. Col. Laurens had been separated from that part of his command that had not entered the Spring Hill ditch by the cavalry, who had borne it before them into the swamp to the left, and when we marched up, inquired *if we had seen them*. Count d'Estaing was wounded in the arm, and endeavouring to rally his men, a few of whom with a drummer he had collected. . . . The Count ordered that we should move more to the left, and by no means to interfere with the troops he was endeavouring to rally; in pursuing this direction we were thrown too much to the left, and before we could reach Spring Hill Redoubt, we had to pass through Yamacraw Swamp, then wet and boggy, with the galley at the mouth annoying our left flank with grape-shot.

While struggling through this morass, the firing slacked, and it was reported that the whole army had retired. I was sent by General M'Intosh to look out from Spring Hill, where I found not an assailant standing. On reporting this to the general, he ordered a retreat, which was effected without much loss, notwithstanding the heavy fire of grape-shot with which we were followed.

The loss of both armies in killed and wounded amounted to 637 French and 457 Americans, 1100. . . . The loss of the British amounted only to fifty-five.

Thus was a fine body of troops sacrificed by the imprudence of the French general, who, being of superior grade, commanded the whole. If the French troops had left their encampment in time for the different corps to have reached their positions, and the whole attacked together, the prospect of success would have been infinitely better, though even then it would have been very doubtful on account of the strength of the enemy's line, which was well supplied by artillery. . . . In fact, the enemy, who were to be assailed at once on a considerable part of their front, finding themselves attacked at one point, very deliberately concentrated their whole fire on the assailing column, and that was repeated as fast as the different corps were brought up to the attack.

General Lincoln had the command of the reserve and covered the retreat; if he had led the attack, I think the event could not have been so disastrous. . . .'[4]

206. Georgia and South Carolina. *Kitchin*

The chief roads and locations lying between the Savannah and Santee rivers are on this map, which appeared in the May number of the *London Magazine* while the news of General Prevost's campaign was still arriving. Tybee lighthouse, Cockspur Fort, Savannah, and Augusta on the Savannah River, Ninety Six at the top left, and the road over which Prevost marched to Charleston are shown.

Inside the town, the loyalist John Harris Cruger was to write of the unhappy note on which the French and American allies parted:

'They came so full of Confidence of succeeding, that they were at some loss where to lay the blame, each abusing the other for deceiving them. . . . We are all hands sufferers by this unfortunate invasion. The only difference is we have acquired glory and our enemies disgrace.'[5]

Lincoln's shattered army limped back to Charleston and began half-heartedly throwing up fortifications in defence of the attack that was almost certain to be made against the city.

In New York, Sir Henry Clinton decided that it was time to move again. Earlier, he had pulled out the 3,000-man garrison stationed at Newport in anticipation of the expedition. On 26 December 1779 he sailed with a force of 7,600 men aboard ninety transports, escorted by fourteen naval vessels. Off the dread Outer Banks of North Carolina, the thin curve of offshore islands known as 'the graveyard of the Atlantic', the fleet sailed into the wild winter storms beating against that section of the continent. The *Russian Merchant* foundered with its cargo of heavy artillery. Horses, terrified by the pitching seas, pawed so frantically in their stalls that many were killed; others were thrown overboard to lighten ship. The *Anna*, with

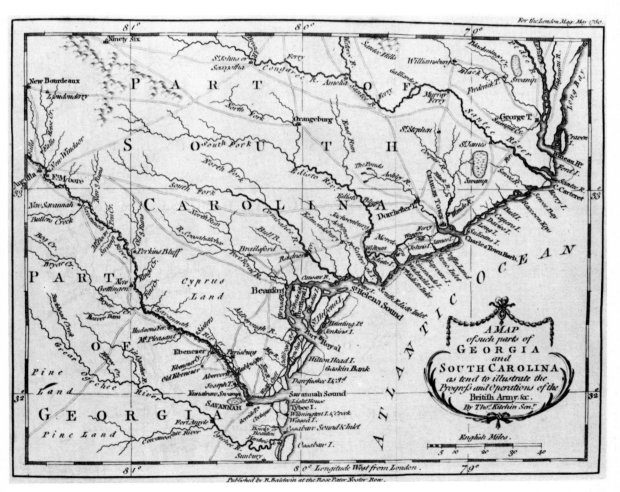

207. The Harbour of Charles Town . . . with a View of the Town from the South Shore of Ashley River

This inset shows Broughton's Battery, the fortified tip end of the Charleston peninsula, seen from James Island across the Ashley River. This is one of the variant forms of the inset found on a large chart of the harbour prepared by Joseph J. W. Des Barres for the *Atlantic Neptune* from careful surveys made by Sir James Wallace, captain in the Royal Navy, in 1776.

a cargo of 200 terrified Hessians, was blown across the Atlantic. After a turbulent voyage of thirty-eight days the demoralized fleet crept into Edisto Inlet and began disembarking their human cargo on Johns Island, some thirty miles below Charleston. This was rice country and cotton country, with black tidal rivers, cypress swamps, gracious plantation houses, and a slave population of Gullah negroes.

The appearance of the city of white tents shook the defenders of Charleston out of their lethargy. Fortifications, 'like mushrooms . . . sprang from the soil', while 600 slaves were brought in from neighbouring plantations to labour on the earthworks.

Lincoln threw up earthworks across Charleston Neck, with a series of strong batteries and redoubts. As the British approached, there was something of a revival of chivalry as soldiers played at knights. After the pickets commanded by Colonel John Laurens had been driven in, Laurens

'was reinforced in the evening by Major Low and about ninety men, with two field pieces. Our officers and men, stimulated in view of both armies and many ladies, vied with each other in acts of firmness and gallantry; particularly in regaining an old breastwork, the enemy took possession of in the evening, after our people were retreating regularly to the garrison. A mere point of honor, without advantage! and afterwards left it about dark, retreating very orderly into the garrison.'[6]

British batteries opened fire on 5 April, but after only three days it became evident that this was to be no replay of the siege of 1776. In an almost insolent fashion, the naval vessels under Vice-Admiral Marriot Arbuthnot demonstrated that Fort Moultrie (old Fort Sullivan) no longer was to be the key

274

to the attack upon the town. From his post on land, Captain Johan Hinrichs of the Hessian *jäger* corps heard the roar of artillery:

'This afternoon our men-of-war passed Fort Moultrie. At four o'clock they came out of Five-Fathom Hole with a splendid wind and a strong tide, and aided by fog. The Admiral went ahead in a jolly boat and piloted each ship. Sir Andrew Snape Hammond led the vanguard with the *Roebuck*. At half past four he passed the fort, which belched fire out of forty pieces, most of them 24-pounders. As soon as this ship in all her glory came under the fort she defiantly replied with a broadside and then sailed by without loss and without delay. After crossing below the city she cast anchor at Fort Johnson. Then came the *Richmond*, . . . She lost her fore-topmast. The *Renown* formed

208. A Sketch of the Environs of Charlestown in South Carolina. *George Sproule*

This survey shows the movements of Clinton's troops from their landing at North Edisto Inlet on 11 February 1780 across the swamps and waterways of John's and James Islands in their advance to Charleston. 'The landing place was Simmons Point on Simmons Island', noted Captain Johann Hinricks of the Hessian Jäger corps in his diary. 'It is a port of Johns Island, desolate and sandy, and full of cabbage trees . . . [Our] column made its way through a wilderness of deep sand, marshland, and impenetrable woods where human feet had never trod . . . Sometimes we had to struggle, singly or two abreast, through marsh and woodland for half a mile. What a land to wage war in!'

This map, engraved for the *Atlantic Neptune* on 1 June 1780, was made 'on the Spot' by Captain George Sproule, assistant engineer in the 16th Regiment. In 1767 he had helped survey the St Lawrence River and Labrador coast under the surveyor general, S. Holland; in 1778 he supervised engineering fortifications around New York; and after the Revolution from 1785 to 1817 he was the first surveyor general of the Province of New Brunswick.

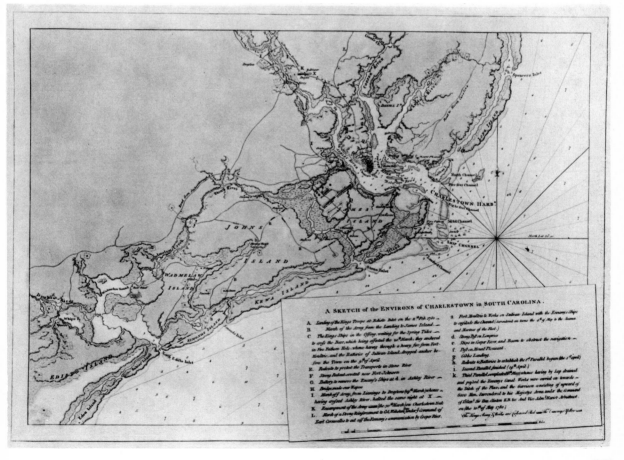

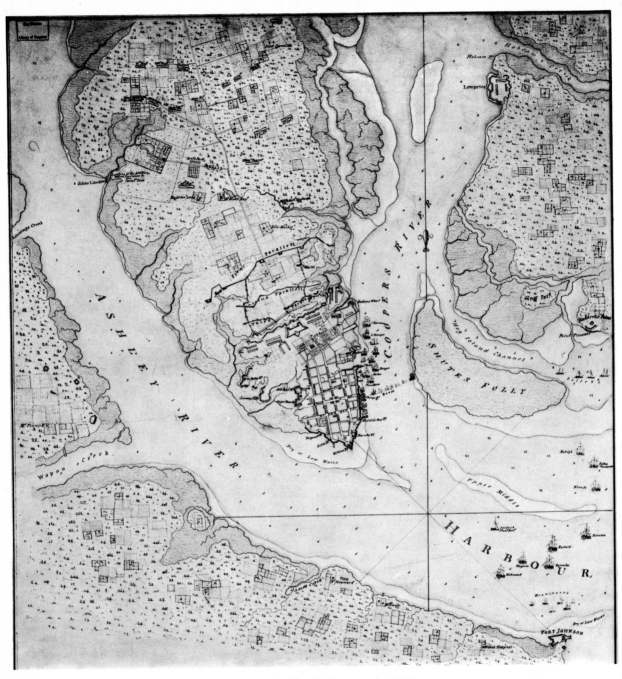

209. The Investiture of Charleston, S.C. by the English army in 1780

The surrender of Lincoln's entire army and capture of the strategic capital was one of the great disasters of the war for the Americans. Clinton's forces and equipment were greatly superior to those of his opponents.

On 20 March 1780, Vice-Admiral Arbuthnot moved his vessels across the bar into Five Fathom Holes and Charleston Harbour. Nine days later Clinton crossed the Ashley River in force from Linning's (Old Town) Creek to Gibbs Landing by transport. From their encampments, which stretched across the peninsula north of the city, the British advanced cautiously by a series of three parallel trenches in classical siege fashion. The Americans had time to repair the defences of the city, neglected since 1776, to dig a broad canal or moat in front of ramparts extending east and west from the Citadel ('O' on the map), fortify the shore line, and make a boom across the Cooper River anchored to a series of sunken ships. Lincoln's situation, however, became increasingly desperate; on 12 May he capitulated.

the rear guard, and when she arrived at the fort she lay to, took in her sails, and gave such an unrelenting, murderous fire that the whole ship seemed to flare up. Thus she covered the rear of the squadron.

One transport ran aground and was so shot to pieces that the sailors had to set her afire and abandon her. Several cannon balls went through the ships without doing any damage. By half-past six our ships lay at anchor on this side, having [twenty-]seven killed and one midshipman and thirteen men wounded, most of whom were on the *Roebuck*. What a trifling loss under so enormous a fire! The enemy suddenly stopped firing and, filled with amazement, saw the proud Briton, the master of the sea, meet and overcome every danger, every obstacle, with scorn and disdain. Horror, astonishment, fear, despondency, and shattered hopes seem to befog their eyes, ears, and hearts to such an extent that they did not fire a single shot at our men, who had jumped upon the parapets of the works!'[7]

Two days later, Clinton sent in summons to which Lincoln replied 'that his duty and inclination led him to hold out to the last extremity'. He had kept an escape route up the Cooper River, where Brigadier-General Isaac Huger was in command at Biggin Bridge near Monck's Corner. Banastre Tarleton, proud commander of the tory unit known as the British Legion, reinforced with Patrick Ferguson's riflemen, was sent to dislodge Huger. Tarleton was later to write of the incident:

'It was evident that the American cavalry had posted themselves in front of the Cooper River, and that the militia were placed in a meeting house which commanded the bridge, and were distributed on the opposite bank. At three o'clock in the morning, the advanced guard of dragoons and mounted infantry, supported by the remainder of the legion and Ferguson's corps, approached the American post. A watch word was immediately communicated to the officers and soldiers, which was closely followed by an order to charge the enemy's guard on the main road, there being no other avenue open, owing to the swamps upon the flanks, and to pursue them into camp.

The order was executed with the greatest promptitude and success. The Americans were completely surprised. Major Vernier, of Pulaski's legion, and some other officers and men who attempted to defend themselves were killed or wounded. General Huger, Colonels Washington and Jamieson, with many officers and men, fled on foot to the swamps close to their encampment, where, being concealed by the darkness, they effected their escape. Four hundred horses belonging to the officers and dragoons, with their arms and appointments (a valuable acquisition for the British cavalry in their present state), fell into the hand of the victors, about one hundred officers, dragoons and hussars, together with fifty wagons loaded with arms, clothing and ammunition, shared the same fate.

Without loss of time, Major Cochrane was ordered to force the bridge and the meeting house with the infantry of the British legion. He charged the militia with fixed bayonets, got possession of the pass and dispersed every thing that opposed him.

In the attack at Monck's Corner, and at Biggin Bridge, the British had one officer and two men wounded, with five horses killed and wounded.'[8]

On 17 April, Clinton received a reinforcement of 3,000 men from New York,

210. Map of North and South Carolina (detail of Charles Town Precinct). *Mouzon*

Henry Mouzon's map, published in London just before the outbreak of the war, with its excellent topographical information about roads, rivers with their tributaries, and plantation owners, was used by General Henry Clinton and his officers in their campaigns. Clinton's own copy is preserved in the William L. Clements Library.

At the top centre of this detail is Monck's Corner, just above Goose Creek, where the Mouzons lived. Lieutenant-Colonel Banastre Tarleton's swift march to Monck's Corner and surprise attack on General Isaac Huger's cavalry force there at three o'clock on the morning of 13 April 1780 resulted in the rout of the Americans and narrowed the possibility of escape for General Lincoln's army in Charleston. The victory gave immediate fame to Tarleton and the green-uniformed British Legion of Tories he had recruited.

and the British dug and scraped even more vigorously in the sandy soil. New batteries added their thunder, yet surprisingly few people were injured. Lincoln, realizing that he could not hold out, considered removing his Continental troops and called a council of general officers:

'When the citizens were informed upon what the council was deliberating, some of them came into council, and expressed themselves very warmly, and declared to General Lincoln, that if he attempted to withdraw the troops, and leave the citizens; that they would cut up his boats, and open the gates to the enemy: this put a stop to all thoughts of evacuation of the troops, and nothing was left to us, but to make the best terms we could.'[9]

211. Mulberry House and Grounds. *Thomas Coram*

The leaders and defenders of Charleston were for the most part planters of rice and indigo, with a country house, a town house, and many Negro slaves. Mulberry House, used as headquarters by British cavalry during the Revolution and by the Continental forces in the spring of 1781 and called 'Castle' because of its medieval aspect, was built in 1714 by Thomas Broughton, governor of the province from 1735–7, and owned by the family until this century. It was a strong point and refuge for other families in the Yemassee War of 1715.

Like other plantations, Mulberry fronted on a river, here the Cooper, near Monck's Corner in Berkeley County. It was patterned after Seaton, a Jacobean brick manor-house of the Broughtons in England, with a hip-on-gable roof, five dormers, and four tower rooms with bell-shaped cupolas. Its name came from a mulberry tree found here when Indians cultivated the land. This view by Coram, a painter from Bristol, England, who came to Charleston in 1769, shows the house at the end of the 'street', a row of cabins for house servants and field hands.

In a show of senseless bravado, the Americans made a sortie in force, but only succeeded in losing a number of men, including General Moultrie's brother. The English ridiculed the effort:

'On the Morning of the 24th, as Monkies mimic Men, we had a Sortie—such a Sortie as the Rebels have only succeeded by, and such a Sortie as a Thief may make his Fortune by—but if he stays to see *who is there*, he is either killed on the Spot, or rewarded with a Halter.'[10]

By 3 May, Clinton's third parallel was almost complete and from their works the Americans could clearly see preparations being made for an assault. Fort Moultrie still stood on Sullivan's Island as a symbol of hope; one British officer commented that 'none but cowardly Rascals would ever give up so strong a Post'. A force of British marines was landed on the island. Around two o'clock in the morning of 5 May,

'Captain Hudson, of the Navy, summoned the fort. Lieut. Col. Scott, who commanded, sent out for Answer, "Tol, lol, derol, lol. Fort Moultrie will be defended to the last Extremity."

The Sixth, Captain Hudson sent word to Col. Scott he had given him Time enough to consider of it, and made his Proposals. If he did not send out an Answer in a Quarter of an Hour, he would storm it, and put every Man to the Sword. At this, Mr. Scott sent out, begging a Cessation of Hostilities, that the Fort would surrender. . . . The seventh they marched out, and Capt. Hudson marched in, took Possession, levelled the Thirteen Stripes with the Dust, and the Triumphant English Flag was raised on the Staff. This shocked the Gentry in Town.'[11]

This was but the beginning of the end. On 6 May, Clinton 'sent proposals of surrender to us, beginning with a preamble, that it proceeded from his humanity and desire to spare the effusion of blood'. Lincoln's proposals in his reply were declared 'utterly inadmissable', and there was the warning that hostilities would 'commence afresh'. William Moultrie, who had known the exhilaration of victory in Charleston, now waited to taste the dregs of defeat:

'We remained near an hour silent, all calm and ready, each waiting for the other to begin. At length, we fired the first gun, and immediately followed a tremendous number of shells; it was a glorious sight, to see them like meteors crossing each other, and bursting in the air; it appeared as if the stars were tumbling down. The fire was incessant almost the whole night, cannon-balls whizzing and shells hissing continually amongst us; ammunition chests and temporary magazines blowing up; great guns bursting, and wounded men groaning along the lines: it was a dreadful night! it was our last great effort, but it availed us nothing; after this, our military ardor was much abated; we began to cool, and we cooled gradually, and on the eleventh of May we capitulated.'[12]

The following day one observer noted 'tears coursing down the cheeks of Gen. Moultrie'. But as the Americans sadly beat a 'Turk's March', one Britisher was elated:

'The LINCOLNADE was acted on the 12th. General Leslie with the Royal English Fusiliers and Hessian Grenadiers, and some Artillery, took possession of the Town, and planted the British Colours by the Gate, on the

212. Lieutenant-General Sir Henry Clinton

Clinton was the only one of the British generals of the Revolution who left a long, detailed account of the entire war as he experienced it, in which he attempted to analyse the reasons for failure and assess blame. This account, 'An Historical Detail of Seven Years' Campaigns in North America from 1775 to 1782', is biased by his ardent desire to clear himself of the responsibility for failure and to lay the blame on others; it is, however, both valuable historically and revealing of the man himself.

One of his fortes was the making of detailed military plans, often of great merit, which were frequently disregarded by others or which failed by his own over-cautious nature. His relationships with neither his superiors nor his subordinates ran smooth; his sense of grievance and of worry for his reputation kept him from firm and audacious action when it was needed, as in the disasters of Burgoyne and Cornwallis. Yet he could plan and execute a military action with brilliance, as in the Battle of Long Island. But he was not strong enough to rise above the enormous difficulties with which he had to cope.

Ramparts, and Lincoln limp'd out at the Head of the most ragged Rabble I ever beheld; it, however, pleased me much better than the Meschianza.

They were indulged with beating a drum and to bring out their Colours cased; they laid down their Arms between their Abattis, and surrendered Prisoners of War. There are seven Generals here. I am told the whole Continentals, including Hospital, amount to Two Thousand three Hundred. The Militia, poor Creatures, could not be prevailed upon to come out. They began to creep out of their Holes the next Day . . . by the Capitulation, they are allowed to go home and plow the ground. There only can they be useful.'[13]

John Mathews, Congressional delegate from South Carolina, was unhappy with the prospect of the fall of Charleston, but still maintained an attitude of defiant rebellion:

'If [it] has fallen or does fall, I fear the whole country goes with it, for having nothing but a few discontented, fluctuating militia to depend on, we shall never be in any condition to check the ravages of a merciless enemy, and I imagine our people have not fortitude enough to see their property destroyed when their submission can be the means of saving it. . . . I shall look on myself (whenever this event happens) as not worth a groat, unless we can retake the country or have it restored by treaty, then the land must remain but nothing else.

As to becoming a British citizen again, if a restoration of my estate is to depend on these terms, why let them keep it, and the Devil help them with it.'[14]

So fell proud Charleston, key port of the South. Now it seemed that the British only had to mop up scattered pockets of resistance, and then go about the business of rolling up the southern states one by one, and at their own pace. One source of possible irritation was Colonel Abraham Buford's force of 300 Virginians who had been marching to the relief of Charleston, but had now begun falling back towards North Carolina. The Legion of Banastre Tarleton was sent galloping off after them. The subsequent engagement in the Waxhaws was to earn for the Green Dragoon the sobriquet of 'Bloody Tarleton' and the term 'Tarleton's Quarters' was to become synonymous with bloodshed and cruelty on the battlefield. Surgeon Robert Brownfield was one of those who laid down their arms and asked for mercy:

'[Tarleton's] ostensible pretext for cruelty for the relentless barbarity that ensued, was, that his horse was killed under him just as the flag was raised. . . . Ensign Cruit, who advanced with the flag, was instantly shot down. Viewing this as an earnest of what they were to expect, a resumption of their arms was attempted, to sell their lives as dearly as possible; but before this was fully effected, Tarleton with his cruel myrmidons was in the midst of them, when commenced a scene of indiscriminate carnage, never surpassed by the ruthless atrocities of the most barbarous savages.

The demand for quarters, seldom refused to a vanquished foe, was at once found to be in vain; not a man was spared, and it was the concurrent testimony of all the survivors that for fifteen minutes after, every man was prostrate. They went over the ground, plunging their bayonets into everyone that exhibited any signs of life and, in some instances, where several had fallen over the others, these monsters were seen to throw off on the point of the bayonet the uppermost, to come at those underneath.'[15]

Better to maintain control of South Carolina a chain of posts was established across the state, stretching as far west as Ninety-Six. With the conqueror's authority seemingly re-established, Clinton returned to New York, leaving Lord Cornwallis in command. On the surface, it appeared that a pattern of government was in force, but there ran beneath the surface an undercurrent of hate.

For the Americans, there was the question of the selection of a successor to Benjamin Lincoln. Washington wished Nathanael Greene to command the Southern Department, but too many members of Congress remembered the glory of Saratoga. So it was Horatio Gates who rode southward, 'dress'd in a grey frock coat and a bob-wig—his suite was two aid de camps and a domestick'. In North Carolina, at Hollingsworth's farm, on Deep River, the general came up with his new command on 25 July 1780. Perhaps his stunning victory over Burgoyne was still too green in his memory and he wished to polish his image in history, for Gates, after little more than a cursory examination of his troops, issued orders for his ragged army to hold themselves in readiness to march at once. To blunt Lord Cornwallis' possible expedition into North Carolina and Virginia, Gates planned to fall upon the post at Camden, South Carolina, at this time under the control of Francis, Lord Rawdon. Protests that provisions were scarce were brushed aside with the assurance, 'Plenty will soon succeed the late unavoidable scarcity ... provisions, rum, salt, and every requisite will flow into camp ... [and] with a liberal hand be distributed.' Rather than swinging through Mecklenburg and Rowan counties where the people were friendly to the cause and supplies were relatively plentiful, Gates chose the more direct route through the pine barrens because it was fifty miles shorter, although food was scarce and its people of royal inclinations. Gates ignored the protests of his officers and on 27 July marched out of camp. The progress of the army was marked by the beat of the drum and the squeal of the fife. Every morning the piney woods shuddered with the boom of the morning gun. Colonel Otho Williams, deputy adjutant-general, wasn't impressed with this show of martial fluff:

'The distresses of the soldiery daily increased—they were told that the banks of the Pee Dee River were extremely fertile—and so indeed they were; but the preceding crop of corn (the principal article of produce) was exhausted, and the new grain, although luxuriant and fine, was unfit for use. Many of the soldiery, urged by necessity, plucked the green ears and boiled them with the lean beef, which was collected in the woods, made for themselves a repast, not unpalatable to be sure, but which was attended with painful effects. Green peaches also were substituted for bread, and had similar consequences. Some of the officers, aware of the risk of eating such vegetables, and in such a state, with poor fresh beef, and without salt, restrained themselves from taking anything but the beef itself, boiled or roasted. It occurred to some that the hair powder which remained in their bags, would thicken soup, and it was actually applied. . . .

As there were no spirits yet arrived in camp. and as ... it was unusual for troops to make a forced march, or prepare to meet an enemy without some extraordinary allowance, it was unluckily conceived that molasses would, for once, be an acceptable substitute.'[16]

William Seymour felt the effects of this diet:

'Instead of rum we had a gill of molasses per man served out to us, which instead of livening our spirits, served to purge us as well as if we had taken a jallap, for the men all the way as we went along, were every moment obliged to fall out of the Ranks to evacuate.'[17]

The intelligence that Gates had not received was that Cornwallis had moved up to Camden to assume personal command. By coincidence, both armies moved out at ten o'clock on the night of 15 August, each taking a route through Gum Swamp. Some time after two o'clock in the morning, in a narrow clearing between two branches of the swamp in 'Parker's Old Field', the two forces blundered into each other. Muskets stabbed fire through the night, shouts split the air, and then all suddenly fell quiet as the two armies stumbled back to await the coming of daylight.

Otho Williams, as adjutant-general, was able to reconstruct the battle of Camden from the reports gathered from the men on the field and his own observations:

'The General's astonishment could not be concealed. He ordered ... another council of war. All the general officers immediately assembled . . . ; the unwelcome news was communicated to them. General Gates said, "Gentlemen, what is best to be done?" All were mute for a few moments, when the gallant Stevens exclaimed, "Gentlemen, is [it] not too late *now* to do anything but fight?" No other advice was offered, and the General desired the gentlemen would repair to their respective commands. . . .

Frequent skirmishes happened during the night between the two advanced parties, which served to discover the relative situation of the two armies, and as a prelude to what was to take place in the morning.

At dawn of day (on the morning of the 16th of August) the enemy appeared in front advancing in column. . . .

The deputy adjutant general requested General Stevens to let him have forty or fifty privates, volunteers, who would run forward of the brigade and commence the attack. They were led forward within forty or fifty yards of the enemy, and ordered to take trees and keep up as brisk a fire as possible. The desired effect of this expedient, to extort the enemy's fire at some distance, . . . was not gained. General Stevens, observing the enemy to rush on, put his men in mind of their bayonets; but, the impetuosity with which they advanced, firing and huzzaing, threw the whole body of the militia into

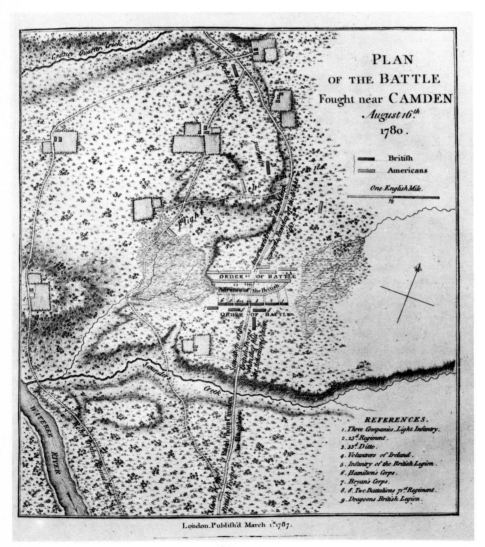

213. Plan of the Battle Fought near Camden August 16*th* 1780

William Faden's engraving in Banastre Tarleton's *History of the Campaigns of 1780 and 1781 in the Southern Department* (London, 1797) shows the route of the British troops northward from Camden to their meeting with the Americans after crossing Saunders Creek, five miles from Camden.

214. A New and Accurate Map of North Carolina, and Part of South Carolina, with the Field of Battle between Earl Cornwallis and General Gates *(detail)*

This map, which appeared in the *Political Magazine* for 30 November 1780, places the Battle of Camden too far to the north of the town; it shows, however, the general topography of the region in which the two armies were operating.

such a panic, that they generally threw down their *loaded* arms and fled in the utmost consternation. The unworthy example of the Virginians was followed by the North Carolinians; only a small part of the brigade, commanded by Brigadier General Gregory, made a short pause. A part of Dixon's regiment, of that brigade . . . fired two or three rounds of cartridge. But a great majority of the militia (at least two-thirds of the army) fled without firing a shot. . . .

The regular troops, who had the keen edge of sensibility rubbed off by strict discipline and hard service, saw the confusion with but little emotion. They engaged seriously in the affair. . . .

Lord Cornwallis, perceiving there was no cavalry opposed to him, pushed forward his dragoons and his infantry charging at the same moment with fixed bayonets, put an end to the contest.

His victory was complete. All the artillery and a great number of prisoners fell into his hands. Many fine fellows lay on the field, and the rout of the remainder was entire (not even a company retired in any order), every one escaped as he could. . . .

The only apology General Gates condescended to make to the army for the loss of the battle was, "A man may pit a cock, but he can't *make* him fight," "The fate of battle is uncontrollable," and such other common maxims as admit of no contradiction. . . .

General Gates perceived no effective succour short of Hillsborough, where the General Assembly of North Carolina were about to convene. Thither he repaired, with all possible expedition. . . .'[18]

The bubble of Saratoga had burst with the force of a cannon shot. Americans could not believe it at first, and then many of those who had sent Gates off to the South with such bold assurances that he would 'Burgoyne' Cornwallis for sure, now began to clamour for his recall. The British were jubilant. James Rivington's Tory newspaper in New York, the *Royal Gazette*, published a derisive advertisement which was said to have been 'stuck up at the public places' in Philadelphia:

'Millions! — Millions! — Millions!
REWARD

STRAYED, DESERTED, OR STOLEN, from the Subscriber, on the 16th of August last, near Camden, in the State of South Carolina, a whole Army, consisting of Horse, Foot, and Dragoons, to the amount of near TEN THOUSAND (as has been said) with all their baggage, artillery, wagons and camp equipage. The subscriber has very strong suspicions, from information received from his Aid de Camp, that a certain CHARLES, EARL CORNWALLIS, was principally concerned in carrying off the said ARMY with their baggage, &c. Any person or persons civil or military, who will give information, either to the Subscriber, or to Charles Thompson. Esq., Secretary to the Continental Congress, where the said ARMY is, so that they may be recovered and rallied again, shall be entitled to demand from the Treasurer of the United States, the sum of THREE MILLIONS OF PAPER DOLLARS as soon as they can be spared from the Public Funds, and ANOTHER MILLION. for apprehending the Person Principally concerned in taking the said Army off. Proper passes will be granted by the President of the said Congress to such persons as incline to go in search of said ARMY. And as further encouragement, no deduction will be made from the above reward on account of any of the Militia (who composed the said ARMY) not being able to be found or heard of, as no dependence can be placed on their services, and nothing but the most speedy flight can ever save their Commander.

HORATIO GATES, M.G.

and late Commander in Chief of the Southern Army, August 30, 1780.'[19]

With Gates crushed and the forces of Thomas Sumter, the South Carolina partisan leader, scattered, Cornwallis pushed out of Camden on 8 September 1780, moving northward towards Charlotte. It was to be a three-pronged invasion. One detachment under Major James Craig was to occupy the port of Wilmington, thereby opening up the Cape Fear River as a supply route into the interior. Major Patrick Ferguson, acting as Inspector of Militia for the Southern Provinces, was to move along the base of the mountains, protecting the west, or left, flank.

Cornwallis had marched into Charlotte on 25 September, and had met opposition from partisan bands operating under the command of William Lee Davidson, Joseph Graham and young William R. Davie, so much so that one British officer admitted, 'The whole of the British army was actually kept at bay for some minutes by a few mounted Americans, not exceeding twenty in number.' And once in town, an aide to his Lordship was to write, 'Charlotte is an agreeable village, but in a damned rebellious country.'

After a skirmish, Ferguson marched through the foothills of the South Carolina Blue Ridge, an area one young lieutenant termed 'composed of the most violent rebels I ever saw, particularly the young ladies'. By 23 September, he was at Gilbert Town, at the time consisting of 'one dwelling house, one barn, a blacksmith's shop, and some out-houses'.

But now word came in that the mountain men, hardened frontiersmen from across the Appalachian chain, were flocking in to a rendezvous, and were planning to march against Ferguson. He began to fall back on Corn-wallis' army at Charlotte, but engaged in a bit of bluster hoping to frighten off his pursuers, issuing an appeal to the 'inhabitants of North Carolina':

'Gentlemen: Unless you wish to be eat up by an inundation of barbarians, who begun by murdering an unarmed son before an aged father, and after-wards lopped off his arms, and who by their shocking cruelties and irregularities, give the best proof of their cowardice and want of discipline; I say, if you wish to be pinioned, robbed, and murdered, and see your wives and daughters, in four days, abused by the dregs of mankind—in short, if you wish or deserve to live and bear the name of men, grasp your arms in a moment and run to camp.

The Back Water men have crossed the mountains; McDowell, Hampton, Shelby, Cleveland were at their head, so that you know what you have to depend upon. If you choose to be degraded forever and ever by a set of mongrels, say so at once, and let your women turn their backs on you, and look out for real men to protect them.'[20]

After a tiring march on 6 October, Ferguson camped near the North Carolina line on an outlying spur of the Blue Ridge rising some sixty feet above the surrounding countryside, called 'Little King's Mountain', from the man who farmed the soil at its base. The summit was more of a plateau some six hundred yards long and ranging from seventy to one hundred and twenty yards wide. The sides were rocky, precipitous and densely wooded. The place looked good to Ferguson, so much so that he supposedly made the statement that 'he was on King's Mountain, and that he was king of that Mountain, and that God Almighty could not drive him from it'.

By the following day the mountain men were at the base of King's Mountain, united under the command of Colonel William Campbell of the Virginia militia, who had been elected 'Officer of the Day'. Isaac Shelby described the beginning of the attack:

'When the patriots came near the mountains they halted, tied all their loose baggage to their saddles, fastened their horses and left them under charge of a few men, and then prepared for an immediate attack. About 3 o'clock the patriot force was led to the attack in four columns. Col. Campbell commanded the right centre column, Col. Shelby the left centre, Col. Sevier the right flank column, and Col. Cleveland the left flank. As they came to the foot of the mountain, the right centre and right flank columns deployed to the right, and the left centre and left flank columns to the left, and thus surrounding the mountain they marched up, commencing the action on all sides.'[21]

The surge up the mountain caught Ferguson unprepared, along with Captain Alexander Chesney, a South Carolina loyalist officer:

'So rapid was the attack, that I was in the act of dismounting to report that all was quiet when we heard their firing about half a mile distant. I imme-diately paraded the men and posted the officers. During this short interval I received a wound, which, however, did not prevent my doing my duty, and on going towards my horse I found he had been killed.

King's mountain, from its height, would have enabled us to oppose a superior force with advantage, had it not been covered with wood, which sheltered the Americans and enabled them to fight in their favorite manner.

In fact, after driving in our pickets, they were enabled to advance in three divisions, under separate leaders, to the crest of the hill in perfect safety, until they took post, and opened an irregular but destructive fire from behind trees and other cover. . . . In this manner the engagement was maintained for near an hour, the mountaineers flying when there was danger of being charged with the bayonet, and returning again so soon as the British detachment had faced about to repeal another of their parties.'[22]

Fighting that day on the American side was sixteen-year-old Thomas Young:

'The orders were at the firing of the first gun, for every man to raise a whoop, rush forward, and fight his way as best he could. When our division came up the northern base of the mountain, and Col. Roebuck drew us a little to the left and commenced the attack. I well remember how I behaved. Ben Hollingsworth and myself took right up the side of the mountain, and fought from tree to tree, our way to the summit. I recollect I stood behind one tree and fired until the bark was nearly all knocked off, and my eyes pretty well filled with it. One fellow shaved me pretty close, for his bullet took a piece out of my gun stock. Before I was aware of it, I found myself apparently between my own regiment and the enemy, as I judged, from seeing the paper which the whigs wore in their hats, and the pine knots the tories wore in theirs, these being the badges of distinction.'[23]

Above the crash of rifle and musket could be heard the thin shriek of the little silver whistle by which Ferguson directed his troops. Suddenly it could be heard no more. Isaac Shelby had just gained the summit:

'It was here that Fergusson . . . was killed—and a white flag was soon after hoisted by the enemy, in token of surrender, They were ordered to throw down their arms; which they did, and surrendered themselves at discretion. It was some time before a complete cessation of the firing, on our part, could be effected. Our men who had been so scattered in the battle were continually coming up, and continued to fire, without comprehending in the heat of the moment, what had happened; and some, who had heard that at Buford's defeat the British had refused quarters to many who had asked it, were willing to follow the bad example. Owing to these causes, the ignorance of some, and the disposition of some to retaliate, it required some time and some exertion on the part of the officers, to put an entire stop to the firing. After the surrender of the enemy, our men gave spontaneously three loud and long shouts.'[24]

One item picked up later was a small leather-bound diary that contained the notation under 7 October: 'The cursed rebels Came upon us killed and Took every Soul and So My Dear friends I bid you farewell for I am Started to the warm Country.'

The prisoners were marched to Gilbert Town where the American Colonel Campbell found himself forced to issue the order: 'I must request the officers of all ranks in the army to restrain the disorderly manner of slaughtering and disturbing the prisoners.' One of these was a military surgeon who witnessed the end of the unlucky loyalists among them:

'*Saturday, Oct. 14, 1780.* Ten o'clock in the morning their guard paraded & formed a circle. Capt. DePeyster & the rest of our officers were ordered within the ring. They proceeded to trying the militiamen for treason. Thirty of them were condemned and bound under the gallows. We were kept throughout the day in the rain, spectators of this disagreeable days work. At seven o'clock in the evening, they began to execute them. Coll. Mills, Capt. Wilson, Capt. Chitwood, and six others were hanged for their loyalty to their sovereign. They died like Romans, saying they died for their King and his Laws.

What increased this melancholy scene was the seeing Mrs. Mills take leave of her husband & two of Capt. Chitwoods daughters take leave of their father. The latter were comforted with being told their father was pardoned, They then went to our fire where we had made a shed to keep out the rain. They had scarce set down when news was brought that their father was dead. Here words can scarce describe the melancholy scene, the two young ladies swoon'd away and continued in fits all night. — Mrs. Mills with a young child in her arms set out all night in the rain with her husbands corps & not even a blanket to cover her from the inclemency of the weather. One of the condemned named Baldwin at the foot of the gallows broke through their guard and made his escape.'[25]

Of those convicted, nine were hanged. The others were reprieved when there was the rumour that Tarleton was on his way to rescue them. But more important, Ferguson, Cornwallis's hoped-for 'great Western Bugbear', was dead, and the British timetable of invasion thrown off schedule.

215. King's Mountain, 7 October 1780. *Graham*

The country surrounding King's Mountain was densely forested; trees covered its precipitous slopes to a gently rounded and sloping top which was comparatively clear. Here Ferguson bivouacked his Rangers and Loyalist troops; it was, he thought, an impregnable position. He did not know the methods of the mountain men; his assumed safety was his undoing.

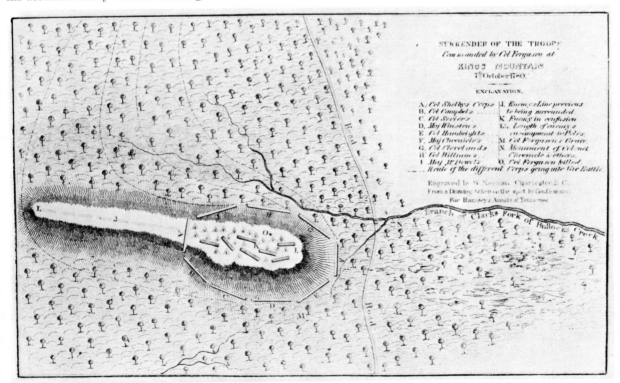

13. The South: Phase Two

AT CHARLOTTE, a small North Carolina town which was a nest of rebels, Lord Cornwallis lay ill, shivering and tossing with fever. In the tents clustered around the village many of his men sickened and clung to their blankets. The news of the defeat of Ferguson was a blow strong enough for the general to issue orders to pull back into South Carolina. After fifteen days of wallowing over roads saturated by almost constant rain, the British army went into camp at Wynnesborough. But it was almost a new South Carolina, for many had wearied of British measures and had taken the field under such dashing partisan leaders as Thomas Sumter, Francis Marion, and Andrew Pickens. Among those who joined Marion in the eastern, sub-tropical, snake-infested swamp country was Captain Tarleton Brown:

'Overtaking General Marion at Kingstree, Black River, S.C., we immediately united with his troops. Marion's route lay then between the Santee and Little Pedee rivers; and being desirous to intercept and defeat Col. Watts [Watson], who was then marching at the head of 400 men between Camden and Georgetown, every arrangement and preparation was made to carry into execution his design. All things being now ready, Watts appeared in sight at the head of his large force, and as they marched down the road with great show and magnificence (hoping, no doubt, to terrify and conquer the country), they spied us; at which time, the British horse sallied forth to surround us.

Marion, with his characteristic shrewdness and sagacity, discovered their manoeuvres, anticipated their object and retreated to the woods, some four or five hundred yards, and prepared for them. In a few moments they came dashing up, expecting to find us all in confusion and disorder, but to their astonishment we were ready for the attack, and perceiving this, they called a halt, at which time Marion and Horry ordered a charge. Col. Horry stammered badly, and on this occasion he leaned forward, spurred his horse, waved his sword and ran fifty or sixty yards, endeavoring to utter the word *charge*, and finding he could not, bawled out, *"Damn it boys, you . . . you know what I mean. Go on!"*

We were then doing what we could, pressing with all rapidity to the strife, and before the British could get back to the main body we slew a goodly number of them. Being eager to do all the damage we could, we pursued the fellows very close to the line of their main body, and as soon as they got in, Watts began to thunder his cannon at us, and to tear down the limbs and branches of the trees, which fell about us like hail, but did no other damage than to wound one of our men. . . . Marion, now finding his force, which consisted only of two hundred men (though sterling to a man, brave, fearless and patriotic), was too small to give Watts open battle, guarded the bridges and swamps in his route, and annoyed and killed his men as they passed.

216. Cornwallis retreats from Charlotte, 'a hornet's nest'.
Nelson

On 26 September 1780 Cornwallis occupied Charlotte in his unsuccessful campaign to annihilate Patriot resistance in North Carolina. Charlotte, with about forty houses, an arms factory, and a court-house at the centre of its crossroads, was a hotbed of rebellion where in May 1775 the 'Mecklenburg Resolves' had been signed. Instead of success Cornwallis found increasing threats from gathering frontiersmen and militia under General William Davidson and others, who attacked his foraging parties. He began a hasty retreat towards Winnsboro, South Carolina, on 12 October. His troops were led astray from the main road by their guide; the mud was so bad that some thirty wagons with supplies and arms were abandoned.

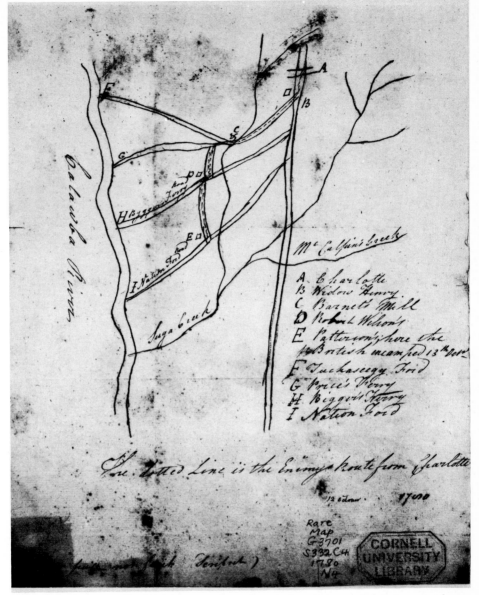

For prudence sake, Marion never encamped over two nights in one place, unless at a safe distance from the enemy. He generally commenced the line of march about sun-set, continuing through the greater part of the night. By this policy he was enabled effectually to defeat the plans of the British and to strengthen his languishing cause. For while the one army was encamping and resting in calm and listless security, not dreaming of danger, the other, taking advantage of opportunity and advancing through the sable curtain of the night unobserved, often effectually vanquished and routed their foes. It was from the craftiness and ingenuity of Marion, the celerity with which he moved from post to post, that his enemies gave to him the significant appellation of the "Swamp Fox".[1]

Partisan warfare was the primary style of fighting in the south. Gates was in North Carolina, nursing his wounded pride and trying to rebuild his army. In response to the increasing cry that he be removed, the Continental Congress suggested to Washington that he select a new commanding general for the Southern Department. He selected Major-General Nathanael Greene, who had but recently been appointed to the command at West Point, and urged him to hasten to his new post, for 'there is an army to be created, the mass of which is at present without any formation at all'. The commander-in-chief regretted that he could not detach sizeable reinforcements to the Army, but he did assign General Steuben and Henry Lee's Legion to Greene's command.

Greene rode south, stopping at Philadelphia for nine days to seek support from the Continental Congress. He was sorely disappointed, for 'poverty was urged as a plea, in bar to every application. They all promised fair, but I fear will do little: ability is wanting with some, and inclinations with others.' If he had seen the *Royal Gazette* a month or so later, Greene may well have agreed with the bit of doggerel that appeared in that paper:

'THE DEVIL AND THE CONGRESS

The Devil loves liberty, and so does the Congress,
The Devil has been a lyar from the beginning, and
* so have the Congress,*
The Devil is a Deceiver, and so are the Congress,
The Devil loves Rebellion, and so do the Congress,
The Devil was chain'd and so will be the Congress,
As the Devil is in Hell; where will be the Congress.'[2]

But there were reasons for Congress' reluctance to make the promises of support that Greene wanted. For one thing, there was the depreciation of paper currency, with the *Royal Gazette*, several months later, describing a demonstration:

'The Congress is finally bankrupt! Last Saturday a large body of the inhabitants with paper dollars in their hats by way of cockades paraded the streets of Philadelphia, carrying colors flying, with a DOG TARRED, and instead of the usual appendage and ornament of feathers, his back was covered with the Congress' paper dollars. This example of disaffection, immediately under the eyes of the rulers of the revolted provinces, in solemn session at the State House assembled, was directly followed by the jailer, who refused accepting the bills in purchase of a glass of rum, and afterwards by the traders of the city, who shut up their shops, declining to sell any more goods but for gold and silver. It was also declared by the popular voice that if the opposition to Great Britain was not carried on by solid money instead of paper bills, all further resistance to the mother country were in vain and must be given up.'[3]

Greene swung by to talk with the governors of Delaware and Maryland, while Steuben rode on towards Virginia where he was to be stationed, forwarding recruits and supplies to the Southern Army. As they paid a visit to Washington's home on the Potomac, Steuben's aide, du Ponceau, remembered:

'On our way, the Baron paid a visit to Mrs. Washington at Mount Vernon. We were most cordially received and invited to dinner. The external appearance of the mansion did not strike the Baron very favorably.

"If," he said, "Washington were not a better general than he was an architect, the affairs of America would be in a very bad condition."[4]

After a visit with Governor Jefferson in Richmond, Greene finally caught up with his army at Charlotte on 2 December 1780. After announcing Greene as his successor, Gates retired to his home, Traveller's Rest, in Virginia, seeking to wipe the smear of Camden from his reputation.

Nathanael Greene was not pleased with his new command nor the condition under which they existed. To his friend, Joseph Reed of Pennsylvania, he complained:

'The appearance of the troops was wretched beyond description, and their distress, on account of provisions, was little less than their sufferings for want of clothing and other necessities. General Gates had lost the confidence of the officers, and the troops all their discipline, and so addicted to plundering that they were a terror to the inhabitants. The general and I met on very good terms and parted so. . . .

The country is so extensive and the powers of government so weak that everybody does as he pleases. The inhabitants are much divided in their political sentiments, and the Whigs and Tories pursue each other with little less than savage fury. The back-country people are bold and daring in their make, but the people upon the sea-shore are sickly and but indifferent militia. The ruin of the State is inevitable if there are such large bodies of militia kept on foot. No army can subsist in the country long if the ravages continue. Indeed, unless this army is better supported than I see any prospect of, the country is lost beyond redemption, for it is impossible for the people to struggle much longer under their present difficulties. There appears a foolish pride in the representation of things from this quarter; the strength and resources of the country are far overrated, and those who are engaged in this business, to indulge their pride, will sacrifice their country. . . .

We are living upon charity and subsist by daily collections. Indian meal and beef is our common diet, and not a drop of spirits have we had with us since I came to the army. An army naked and subsisted in this manner, and not more than one-third equal to the enemy in numbers, will make but a poor fight, especially as one has been accustomed to victory and the other to flight. It is difficult to give spirits to troops that have nothing to animate them.'[5]

Thaddeus Kosciusko, a Polish officer serving with the Southern Army and later to become a famous Polish patriot, had been ordered by Gates to seek a site that had not been depleted by two armies. Returning, he informed Greene that the crops of the country along the Pee Dee River in south-eastern South Carolina promised a partial solution to the food problem. Greene decided to split his army, with the larger segment to take position on the Pee Dee, and a smaller detachment under Brigadier Daniel Morgan swinging to the south-west, to operate in the foothill area between the Broad and Pacolet rivers. Not only would this alleviate the supply situation, but Morgan could discourage Tory raids, give protection to the Whigs, and, in general, 'spirit up the people'. And should Cornwallis undertake another invasion of North Carolina, this detachment could fall in on his flanks. Within five days, Morgan was encamped on the banks of the Pacolet. Colonel William Washington was sent off to scatter the 350 Tories who were plaguing the neighbourhood of a place called 'Fair Forest'. Among the Americans was Thomas Young:

'When we came in sight, we perceived that the Tories had formed a line on the brow of the hill opposite to us. We had a long hill to descend and another to rise. Colonel Washington and his dragoons gave a shout, drew swords, and charged down the hill like madmen. The Tories fled in every distance without firing a gun. We took a great many prisoners and killed a few.

Here I must relate an incident which occurred on this occasion. In Washington's corps there was a boy of fourteen or fifteen, a mere lad, who in crossing Tiger River was ducked by a blunder of his horse. The men laughed and jeered at him very much at which he got mad and swore that, boy or no boy, he would kill a man that day or die. He accomplished the former. I remember very well being highly amused at the little fellow chasing around a [corn] crib after a Tory, cutting and slashing away with his puny arm, till he brought him down.'[6]

Cornwallis could not allow Morgan to manoeuvre undisturbed. On 1 January 1781, Banastre Tarleton with his British Legion, the first battalion of the 71st Regiment, and two light artillery pieces were ordered to find Morgan and 'push him to the utmost'. Morgan fell back before this superior force, allowing militia to come in and seeking a suitable place to fight. Despite his men cursing him for a coward, he continued his retreat until he reached a place near the North Carolina border called 'Hannah's Cowpens', an unlikely site for battle as the Broad River ran not too distant to the rear, eliminating a route of withdrawal. Even Tarleton was delighted with the terrain which was 'disadvantageous for the Americans, and convenient for the British. An open wood certainly as good a place for action as Lieutenant-Colonel Tarleton could desire; America does not produce any more suitable to the nature of the troops under his command.' Morgan later explained his reason for selecting the place:

217. A real representation of the Dress of An American Rifle-man

'I would not have had a swamp in view of my militia on any consideration; they would have made for it, and nothing could have detained them from it. And as to covering my wings, I knew my adversary and was perfectly sure I should have nothing but downright fighting. As to retreat, it was the very thing I wished to cut off all hope of. I would have thanked Tarleton had he surrounded me with his cavalry. It would have been better than placing my own men in the rear to shoot down those who broke from the ranks. When men are forced to fight, they will sell their lives dearly; and I knew the dread of Tarleton's cavalry would give due weight to the protection of my bayonets, and keep my troops from breaking as Buford's regiment did. Had I crossed the river, one-half of the militia would immediately have abandoned me.'[7]

At the crest of a long, gently rising slope, some 700 yards in length, Morgan placed his crack troops, the Maryland, Delaware, and Virginia Continentals, under Colonel John Eager Howard, and flanked by the Virginia and Georgia militia. Nearly 150 yards down the hill were the militia of North Carolina, South Carolina, and Georgia, while 150 men were thrown out another 150 yards as skirmishers. Behind the third line, and under the crest of the hill, rested William Washington and his dragoons, guarding the militia horses and ready to act in support. Morgan addressed the militia, asking them only to deliver two volleys and they then would be free to leave. Private Thomas Young was nervous as Tarleton came in view:

'The morning of the 17th of January, 1781, was bitterly cold. We were formed in the order of battle, and the men were slapping their hands together to keep warm—an exertion not long necessary. . . .

About sunrise the British line advanced at a sort of trot, with a loud halloo. It was the most beautiful line I ever saw. When they shouted, I

218. The Battle of Cowpens. *A. Dupré*

On a hill near Cowpens, South Carolina, with the Broad River at his back, Daniel Morgan deployed his men in a 'masterly manoeuvre' which resulted in the complete defeat of Banastre Tarleton. Morgan stationed his Continentals at the top of the ridge; the militia, on whom Morgan like Greene placed little dependence, were stationed in front, with orders to fire two or three volleys and then retreat. Tarleton's initial ranks charged the militia, who fired and then retired; the British volunteers, sensing victory, rushed forward pell-mell, and Tarleton sent in his reserves. Colonel William Washington then attacked the right flank with his cavalry, while the militia, having circled the hill behind the Continentals, reformed and attacked the left flank. Tarleton escaped with some of his cavalry; most of his forces were killed, wounded, or taken prisoner.

Morgan 'went among the volunteers,' wrote Thomas Young, 'helped them with their swords, joked with them about their sweethearts, told them to keep in good spirits, and the day would be ours. And long after I laid down, he was going among the soldiers, encouraging them and telling them that the old wagoner would crack his whip over Ban. in the morning, sure as they lived.'

heard Morgan say, "They give us the British halloo, boys, give them the Indian halloo, by God!" and he galloped along the lines, cheering the men and telling them not to fire until we could see the whites of their eyes. Every officer was crying, "Don't fire!" for it was a hard matter for us to keep from it. . . .

The militia fired first. It was for a time, pop-pop-pop—and then a whole volley; but when the regulars fired, it seemed like one sheet of flame from right to left. Oh! it was beautiful!'[8]

Among the militia was young James Collins, who had come into Morgan's camp to escape his Tory neighbours and now found himself in a worse predicament:

'We gave the enemy one fire; when they charged us with their bayonets, we gave way and retreated for our horses. Tarleton's cavalry pursued us. "Now," thought I, "my hide is in the loft."

Just as we got to our horses, they overtook us and began to make a few hacks at some, however without doing much injury. They, in their haste, had pretty much scattered, . . . but in a few moments Colonel Washington's cavalry was among them like a whirlwind, and the poor fellows began to keel from their horses without being able to remount. The shock was so sudden and violent they could not stand it, and immediately betook themselves to flight. There was no time to rally, and they appeared to be as hard to stop as a drove of wild Choctaw steers, going to a Pennsylvania market.

In a few moments the clashing of swords was out of hearing and quickly out of sight. By this time both lines of infantry was warmly engaged, and we being relieved from the pursuit of the enemy began to rally and prepare to redeem our credit, when Morgan rode up in front and waving his sword, cried out, "Form, form, my brave fellows! Give them one more brisk fire and the day is ours! Old Morgan was never beaten!"'[9]

The British infantry drove hard to the third line. The American Colonel Howard reported the mistake that made Cowpens a little gem of a battle:

'Seeing my right flank was exposed to the enemy, I attempted to change the front of Wallace's company (Virginia regulars). In doing this, some confusion ensued, and first a part and then the whole of the company commenced a retreat. The officers along the line seeing this, and supposing that orders had been given for a retreat, faced their men about and moved off. Morgan, who had mostly been with the militia, quickly rode up to me and expressed apprehension of the event, but I soon removed his fears by pointing to the line, and observing that men were not beaten who retreated in that order. He then ordered me to keep up with the men until we came to the rising ground near Washington's horse, and he rode forward to fix on the most proper place for us to halt and face about.

In a minute we had a perfect line. The enemy were now very near us. Our men commenced a very destructive fire, which they [the British] little expected, and a few rounds occasioned great disorder in their ranks. While [they were] in this confusion I ordered a charge with the bayonet, which order was obeyed with great alacrity. As the line advanced, I observed their artillery a short distance in front, and called to Captain Ewing to take it. Captain Anderson, hearing the order, also pushed for the same object, and both being emulous for the prize, kept pace until near the first piece, when

219. Brigadier-General Daniel Morgan.
John Trumbull

Morgan of Virginia was a folk-hero of the Revolution, like Israel Putnam in New England. He used to rally his riflemen with a turkey call.

In 1775 Morgan and his company were dispatched on Arnold's desperate trek through the wilderness of Maine and Canada to Quebec. He fought with furious courage at the barriers there, and won the esteem of Washington. Captured and exchanged, he was given command of a company of light infantry and sent in 1777 to help Gates stop Burgoyne's invasion. Back in the middle states, Morgan met Lafayette at Whitemarsh; the elegant young French officer had great admiration for the rugged rifleman, and a warm friendship developed.

After a rest he was recalled in 1779 to active service in the southern campaign, delighted that his old friend Gates had the command. 'Would to god youd a had it six months ago,' he wrote to him; 'our affairs would have wore a more pleasing aspect at this day than they do.' Though racked with sciatica and rheumatism, Morgan made a contribution to changing that aspect, especially in his victory at Cowpens, where he showed himself a brilliant tactician as well as an officer of courage and endurance.

Anderson, by putting the end of his spontoon forward into the ground, made a long leap, which brought him upon the gun and gave him the prize. . . .

In the pursuit I was led to the right, in among the Seventy-First, who were broken into squads and, as I called to them to surrender, they laid down their arms, and the officers delivered up their swords. Captain Duncanson, of the Seventy-First Grenadiers, gave me his sword and stood by me. Upon getting on my horse, I found him pulling at my saddle and he nearly unhorsed me. I expressed my displeasure, and asked him what he was about. The explanation was that they had orders to give no quarter, and they did not expect any, and as my men were coming up, he was afraid they would use him ill. I admitted his excuse and put him in care of a sergeant.'[10]

It was a magnificent victory. Taken were the two artillery pieces, two standards, 800 muskets, one travelling forge, thirty-five wagons, 100 horses, and 'all their music'. British losses were staggering: ten British officers were among the 100 killed and among the 700 captured rank and file, 200 had suffered wounds. By contrast, Morgan's losses were twelve killed and sixty wounded.

Realizing that victory had made him a prime target for Lord Cornwallis and the entire British army, Morgan wasted little time. Leaving the local militia to care for the wounded and bury the dead of both forces, the brigadier moved northward. When he received the news, General Greene placed his army under the command of Brigadier-General Isaac Huger of South Carolina and, accompanied by a sergeant's guard, sped across country to direct Morgan's retreat.

Waiting only until he was joined by recently arrived reinforcements, Cornwallis took up the pursuit in full cry, floundering through rain-swollen streams and muddy roads. On 25 January, the British column crawled into Ramsour's Mill and encamped on the hill where, on the preceding 20 June, the Whigs and Tories of North Carolina had settled their political differences with gunpowder. Cornwallis remedied the loss of his light troops at Cowpens through a drastic step. He wrote to Clinton:

'I therefore assembled the army on the 25th at Ramsoure's Mill, on the south fork of the Catawba, and as the loss of my light troops could only be remedied by the activity of the whole corps, I employed a halt of two days in collecting some flour, and in destroying the superfluous baggage and all my waggons, except those loaded with hospital stores, salt, and ammunition, and four reserved empty in readiness for sick and wounded. In this measure, though at the expense of a great deal of officer's baggage, and of all prospect in future of rum, and even a regular supply of provisions to the soldiers, I must, in justice to this army, say that there was the most general and cheerful acquiescence. . . .

The rains had rendered the North Catawba impossible, and General Morgan's corps, the militia of the rebellious counties of Rowan and Mecklenburg under General Davidson, or the gang of plunderers usually under the command of General Sumpter, not then recovered from his wounds, had occupied all the fords in a space of more than forty miles upwards from the fork. During its height I approached the river by short marches, so as to give the enemy equal apprehension at several fords; and after having procured the best information in my power, I resolved to attempt passage. . . .'[11]

Making a feint at Beatty's ford near Charlotte, Cornwallis led his main force to Cowan's ford, reported to be lightly guarded. On the far shore, inexperienced Scotch-Irish militia under Brigadier William Lee Davidson waited during a sleepless night. Ordering his men into the swollen water under cover of darkness, 'Lord Cornwallis, according to his usual manner, dashed first into the river, mounted on a very fine spirited horse'. To Sergeant Roger Lamb the Catawba seemed

'about half a mile over. The enemy stood on the hills of the opposite shore, which was high and steep, hanging over the river, so that they had every advantage over us, to facilitate their firing on those who attempted to cross there. Lord Cornwallis' fine horse was wounded, under him, but his lordship escaped unhurt. Amidst these dreadful oppositions, we still urged through this rapid stream, striving with every effort to gain the opposite shore; just in the centre of the river, the bombardier who was employed in steering one of the three pounders, unfortunately let go his hold on the helm of the gun, and being a low man, he was forced off his feet, and immediately carried headlong down the river. . . . I was determined to save his life or perish in the attempt. I therefore quitted my hold on the right man of my division, and threw myself on my belly on the surface of the water, and in nine or ten strokes I overtook him. . . . I got him on his feet, and led him back in safety to his gun. It was very remarkable, and taken particular notice of by the

220. The Marches of Lord Cornwallis in the Southern Provinces *(detail).* *Tarleton*

The routes followed by Cornwallis in 1780 and 1781 are marked on this map which includes the names of local places and fords along the way not found on other printed maps of the war period. Cornwallis left Charleston, marched to Charlotte, NC, turned back to winter in Winnsboro, SC and resumed his campaign in a pursuit of Greene to the Dan River in Virginia; after the encounter with Greene at Guildford (Guilford) he turned to the coast at Wilmington, NC, on the Cape Fear River. From there he marched north to Petersburg, Virginia, followed the James River down to Portsmouth, and from there sailed around the peninsula to York (Yorktown). The excursions of Tarleton's cavalry legion to the Dan River in Virginia and from Petersburg through Virginia are shown.

THE MARCHES
OF
LORD CORNWALLIS
IN THE
SOUTHERN PROVINCES,
NOW
STATES OF NORTH AMERICA;
Comprehending
THE TWO CAROLINAS,
WITH
VIRGINIA AND MARYLAND,
and THE DELAWARE COUNTIES.
BY *WILLIAM FADEN*
Geographer to the King

British troops, that during this transaction not one shot was fired at us by the Americans; indeed they might have easily shot us both in the head, as the current of the river carried us very near to them. After this affair the enemy began again a very heavy fire upon us, nevertheless our division waded on, in a cool intrepid manner, to return their fire, being impossible, as our cartouch boxes were all tied at the backs of our necks. This urged us on with greater rapidity.'[12]

As the dripping British emerged from the river, they gave the rebels a volley. General Davidson fell dead. The militia drifted off so fast that they 'made straight shirt tails', and, as one Tory put it, 'I tell you his Lordship . . . was the best dog in the hunt and not a rebel to be seen.'

A short time later, Tarleton charged a group of militia at Torrance's

299

Tavern and scattered them, some running off clutching tightly their 'pails of whiskey'. These two engagements, little more than skirmishes, became important as the militia grew discouraged and forced Greene to continue his retreat out of the state. Huger and the army of the Pee Dee were to make a junction with Greene at Guilford Court House. Greene wished to make a stand at that place, but was overruled by a council of officers. Crossing the Yadkin and other streams, the army raced for the Dan River, separating North Carolina from Virginia.

Colonel Otho Williams was given the command of the light troops with instructions to delay the enemy as much as possible. On 12 February, the British vanguard under General O'Hara almost came to blows with Henry Lee, and from this time the two forces were almost always in sight of each other. At every stream crossing, or favourable spot, Williams would draw up his command and delay the enemy by forcing them to deploy. Greene's army reached the Dan and on 13 and 14 February crossed over into Virginia at Boyd's and Irwin's ferries. Frustrated, Cornwallis rested his tired army before pulling back to set up camp at Hillsborough.

While awaiting the strength of his army to be bolstered by Virginia militia, Greene sent Henry Lee's Legion and the militia back across the Dan River. On their way to attack Tarleton, they ran into and massacred a sizeable group of Tories, under Dr John Pyle, who were on the march to

join the British army. Ninety Tories lay dead, convincing many loyalists that the British army could not protect its own.

On 23 February, Greene recrossed the Dan into North Carolina and for the next two weeks danced away before an impatient Cornwallis. Skirmishes between scouting parties were frequent, and there was a fight at the ford across Reedy Fork Creek at Wetzel's Mill on 6 March that almost developed into a full-scale battle. Both armies manoeuvred, often on parallel course, but eventually Cornwallis worked his way to the Quaker Meeting House between the forks of Deep River, while Greene moved into the area around High Rock Ford on Haw River.

On 13 March, his army swelled by reinforcements, Greene marched along the banks of the Haw, then up to Troublesome Creek. The following night he lay at Guilford Court House, the baggage dispatched to Speedwell Furnace, the iron works on Troublesome Creek. The night was spent in councils of war.

The following morning Greene positioned his army in a pattern similar to that used by Daniel Morgan at Cowpens. The ground sloped westward for near half a mile, its toe dangling in a small stream. Old fields spotted the dense trees that clung to the slope. The 'Great Road' from Salisbury to Hillsborough split the area.

At the crest, in the clearing around the courthouse, Greene stationed the

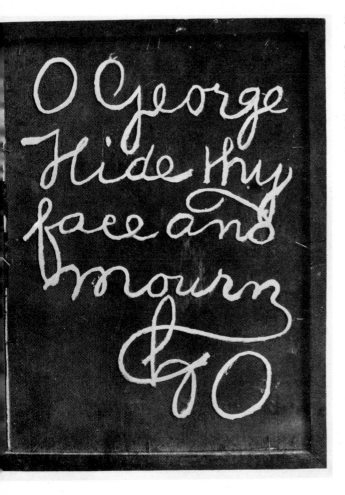

221-3. General Greene turns George III's face to the wall

The night of the Battle of Cowan's Ford, a messenger reached Nathanael Greene and reported, 'General Davidson is dead, and the militia dispersed, and Cornwallis over the Catawba.' Greene mounted his horse and shortly after midnight reached Steel's Tavern in Salisbury, where his friend Dr Read greeted him, 'What, alone, General?' 'Yes', said Greene, 'tired, hungry, alone, and penniless.' As Greene was sitting at a table in his room, discouraged, the mistress of the tavern, Mrs Elizabeth Steel, entered the room with a small sack in each hand. According to local tradition, 'These', she said, as she dropped them on the table, 'are my life's savings; take them if they will help.' Greene, cheered by her generous patriotism, looked up to see the portraits of George III and Queen Charlotte. He rose, turned the royal face against the wall, and wrote on the back 'O George Hide thy face and mourn'. The next morning Greene's distress returned; the military supplies gathered at Salisbury had been so carelessly stored that 1,700 muskets were rusted almost beyond use. 'These are the happy effects', he exclaimed, 'of defending the country with militia from which the good Lord deliver us.'

Delaware and Maryland Continentals, the steadiest troops under his command. Some 400 yards down the slope were the Virginia militia of generals Stevens and Lawson, considered a cut above the average militia units because of the number of ex-Continental soldiers in their ranks. At the foot of the slope, behind a rail fence at the skirt of the woods, were two brigades of North Carolina militia under Generals Butler and Eaton. Several companies of riflemen along with the mounted troops of Washington and Lee steadied the flanks. General Stevens had been humiliated at Camden by the flight of his militia. He was determined that there would not be a repeat performance:

'To guard against my men breaking, I informed them they must not be alarmed at seeing the Carolinians retreat, as perhaps, after giving a fire, they would be ordered to do so. I posted in my rear a number of riflemen, behind trees, . . . we were formed in a skirt of woods. I informed my men they were placed there to shoot the first man that might run, and at the same time they would serve to cover their retreat if necessary.'[13]

224. Battle of Guilford

The British in this battle scene are advancing across open fields towards the North Carolina militia at the left, where the fighting has commenced. The engraving is inaccurate in detail. Except for the first attack, in which the British were almost mired in newly ploughed rain-soaked red clay, they fought through wooded terrain which stretched away on either side of the Hillsboro–Guilford County courthouse road. Tarleton's dragoons, here shown emerging from a wood, were actually held in reserve by Cornwallis throughout the battle. Cornwallis did not use his two three-pounders until after the British had reached a knoll about 250 yards from the courthouse. He then ordered them to fire the cannon in spite of protests from his officers; the shot killed his own men as well as the enemy. The artillery played a crucial part, however, in driving the Americans back.

225. Battle of Guildford, Fought on the 15th of March 1781

Cornwallis had advanced to Hillsboro in pursuit of Greene. 'His lordship', wrote Tarleton, 'decided to advance upon the Americans . . . The continentals were . . . posted facing the wood where the two lines of militia were drawn up. . . . The King's troops threw in their fire, and charged rapidly with bayonets: The shock was not waited for by the militia, who retreated behind their second line. . . . At this period the event of the action was doubtful, and victory alternately presided over each army . . . At this crisis, the judicious use of the three pounders, the firm countenance of the British infantry, and the appearance of the cavalry, obliged the enemy to retreat, leaving their cannon and ammunition waggons behind them.'

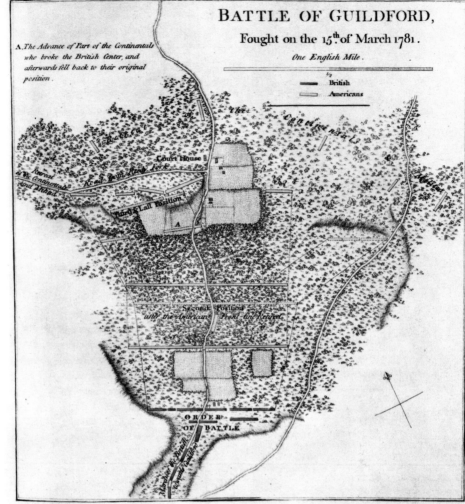

BATTLE OF GUILDFORD,

Fought on the 15th of March 1781.

One English Mile.

British
Americans

A. *The Advance of Part of the Continentals who broke the British Center, and afterwards fell back to their original position.*

London Publifh'd March 1st 1787.

Cornwallis, the day before, had learned of Greene's position. He sent off his baggage to Bell's Mill on Deep River. At daybreak, on 15 March, he marched from New Garden Meeting House, with Tarleton ranging out in front of the army. Henry Lee had sallied forth and there was a sharp skirmish between the two units before the engagement was broken off and both legions galloped back to their own armies. Sir Thomas Saumarez, a lieutenant in the Royal Welsh Fusiliers, described the beginning of the battle of Guilford Court House:

'About one o'clock, the action commenced. The Royal Welsh Fusiliers had to attack the enemy in front, under every disadvantage, having to march over a field lately ploughed, which was wet and muddy from the rains which had recently fallen. The enemy, greatly superior in numbers, were most advantageously posted on a rising ground and behind rails. The regiment marched to the attack under a most galling and destructive fire, which it could return only by an occasional volley. No troops could behave better than the regiment and the little army did at this period, as they never returned the enemy's fire but by word of command, and marched on with the most undaunted courage.

When at length they got within a few yards of the American first line, they gave a volley, and charged with such impetuosity as to cause them to retreat, which they did to the right and left flanks, leaving the front of the British troops exposed to a second line of the enemy, which was formed behind brushwood.'[14]

The long red line, advancing at a slow trot across the field, their bayonets at the ready, was too much for the North Carolina militia, especially when they remembered that few had bayonets of their own with which to parry the thrusts of the enemy. Henry Lee was among those who attempted to rally the fugitives:

'When the enemy came within long shot, the American line, by order, began to fire. Undismayed, the British continued to advance, and having reached a proper distance, discharged their pieces and rent the air with shouts. To our infinite distress and mortification, the North Carolina brigade took flight, a few only of Eaton's brigade excepted, who clung to the militia under Campbell which, with the Legion, manfully maintained their ground. Every effort was made by . . . the officers of many grades, to stop this unaccountable panic, for not a man of the corps had been killed or wounded. Lieutenant Colonel Lee joined in the attempt to rally the fugitives, threatening to fall upon them with his cavalry. All was in vain; so thoroughly confounded were these unhappy men that, throwing away arms, knapsacks, and even canteens, they rushed like a torrent headlong through the woods.'[15]

Sergeant Lamb was with the Royal Welsh Fusiliers that day:

'I saw Lord Cornwallis riding across the clear ground. His Lordship was riding on a dragoon's horse (his own having been shot) the saddlebags were under the creature's belly, which much retarded his progress, owing to the vast quantity of underwood that was spread over the ground. . . . I immediately laid hold of the bridle of his horse and turned his head. I then mentioned to him, that if His Lordship had pursued the same direction he would, in a few moments have been surrounded by the enemy and perhaps cut to pieces or captured. I continued to run alongside the horse, keeping the bridle in my hand, until His Lordship gained the 23rd Regiment, which at [that] time were drawn up in the skirts of the woods.'[16]

Captain John Smith of the Marylanders and Lieutenant-Colonel Duncan Stuart of the first battalion of Guards engaged in mortal combat when the British reached the third line on the crest of the hill:

'In the midst of the Battle at Guilford, while the Americans and British Troops were intermixed with a charge of Bayonets, Smith and his men were in the throng killing the Guards and Grenadiers like so many Furies. Colo. Stewart, seeing the mischief Smith was doing, made up to him through the crowd, Dust and Smoke unperceived and made a violent Lunge at him with his Small Sword. The first that Smith saw was the shining Metal like lightning at his Bosom, he only had time to lean a little to the right, and lift up his left arm so as to let the polished Steel pass under it when the Hilt struck his Breast. It would have run through his Body but for the haste of the Colo., and happening to set his foot on the Arm of a Man Smith had just cut down, his unsteady Step, his violent Lunge, and missing his arm brot him with one knee on the dead man. The Guards came rushing up very strong. Smith had no alternative but to wheel around and give Stewart a back handed Blow over or across the Head, on which he fell.

His Orderly Sergeant attacked Smith, but Smith's Sergeant dispatched him: a 2d attacked him. Smith hewed him down: a 3d behind him threw down a Cartridge and shot him in the back of the Head. Smith now fell among the Slain, but was taken up by his men and brot off: it was found to be only a Buck Shot lodged against the Skull and had only stunned him.'[17]

Greene pulled his army back to the iron works on Troublesome Creek. There was a short pursuit by the British; St George Tucker considered it to be of little import:

'We were soon after ordered to retreat. Whilst we were doing so, Tarleton advanced to attack us with his horse; but a party of continentals, who were fortunately close behind us, gave him so warm a reception that he retreated with some degree of precipitation. A few minutes after we halted by the side of an old field fence, and observed him surveying us at a distance of two or three hundred yards. He did not think it proper to attack us again, as we were advantageously posted; and the continentals, who had encountered him just before, were still in our rear. After this, the whole army retreated in good order to the iron works, fifteen miles from the field of battle, having lost the field and our artillery. . . . Cornwallis undoubtedly gained a dear bought victory.'[18]

Greene, expecting a follow-up attack by Cornwallis, threw up fortifications on Troublesome Creek. But the British were sorely hurt. After issuing a proclamation claiming a 'compleat victory over the rebels', Cornwallis pulled out of Guilford on 18 March, marching towards Wilmington, on the coast of North Carolina.

Greene followed as far as Ramsey's Mill on Deep River. His militia were going home 'to kiss their wives and sweethearts', and his strength was fast diminishing. He suddenly swerved southward, hoping to lure the British back into South Carolina. Cornwallis refused to take the bait and continued on to the coast. He had neither the strength nor the inclination to fight another battle in the near future. As Horace Walpole was to comment, 'Lord Cornwallis's triumphs have increased our losses, without leaving any hopes.'

Nathanael Greene planned to strike at Camden, still under the command of Lord Rawdon. Marching through the warming rays of the spring sun, he was within four miles of the town by 19 April. Camden was too well fortified to make a direct assault, and the army bivouacked on Hobkirk's Hill, a long, narrow, sandy ridge about a mile and a half from the square stockade around the town. Rawdon, watching nervously, decided to take the initiative when an American deserter by the name of Jones came in with the intelligence that Greene, while shifting his position around the town, had sent off his wagons and artillery. Gathering not only his garrison and convalescents but all noncombatants who could shoulder a musket, Rawdon made a sudden sortie out towards Hobkirk's Hill. A native of Camden, Samuel Mathis, later reconstructed the battle from the testimony of those engaged that 25 April:

'Kirkwood's muskets gave the alarm to the Americans, several of whom were at the spring cooking and washing, and had to run a considerable distance before they got to their arms which were stacked in the very line they had to form. . . .

The British, when they first attacked near the spring, pressed directly forward and succeeded in turning our left. . . . A well-directed fire with canister and grape did great execution and soon cleared the road so that all their doctors were sent to take care of the wounded. Washington's

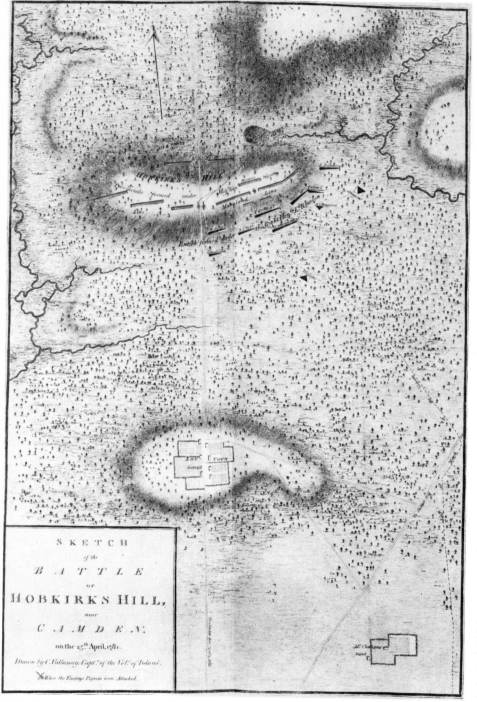

226. Sketch of the battle of Hobkirk's Hill, near Camden, on the 25th April, 1781. *Vallancey*

At Hobkirk's Hill, or the second battle of Camden, Greene deployed his troops along the ridge, a mile and three-quarters from the British forces in the stockaded town. Lord Rawdon decided to attack and at the end of the day had gained the ridge; Greene retreated three miles to Sanders Creek. But the British, their communications with Charleston threatened, soon abandoned Camden. As Greene wrote to the French minister, the Chevalier La Luzerne, 'We fight, get beat, rise, and fight again.'

This plan from a drawing by Captain C. Vallancey of the Volunteers of Ireland, who fought on the right flank, was engraved by W. Faden and published in London on 1 April 1783. The same plate, with slight changes, was used in Stedman's *History of the American War* in 1794.

cavalry, coming up at this moment, completed the route . . . took all the British doctors or surgeons and a great many others (alas! too many) prisoners—more than one third of Washington's men were encumbered with prisoners, who hindered their acting when necessary. . . .

Our left was somewhat turned or yielding, then our Colonel (Ford) was wounded. . . . The left of the British, at least their cavalry, were routed, many killed and many prisoners. Lord Rawdon, hearing the cannon and seeing his horse dispersed, was stunned and astonished beyond measure, ordered the deserter [Jones] hung and, galloping up to the scene of disaster, was quickly surrounded by Washington's horse and his sword demanded. One of his aides received a severe wound from the sword of a dragoon. . . .

Lord Rawdon . . . saw the scene, and also that some of his cavalry had rallied and with the infantry was coming to his relief, while he very politely bowed and seemed to acquiesce with the demands of the dragoons around him, pretended that his sword was hard to get out of the scabbard, feigned to endeavour to draw it or unhook it . . . until the party that took him were attacked and had to fly. . . .

The scene was quickly changed. Washington's dragoons were now attacked by horse and foot, and the very prisoners they had mounted behind them seized the arms of their captors and overcame them. General Greene now ordered a retreat, and pushed on Washington's cavalry to Saunder's Creek (which lay four miles in the rear), to halt the troops and stop the stragglers. . . . In this he succeeded, carrying off with him all the British surgeons and several officers. . . .

General Greene galloped up to Captain John Smith and ordered him to fall in to the rear and save the cannon. Smith instantly came and found the artillery men hauling off the pieces with the drag-ropes. He and his men laid hold, and off they went at a trot, but had not gone far until he discovered the British cavalry were in pursuit. He formed his men across the road, gave them a full fire at a short distance and fled with the guns as before. This volley checked the horses and threw many of the riders, but they, after some time, remounted and pushed on again. . . . This he repeated several times until they had got two or three miles from the field of action. Here one of Smith's men fired, or his gun went off by accident, before the word was given, which produced a scattering fire, on which the cavalry rushed in among them and cut them all to pieces. They fought like Bull Dogs and were all killed or taken . . . the artillery escaped. Smith had a stout, heavy cut and thrust, and a very strong arm with which he did great execution. . . . At length not having a man to support him, being overwhelmed with numbers, he surrendered.

On the next day, Captain Smith was put in close confinement, locked up in jail without being informed what it was for. After lying there twenty-four hours, it was announced to him by the jailer that he should be hung the next morning at 8 o'clock. . . . That night a deserter went out and informed General Greene of his situation. General Greene immediately sent in a flag to know the truth of the tale, threatening retaliation. Lord Rawdon informed the officer bearing the flag that two or three women of the British Army had come from Guilford, North Carolina, since the battle there and related that Captain Smith had killed Colonel Stewart of the King's Guards in cold blood two hours after the battle, on his knees begging for mercy. This was found to be false. . . they liberated Captain Smith from jail, and soon afterwards on their leaving Camden they left him, and left in his care several of their officers who had been wounded in the late action. . . .'[19]

Although forced to retire from the field, Greene gained a victory in one sense. On 10 May, Rawdon evacuated Camden, thereby establishing a pattern. Greene was not to win a clear-cut victory, but after every battle the British were to pull in their forces in an ever-tightening circle around Charleston.

And the partisan chieftains began to win glory for themselves in the reduction of the chain of British posts stretching across the state and Georgia. Fort Watson on the Santee and Fort Motte on the Congaree fell to Marion, aided by Lee's Legion. Lee took Fort Granby on the Congaree. Marion did no more than demonstrate before Georgetown and the garrison evacuated that port. Thomas Sumter took Orangeburg with little effort. Fort Galpin on the Congaree, then the two forts in Augusta fell to Lee, aided by the South Carolina and Georgia militia under Andrew Pickens and Elijah Clark. Lee hastened to join Greene who had laid siege to the western-most British post, a village by the name of Ninety-Six.

Ninety-Six lay surrounded by a strong stockade, on the east side of which lay the as yet unfinished 'Star' redoubt, containing three three-pounders. A dry ditch worked its way around the walls; outside lay the tangled trees of an abatis. Lieutenant-Colonel John Harris Cruger, who had breathed gunpowder during the siege of Savannah, commanded nearly 550 men, some 200 of whom were loyalists.

On 21 May 1781, Greene's army sat down in front of the town and the following day began siege operations with an army of almost 1,000 troops. Greene, who demonstrated much ability on the open battlefield, lacked practice in siege operations. As the hot June days droned by, his inexperience became more evident, but his men still plied pick and shovel in working parallels nearer the walls. Lieutenant Hatton, of the New Jersey Volunteers, a loyalist unit within the fort at Ninety-Six, later told his story to Roderick Mackenzie:

'On the 8th of June, the garrison had the mortification to see that of Augusta marched by them prisoners of war. . . . Colonel Lee, by whom they were taken, enjoyed the gratification of a little mind in exhibiting them before Ninety Six, with a British standard reversed, drums beating and fifes playing, to ridicule their situation. This pitiful recourse had an effect quite contrary to that which it was intended to produce. The soldiers were easily convinced by their officers that death was preferable to captivity with such an enemy. Having enjoyed his triumph, Colonel Lee, with his corps called the Legion, next sat down to reduce the stockade upon the left, which preserved a communication with the water . . . while the operations of General Greene were directed against the Star.

On the evening of the 9th of June, in the apprehension that something extraordinary was going on in the enemy's works, two sallies, with strong parties, were made. One of these, entering their trenches upon the right and penetrating to a battery of four guns, were prevented from destroying them for want of spikes and hammers. They here discovered the mouth of a mine, designed to be carried under a curtain to the Star, upon springing of which the breach was to be entered by the American army, sword in hand. The

227. Francis Rawdon Hastings, Earl of Moira. *Gilbert Stuart*

Lord Rawdon had his baptism of fire at Bunker Hill at the age of twenty-one. 'I was everywhere in the thickest of the fire', he wrote home exuberantly to his uncle, 'and flatter myself that I behaved as you could wish.' He was very scornful of his opponents in the early days of the American war. 'An army composed as theirs is cannot bear the frown of adversity', he wrote from Staten Island. As six long years of war dragged by, he presumably modified his opinions; but he himself bore 'the frown of adversity' well, and became an able commander. In Philadelphia, he raised a Tory legion, called the Volunteers of Ireland. He was eventually captured by de Grasse when sailing for home.

Back in England, he was active in the House of Lords and in 1812 became governor-general of India, where, as the Marquess of Hastings, he fought victoriously, completing British domination of India.

other division that marched upon the left fell in with the covering party of the besiegers, a number of whom were put to the bayonet. Both divisions returned to the garrison with little loss. . . . Never did luckless wight receive a more inglorious wound, than Count Koziusco did on this—it was in that part which Hudibras has constituted the seat of honour, and was given just as this engineer was examining the mine which he had projected! . . .

The suffering of the garrison were now extreme. With infinite labour a well was dug in the Star, but water was not obtained, and the only means of obtaining this necessary element in a torrid climate in the month of June was to send out naked Negroes, who brought in a scanty supply from within pistol shot of the American pickets, their bodies not being distinguishable in the night from the fallen trees with which the place abounded. . . .

Whilst the commandant was using these endeavours, an American Loyalist, in open day, under the fire of the enemy, rode through their pickets and delivered a verbal message from Lord Rawdon: "That he had passed Orangeburg and was in full march to raise the siege." . . .

On the morning of this day the third parallel of the besiegers was completed; they turned the abbatis, drew out the pickets and brought forward two trenches within six feet of the ditch of the Star. General Greene, well informed of the advance of Lord Rawdon and knowing that the garrison was equally apprised of it, determined upon a general assault, which he commenced at noon. . . .

The main body of the Americans could not be brought forward to the assault; they were contented with supporting the parties in the ditch by an incessant fire from the lines.

At length the garrison became impatient. Two parties . . . issued from the sally port in the rear of the Star. They entered the ditch, divided their men and advanced, pushing their bayonets till they met each other. . . . General Greene, from one of the advanced batteries, with astonishment beheld two parties, consisting only of thirty men each, sallying into a ditch, charging and carrying every thing before them, though exposed to the fire of the whole army. It was an exertion of officers leading troops ardent in the cause of their sovereign, and steeled with the remembrance of injuries which they and their connections had so often received from the subverters of law and good government.

The Americans covered their shame in the trenches, nor was it till the next day that they recollected themselves so far as to ask permission to bury their dead. The groans also of their wounded assailed their ears and called aloud for that relief which ought to have been much earlier administered.

General Greene raised the siege upon the evening of the 19th, and on the morning of the 21st the army under Lord Rawdon made its appearance.'[20]

The gallant defence of Ninety-Six proved in vain, for Rawdon ordered the post evacuated. But Rawdon himself was feeling the strain of six years of campaigning in North America. Falling ill, he placed his troops under the command of Lieutenant-Colonel Alexander Stuart and took passage for England, only to be captured by a French 74-gun ship of the line.

Charles Stedman, although with Cornwallis, reconstructed the battle of Eutaw Springs from official reports and personal accounts:

'In the mean time general Greene was reinforced by a brigade of continental troops from North Carolina, and intent upon prosecuting his plan for the recovery of South Carolina, put his forces in motion as soon as the extreme heat began to abate. On the twenty-second of August he marched from the high hills of Santee with an intention to give battle to the British army, and proceeding up the northern banks of the Wateree, crossed it near Camden. From thence he directed his march to Friday's Ferry on the Congaree, where he was joined by general Pickens with the militia of Ninety-six, and by the South Carolina State troops under colonel Henderson.

The British commander, upon receiving intelligence that general Greene was on his march to attack him, fell back with his whole force to Eutaw, about forty miles from the Congaree. This movement was made for the purpose of meeting a convoy of provisions then on the road from Charlestown, rather than weaken the army whilst an attack was expected, by sending off so strong an escort as would be necessary for securing its safe arrival.

General Greene having passed the Congaree, continued to advance towards Eutaw, but by very slow marches, that he might give time to general Marion to join him with his brigade of militia. This junction was made on the seventh of September, about seven miles from Eutaw; and at four in the morning of the following day, general Greene marched with his whole force to make his projected attack. . . .

The enemy attacked with great impetuosity; the chief impression seemed to be designed against the artillery on the road, and to turn the left of the British. The pressure of the enemy's fire was such as compelled the third regiment, or Buffs, to give way, the regiment being composed of new troops. The remains of those veteran corps, the sixty-third and sixty-fourth regiments, who had served the whole of the war, lost none of their fame in this action. They rushed with bayonets into the midst of the enemy; nor did they give ground, until overpowered by numbers and severe slaughter. Various was the success in the centre and on the right.

At this time colonel Washington, endeavouring to pass through the right of the flank corps and the rivulet, led his cavalry with great gallantry to the charge. The flank corps received this charge with great steadiness. At the first fire, colonel Washington was wounded and taken prisoner, and several of his men fell, which prevented a similar attack. The artillery on both sides was several times taken and retaken.

At this time the flank battalion, whose post had been passed undiscovered by the main body of the enemy, wheeled round, and coming in the rear of the enemy, threw them into confusion, which being increased by a fire from the New York volunteers, under the command of major Sheridan, who had taken post in a stone house on the open ground upon the right of the road, decided the action. Incessant peals of musquetry from the windows poured destruction upon the enemy, and effectually stopped their further progress.

Although severely checked, the Americans were not discouraged, and brought up four six pounders to batter the house; but the fire of the detachment within continued to be so well supported, that the American artillery became useless, and most of the officers and men that were attached to it, were either killed or wounded. . . .

They were obliged to abandon two of the four pieces of cannon that had been brought up against the house, and they left behind them, according to their own account, one hundred and thirty nine of their number killed on the field of battle. . . .

The incidents attending this action gave occasion to both commanders to claim the victory. . . . The British commander remained upon the ground the night after the action and the following day, without any attempt being made by general Greene to molest him; and when he afterwards retired to Monk's Corner for the safety and protection of his wounded, the American commander contented himself with advancing to the ground left by the British troops, and soon afterwards retreated to his former encampment on the high hills of Santee, placing a large river between him and the British army. . . .

Indeed this was the last action of any consequence that happened in South Carolina between the king's troops and the Americans. The former from this time, chiefly confined themselves to Charlestown Neck and some posts in its neighbourhood; the security of the town appearing to be their principal object; and General Greene either was not, or did not think himself in sufficient force to reduce it.'[21]

Nathanael Greene never won a battle in the South, yet after every action he forced the British to pull in their lines. He had looked upon the department as a place to gain his niche in history. When he heard that Washington was marching to attack Cornwallis in Virginia, he rather sadly wrote, 'We have been beating the bush, and the General has come to catch the bird.'

14. Yorktown

ON 25 APRIL 1781, Cornwallis led his troops out of Wilmington, taking the road to Virginia. Since the first of the year there had been a force operating in that state under the direction of Brigadier-General Benedict Arnold, now commanding British troops in America. They had reached Richmond on 5 January, and Governor Jefferson's account of their destructiveness appeared in the *Virginia Gazette*:

'A regiment of infantry and about fifty horse, continued on without halting to the foundery, they burnt that, the boring mill, the magazine, and two other houses, and proceeded to Westham, but nothing being in their power there, they retired to Richmond. The next morning they burnt some buildings of publick and some of private property, with what stores remained in them; destroyed a great quantity of private stores and about 12 o'clock retired towards Westover, where they encamped within the neck the next day.

The loss sustained is not yet accurately known. At this place about 300 muskets, some soldiers clothing to a small amount, sulphur, some quarter masters stores, of which 120 sides of leather was the principle article, part of the artificers tools, and 2 wagons; besides which five brass four pounders which had been sunk in the river, were discovered to them, raised and carried off. At the foundery about 5 tons of powder was thrown into the canal, of which there will be a considerable saving by remanufacturing it. Part of the papers belonging [to] the Auditors office, and the books and papers of the Council office, which were ordered to Westham, but in the confusion carried by mistake to the foundery, were also destroyed.

The roof of the foundery was burnt, but the stacks of chimnies and furnaces not at all injured. Within less than 48 hours from the time of their landing and 19 of our knowing of their destination, they had penetrated 33 miles, done the whole injury, and retired. Our militia dispersed over a large tract of country can be called in but slowly.'[1]

Arnold fell back down to Portsmouth. Over in Berkeley County, Horatio Gates sat grieving the death of his only son and, still sulking over his treatment after Camden, wrote a bitter letter to Governor Jefferson:

'If Lord Cornwallis Conquers the Southern, and Eastern Parts of No: Carolina, and extends his Posts of Communication to Portsmouth, you must expect the weight of the War will penetrate into your Bowels, and Cause such an Inflamation there, as may (if Timely remedies are not applied) consume the Life Blood of the State. Have you cried aloud to Congress, and to *The Commander in Chief of the Army*, for Succour; have they Listen'd to your Cry? If they have not, are you doing the best thing for Yourselves? Military Wisdom has ever heretofore, been imputed to Virginia; is there a Rotteness in the State of Denmark? Find it out, and Cut it off. This is a letter of one Chess Player to Another, not the letter of General Gates, to Governor

Jefferson; I am now at my unhappy private House, you are acting in the busy Scene of Public Life, and in the most Exalted Station; in which I sincerely wish you all the Honour and Success; Happiness, I know you cannot have.'[2]

To curb Arnold's range, Washington dispatched the Marquis de Lafayette with 1,200 men to Virginia, and on 8 March a French fleet sailed from Newport to bottle up Arnold in the Chesapeake. Upon discovering this, Clinton immediately dispatched a 3,000-man force under Major-General William Phillips to assume the command in Virginia. An English fleet under Admiral Arbuthnot sailed against the French squadron under

228. Skirmish at Richmond. 5th Jany 1781. *Allen*

Richmond, at the head of navigation on the James River, was the recently established capital of Virginia, where 'a great variety of military stores' had been collected. Benedict Arnold, upon reaching its outskirts with his army (F, right centre of map), ordered Simcoe (C) to dislodge several hundred rebels on the heights (A, A). The cavalry of the Queen's Rangers dispersed the rebels on the summit above Gilleys Creek and proceeded to Westham (dotted route), where they drove off a cavalry unit (B, extreme left, centre) and destroyed the warehouses and their contents. Arnold's troops also destroyed private dwellings and valuable colonial records.

This manuscript map is copied from a sketch by the Loyalist Lieutenant Adam Allen of the Queen's Rangers, which Simcoe inserted in a copy of his *Journal* presented to George III.

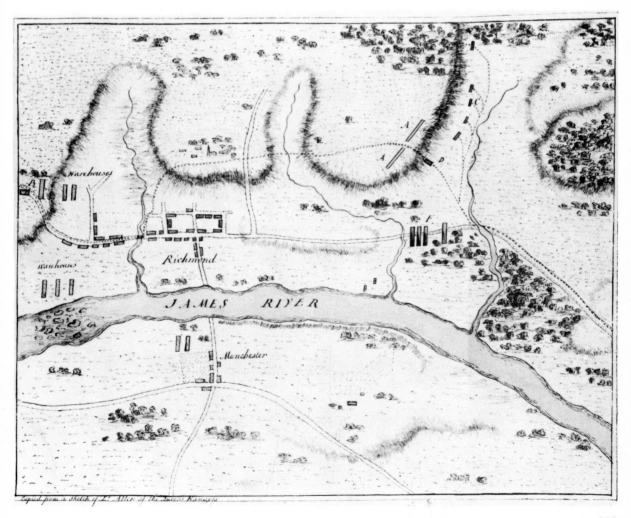

Admiral Destouches, and in a one-hour battle neither officer could claim victory, although Destouches pulled off and left the sea lanes open to the British.

Cornwallis wanted to take over the troops under Phillips to bolster his own sadly mauled force. When he made the junction at Petersburg he discovered that Phillips had died of a 'putrid' fever just a week earlier. In this operation his Lordship was going against the wishes of Clinton, who had written to Germain, 'I hope Cornwallis may have gone back to Carolina. . . . If he joins Phillips I shall tremble for every post except Charlestown, and even for Georgia.'

Cornwallis struck at Lafayette, but the Marquis slid back before him, trying to allow time for the Virginia militia to come in and gaining time until Anthony Wayne and his Pennsylvania Line could join him. Tarleton was sent off raiding towards Charlottesville where the legislature was sitting. Jefferson later recalled his narrow escape:

'[As Tarleton] was passing through Louisa on the 3d of June, he was observed by a Mr. Jouett, who suspecting the object, set out immediately for Charlottesville, and knowing the by-ways of the neighborhood, passed the enemy's encampment, rode all night, and before sun-rise of the 4th. called at Monticello with notice of what he had seen, and passed on to Charlottesville to notify the members of the Legislature.

The Speakers of the two houses, and some other members were lodging with us. I ordered a carriage to be ready to carry off my family; we breakfasted at leisure with our guests, and after breakfast they had gone to Charlottesville; when a neighbor rode up at full speed to inform me that a troop of horse was then ascending the hill to the house.

I instantly sent off my family, and, after a short delay for some pressing arrangements, I mounted my horse, . . . went thro' the woods, and joined my family at the house of a friend where we dined.'[3]

After this, Cornwallis pulled back eastward to occupy Williamsburg. On 22 June, Anthony Wayne and his Pennsylvanians joined Lafayette. The Virginian St George Tucker was taken with their military smartness:

'They were a splendid and formidable corps. If the laurels which they win bear any proportion to the plumes they were adorned with, the heroes of antiquity will soon sink into oblivion. Were I a native of Laputa, with the assistance of a quadrant I might possibly calculate the altitude of that which nods over the brow of their General. Their military pride promises much, for the first step to make a good soldier is to entertain a consciousness of personal superiority; and this superiority is said to prevail in the breasts of these men, even to the meanest private in the ranks.'[4]

Wayne's men and their jaunty plumes were soon tested. It was at Green Spring, on 6 July, that they 'pick'd a Quarrell with the British'. A newspaper carried the story how Cornwallis, pretending to ferry his army across the James River, drew Anthony Wayne into a trap:

'Cornwallis having encamped near Jamestown . . . , the Marquis Lafayette sent General Wayne, with the Pennsylvania Line, to take their station within a small distance of the British army and watch their operations. About three hundred riflemen occupied the ground between General Wayne and Lord Cornwallis, who were directed to scatter themselves in the woods,

229. 'Le Marquis de la Fayette. Conclusion de la Campagne de 1781 en Virginie.' *L. le Paon*

'Liberté' reads the legend below this picture; 'America was enslaved, this hero came to break the chains; his successes beyond the seas presage those of the Homeland.' This Lafayette is a much older man than the ardent youth who arrived in 1777 (plate 157). He has stood the fortunes of the war and become an able and trusted commander. As he stands with his black equerry watching the troops move down to the siege of Yorktown, he has just finished playing watchdog to Cornwallis in Virginia, adroitly avoiding a confrontation at the wrong time and place.

In the difficult days of the French Revolution and the Napoleonic Era, Lafayette stood firmly for his principles of representative, constitutional government. He revisited the United States in 1784 and again in 1824, receiving an honoured welcome. He died in 1834. When the United States went to the aid of beleaguered France in 1917, the slogan chosen was 'Lafayette, we are here'.

without order, and annoy the enemy's camp. This they did with such effect, that a small party was sent out against them to dislodge them; each side continuing to reinforce—at length the whole of General Wayne's division were engaged.

They drove the advance detachment back to their lines and, without stopping there, attacked the whole British army, drawn up in order of battle, and charged them with their bayonets. The action was obstinate for the little time it lasted, but the disproportion of numbers was too great. The Marquis arrived, in person, in time enough to order a retreat, and to bring off the Pennsylvania troops before they were surrounded, which the enemy were endeavoring to effect, being able greatly to outflank them. Cornwallis did not pursue them more than half a mile in the retreat, apprehending the rest of the Americans were near enough to support them, and not choosing to risk a general engagement. . . . The British, immediately after the action, which ended about nine o'clock in the evening, crossed James River.'[5]

Cornwallis' army shuffled down to Portsmouth to receive Clinton's dispatches directing him to establish a base on Chesapeake Bay to provide protection for the British fleet. Neither Portsmouth nor Point Comfort satisfied Cornwallis or his engineers, and the General made the decision to occupy and fortify the little tobacco port of Yorktown, some eleven miles from the mouth of the York River. It was a small town, located atop marl bluffs rising some forty feet above the river. Across the York, Gloucester Point lunged out to narrow the stream to less than a mile. On two sides of the village two sprawling swamps protected the approaches to the town from those directions. By 22 August, Cornwallis had his army, aided by near 2,000 slaves, throwing up earthworks around Yorktown. This was the Tidewater country of the old plantations, just a few miles from Jamestown where the British had made their first permanent settlement in America.

Washington had been keeping an eye on the developments in Virginia. So far, 1781 had not been a very happy year for him. In his headquarters, at New Windsor on the Hudson, the General had suffered experiences that no commanding general welcomes. Inactivity had allowed the troops to take inventory of their situation and to come to the conclusion that their country had forgotten them. The Pennsylvania Line, ragged, hungry, and cold, and paid in depreciated currency, tugged at and broke the bonds of discipline on New Year's day, when they learned that raw recruits were distributed enlistment bounties of hard money. The eventual compromise, allowing many of the dissatisfied their discharges, led to wasting of the line, so much so that Wayne had practically to rebuild his regiments. Not until then were they detached to Lafayette in Virginia, where they displayed good training and discipline when they charged the British at Green Spring.

But the seed had been planted. Near the end of January the New Jersey Line, billeted at Pompton, suddenly exploded in defiance of their officers. Upon this occasion Washington acted swiftly, sending General Robert Howe and a detachment of 500 men marching through the night to surround the camp of the insurgents. The mutineers submitted tamely; two of the three leaders were executed before a firing squad, a third, 'to his unspeakable joy', was pardoned.

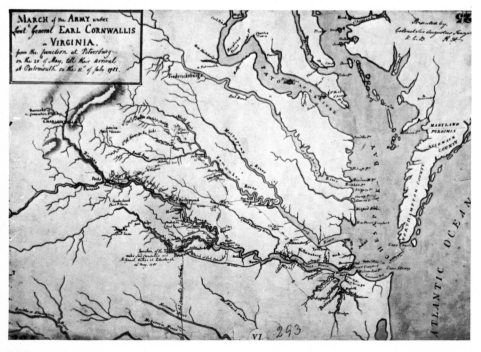

230. March of the army under Lieutenant General Earl Cornwallis in Virginia from the junction of Petersburg on the 12th of May till their arrival at Portsmouth on 12th July 1781

This manuscript map shows Cornwallis's movements in Virginia, including expeditions he sent out from Petersburg after 12 May, and traces his route to Portsmouth. It was apparently made by a British officer before Cornwallis made the decision to move his troops to Yorktown.

231. Earl Cornwallis.
I. Jones

Most Americans, if asked to name one British commander of the American Revolution, would name Cornwallis. This is partly because it was his sword which, after eight long years, was given in surrender, and partly because he fought through the whole war, up and down the length and breadth of the land. 'I am quite tired of marching about the country in search of adventures', he wrote to General William Phillips in 1781; and well he might be.

In 1776 he suffered the defeat at Charleston, after which he was eager to conquer the South. Always believing the Tories would rally in strong support, he was always disappointed. He happily played a part in the taking of Charleston in 1780, and ruined Gates' career by his victory at Camden. Brave and thorough, he was at his best in pitched battles, not brilliant in the hit-and-run guerrilla campaigns which next befell. Stubbornly determined to keep his army in the South, and allowed to do so by Clinton's indecisiveness, he allowed himself to be caught in the Franco-American trap of Yorktown. He had, however, a long and distinguished career after defeat, as viceroy of Ireland and twice governor-general of India.

With his army under control, but still grumbling, Washington planned to initiate operations against the enemy lest his army fall to pieces. Despite the great admiration the General and Rochambeau held for each other, de Fersen wrote to his father:

'There is a coolness between Washington and M. de Rochambeau; the dissatisfaction is on the part of the American General, ours is ignorant of the reason. He has given me orders to go with a letter to him, and to inform myself of the reason for his discontent, to heal the breach if possible, or if the affair be more grave to report to him the cause.'[6]

Apparently the Count was a good arbitrator, for Washington and Rochambeau met amiably at Wethersfield, Connecticut, to plan a move against Clinton in New York. Matters bore a happier outlook with the reception of dispatches from Comte de Grasse stating that he would be operating off the coast of North America during July and August, but was forced by previous commitments to the Spanish to leave no later than 15 October. On 10 July, the two armies made a junction at White Plains with the French general reporting, 'We have made the most rapid march, without any dissatisfaction, without leaving a man behind us, except ten love-sick soldiers from the regiment of Soissonais who wanted to see their sweethearts at Newport and for whom I am going to send. Our junction was made with great acclamation on the part of the Americans.'

The New York defences were stronger than anticipated, and the proposed attack came to but little more than a staring match, as the New England militia, who held little love for the New Yorkers, took their time in coming in. Dispatches arrived from de Grasse on 14 August, stating that he planned to operate in the Chesapeake, an option secretly granted him by Rochambeau who had never favoured an attack on New York. Washington was forced to agree. But Clinton had to be entertained, even as preparations were made to march against Cornwallis. Chief Justice Smith wrote to Colonel Charles Stuart:

'When the French Troops left Rhode Island, and marched towards this place, the prevailing opinion here and in the country was that an attack was intended on New York. Sir Henry Clinton seemed to be confirmed in this idea when Gen. Washington joined the French and advanced nearer to us.

We had instantly a period of great confusion; much appeared necessary to be done to strengthen the fortifications, new walls to be constructed, the Militia to be called out.

General Robertson advised that the shops should be closed. The number of the enemy, we were told, and it was believed at Head-quarters, were upwards of 11,000. They drew near Kingsbridge, then retreated to West Chester, and the White Plains—at length they burnt their Barracks, broke up their camp, and marched into New Jersey—then to Philadelphia, and so on to the Chesapeake.'[7]

Intercepted letters had provided Clinton with allied plans for an assault against New York. In the midst of feverish preparations he received a reinforcement of 3,000 Hessians, but also a visitor who could not be allowed to fall into the hands of the Americans, Prince William, son of George III. Doctor John Cochran passed on the news to a colleague:

'[Admiral Robert] Digby is arrived at N.Y. with 3 ships of the Line and some Frigates. With him came one of the Royal Whelps from Great Britain. . . . A young Lad who came out of N.Y. some Days ago being examined by General Heath was asked if he saw the Young Prince, he answered Yes; he saw many go to look at him and he thought he might as well see him as the rest, he said he expected to have seen something more in him than other people but was Disappointed excepting his being the Ugliest person he ever saw, with a very large Nose, his eyes resembling those of a Wall Eyed Horse and his leggs all of a thickness from his knees to his Ankles, but that he had a fine Gold Coat. A pretty representative this Fellow will make to cause a Rebellion to sink at his Approach. I think from the description given him he is much better to cause an Abortion in the Fair Sex than to Quell a Rebellion.'[8]

While Sir Henry Clinton was minding his social amenities, the allied armies, marching swiftly, crossed New Jersey and in the afternoon of 2 September strutted through Philadelphia. Surgeon Thacher thought it a good show:

'The streets being extremely dirty, and the weather warm and dry, we raised a dust like a smothering snowstorm, blinding our eyes and covering our bodies with it. This was not a little mortifying, as ladies were viewing us from the open windows of every house we passed through this splendid city. The scene must have been exceedingly interesting to the inhabitants, and contemplating the noble cause in which we were engaged, they must have experienced in their hearts a glow of patriotism, if not emotions of military ardor.

Our line of march, including appendages and attendants, extended nearly two miles. The general officers and their aides, in rich military uniforms, mounted on noble steeds elegantly caparisoned, were followed by their servants and baggage. In the rear of every brigade were several field pieces, accompanied by ammunition carriages. The soldiers marched in slow and solemn step, regulated by the drum and fife. In the rear followed a great number of wagons, loaded with provisions, and other baggage, such as a few soldiers' wives and children, though a very small number of these were allowed to encumber us on this occasion.

The day following the French troops marched through the city, dressed in complete uniforms of white broadcloth, faced with green, and besides the drum and fife, they were furnished with a complete band of music, which operates like enchantment.'[9]

Leaving Philadelphia, the two armies marched by different roads, meeting at Chester, where Rochambeau saw Washington cast aside his dignity:

'I caught sight of General Washington waving his hat at me, with demonstrative gestures of the greatest joy. When I rode up to him he explained that he had just received a dispatch from Baltimore, informing him that de Grasse had arrived in the Chesapeake with 28 ships of the Line and Lauzan, who was also present, said, "I never saw a man more thoroughly and openly delighted than was General Washington at this moment." '[10]

The following day, 5 September, the French squadron of thirty ships was to prove its usefulness. Ships rode gentle swells inside the Capes, and Pierre Sordelet was on deck early that morning when 'the frigate gave the signal to the squadron of strange ships outside. Immediately the Admiral gave the signal to clear the decks for action and to crowd on sail as quickly as possible. All the ships cut their cables and left their anchors. By noon all the squadron was under sail, being short of 1800 men and 90 officers. . . . The wind was behind us and we were able to come near them without recognizing them.

Finally they broke their colors and it was seen that it was the English squadron. The Admiral signalled to crowd on sail on the ships. At noon we counted 29 ships of which 7 were frigates. All our ships raised their colors to their mastheads. All the squadron changed their course. . . . The last of our ships were sailing close to the wind. At 3:00 the English hoisted their signals. Our Admiral gave the signal to our ships to crowd on sail. All the English ships tried to come broadside to us. All our squadron crowded on sail to get into line of battle. About 3:45 our ships were coming up together to the last of the enemy very cleverly.

At 4:02 the ships of England and France began the battle. We saw that 15 of our ships engaged a similar number of English while all the other ships put on sail to go to their aid. By 5:00 only 7 French ships were not engaged. The battle was very violent, one could not see whether the English or French fire was the heaviest, and through the heavy smoke one could hear the thunder of the guns. There were a number of English ships, which as we were in the open, fired a quantity of shots at us which did not come half way. There was a two decked English ship broadside to us which threw a terrible fire on us. All of their bombs dropped in the water. The battle lasted until almost 6:45, as night fell, otherwise it would not have ceased. All night we followed them, waiting for the morrow to see the damage to each one. All night the weather was fine, the wind fresh, the sea quiet. It is a surprising thing that the noise of the cannon seemed to quiet the wind and sea. . . .

[Sept.] 7. The Carolinas were visible all morning. We saw the English squadron which was to our north. About noon the wind freshened. Our Admiral gave the sign to put the wind behind us and to get into battle formation to give pursuit to the English. At 1:00 PM all our squadron crowded on sail. The weather fine, the sea very quiet. It has appeared that the English did not wish to fight. They crowded on sail and turned away from us. All day we pursued them to the windward. They changed their course, we did the same. . . .

[Sept.] 11. Early in the morning one of our ships signalled many ships to the leeward. I made out the names of some and signalled to the two other ships that a number of ships were ready to give chase to them. About noon the Admiral gave the signal to go into anchorage and prepare to drop anchor in the passage where our ships lay at anchor when the English came up to take us. The weather fine, the wind fresh, the sea fairly calm. About 3:00 PM these two vessels which our ships had given chase to, were taken, one of them was an English frigate of 32 pieces, named in English, the Richmond. The other was another English frigate which had only been sent up by Admiral Graves to carry dispatches. It had come into the midst of our squadron. . . . It was the frigate called L'Iris of 32 guns, double sheathed in copper. All of our ships dropped anchor safely. . . . We also found M. de Barras at anchor with his squadron composed of 7 ships.'[11]

Even as the battered English fleet under Admiral Graves was putting about for New York and repairs, the French were busily putting the white-uniformed soldiers of Louis XVI ashore at Jamestown Island. Washington, after swinging by for a visit to Mount Vernon, hurried on to Williamsburg where the armies were gathering. Among the 3,000 Virginia militia assembled there under General Thomas Nelson, Governor of Virginia, was St George Tucker, who described the General's arrival:

'About four o'clock in the afternoon his approach was announced. He had passed our camp—which is now in rear of the whole army—before we had time to parade the militia. The French line had just time to form. The Continentals had more leisure. He approached without any pomp or parade,

232. 'Carte de la Partie de la Virginie ou l'armée combinée de France & des États-unis de l'Amérique a fait prisonnière l'armée Anglaise.'

This graphic and charming map of Yorktown and the Battle of the Capes, published in Paris shortly after the surrender, is pictorially effective but generally inaccurate. The French fleet never took station between the capes; the 'Middle Ground' was too shallow for ships of the line to cross; and the ships, when they tacked out against the NNE wind by Cape Henry, met the east–west British column of ships to their south and not to the north-west, as here.

The relative position of the French and American ground troops investing Yorktown and Gloucester is correctly shown, but the topography and the location of the forces are erroneous. The map was evidently not 'surveyed and drawn on the spot' as claimed in the cartouche.

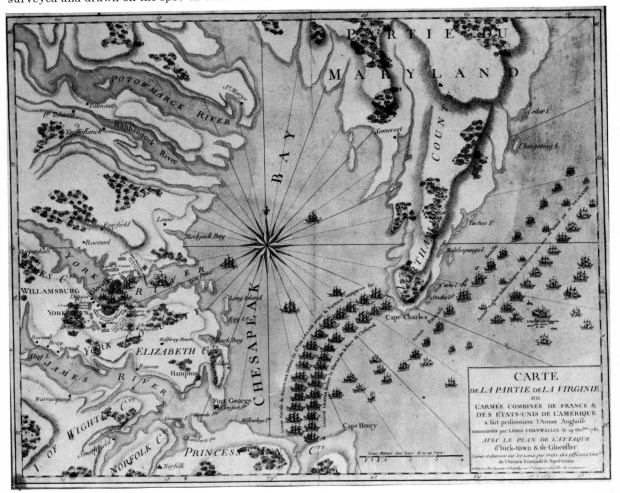

attended by only a few horsemen and his own servants. . . . The Marquis rode up with precipitation, clasped the General in his arms, and embraced him with an ardor not easily described.

The whole army and all the town were presently in motion. The General . . . rode through the French lines. The troops were paraded for the purpose, and cut a most splendid figure. He then visited the Continental line. As he entered the camp the cannon from the park of artillery and from every brigade announced the happy event. His train by this time was much increased; and men, women and children seemed to vie with each other in demonstrations of joy, and eagerness to see their beloved countrymen. . . . Cornwallis may now tremble for his fate, for nothing but some extraordinary interposition of his guardian angels seems capable of saving him and his whole army from captivity.'[12]

Few natives were awake at five o'clock on the morning of 28 September when the army marched down the road to Yorktown, thirteen miles away. A few dogs barked, and a child cried in wonderment at the sound of scuffling feet and crunching wheels through the sandy streets. At Yorktown, the British Captain Samuel Graham of the 76th Regiment knew they were coming and had been waiting:

'Our army continued strengthening their posts as well as they could, felling trees and causing such other obstructions to the advance of the enemy as were in their power when, on 28th September, information was given by a picket in front of a working party that the enemy were advancing in force by the Williamsburg road. The army immediately took post in the outward position.

The French and Americans came on in the most cautious and regular order. Some shots were fired from our field pieces. The French also felt the redoubt on our right flank, defended by the 23rd and a party of marines, but did not persist. The two armies remained some time in this position observing each other. In ours, there was but one wish, that they would advance. While standing with a brother captain, we overheard a soliloquy of an old Highland gentleman, a lieutenant, who drawing his sword, said to himself, "Come on, Maister Washington, I'm unco glad to see you; I've been offered money for my commission, but I could na think of gangin' home without a sight of you. Come on."'[13]

But the old Highlander could only gaze out across the parapet as the marching column slowly unfolded itself and began to wind around the town. The following day, British artillery lofted a few shells from their advanced redoubts, and scouting parties let fly a few shot at advanced posts. But on the night of Saturday 29 September Cornwallis pulled in his garrisons from the outer redoubts on the south and east sides of town. Captain James Duncan's men were among those assigned to pick and shovel duty on 1 October:

'The engineers having fixed on and chained off the ground in two different places to erect their works within point blank shot of the enemy. . . . At dusk of evening we all marched up, and never did I see men exert themselves half so much or work with more eagerness. Indeed, it was to their interest, for they could expect nothing else but an incessant roar of cannon the whole night. I must confess I too had my fears, but fortunately for us they did not fire a shot the whole night. . . .

322

233. Washington and Rochambeau give final orders for the attack on Yorktown. *Coudert*

On 28 September the allied troops marched from Williamsburg to within two miles of Yorktown. The next day the siege began: 'The American troops take their station in front of the enemies works', wrote Trumbull, Washington's secretary. 'The French occupy the left of the Americans and extend to the river above the town.'

Here Rochambeau is giving a direction with Washington to his left in front of the American headquarters tent. The details of the scene may be imagined; the uniforms of the Americans and French are authentic.

Oct. 2.—The works were so far finished in the course of the preceding night that the men worked in them this day with very little danger, although the enemy kept up an almost incessant fire from two pieces of artillery. A drummer, rather too curious in his observation, was this day killed with a cannon ball.

Oct. 3.—Last night four men of our regiment . . . were unfortunately killed (on covering party) by one cannon ball. . . . A militia man this day, possessed of more bravery than prudence, stood constantly on the parapet and d—— his soul if he would dodge for the balls. He had escaped longer than could have been expected, and growing foolhardy, brandished his spade at every ball that was fired till, unfortunately, a ball came that put an end to his caper. . . .'[14]

On the far side of the York River the British had established a post on Gloucester Point. On 2 October, Tarleton's Legion and Simcoe's Rangers had been ferried across for garrison duty. The following day there was a clash with the legion and the Duke de Lauzun. The American colonel Butler heard of the skirmish in the lines before Yorktown:

'The ruffian Tarleton, with a body of troops, went to Gloster yesterday; after killing all his poor horses and mounting men on the officers' horses, (who Lord Cornwallis ordered to part with them) pushed out to forage, but fell in with the Duke de Lauzun and his legion who treated them roughly, and obliged them to retire to their lurking places with the loss of above fifty killed, wounded and taken. Tarleton himself was rode down by his own men, whose hurry caused them to be very impolite to their commander.'[15]

Many Americans, brimming with overconfidence, indulged their bravado. Even Washington seemed careless:

'That morning the Commander-in-Chief, with almost all the general officers, came to my picket, and was in my front. While I was seated on the platform of the popular redoubt viewing their battery, the enemy fired over their heads and cut the branches of the tree, which fell about me; but as the Generals did not move, the second ball struck directly in my front, and went into the ground about three rods before the Generals (had it raised it must have passed through the cluster, and have killed several), when they all retreated except the Commander-in-Chief, who remained with his spying-glass observing their works, and although he remained some time alone, directly in their view, they did not fire again.'[16]

Day by day, the first parallel, the long trench that gradually encircled the town, and was broken only by batteries for heavy artillery, worked its way towards the river. Captain Duncan felt that Colonel Alexander Hamilton carried fanfaronade a bit too far on 7 October:

'The trenches were this day to be enlivened with drums beating and colors flying, and this honor was conferred on our division of light infantry. . . . Immediately upon our arrival the colors were planted on the parapet with this motto: *Manus Haec inimica tyrannis.*

   Our next maneuver was rather extraordinary. We were ordered to mount the bank, front the enemy, and there by word of command go through all the ceremony of soldiery, ordering and grounding our arms; and although the enemy had been firing a little, they did not give us a single shot. I suppose their astonishment at our conduct must have prevented them, for I can assign no other reason. Col. Hamilton gave these orders, and although I esteem him one of the first officers in the American army, must beg leave in this instance to think he wantonly exposed the lives of our men. Our orders were this night that if the enemy made a sortie and attempted to storm the trenches we were to give them one fire from the banquet, rush over the parapet and meet them with the bayonet.'[17]

As the allies completed their batteries, the little town of York was saturated with bombardment. Captain Graham lost a friend:

'They had constructed a battery of heavy guns opposite the redoubts on our right flank, and on the evening of the 9th they fired an eighteen pound cannon ball into the town as a beginning, which, entering a wooden house where the officers of the 7th Regiment were at dinner, badly wounded the old Highland lieutenant whose soliloquy is before narrated, also slightly the quarter-master and adjutant, and killed the Commissary-General Perkins who was at table.

The incessant cannonade now commenced on both sides, but our batteries and newly constructed works soon began to feel the effects of the powerful artillery opposed to them, and on the 10th scarcely a gun could be fired from our works, fascines, stockade platforms, and earth, with guns and gun-carriages, being all pounded together in a mass. The Hon. Major Cochrane, of the legion who came express from New York through the French fleet, and was appointed to act as an aid-de-camp to Lord Cornwallis, being led by zeal to fire a gun from behind the parapet in the horn work "en ricochet," and anxious to see its effect, looked over to observe it, when his head was carried off by a cannon ball.'[18]

On Friday 12 October, 'Secretary' Thomas Nelson, former Secretary of the colony of Virginia and uncle of Governor Thomas Nelson, was allowed to come out to the allied lines. The following day St George Tucker watched the artillery duel before he dined with the Secretary:

'Last Evening and during the night the Cannonade & Bombardment from ours & the french Batteries were kept up with very little Intermission. Red hot Balls being fired at the Shipping from the french Battery over the Creek, the Charon and forty four Gun ship and another ship were set fire to & burnt during the night & a Brig in the morning met with the same Fate. . . . The Enemy threw a few shells from five mortars. . . . Most of these burst in the Air at a considerable Height. . . . After this their shells were directed apparently towards the place where we this Evening begun to open our second parallel. . . .

I this day dined in Company with the Secretary. He says our Bombardment produced great Effects in annoying the Enemy & destroying their Works—Two Officers were killed & one wounded by a Bomb the Evening we opened—Lord Shuten's [Chewton] Cane was struck out of his Hand by a Cannon Ball—Lord Cornwallis has built a kind of Grotto at the foot of the Secretary's Garden where he lives under Ground.—A negroe of the Secretary's was kill'd in his House—It seems to be his Opinion that the British are a good deal dispirited altho' he says they affect to say they have no Apprehension of the Garrison's falling—An immense number of Negroes have died in the most miserable Manner in York.'[19]

With possible victory in sight, men dug lustily in extending the second parallel. Two redoubts, known only as nine and ten, blocked the extension of the line to the river. Sunday night, 14 October, was selected as the night when the two strongpoints were to be overrun. Baron de Vioménil was to storm number nine with the Royal Deux-Ponts and Gatenois regiments. Alexander Hamilton, as field officer of the day, demanded that he be allowed to lead the picked detachment of Lafayette's light infantry against number ten. Count Deux Ponts led his regiment forward:

'I advanced in the greatest silence. At a hundred and twenty or thirty paces we were discovered, and the Hessian soldier who was stationed as a sentinel on the parapet, cried out "Wer da?" (Who comes there?), to which we did not reply, but hastened our steps. We lost not a moment in reaching the abatis, which being strong and well preserved at about twenty-five paces from the redoubt, cost us many men, and stopped us for some minutes, but was cleared away with brave determination. We threw ourselves into the ditch at once, and each one sought to break through the fraises, and to mount the parapet.

We reached there at first in small numbers and I gave the order to fire. The enemy kept up a sharp fire and charged us at the point of the bayonet, but no one was driven back. The carpenters . . . had made some breaches in the palisades, which helped the main body of troops in mounting. The parapet was becoming manned visibly. Our fire was increasing and making terrible havoc among the enemy, who had placed themselves behind a kind of entrenchment of barrels, where they were well massed, and where all our shots told. We succeeded at the moment when I wished to give the order to leap into the redoubt and charge upon the enemy with the bayonet; then they laid down their arms and we leaped in with more tranquility and less risk. I shouted immediately the cry of *"Vive le Roy,"* which was repeated by all the Grenadiers and Chasseurs who were in good condition, by all troops in the trenches, and to which the enemy replied by a general discharge of artillery and musketry. I never saw a sight more beautiful or more majestic.'[20]

Joseph Plumb Martin, now a sergeant, did not know that he was to storm redoubt ten until he arrived in the lines a little before sunset and saw officers tying bayonets on long staves:

'The Sappers and Miners were furnished with axes and were to proceed in front and cut a passage for the troops through the abatis, which are composed of the tops of trees, the small branches cut off with a slanting stroke which renders them sharp as spikes. These trees are then laid at a small distance from the trench or ditch, pointing outwards, and the butts fastened to the ground in such a manner that they cannot be removed by those on the outside of them. It is almost impossible to get through them. Through these we were to cut a passage before we or the other assailants could enter.

At dark the detachment was formed and advanced beyond the trenches and lay down on the ground to await the signal for advancing to the attack. . . . Our watchword was "Rochambeau," . . . a good watchword, for being pronounced *Ro-sham-bow*, it sounded, when pronounced quick, like *rush-on-boys*.

We had not lain here long before the expected signal was given . . . by the three shells with their fiery trains mounting the air in quick succession. The word *up, up*, was reiterated through the detachment. We immediately moved silently on toward the redoubt we were to attack, with unloaded muskets. Just as we arrived at the abatis, the enemy discovered us and directly opened a sharp fire upon us. We were now at a place where many of our larger shells had burst in the ground, making holes sufficient to bury an ox in. The men, having their eyes fixed upon what was transacting before them were every now and then falling into these holes. I thought the British were killing us off at a great rate. At length, one of the holes happening to pick me up, I found out the mystery of the great slaughter.

As soon as the firing began, our people began to cry, "The fort's our own!" and it was "Rush on boys." The Sappers and the Miners soon cleared a path for the infantry, who entered it rapidly. Our Miners were ordered not to enter the fort, but there was no stopping them. "We will go," said they. "Then go to the d---l," said the commanding officer of our corps, "if you will." I could not press for the entrance we had made, it was so crowded. I therefore forced a passage at a place where I saw our shot had cut away some of the abatis; several others entered at the same place. While passing, a man at my side received a ball in his head and fell under my feet, crying out bitterly. While crossing the trench, the enemy threw hand granades. . . . In the heat of the action I saw a British soldier jump over the walls of the fort next the river and go down the bank, which was almost perpendicular and twenty or thirty feet high. When he came on the beach he made off for the town, and if he did not make good use of his legs I never saw a man that did.'[21]

Shortly after the redoubts were taken, there was an amusing incident in number ten involving General Henry Knox and Alexander Hamilton:

'The blinds . . . were made of hogshead and pipes filled with sand—they were placed there by the British. . . . With Hamilton, Knox and others, there were present in that redoubt about four hundred American troops—the French troops were in another redoubt. A general order had been given, that when a shell was seen, they might cry out *a shell*—but not cry *a shot* when a shot was seen. The reason of this distinction was, that a shell might be avoided, but to cry *a shot* would only make confusion and do no good. The order was just then discussed, Col. Hamilton remarking that it seemed unsoldier-like to halloo *a shell*, while Knox contended the contrary, and that the order was wisely given by General Washington, who cared for the life of his men.

The argument . . . was progressed with a slight degree of warmth, when suddenly *spat! spat!* two shells fell and struck within the redoubt. Instantly a cry broke out on all sides, *"a shell! a shell!"* and such a scrambling and jumping to reach the blinds and get behind them for defense. Knox and Hamilton were united in action, however differing in word, for both got behind the blinds, and Hamilton to be yet more secure, held on behind Knox, (Knox being a very large man and Hamilton a small man). Upon this Knox struggled to throw Hamilton off, and in the effort himself (Knox) rolled over and threw Hamilton off towards the shells. Hamilton however scrabbled back again behind the blinds. All this was done rapidly, for in two minutes the shells burst, and threw their deadly missiles in all directions. It was now safe and soldier-like to stand out. "Now," says Knox, "now what do you think, Mr. Hamilton, about crying *shell*—but let me tell you not to make a breastwork of me again." . . . on looking around and finding not a man hurt out of the more than 400, Knox exclaimed, *"it is a miracle."* '[22]

Colonel Butler recorded the last bit of swashbuckling by the British which did little but gain the admiration of the allies for a brave deed. It was on 15 October:

'About 12 o'clock at night, Maj. Abercrombie, of the British, with a party of the Light Infantry and Guards, made a sally . . . pushed rapidly to a French battery, and spiked the guns and drove out the people, having killed four or five; Thence to the covert way or communication leading from the first to the second parallel, where they halted.

They then discovered a battery commanded by Capt. Savage, of the Americans and challenged, What troops? The answer was French—on which the order of the British Commandant was "Push on, my brave boys, and skin the b——ds." This was heard by Count De Noailles, who had the command of a covering party, which he ordered to advance, and was guided by the *Huzza* of the British. He ordered grenadiers to "charge bayonets and rush on," which they did with great spirit crying "Vive Le Roy," and to use the British phrase skivered eight of the Guards and Infantry, and took twelve prisoners, and drove them quite off. The British spiked Savage's three guns with the points of bayonets, but our smiths and artillery men soon cleared all the guns, and in six hours chastised the enemy for their temerity with the same pieces.'[23]

During the dark night of 16 October, Cornwallis made a desperate attempt to ferry his troops across to the Gloucester side and break out from there to fight his way to New York. A sudden squall, carrying slanting sheets of rain, frustrated that attempt when only a portion of the troops were on the far side of the York. At two o'clock the following morning they were ordered back to Yorktown. A young Hessian soldier was on duty in the lines the following day:

'this morning right after reveille, General Cornwallis came into the hornwork and observed the enemy and his works. As soon as he had gone back to his quarters, he immediately sent a flag of truce, with a white standard over to the enemy. The light infantry began to cut their new tents in the hornwork to pieces and many were altogether ruined, so one expected an early surrender.'[24]

Major Ebenezer Denny was on the far side of the field gazing across the parapet:

'In the morning before relief came, had the pleasure of seeing a drummer mount the enemy's parapet, and beat a parley, and immediately an officer, holding up a white handkerchief, made his appearance outside their works;

234. This Representation of Peter Franciscos Gallant Action with Nine of Tarletons Cavalry in Sight of a Troop of Four Hundred Men Took place in Amelia County Virginia 1781

Francisco's exploit shown here is authentic although the engraving was made much later. He was an enlisted soldier of unusual size and strength who had dragged a 1,100-pound cannon across the field, in default of horses, at the battle of Camden. On this occasion he was reconnoitring alone when surrounded and taken prisoner by a marauding party. Francisco stepped back when one of the troopers bent down to rob him of his prized silver shoe buckles, drew his sword, and struck him across the skull. He seized the musket of the mounted trooper when it missed fire; he wounded him also and shouted 'Come on, my brave boys; now's your time; we'll soon dispatch these few and then attack the main body.' Tarleton's soldiers fled panic-stricken, and Francisco appropriated six of the eight horses left behind.

235. (Overleaf) The Siege of Yorktown, with the arrival of French troops, 14 September 1781. *L. N. Van Blarenberghe*

The scene is the arrival of the French army under Comte de Rochambeau, on their way to take up their positions before Yorktown. They are resplendent in their white uniforms, which had amazed the citizenry along the way, accustomed to the drab equipment of the American forces. In the distance is York River and the Gloucester Point shore beyond. In the centre are the Continental and French staffs, discussing the plans.
    The details are based on an eyewitness drawing by Louis Alexandre Berthier of Rochambeau's staff, later to become Napoleon's chief-of-staff, marshal of the Empire, and Prince of Neuchâtel and Wagram.
    Louis Van Blarenberghe was appointed in 1778 as the official draftsman of the Ministry of War in Paris.

The British troops are
marching between
rows of French and
Continental soldiers;
in the field beyond the
British and Hessians
are laying down their
arms. The accuracy of
the painting is
supported by the
journal of Dr James
Thacher, who
observed the ceremony
from horseback: 'This
is to us a most glorious
day, but to the
English, one of bitter
chagrin and
disappointment. . . .
The Americans were
drawn up on the right
side of the road, and
the French occupied
the left. At the head
of the former, the
great American
commander, mounted
on his noble courser,
took his station,
attended by his aids,
at the head of the
latter was posted,
the excellent Count
Rochambeau and his
suite . . . every
countenance beamed
with satisfaction and
joy. The concourse of
spectators from the
country was
prodigious . . . Many
of the [British]
soldiers manifested a
sullen temper,
throwing down their
arms on the pile with
violence, as if deter-
mined to render them
useless . . . this
irregularity was
checked, however, by
the authority of
General Lincoln.'

the drummer accompanied him, beating. Our batteries ceased. An officer
from our lines ran and met the other, and tied the handkerchief over his
eyes. The drummer sent back, and the British Officer conducted to a house
in rear of our lines. Firing ceased totally.'[25]

The sudden silence swept across the battlefield. St George Tucker gloried
in the scene on 18 October, as commissioners of both armies were hammering
out the terms of capitulation in the house of Augustine Moore:

'At dawn of the day the British gave us a serenada with the Bag pipe . . . &
were answered by the French with the Band of the Regiment of deux ponts.
As soon as the Sun rose one of the most striking pictures of War was
display'd that Imagination can paint—From the point of Rock Battery on
our side our Lines compleatly mann'd and our Works crowded with soldiers
were exhibited to view—opposite these at the Distance of two hundred
yards you were presented with a sight of the British Works; their parapets
crowded with officers looking at those who were assembled at the top of
our Works—the Secretary's house with one of the Corners broke off, &
many large holes thro the Roof & Walls part of which seem'd tottering with
their Weight afforded a striking Instance of the Destruction occasioned by
War—Many other houses in the vicinity contributed to accomplish the
Scene.
    On the beach of York directly under the Eye hundreds of busy people
might be seen moving to & fro—At a small distance from the Shore were
seen ships sunk down to the Waters Edge—further out in the Channel the
Masts, Yards & even the top gallant Masts of some might be seen, without
any vestige of the hulls.'[26]

The rays of the warm autumn sun filtered through red and brown leaves
around two o'clock on 19 October 1781. For a mile on either side of the
Hampton road troops were lined, the Americans on the right, the French
on the left. Washington sat waiting to accept his first surrender ever.
Beside him was Major-General Benjamin Lincoln who, having been ex-
changed, was now acting as second-in-command of the American army.
Cornwallis, pleading illness, sent his second-in-command, Brigadier-
General Charles O'Hara, to hand over his sword. The redcoated column
drew nearer, its music playing a tune called 'The World Turned Upside
Down', subtitled 'The Old Woman Taught Wisdom', although Major Denny
thought their 'drums beat as if they did not care how'. Lieutenant William
McDowell observed, 'The British prisoners appeared much in liquor.'
Count Mathieu Dumas was in the official party as the generals met:

'I had orders to go and meet the troops of the garrison, and to direct the
columns. I placed myself at General O'Hara's left hand. As we approached
the trenches, he asked me where General Rochambeau was. "On our left,"
I said, "at the head of the French line."
    The English general urged his horse forward to present his sword to the
French general. Guessing his intentions, I galloped on to place myself
between him and M. de Rochambeau, who at the moment made me a sign,
pointing to General Washington, who was opposite him, at the head of the
American army.
    "You are mistaken," said I to General O'Hara, "the Commander-in-Chief

of our army is to the right." I accompanied him, and the moment he presented his sword, General Washington, anticipating him, said "Never from such a good hand." '[27]

Later, old 'Papa' Rochambeau explained that 'the French army being only an auxilliary on this continent, it devolved on the American General to tender him his orders'. Earlier in the day, Ebenezer Denny had been among the party who went in to take possession of the town:

'Detachments of French and Americans took possession of British forts. Major Hamilton commanded a battalion which took possession of a fort . . . on the bank of the York river. I carried the standard of our regiment upon this occasion. On entering the fort, Baron Steuben, who accompanied us, took the standard from me and planted it himself. . . . Much confusion and riot among the British through the day; many of the soldiers were intoxicated; several attempts in course of the night to break open stores; an American sentinel killed by a British soldier with a bayonet; our patrols kept busy. Glad to be relieved from this disagreeable station. Negroes lie about, sick and dying, in every stage of small pox. Never was in so filthy a place—some handsome houses, but prodigiously shattered.'[28]

Sergeant Martin, helping round up the slaves with Cornwallis, received a dollar, or rather its equivalent in continental currency: 'it amounted to twelve hundred dollars, all of which I afterwards paid for one single quart of rum'. A great chuckle ran through American ranks when Banastre Tarleton got his due:

'A Mr. Day came to our tent and said he was steward to Sir Peyton Skipwith, and that the horse that Colonel Tarleton was riding belonged to his master; that moreover the horse was worth 500 pounds, and he had come all the way from Dan River, determined to get it. Mr. Day went into a marshy place near by and cut him a sweet gumstick as thick as a man's wrist.

It was not long before the mighty Tarleton with his servant, came riding along in high style. Mr. Day was in the road, and said, "Good morning, Colonel Tarleton, this is my horse, dismount." Holding the horse, he drew his cudgel as if to strike. Colonel Tarleton jumped off quicker than ever I saw a man in my life. . . . Mr. Day went off in a very long trot towards Williamsburg. . . .

Oh! how we did laugh to think how the mighty man who had caused so much terror and alarm in Virginia, had been made to jump off the wrong side of his horse so quickly, with nothing but a sweet gum stick and a chunky little man against him, while he, who was a tall, large, likely man had a fine sword by his side.'[29]

Out beyond the Capes of the Chesapeake, a rescue squadron with Clinton on board began tacking about for the return voyage to New York. On 19 October, the day that Cornwallis' army had marched out to surrender field, the fleet had upped anchor in New York. Even as they beat against the wind, the Marquis de Lafayette was writing to his friend Washington:

'The play, sir, is over—and the fifth act has just been closed. I was in a somewhat awkward situation during the first acts; my heart experienced great delight at the final one—and I do not feel less pleasure in congratulating you, at this moment, upon the fortunate issue of this campaign.'[30]

330

15. Rebellion becomes Revolution

THERE WAS NO WAY of knowing that victory at Yorktown meant the end of the war, but it provided a cause for celebration throughout the country. No longer were the French the villains of Newport and Savannah, but valued allies. And there was a need to bolster confidence. Although the Articles of Confederation, ratified on 1 March 1781, had given the Continental Congress some stability, that body had become almost a political shell, financially destitute and not always looked upon as the oracle of freedom. Washington's aide, Tench Tilghman, carried the news of Yorktown to Philadelphia, but discovered that rather than receiving a reward as the bearer of cheerful news, it was difficult to gain reimbursement for his expenses:

'When the messenger brought the News of this Capitulation to Congress, it was necessary to furnish him with hard money for expenses. There was not a sufficiency in the Treasury to do it, and the Members of Congress of which I was one, each paid a dollar to accomplish it.'[1]

In a nation starved for victories, Yorktown was an occasion. The *New York Packet* of 1 November carried accounts of festivities in other areas of the state:

'At Fishkill, New York, the glorious victory was observed with exhuberant joy and festivity. A roasted ox and plenty of liquor formed the repast; a number of toasts were drank on the occasion. French and American colors were displayed, cannon were fired, and in the evening, illuminations, bonfires, rockets, and squibs, gave agreeable amusement to the numerous spectators.

    At Newburgh the occasion was observed in the same joyous manner, and to enliven the entertainment, they hanged and burnt in effigy the traitor Arnold.'[2]

As might be expected, the news was received with less gaiety in England. Lord George Germain as Secretary of State for the Colonies was responsible for conveying the information to Lord North, the First Minister:

'On Sunday, the 25th [November], about noon, official intelligence of the surrender of the British forces at York Town, arrived from Falmouth, at Lord Germain's house in Pall-Mall. . . . After a short consultation, they determined to lay it, in person, before Lord North.

    He had not received any intimation of the event, when they arrived at his door, in Downing-street, between one and two o'clock. The first minister's firmness, and even his presence of mind . . . gave way for a short time, under this awful disaster. I asked Lord George afterwards, how he took the communication when made to him? "As he would have taken a ball in his breast," replied Lord George. For, he opened his arms, exclaiming wildly, as he paced up and down the apartment during a few minutes, "Oh, God!

it is all over!" Words which he repeated many times, with emotions of the deepest consternation and distress.'[3]

Cornwallis, paroled, was allowed to return to England. As he sailed, American wits marshalled their talents to heap further coals of humiliation upon his troubled head:

'*Farewell, my lord; may zephyrs waft thee o'er*
In health and safety to thy native shore;
There seek Burgoyne, and tell him, though too late,
You blamed unwisely his unhappy fate:
Tell your deluded monarch that you see
The Hand of Heaven upraised for liberty:
Tell your exhausted nation, tell them true,
They cannot conquer those who conquer'd you.'[4]

The allied army had broken up after Yorktown, with some American units detached to South Carolina to aid Greene, the remainder to go to New Jersey to winter in the Hudson Highlands, while the French troops under Rochambeau went into winter quarters in Williamsburg. Shortly after the surrender, the French naval squadron sailed off to the West Indies to meet eventual defeat at the hand of Admiral Rodney in the Battle of the Saints in April 1782. Before they set their sails, one French officer recorded his impressions of the Americans:

'Before leaving this country I wish to say something of North America and its people. The Americans are generally large, strong and well made: the women are handsome, tapering in form, have very little bust, of a disposition the more gentle from the fact of their having among them many Anabaptists, known to be the most charitable of all sects. Hospitality is greatly practiced, as travellers in this extensive country are few, scarcely any in fact.

The servants are negroes, certainly the least unhappy of their kind, being treated with more kindness than our lackeys in France; hence we never hear in this country of masters poisoned by their negroes, so common an occurrence in our West India islands. The Anglican is the dominant religion; all are suffered here; the language is English. I believe these two things may well make them give the English the preference over us in a few years.

The Americans are phlegmatic, extremely serious, always engaged in their business, and that of state. They are with their wives only to take tea or some other drink. The girls are very free, and can have a lover without their parents finding it amiss; but if they are unfortunate enough to have a child, they must leave the country, unless they get married: but woe to the stranger who in such cases refuses to marry, for he refuses at the risk of his life. The women are as reserved as the girls are unreserved, and I do not think the unfaithful ones can be cited: at all events they behave with the greatest reserve; yet they were fond of the French officers, whom they preferred to their own countrymen, but with all possible decency.'[5]

Washington, after remaining four months in Philadelphia, rejoined his army at Newburgh on the Hudson, arriving there on 1 April 1782. There was a definite smell of peace in the air, and in Paris, Benjamin Franklin, John Adams, and John Jay were hammering out a treaty with representa-

237. The American Peace Commissioners. *Benjamin West*

By means of a combination of stubbornness, tact, and recently won diplomatic skill, the American commissioners won a highly favourable peace treaty for America in 1783, in the face not only of British opposition, but self-serving compromises favoured by her allies France and Spain. As here painted by Benjamin West, the teacher of many of the Revolutionary painters, they are, from left to right, John Jay of New York, John Adams of Massachusetts, Benjamin Franklin of Pennsylvania, and Henry Laurens of South Carolina. The young man at the right is their secretary, Franklin's grandson, William Temple Franklin. The painting is unfinished because the British commissioners refused to pose.

tives of the government of Lord Rockingham, successors to the North Ministry. There was not a great deal to do other than watch the British, now under the command of Sir Guy Carleton, Clinton's replacement as Commander-in-Chief of the British Army in North America. Washington's primary concern was driving off the boredom that he feared would infect his troops; drills and parades would keep them out of mischief. On 18 September, his general order ran:

'There will be a general review on Saturday next. No officer (or soldier who has a uniform suit, and ought to be in the ranks) is to be absent. The Commander-in-Chief gives this early notice, that the men may appear clean and to advantage. The General, at some of the late manoeuvring, has discovered in some instances an inattention in marching; for, besides the loss of step, which is alone sufficient to give an awkward movement to a division or platoon, he has remarked that many of the soldiers do not step boldly and freely, but short, and with bent knees. The officers commanding platoons and divisions will see that these defects are remedied, and that their men, while marching by the reviewing officer, carry their body erect, look well up, incline their heads to the right, and look full in the face of that officer—this last to be considered a standing order.'[6]

Officers sought their own amusement, as suggested by an advertisement in the *New York Packet*:

'A Fox Hunt. The Gentlemen of the Army, with a number of the most respectable inhabitants of Ulster and Orange, purpose a Fox Hunt on the twenty third of this instant, where all gentlemen are invited, with their hounds and their horses. The game is plenty, and it is hoped the sport will be pleasant.'[7]

Sergeant Joseph Martin was kept busy when he was given two men and ordered to roam through New Jersey taking up deserters:

'We this forenoon passed through a pretty village called Maidenhead; (don't stare, dear reader, I did not name it). An hour or two before we came to this place, I saw a pretty young lady standing in the door of a house, just by the road side. I very innocently inquired of her how far it was to Maidenhead; she answered, "five miles." One of my men, who, though young, did not stand in imminent danger of being hanged for his beauty, observed to the young woman, that he thought the commodity scarce in the market, since he had to go so far to see it. "Don't trouble yourself," said she, "about that, there is no danger of its being more scarce on your account." The fellow leered, and, I believe, wished he had held his tongue.'[8]

All that summer Sir Guy Carleton prepared for the evacuation of the southern states. Savannah saw the last British sail creep over the horizon on 11 July 1782, and all that fall there were rumours that Charleston would soon be rid of its unpopular tenants. A Hessian soldier heard what he thought were rumours, until on 14 December 1782:

'It was first posted up at Charleston that in case the Hessians and the English should go to sea and abandon the City, no citizen should open a door or window in three days, much less let himself be seen on the street on pain of punishment until the end. Moreover if any one transgresses in other respects by firing guns and other excesses during the out-march to the water, he will at once be taken into custody and sent to Nova Scotia upon a wild, wild island, where there is no wood. Early in the morning an alarm was struck and when we moved out of camp and stood in the streets under arms, we were notified of going upon water. Although every soldier had packed up everything in his quarters, one had forgotten this, another that. It happened also in the beginning, but many remained behind and forgot to come back. The subordinate officers were therefore obliged to bring in all that were to be found, and then we went forward. When we came to the water, some small vessels lay there on which we proceeded to the big ships and then departed from the city up the harbor.'[9]

Young Lewis Morris of New York, Greene's aide, took time off from his courtship of a wealthy young South Carolina widow to describe the event for his father:

'This joyful event took part on the 14th Instant and a great regularity was observed by both parties, which was happily agreed to between Gen*l* Wayne

238. Americaner Soldat

There are not many contemporary pictures in existence of the uniforms of the American Revolutionary soldier. This one, if correctly dated, must be one of the earliest to show a Congress cap. The fringe appears in several contemporary paintings.

Americaner Soldat.

who commanded the light corps in advance and Gen*l* Leslie the day before the embarkation; that when the rear guard retired, Gen*l* Wayne should advance about two hundred paces in its rear, and that all hostilities should cease, till the troops were on board of the ships—the whole fleet is now about five miles off waiting for a fair wind and spring tide to pass the bar. It is a most grateful sight to the distressed people of this country, and they have now the pleasing prospect of enjoying that little they have left in peace and tranquility.'[10]

In the genial air that seemed to float about the American camp to the north, old animosities seemed to be forgotten. Horatio Gates, once again in good graces and second-in-command of the army, wrote to Robert Morris:

'I am well, and as happy as an Old Soldier can be, in a Tent the latter end of October, we move in a day to Winter Quarters; when I hope to get warm for once since I arrived in Camp. Upon talking with the General, I have sent for Mrs. Gates to keep me from freezing this Winter. . . . Mrs. Washington is, I understand, upon the road. All is secret, and uncertain in Regard to the Enemy. Sir Guy is so Damn'd close, that he must be doing something He is ashamed of, for every thing Offensive on his part, is at an End, and things must strangely Alter, before the power of G. Britain can revive. I verily think that is departed never to rise again in this Hemisphere.'[11]

But an old friend of Gates' was neither forgiven, nor could he return to the army. Just a little over three weeks before Gates wrote the above, Charles Lee died in Philadelphia's 'Conestoga Wagon'. Ebenezer Hazard sent the details to Jeremy Belknap:

'General Lee died in the second story of a tavern, after a few days' illness, in some degree his own physician and but badly attended, except by two faithful dogs, who frequently attempted in vain to awaken their dead master. They laid themselves down by his corpse for a considerable time, so long that it became necessary for new masters to remove them. He lies buried in Christ's Church yard. No stone marks his bed. Indeed, those who saw his open grave can scarcely mark the site, as it is continually trodden by persons going into and coming out of church. Behold the honor of the great!'[12]

And only Charles Lee would have left such a last will and testament:

'I desire most earnestly that I may not be buried in any church, or church yard, or within a mile of any Presbyterian or Anabaptist meeting house; for since I have resided in this country, I have had so much bad company while living, that I do not choose to continue it when dead.

I recommend my soul to the Creator of all worlds and of all creatures, who must, from his visible attributes, be indifferent to their modes of worship or creeds, whether Christian, Mohammedans, or Jewish whether instilled by education, or taken up by reflection; whether more or less absurd; as a weak mortal can no more be answerable for his persuasions, notions, or even skepticism in religion, than for the color of his skin.'[13]

But as peace became more of a certainty, discontent swelled into a smouldering rage among those officers who felt they were unappreciated by their country. Their pay was in arrears, and Congress had done little other than make recommendations to the various states. In December 1782, a representation of officers had appeared before Congress demanding that, upon disbandment of the army, they be granted half pay for life, after the European custom. Several motions to that effect died in Congress. Two anonymous and inflammatory declarations, to become known as the 'Newburgh Addresses', circulated through camp. The author was believed to have been Major John Armstrong, aide to General Gates. A mass meeting of officers was called for 11 March. Washington, in turn, issued an officers' call for 15 March, supposedly to hear the report of the committee to Congress. Gates was to preside, while the commanding general was not expected to attend. Major Samuel Shaw described the proceedings for the Rev. Mr Eliot:

'The meeting of the officers was in itself exceedingly respectable, the matters they were called to deliberate upon were of the most serious nature, and the unexpected attendance of the Commander-in-Chief heightened the solemnity of the scene. Every eye was fixed upon the illustrious man, and attention to their beloved General held the assembly mute. He opened the meeting by apologizing for his appearance there, which was by no means his intention when he published the order which directed them to assemble. But the diligence used in circulating the anonymous pieces rendered it necessary that he should give his sentiments to the army on the nature and tendency of them, and determined him to avail himself of the present opportunity; and, in order to do it with greater perspicuity, he had committed his thoughts to writing, which, with the indulgence of his brother officers, he would take the liberty of reading to them.

It is needless for me to say any thing of this production; *it speaks for itself*. After he concluded his address, he said, that, as a corroborating testimony of the good disposition in Congress towards the Army, he would communicate to them a letter received from a worthy member of that body, and one who on all occasions had ever approved himself their fast friend. This was an exceedingly sensible letter; and while it pointed out the difficulties and embarrassments of Congress, it held up very forcibly the idea that the army should, at all events, be generously dealt with.

One circumstance in reading this letter must not be omitted. His Excellency, after reading the first paragraph, made a short pause, took out his spectacles, and begged the indulgence of his audience while he put them on, observing at the same time, that he had grown gray in their service, and now found himself going blind. There was something so natural, so unaffected, in this appeal, as rendered it superior to the most studied oratory; it forced its way to the heart, and you might see sensibility moisten every eye. The General, having finished, took leave of the assembly. . . . Had this day been wanting, the world had never seen the last stage of perfection to which human nature is capable of attaining.'[14]

As Washington made his way back to his quarters, the officers voted to leave their problems to the care of the General. Congress eventually agreed to pay officers five years' pay in cash, or in bonds bearing an interest rate of six per cent. Enlisted men were to receive full pay for four months.

Shortly after this incident, Washington received a letter from Lafayette who had returned to France. In this, the young Frenchman reported that a preliminary peace treaty had been signed, a fact soon confirmed in a letter from Sir Guy Carleton. Congress ratified the provisional treaty on 15 April and two days later published a proclamation to that effect. Surgeon James Thacher heard the news on 19 April:

'On the completion of eight years from the memorable battle of Lexington, the proclamation of the congress for a cessation of hostilities was published at the door of the public building followed by three huzzas; after which, a prayer was offered to the Almighty Ruler of the World, by the Rev. Mr. Ganno, and an anthem was performed by voices and instruments.'[15]

The young Hessian Stephen Popp had been confined in Frederick, Maryland, a prisoner of war since Yorktown. He was as happy as the townspeople:

'Learned of peace between England and the Provinces of North America,— and could not at first believe the news told us by some of our men, until it was confirmed by people of the town. The Two Companies of Militia got orders to go home—we heard the bells of the town ringing and the people hurraing and the two Militia Companies marched through the town with white flags as emblems of peace. Then came a message from Philadelphia to the Commander of the Militia in Fredericktown, which he sent us. The Reformed Church celebrated peace on the 13th,—Palm Sunday, and the Pastor preached on a text from Judges verse 24. On the 3rd day of the Easter holidays there was a general celebration,—cannon firing all day,—the two City Companies and the Militia paraded with white flags with thirteen stripes for the thirteen Colonies. Our American guard was withdrawn and we were left quite free. The American officers and gentlemen gave a great ball,—at 9 P.M. there were fire works,—which our cannoniers made,—the whole town was illuminated and there was a great fire of small arms,— we shared in the rejoicing, for we knew we should soon be free.'[16]

During the celebration, someone took the time to note the weight of officers then in camp. It would seem they had not suffered much from lack of provisions:

'General Washington	209 lbs.	Colonel Henry Jackson	238 lbs.
General Lincoln	224 lbs.	Colonel Swift	219 lbs.
General Knox	280 lbs.	Lt. Colonel Huntington	232 lbs.
General Huntington	132 lbs.	Lt. Colonel Cobb	186 lbs.
General Greaton	166 lbs.	Lt. Colonel Humphreys	221 lbs.'[17]
Colonel Michael Jackson	252 lbs.		

Many of the troops were furloughed and allowed to go home. Sergeant Joseph Martin assembled with his men for the last time:

'I confess, after all, that my anticipation of the happiness I should experience upon such a day as this was not realized . . . there was as much sorrow as joy transfused on the occasion. We had lived together as a family of brothers for several years, setting aside some little family squabbles, like most families, had shared with each other the hardships, dangers and sufferings incident to a soldier's life; had sympathized with each other in trouble and sickness; had assisted in bearing each other's burden or strove to make them lighter by council and advice; had endeavored to conceal each other's fault or make them appear in as good a light as they would bear. . . . And now we were to be, the greater part of us, parted forever; as unconditionally separated as though the grave lay between us.'[18]

Joel Shepard, a happy-go-lucky private from Hinsdale, New York, held few regrets as to the end of his tour of duty and seemed determined to take his fun where he found it:

'[At a dance at Fort Herkimer] These duchmen took but very little notis of the young women. Finally wee, the young soldiers, used them with good manners and we treated them and were sociable to them, and the young women took notis ouf our Behaviour, and it them. Well, I had a discourse with one of the girls. She said that her father and mother did not like to have their daughters keep Company with the soldiers but they often did privately. We had some discours on the subject and said that the English people were more tender of their wifes than the Dutch were. Finally, I found she had a good opinion of the Yankeys and finally we concluded [to stay] together that night and we did, But was very privately. She returned home and let me in at a back window all as stil as possible, and we had a sociable nights discours. About the break of day I got out of the window and started to my quarters.'[19]

In October, a proclamation of Congress provided for the discharge of all soldiers except a small force, to be maintained 'until the peace establishment be organized'. Sir Guy Carleton was making his plans to evacuate New York on 25 November. Inside the city, one F. Michelis set down his impressions of the principals now involved:

'Sir Guy Carleton—Held in high esteem. Had he come sooner he would have made Tories of all the Whigs. Many wish he might be British Ambassador at Philadelphia. The French respect, fear and hate him.

Lord Cornwallis—Hated and despised by the allied nations, considered no general.

General Washington—Soon the Protector of America. A deep, endless ambition, too thinly veiled to escape penetration of some who see him behind the coulisse as well as on the stage makes the basis of this man who has for ever inscribed his name in the annals of the world; great not by shining talents, but by a happy occurrence of circumstances, a useful understanding, a passive perseverance, the mediocrity of his competitors, the weakness and perfidy of his antagonists. Genius it seems is not the growth of the western world. He is without a spark of imagination, enthusiasm or that torrent of talent that carries everything before it, cold, deliberate, patient, persevering, he finds himself elevated to a pitch of grandeur he never dreamed of, and would not grasp at the supreme power if to obtain it he must as Cromwell surround the State-house and tell them, "be gone, the Lord you seek has left this place." But no such exertion will be required, the nation is sick of Congress. Congress is tired of its situation. I know they *all* expect and most *desire* a revolution.

Congress—Its members of little respectability and acknowledge they have no power at all, but the persecution of the loyalists springs from them.'[20]

English observers were not the only persons who thought that Congress was too weak to carry the banner of government. Ebenezer Huntington, moody of nature and disgusted with the treatment of the military, registered his annoyance and a prediction with his brother:

'We most earnestly wish it [Treaty of Peace], that we may return to private Life with all the care & Comfort, that an ungrateful Countryman will permit—how much that will be, God knows when we are become not only the objects of abuse in the publick prints, and called the Harpies & Locusts of the Country, but am even so Obnoxious as to be Mobbed, and that under the Eyes of the Civil Authority if not under their Direction—God grant us Government, as States, free & independent, or give us a king, even tyranny is better than Anarchy—and I am well convinced the people do not know how to distinguish between Liberty and licentiousness—if you have no particular cloth procured for me, I wish you would get me enough to replace that you had of me of the same Colour or nearly so, that I may get my regimentals aside soon after I get home, & lay them up against a revolution, which will happen in Eighteen Months, unless government is supported.'[21]

But with the evacuation of New York and the sailing of the last British garrison, few thought of the future. Colonel Benjamin Tallmadge was well pleased with the present:

'The 25th of November, 1783, was appointed for the British troops to evacuate the city, and for the American troops to take possession of it. Gen. Knox, at the head of a select corps of American troops, entered the city as the rear of the British troops embarked; soon after which the Commander-in-Chief, accompanied by Gov. Clinton and their respective suites, made their public entry into the city on horseback, followed by the Lieut.-Governor and members of the Council. The officers of the army, eight abreast, and citizens on horseback, eight abreast, and citizens on foot, eight abreast, followed. . . . So perfect was the order of March, that entire tranquility prevailed, and nothing occurred to mar the general joy. Every countenance seemed to express the triumph of republican principles over the military despotism which had so long pervaded this now happy city. Most of the [loyalist] refugees had embarked for Nova Scotia, and the few who remained, were too insignificant to be noticed in the crowd. It was indeed a joyful day to the officers and soldiers of our army, and to all the friends of American independence, while the troops of the enemy, still in our waters, and the host of tories and refugees, were sorely mortified. The

239. 'Amérique Septentrionale', third French edition, fifth impression 1777. *John Mitchell*

No map delineating the boundaries was attached to the Treaty of Paris, signed on 3 September 1783. The English and American commissioners had signed a preliminary treaty on 30 November 1782. A Mitchell map, according to Benjamin Franklin, was used in these negotiations. The map here reproduced, with lines hachured from Franklin's own red-line marking on the map he gave to Vergennes, the French foreign minister, is therefore of especial interest. It was sent to Floridablanca, the Spanish foreign minister, by Aranha, the Spanish minister at Paris, with the following letter dated 1 January 1783: 'I now send you a map just like the one I sent you 10 August 1782, when I began negotiating with John Jay concerning the boundary between the United States and the Spanish possessions in North America. It is marked in accordance with the boundary articles of the treaty of 30 November 1782, between the United States and England. The boundaries upon this map are copied from the very map upon which Benjamin Franklin marked the boundaries for Monsieur Vergennes, less than four weeks ago on 6 December 1782.'
Mitchell's 'A Map of the British and French Dominions' was frequently corrected in the years following its first appearance; at least twenty-one variants, with changes on the plates, have been identified. In the production of his map the author was able to examine the records and maps of the Board for Trade and Plantations; by official order he was furnished with information by the governors of the provinces; he had access to the navigational reports in the Admiralty; and he called upon numerous explorers, traders, and scientists for their specific knowledge. With all its errors and omissions, the necessary result of the ignorance in which the topography of the continent was still shrouded, it was a magnificent achievement.

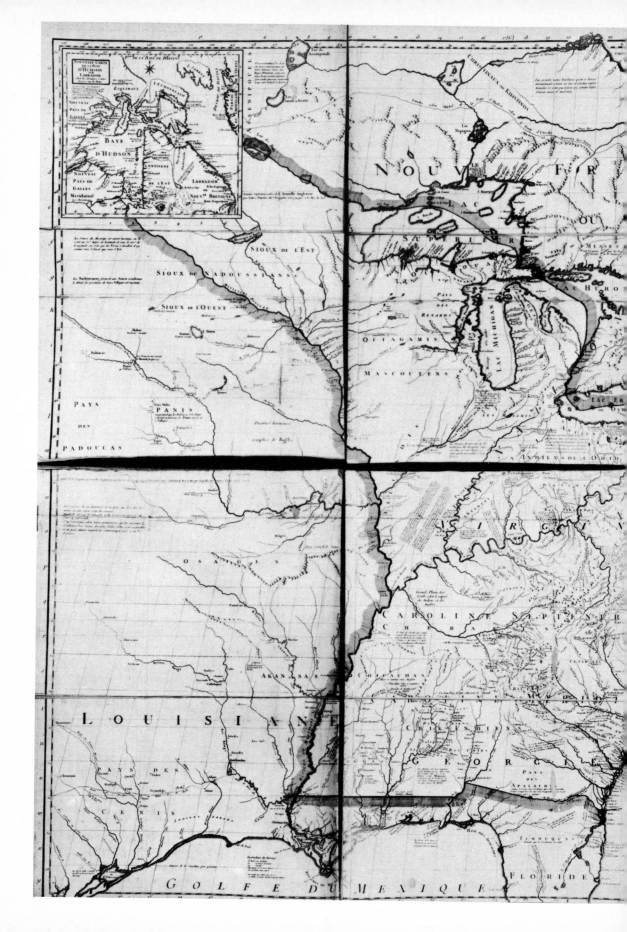

joy of meeting friends, who had long been separated by the cruel rigors of war, cannot be described.

Gov. Clinton gave a public dinner, at which Gen. Washington and the principal officers of the army, citizens, etc., were present. On the Tuesday evening following, there was a most splendid display of fireworks, at the lower part of Broadway, near the Bowling Green. It far exceeded anything I had ever seen in my life.

The time now drew near when the Commander-in-Chief intended to leave this part of the country for his beloved retreat at Mount Vernon. On Tuesday, the 4th of December, it was made known to the officers then in New York that Gen. Washington intended to commence his journey on that day. At 12 o'clock the officers repaired to *Francis'* [Fraunces] *Tavern*, in Pearl Street, where Gen. Washington had appointed to meet them, and to take his final leave of them.

We had been assembled but a few minutes when His Excellency entered the room. His emotion, too strong to be concealed, seemed to be reciprocated by every officer present. After partaking of a slight refreshment, in almost breathless silence, the General filled his glass with wine, and turning to the officers, he said: "With a heart full of love and gratitude, I now take leave of you. I most devoutly wish that your latter days may be as prosperous and happy as your former ones have been glorious and honorable."

After the officers had taken a glass of wine, Gen. Washington said: "I cannot come to each of you, but shall feel obliged if you will come and take me by the hand." . . .

The *simple thought* that we were then about to part from the man who had conducted us through a long and bloody war; and under whose conduct the glory and independence of our country had been achieved, and that we should see his face no more in this world, seemed to me utterly insupportable. But the time of separation had come, and waving his hand to his *grieving children* around him, he left the room, and passing through a corps of light infantry who were paraded to receive him, he walked silently on to Whitehall, where a barge was in waiting. We all followed in mournful silence to the wharf, where a prodigious crowd had assembled to witness the departure of the man who, under God, had been the great agent in establishing the glory and independence of the United States. As soon as he was seated, the barge put off into the river, and when out in the stream, our great and beloved General waved his hat, and bid us a silent adieu. . . .

In a few days, all the officers who had assembled in New York to participate in the foregoing heart-rending scene, departed to their several places of abode, to commence anew their avocations for life.'[22]

After his dramatic departure from New York, Washington galloped southward, down the road to Annapolis where the Continental Congress was now sitting. On 22 December, there was 'an elegant public dinner', conducted to the booming of thirteen cannon outside the hall, and glasses were lifted high in response to the now traditional thirteen toasts. That evening, at a ball given by the Governor at the State House, Washington danced every set, 'that all the ladies might have the pleasure of dancing with him, or as it since has been handsomely expressed, *get a touch of him*'.

It was exactly noon the following day when the General presented himself at the State House, his purpose to resign his commission. His speech was short, but David Howell said after the proceedings, 'The farewell of General

Washington was a most solemn Scene. . . . And many testified their affectionate attachment to our illustrious Hero and their gratitude for his Services to his country by a most copious shedding of tears.' Young James McHenry, who had served in the military under Washington, described the scene for his betrothed:

'To day, my love, the General, at a public audience made a deposit of his commission and in a very pathetic manner took leave of Congress. It was a solemn and affecting spectacle; such a one as history does not often present. The spectators all wept, and there was hardly a member of Congress who did not drop tears.

The General's hand which held the address shook as he read it. When he spoke of the officers who had composed his family, and recommended those who had continued in it to the present moment to the favorable notice of Congress, he was obliged to support the paper with both hands. But when he commended the interests of his dearest country to almighty God, and those who had the superintendence of them to his holy keeping, his voice faltered and sunk, and the whole house felt his agitations. After a pause which was necessary for him to recover himself, he proceeded to say in the most penetrating manner,

"Having now finished the work assigned me, I retire from the great theatre of action, and bidding an affectionate farewell to this august body under whose orders I have so long acted, I here offer my commission and take my leave of all the employments of public life."

So saying he drew from his bosom his commission and delivered it up to the president of Congress. He then returned to his station, when the president read the reply that had been prepared—but I thought without any shew of feeling, tho' with much dignity.'[23]

It was late in the afternoon the following day when hoof beats were heard in the lane leading to the back door of Mount Vernon. Shortly, a tall, tired, drawn man was stiffly dismounting from his horse. Citizen George Washington was home in time for Christmas.

And now the nation had a hero, a government, and a future.

240. South Prospect of the City of New York

An unidentified artist painted this picture of the harbour of New York filled with British ships. So it looked for the last time in early December 1783, when Sir Guy Carleton, who had succeeded Clinton as commander, evacuated his troops from the city which had been their stronghold ever since it was taken by Sir William Howe in 1776. In these ships with the departing British went many of the journal records, letters, maps and pictures which are still being found in English homes and repositories to form a basis for our knowledge of the War of American Independence.

Notes

CHAPTER 1

1. *Am. Hist. Rev.*, XXVI, 726–7.
2. Deposition, Samuel Bostwick, 17 March 1770, Doggott, *Horrid Massacre*, p. 48.
3. Deposition, Jeffrey Richardson, 19 March 1770, *Ibid*, pp. 39–40.
4. Deposition, William Palfrey, 17 March 1770, *Ibid*, p. 54.
5. Deposition, Thomas Cain, 20 March 1770, *Ibid*, p. 64.
6. Deposition, William Wyat, 13 March 1770, *Ibid*, pp. 73–4.
7. *Proc. Mass. Hist. Soc., 1862–1863*, pp. 174–5.
8. Drake, *Tea Leaves*, pp. xxi–xxii.
9. Arthur Iredell to James Iredell, 31 Jan. 1775, Charles E. Johnston Coll., N.C. Dept. Arch. & Hist.
10. Duane (ed.), *Marshal Diary*, pp. 6–7.
11. Bolton (ed.), *Hugh Percy Letters*, pp. 28–9.
12. Willard, *Letters Am. Rev. 1774–1776*, pp. 14–15.
13. *Va. Mag. Hist.*, XV (April 1908), 356.
14. Adams (ed.), *Familiar Letters*, pp. 40–1.
15. Dexter (ed.), *Stiles Diary*, I, 483–4.
16. *Ibid*, I, 467.
17. *Ibid*, I, 522–3.

CHAPTER 2

1. Belknap, 'Journal', *Proc. Mass. Hist. Soc., 1858–1860*, pp. 84–6.
2. *Mass. Hist. Soc. Colls.*, 1st ser., V, 106–8.
3. Dawson, *Battles*, I, 22–3.
4. Barrett, *Concord Fight*, pp. 12–14.
5. —— to Rogers, 23 April 1775, Wentworth Woodhouse MSS, R-150-2, Sheffield Public Library, Sheffield, England.
6. Willard, *Letters Am. Rev.*, p. 120.
7. French, *Taking of Ticonderoga*, pp. 43–4.
8. *N.E. Hist. and Gen. Reg.*, XI, 156.
9. Sparks (ed.), *Writings of Washington*, III, 491–2.
10. Heath, *Memoirs*, p. 35.
11. *Ibid*, pp. 32–3.
12. Trumbull, *Autobiography*, pp. 24–5.
13. Serle, *Journal*, pp. 20–1.

CHAPTER 3

1. Force, *Am. Arch.*, 4, III, 1343.
2. *Am. Hist. Record*, I, 548.
3. Beatson, *Mil. and Naval Memoirs*, VI, 234–6.

4. Force, *Am. Arch.*, 4, IV, 656.
5. Diary Siege Quebec, 16 Nov. 1776–6 May 1776, Brit. Mus. Add. Mss. 46840.
6. Fore, *Am. Arch.*, 5, III, 253–4.
7. Dawson, *Battles*, I, 172.
8. *Pa. Mag. Hist. & Biog.*, XXV, 510–12.

CHAPTER 4

1. 'J.D.' to Earl of Dumfries, 14 Jan. 1776, PRO CO5/140.
2. Schaw, *Lady of Quality*, 190–1.
3. McLean, Loyalist Narrative, Loyalist Transcripts, N.C. Dept. Arch. & Hist.
4. Moultrie, *Memoirs*, I, 141–4, 174–81.
5. —— to ——, 7 July 1776, Erskine-Murray Correspondence, Ms. 5083, National Library of Scotland.
6. *Proc. Mass. Hist. Soc., 1926–1927*, LX, 239.

CHAPTER 5

1. Webb, *Corres. & Journals*, I, 153.
2. Bangs, 'Journal', *N.J. Hist. Soc. Proc.*, VIII, 125.
3. Collier, Ms. Journal, Nat'l Maritime Mus., Greenwich, England.
4. Robson, ed., *Letters From America*, pp. 31–4.
5. Tallmadge, *Memoir*, pp. 11–13.
6. *Memoirs L.I. Hist. Soc.*, II, 413–14.
7. Force, *Am. Arch.*, 5, I, 1259–60.
8. Grt. Brit. Hist. Mss. Comm., *Rawdon Hastings Mss*, III, 179–80.
9. Martin, *Narrative*, pp. 33–4.
10. Mackenzie, *Diary*, I, 159–60.
11. Heath, *Memoirs*, p. 55.
12. Duncan, 'Journals', *Naval Miscellany*, I, 131–3.
13. *Pennsylvania Evening Post*, 14 Nov. 1776.
14. Weiderhold, 'Fort Washington', *Pa. Mag. Hist. & Biog.*, XXII, 95.
15. Perry, *Reminiscences*, p. 15.
16. Grt. Brit. Hist. Mss. Comm., *Rawdon Hastings Mss*, III, 189–92.
17. Cochrane to Lord Cochrane, 8 Jan. 1777, Laing Mss, (Dundonald) II, 98/5, Univ. Edinburgh Lib.

CHAPTER 6

1. Moore, *Diary of Rev.*, I, 350.
2. Anderson, *Recollections*, p. 28.
3. *Lee Papers*, II, 348.
4. Wilkerson, *Memoirs*, I, 105–6.
5. Webb, *Corres. & Journals*, I, 175.
6. Force, *Am. Arch.*, 5, III, 1188.

7. *Ibid.*, 5, III, 1290.
8. *Continental Journal*, 21 Aug. 1777.
9. Rush, *Autobiography*, pp. 124–5.
10. Greenwood, *Rev. Services*, pp. 38–43.
11. Sgt. R, 'Princeton', *Pa. Mag. Hist. & Biog.*, XX, 515–19.

CHAPTER 7

1. O'Callaghan, ed., *Burgoyne Ord. Bk.*, p. 17.
2. Anburey, *Travels*, I, 190–1.
3. Stone, *Letters of Hessian Officers*, p. 90.
4. *Ibid.*
5. Baxter, *Invasion From North*, pp. 261–5.
6. Thacher, *Journal*, p. 103.
7. Adams, *Familiar Letters*, pp. 292–3.
8. *Continental Journal*, 28 Aug. 1777.
9. *Ibid.*, 21 Aug. 1777.
10. Dwight, *Travels*, III, 196–8.
11. *Colls. Vt. Hist. Soc.*, I, 212–14.
12. *Ibid.*, I, 223–5.
13. *Colls. Mass. Hist. Soc.*, 7, IV, 148.
14. Guild, *Chaplain Smith*, p. 213.
15. Anburey, *Travels*, I, 250–1.
16. Baxter, *Invasion From North*, pp. 270–1.
17. Anburey, *Travels*, I, 249–50.
18. Thacher, *Journal*, pp. 126–7.
19. Burgoyne, *State of Expedition*, p. 166.
20. Stone, *Campaign of Burgoyne*, pp. 371–5.
21. Riedesel, *Letters and Journals*, pp. 126–33.
22. Baxter, *Invasion From North*, pp. 319–23.
23. *Mag. Am. Hist.*, VI, 57.

CHAPTER 8

1. Cresswell, *Journal*, pp. 244–5.
2. Jones, *Hist. N.Y.*, I, 189.
3. Fitzpatrick, *Washington Writings*, IX, 17.
4. Ferguson, *Two Scottish Soldiers*, pp. 66–7.
5. Ferguson to George Ferguson, 8 Oct. 1777, Laing Mss. II, 456, Univ. Edinburgh.
6. *Bull. Hist. Soc. Pa.*, I, 69.
7. *Ibid.*, 58–9.
8. *Ibid.*, 24–5.
9. Moore, *Materials Hist.*, p. 368.
10. *Hist. Mag.*, IV, 346.
11. *Pa. Mag. Hist. & Biog.*, I, 3–4.
12. *Proc. Am. Antiq. Soc.*, XL, 83–4.
13. *Pa. Mag. Hist. & Biog.*, XVI, 152.
14. *Ibid.*, XXIX, 269.
15. Martin, *Narrative*, p. 53.

16. *Hist. Mag.*, IV, 346–7.
17. *North Am. Rev.*, XXII, 427–8.
18. Martin, *Narrative*, pp. 53–4.
19. *Pa. Mag. Hist. & Biog.*, II, 290.
20. Chastellux, *Travels*, I, 260–2.
21. Martin, *Narrative*, pp. 64–8.

CHAPTER 9

1. *Pa. Mag. Hist. & Biog.*, I, 40–1, 43.
2. Fitzpatrick, *Washington Writings*, X, 168.
3. Kapp, *Kalb*, pp. 137–43.
4. Marshal, *Diary*, pp. 172–3.
5. Adams, *Familiar Letters*, pp. 267–8.
6. *Pa. Mag. Hist. & Biog.*, LXIII, 205.
7. Fitzpatrick, *Washington Writings*, X, 29.
8. Sparks, *Washington Writings*, V, 517.
9. Thacher, *Journal*, p. 154n.
10. Kapp, *Steuben*, pp. 128–9.
11. *Pa. Mag. Hist. & Biog.*, XL, 457–8.
12. Boudinot, *Journal*, pp. 76–8.
13. *Penn. Gazette*, 16 May 1778.
14. *Pa. Mag. Hist. & Biog.*, XL, 342–3.
15. *Continental Journal*, 19 Feb. 1778.
16. Serle, *Journal*, pp. 263–4.
17. *Pa. Mag. Hist. & Biog.*, II, 140–1.
18. Balch, *Md. Line*, pp. 103–4.
19. *Mag. Am. Hist.*, III, 356.
20. Martin, *Narrative*, pp. 92–6.
21. *Ibid.*, 96–7.

CHAPTER 10

1. Moré, *Pontgibaud*, pp. 66–7.
2. Hammond, *Sullivan Letters*, II, 282–3.
3. Greene, *Greene*, II, 143–4.
4. Thacher, *Journal*, pp. 179–80.
5. *Hist. Mag.*, I, 180.
6. Huntington, *Letters*, p. 81.
7. *Mag. Am. Hist.*, II, 169.
8. *Cont'l Journal*, 19 Feb. 1778.
9. Thacher, *Journal*, p. 192.
10. *Mag. Am. Hist.*, II, 169.
11. N.Y. *Journal*, 2 Aug. 1779.
12. *Pa. Mag. Hist. & Biog.*, XL, 298.
13. *Hist. Mag.*, I, 181–2.
14. Moore, *Diary*, I, 212.
15. Hist. Ms. Comm., *Verulam Mss*, p. 127.
16. Hughes, *Journal*, p. 69.
17. *Hist. Mag.*, I, 207.
18. Fisher, *Journal*, p. 12.
19. *Hist. Mag.*, VI, 322.
20. Martin, *Narrative*, pp. 124–5.
21. *Colls. N.Y. Hist. Soc.*, XV, 139–40.
22. *Mag. Am. Hist.*, III, 570–1.
23. *Bogart Letters*, p. 26.
24. *R.I. Hist.*, I, 82.
25. *Mag. Am. Hist.*, XVI, 62–3.
26. *Pa. Mag. Hist. & Biog.*, XVI, 62–3.
27. *Mag. Am. Hist.*, III, 306.
28. *Cont'l Journal*, 26 Oct. 1780.
29. *N.E. Mag.*, VI, 363–4.
30. *Aspinwall Papers: Mass. Hist. Soc. Colls.*, 4 ser., X, 813.
31. N.Y. *Royal Gazette*, 30 Aug. 1780.

CHAPTER 11

1. *Sullivan Journals*, pp. 251–2.
2. Dawson, *Battles*, I, 470.
3. *Colls. Ill. Hist. Soc.*, VIII, xxxiii.
4. *Ibid.*, pp. 120–2.
5. *Ibid.*, p. 122.
6. *Ibid.*, pp. 270–1.
7. *Ibid.*, pp. 273–4.
8. *Ibid.*, pp. 159–60.
9. Hist. Ms. Comm, *Stopford-Sackville Mss.*, II, 231–41.
10. *Sullivan Journals*, pp. 229–30.
11. *Hist. Mag.*, XIII, 199.
12. *Sullivan Journals*, p. 87.
13. *Hist. Mag.*, 2d ser., III, 200–1.
14. *Sullivan Journals*, p. 30.
15. *Ibid.*, pp. 31–2.
16. *Ibid.*, p. 99.
17. *Ibid.*, p. 101.

CHAPTER 12

1. Hist. Mss. Comm, *Stopford-Sackville Mss*, II, 99.
2. Dawson, *Battles*, I, 478–9.
3. Moore, *Diary*, II, 224–8.
4. Hough, *Savannah*, pp. 164–70.
5. *Mag. Am. Hist.*, II, 489.
6. *Magnolia*, I, 366.
7. Uhlendorf, *Charleston*, pp. 242–4.
8. Tarleton, *Campaigns*, pp. 16–17.
9. Moultrie, *Memoirs*, II, 80.
10. Hough, *Charleston*, p. 126.
11. *Ibid.*, pp. 166–7.
12. Moultrie, *Memoirs*, II, 96–7.
13. Hough, *Charleston*, pp. 129–30.
14. Burnett, *Letters*, V, 204.
15. James, *Marion*, app., pp. 3–7.
16. Johnson, *Greene*, I, 387.
17. *Pa. Mag. Hist. & Biog.*, VII, 287–8.
18. Johnson, *Greene*, I, 494–8.
19. *Royal Gazette*, 16 Sept. 1780.
20. Draper, *King's Mtn.*, p. 204.
21. *N.C. St. Recs.*, XV, 106.
22. Chesney, *Essay*, pp. 330–1.
23. *Orion*, III, 86.
24. Shelby, *King's Mtn.*, p. 6.
25. Boudinot diary, Princeton Univ.

CHAPTER 13

1. Brown, *Memoirs*, pp. 34–8.
2. *Royal Gazette*, 23 Dec. 1780.
3. *Ibid.*, 12 May 1781.
4. *Pa. Mag. Hist. & Biog.*, LXIII, 312.
5. Reed, *Reed*, II, 334–6.
6. *Orion*, III, 87–8.
7. Johnson, *Greene*, I, 376.
8. *Orion*, III, 100.
9. Collins, *Autobiography*, pp. 5–7.
10. *Mag. Am. Hist.*, VII, 279.
11. Ross, *Cornwallis Corres.*, I, 503.
12. Lamb, *Journal*, p. 344.
13. Lee, *Campaigns*, pp. 181–2.
14. Broughton-Mainwaring, *Fusiliers*, pp. 100–1.
15. Lee, *Memoirs*, pp. 277–8.

16. Lamb, *Journal*, pp. 361–2.
17. *Am. Hist. Rec.*, II, 109.
18. *Mag. Am. Hist.*, VIII, 41.
19. *Am. Hist. Rec.*, II, 106–9.
20. Mackenzie, *Strictures*, pp. 153–64.
21. Stedman, *Hist. Am. War*, II, 421–5.

CHAPTER 14

1. *Va. Gazette* (D & N), 13 Jan. 1781.
2. Boyd, *Jefferson Papers*, IV, 501.
3. *Ibid.*, 265.
4. *Mag. Am. Hist.*, VII, 204.
5. Moore, *Diary*, II, 450–3.
6. *Mag. Am. Hist.*, III, 373.
7. Stuart Wortley, *Prime Minister*, pp. 173–4.
8. *N.Y. Hist.*, XXV, 364.
9. Thacher, *Journal*, pp. 325–6.
10. Bonsal, *French*, p. 130.
11. Sordelet Diary (copy, Nat. Park Service).
12. *Mag. Am. Hist.*, VIII, 212–13.
13. Graham, *Memoirs*, pp. 58–9.
14. *Mag. Am. Hist.*, XXV, 411.
15. *Hist. Mag.*, VII, 107.
16. *Mag. Am. Hist.*, II, 294.
17. *Ibid.*, XXV, 412.
18. Graham, *Memoirs*, pp. 58–9.
19. *W & M Quart.*, 3d ser., V, 386–7.
20. Deux-Ponts, *Campaigns*, pp. 144–7.
21. Martin, *Narrative*, pp. 169–71.
22. *Va. Hist. Reg.*, V, 229–30.
23. *Hist. Mag.*, VII, 110.
24. Doehla, *Journal*, p. 148.
25. Denny, *Journal*, p. 44.
26. *W & M Quart.*, 3d ser., V, 391–2.
27. Dumas, *Memoir*, I, 152–3n.
28. Denny, *Journal*, pp. 44–5.
29. Harper, *Colonial Men*, p. 115.
30. Lafayette, *Memoirs*, p. 444.

CHAPTER 15

1. Boudinot, *Journal*, pp. 38–9.
2. Moore, *Diary*, II, 527.
3. Wraxall, *Memoirs*, p. 246.
4. *Potter's Am. Monthly*, IV, 388.
5. Shea, *French Fleet*, pp. 86–8.
6. *Potter's Am. Monthly*, IV, 189.
7. *Mag. Am. Hist.*, IV, 389.
8. Martin, *Narrative*, p. 184.
9. *Mag. Am. Hist.*, VIII, 830
10. *Colls. N.Y. Hist. Soc.*, VIII, 509.
11. Henkels, *Corres. Robert Morris*, pp. 108–9.
12. *Mass. Hist. Soc. Colls.*, 5 ser., II, 184.
13. *Colls. N.Y. Hist. Soc.*, *1874*, pp. 31–2.
14. Shaw, *Journals*, pp. 103–5.
15. Thacher, *Journal*, p. 343.
16. *Pa. Mag. Hist. & Biog.*, XXV, 252.
17. *Mag. Am. Hist.*, X, 513.
18. Martin, *Narrative*, p. 208.
19. *N.E. Quart.*, I, 489–90.
20. Hist. Ms. Comm., *Am. Mss*, IV, 395–6.
21. Huntington, *Letters*, p. 106.
22. Tallmadge, *Memoir*, pp. 95–8.
23. Steiner, *McHenry*, pp. 69–70.

List of Illustrations

Abbreviations used

AAS American Antiquarian Society; AHR American Historical Review; BM British Museum, published by permission of the British Library; BMC Anne S. K. Brown Military Collection, Brown University Library, Providence; CHS Connecticut Historical Society, Hartford; DAB Dictionary of American Biography; DNB Dictionary of National Biography; HSP Historical Society of Pennsylvania, Philadelphia; JCBL John Carter Brown Library, Brown University; LC Library of Congress; MHS Massachusetts Historical Society; NYHS New-York Historical Society; NYPL New York Public Library, Astor, Lenox and Tilden Foundations; PG Pennsylvania Gazette; PMHB Pennsylvania Magazine of History & Biography; PRO Public Records Office, London; WLCL William L. Clements Library, University of Michigan, Ann Arbor.

47. C. Corbett: Sir William Howe. 1777. (BMC. *Gruber 1972, p. 57, quoting Howe's letter of 23 Nov. 1758 in Howe Coll.,* WLCL)

48. W. Chandler: Battle of Bunker Hill. *c.* 1777. (*Mrs Gardner Richardson, Woodstock, Conn. Little 1947, pl. 36; Rankin 1954, pp. 339–53*)

49. Barron: General Howe prepares his troops for the invasion of New York. 1776. (*Alnwick Castle, Percy Coll.*)

50. The Boston-Albany Road (detail). Map, *c.* 1765. (*Nether Winchendon, Bernard Coll., MP 22. Cumming 1974, pp. 29–30, 76–7*)

51–3. A. Robertson: Panoramic Sketches of Boston and Vicinity from Mount Whoredom. 1776. (NYPL, *Spencer Coll. Robertson 1930, pp. 93–7*)

54. J. Trumbull: Israel Putnam. Sketch, 1790. (*Connecticut State Library, Hartford. 'Israel Putnam',* DAB, *15. 281*)

55. General Richard Montgomery. Engraving, 1789. (BM. *Murray, II:193.* DAB, *XIII:98*)

56. W. Brasier: A Survey of Lake Champlain, including Lake George. Map of 1776. (BM. *Cumming 1974, pp. 61–2*)

57. Anburey: St John's, on the Sorel River. 1789. (BM. *Force, 4th Ser, 1837–46, 13:1343; Anburey 1789, I:268–71*)

58. Benedict Arnold's route to Quebec, 1775. Sketch, 1776. (BM: *London Magazine Sept. 1776, opp. p. 480*)

59. G. B. Fisher: View of the Falls of the Chaudière. Aquatint by J. W. Edy, 1795. (BM: *K. Top. CXIX. 30B. Stocking 1921, pp. 9–13; Senter 1915, pp. 25–37*)

60. Rocque: A Plan of Quebec. 1759. (BM)

61. Hervey Smith: A View of the City of Quebec. 1760. (JCBL)

62. Antill: Siege of Quebec. Map of 1776. (*Cornell University Library, Sparks Coll.*)

63. T. Hart: Col. Arnold Wounded at Quebec. Engraving, 1776. (JCBL. DAB, *I:362–7*)

64. Trumbull: The Death of General Montgomery at Quebec. Engraving by W. Ketterlinus, 1808. (BMC)

65. The *Royal Savage.* 1776. (NYPL, *Schuyler Papers, Ms & Archives Div. Allen 1913, I:164, 169, 171*)

66. Trumbull: Ticonderoga and its Dependencies. Map of 1776; engraved 1841. (BM: *Trumbull*)

67. General Guy Carleton. 1789. (BM: *Murray 1789, II:337.* DNB, *1917, III:1002–4*)

68. Reynolds: Portrait of Governor Dunmore. Oil painting. (*Scottish National Portrait Gallery, Edinburgh, Mrs Elizabeth Murray Loan Coll.*)

69. J. Stratton: Plan of the Post at Great Bridge. Copy by George Spencer. 1781. (BM: *Simcoe 1787,* BM *194. a.18. Force 4th Ser. 1837–46, IV:228*)

70. J. Bew: Virginia and Maryland (detail). Map of 1780. (BM: *Political Magazine I, 1780, opp. p. 786*)

71. R. Wilson: Flora MacDonald. Oil painting. (*Scottish National Portrait Gallery, Edinburgh. McLean 1909, p. 45*)

72. J. Price and J. Strother: North Carolina (detail). Map of 1805. (LC. *Cumming 1966, pp. 23–4, and Pl. IX*)

73. C. J. Sauthier: Plan of the Town of Cross Creek in Cumberland County, North Carolina. March 1770. (BM: *K. Top CXXII. 56*)

74. L. T. Abott: Sir Peter Parker. (*National Maritime Museum, Greenwich Hospital Coll. 'Sir Peter Parker',* DNB, *15:265*)

75. An Exact Plan of Charles-Town-Bar and Harbour. 1776. (BM: *K. Mar. VII. 26*)

76. An Exact Prospect of Charles Town. Engraving, 1762. (BM: *London Magazine 1762, p. 296. Rutledge 1947, pp. 100–3*)

77. A N.b.E. View of the Fort on the Western end of Sulivans Island. Engraving by William Faden, 1776. (LC)

78. C. W. Peale (?): William Moultrie. Oil painting, after 1782. (*Carolina Art Association, Gibbes Art Gallery, Charleston. Moultrie 1802, I. 140–4*)

79. A N.W.b.N. View of Charles Town. Engraving by William Faden, 1776. (BM)

80. Miss Carolina Sulivan. Cartoon, 1776. (BM)

81. Lt. H. Gray: The morning after the engagement on Sullivan's Island (detail). Watercolour, 1776. (*Carolina Art Association*)

82. C. J. Sauthier: New York, as it was when his Majesty's Forces took Possession of it in 1776. Map of 1776. (*Alnwick Castle, Percy Coll.*)

83. A. Robertson: View of the Narrows between Long Island & Staaten Island. (NYPL, *Spencer Coll.*)

84. F. X. Habermann: The Destruction of the Royal Statue in New York. Engraving, 1776. (BM. *Wertenbaker 1948, pp. 13, 84–5*)

85. Jefferson: The Declaration of Independence, 4 July 1776. (*Photo: Radio Times Hulton Picture Library, London.* LC. *Jefferson, ed. Ford, 1894, X:344*)

86. R. Peale: Thomas Jefferson. Engraving, 1800 or 1801. (*Radio Times Hulton Picture Library, London. Bush 1962, pp. 53–5; Jefferson 1942, pp. 5, 211*)

87. Hamilton: The Manner in which the American Colonies Declared themselves Independent of the King of England, throughout the different Provinces on 4 July, 1776. Engraving by Noble, 1790. (BM: *Barnard 1790*)

88. View of New York. *c.* 1777. (*National Maritime Museum, London:* Atlantic Neptune)

89. Saint-Mémin: View of the City of New York taken from Long Island. Etching, 1796. (NYHS. *Stokes & Haskell 1933, p. 41*)

90. Battle of Long Island, August 1776. (*American Philosophical Society, Philadelphia*)

91. J. Ainslie: A Map of the Environs of New York. *c.* 1776. (*Alnwick Castle, Percy Coll.*)

92. News from America, or the Patriots in the Dumps. Engraving, 1776. (BMC. *London Magazine XLV, 1776: 599. George, 1935, V, No. 5340, p. 223*)

93. The *Phoenix* and the *Rose* attacked by fireships in 1776. Engraving, 1778. (*National Maritime Museum, London:* Atlantic Neptune)

94. Habermann: Landing of the English Troops at New York. Engraving, 1776. (BM. *Serle 1940, p. 104*)

95. Trumbull: The Declaration of Independence submitted to the Congress. 1786–94. (*Yale University Art Gallery, Trumbull Coll. Morgan 1926, pp. 35–43*)

96. J. Story: A Sketch of Fort Lee from York Island. *c.* 1776. (*Alnwick Castle, Percy Coll.*)

97. J. Story: A View from near Fort Washington in York Island. *c.* 1776. (*Alnwick Castle, Percy Coll.*)

98. Habermann: The triumphal entrance of the King's troops in New York. Engraving, 1776. (BM. *Wertenbaker 1948, p. 104*)

99. Habermann: The terrible fire in New York. Engraving, 1776. (BM. *Force 1848, 2:462*)

100. The Royal Navy in New York harbour, 1776. Chart, *c.* 1777. (*National Maritime Museum, London:* Atlantic Neptune)

101. T. A. Williams: East View of Hell Gate. 1778. (BM: *London Magazine, 1778*)

102. C. J. Sauthier: Operations of the King's army, 1776. The Engagement on the White Plains (detail). Engraving by William Faden, 1777. (BM)

103. C. J. Sauthier: A Topographical Map of the North Part of New York Island. 1777. (BM)

104. C. J. Sauthier: Operations of the King's Army (Plate 102)

105. Davies: The Landing of the British Forces in the Jerseys under Cornwallis. Watercolour, 1776. (NYPL, *Emmet Coll., Ms & Archives Div. Hastings 1930–47, 3:193*)

106. Gray's Ferry, Schuylkill River, Pennsylvania. Engraving by Trenchard, 1787. (HSP: *Columbian Magazine, August 1787, frontispiece*)

107. R. Cleveley: Occupation of Newport. 1777. (*National Maritime Museum, London. Tuttle 1889, pp. 262–5; Cumming 1969, 101;* DAB. *1885, XI:53–4*)

108. W. Mercer: Battle of Princeton. After 1786. (HSP. *Harcourt 1905, XI:208; Smith 1967, p. 26*)

109. Hamilton: The Capture of General Lee. Engraving by Hawkins, 1790. (BM: *Barnard 1790, opp. p. 690. Bass 1957, pp. 21–2*)

110. Cartright: Take Your Choice! 1776. (BM: *Cartwright, London 1776, frontispiece*)

111. T. Pickering: An Easy Plan of Discipline for a Militia. 1775. (MHS. DAB. *1932, XIV:565–8*)

112. Operations of General Washington, against the Kings Troops in New Jersey. 1777. (BM: *Faden 1777*)

113. L. Heister: Amputation techniques. 1768. (*Royal Society* of Medicine, London: Heister 1768, I:372, Pl. XIV. Rush, ed. Butterfield, I:154)

114. Gunnery. Engraving, 1798. (AAS: Encyclopedia 1798, VIII: opp. p. 196, Pl. CCXXIV)

115. W. H. Bunbury: Recruits. Engraving, 1780. (BM. Stephens & Hawkins 1883, IV:809, No. 4766)

116. General John Burgoyne. Engraving by J. Chapman, 1801. (Radio Times Hulton Picture Library. DNB, 1890, VII: 340–2)

117. Woodruff: General Burgoyne addressing the Indians at their War Feast in Canada. Engraving by J. Taylor, 1804. (BMC. Winsor, 1887, 6:295, n. 3)

118. Medcalfe: Country in which the Army under Lt General Burgoyne acted in the Campaign of 1777 (detail). Engraving by Faden, 1780. (BM)

119. T. Jefferys: The American method of bush fighting (detail). Engraving, 1755. (JCBL: American Printmaking 1969, Pl. 22)

120. Murray: General Horatio Gates. Engraving, 1778. (BM: Murray 1778, II, frontispiece. DAB, VII:184)

121. Anburey: A View of a Saw Mill & Block House upon Fort Anne Creek the property of Genl Skeene. 1789. (BM)

122. The Closet. Cartoon of 1778. (BM. George 1935, V: 281, No. 5470)

123. A south view of Oswego. 1760. (BM: London Magazine 1760, opp. p. 232)

124. C. J. Sauthier: A Map of the Province of New York (detail). Engraving by William Faden, 1776. (BM)

125. J. Williams: Fort Stanwix. c. 1760. (BM: K. Top. CXXI.91)

126. Medcalfe: Lieutenant-Colonel Baum's expedition to Bennington (detail of Plate 127). 1780. (BM)

127. Medcalfe: Baum's defeat at Walmscock (Walloomsack) near Bennington on 16 August 1777. Engraving by Faden, 1780. (BM. Gates Papers, NYHS, Box VII, No. 33, quoted from Commager & Morris 1958, I:572–3)

128. A Real American Rifle Man. 1780. (BMC. Murray 1780, p. 212)

129. Stedman: Saratoga, 17 October 1777. Map of 1793. (JCBL: Stedman 1794, I:352)

130. T. Machin: Fortifications along the Hudson River Highlands. Map of 1778. (Cornell University Library, Sparks Coll. Winsor 1887, 6.642, n.2)

131. Anburey: View of General Burgoyne's Camp on the Hudson River, Sept.–Oct. 1777. Engraving, 1789. (BM: Anburey 1789, p. 148. Nelson 1844, pp. 254–7; Riedesel 1935, p. 53)

132. R. Pollard: Lady Harriet Acland crossing the Hudson to attend her wounded husband, prisoner in the American camp. Aquatint by Pollard and Jules, 1784. (BMC. M.L. Brown 1965, p. 52)

133. H. Gilder: The Engagement on Lake Champlain at Valcour Island. c. 1776. (Windsor Castle, Royal Library, Cumberland Coll. By Gracious Permission of Her Majesty The Queen. Hadden 1884, pp. 31–2; Force 1848–53, 3:254; Mahan 1913, p. 18)

134. J. Hunter: A View of Ticonderoga, from a Point on the North Shore of Lake Champlain. 1777. (BM. K. Top. CXXI. 107.b)

135. J. Trumbull: The Surrender of General Burgoyne at Saratoga, New York, 17 October 1777. c. 1816. (Yale University Art Gallery)

136. A. Robertson: Hudson's River From Chambers, Looking toward the north gate of the Hudson Highlands. Engraving by F. Jukes, London. (NYHS)

137. The Generals in America doing nothing, or worse than nothing. Cartoon of 1779. (BM)

138. Anburey: Encampment of the Convention Army at Charlotte Ville in Virginia. Engraving, 1789. (BM: Anburey 1789, II: 442)

139. A section of a First Rate Ship of War, Showing its various Timbers and Apartments. 1783. (BM: Encyclopaedia Britannica, 2nd ed. 1778–83, X: 'Ships', Pl. CCLXIII)

140. J. Hunter: A Sketch of the Navigation from Swan Point to the River Elk. Map of 1777. (LC, Howe Coll.)

141. J. André: Progress of the British Army. Drawing, 1777. (Henry E. Huntingdon Library and Art Gallery, San Marino)

142. X. della Gatta: The Battle of Paoli. 1782. (Valley Forge

Historical Society. Pennsylvania Archives, 2nd Series, I:598–9)

143. X. della Gatta: The Battle of Germantown. 1782. (Valley Forge Hist. Soc. Pickering 1867, I:166–70)

144. The Taking of Miss Mud I'land. 1777. (BM. George 1935, V:252, No. 5402)

145. Battle of Brandywine. Map of c. 1777. (LC: Faden Coll., no. 79)

146. The Flight of the Congress. Cartoon of 1777. (BM. George 1935, V:251, No. 5401)

147. E. C. V. Colbert: 'Passage d'York sur la Susquehanna'. (BM. Colbert 1935, p. 20; Lafayette 1837)

148. View from Bushongo Tavern 5 miles from York Town on the Baltimore Road. Engraving, 1788. (NYHS: Columbian Magazine, July 1788)

149. All intrepid able-bodied HEROES . . . Poster 1777. (HSP)

150. Battle of Germantown, 4 October 1777. Map of c. 1777. (LC)

151. W. Birch: Philadelphia; Second Street North from Market Street. 1799. (HSP)

152. G. Stuart: George Washington. 1796. (Museum of Fine Arts, Boston, loan of Boston Athenaeum. Adams 1876, p. 79; DAB 1932, XVIII:164–8)

153. Duportail: 'Plan Du Camp De Vallée forge'. Map of 1778. (HSP. Smith 1969, p. 21)

154. Romans: A Chorographical Map of the Country round Philadelphia (detail). 1778. (JCBL. Cumming 1974, p. 52)

155. Proclamation by General Washington, dated Valley Forge, 20 December 1777. (HSP)

156. Cochin: 'D. Beniamin Fraencklin, Grand Comissaire plenipotentiaire du Congres d'Amérique en France'. Mezzotint, 1777. (JCBL. JCBL Annual Report, 1955–6, p. 15)

157. F. G. Casanova: Lafayette. (NYHS. Lafayette 1837, pp. 4–5, 9–19, 17)

158. M. Capitaine du Chesnoy: 'Brouillion ou Plan de la Retraite de Barrenhill en Pensilvanie'. Map of 1778. (JCBL. Reed 1969, pp. 61–3)

159. André: Ticket for the Meschianza; proper lady's headgear. Drawing of 1778, engraved in 1850. (BM. Smith & Watson, 1850, Pl. XXVII; Trevelyan 1899–1907, IV, pp. 286–7)

160. Plan of the Country between New York and Philadelphia (detail). 1778. (BM: 194.a.18, end)

161. G. Spencer: Battle of Monmouth. Map of 1778. (BM: Simcoe 1787, insert. Smith 1964)

162. Rushbrooke: Major General Charles Lee with his black poodle. Drawn in 1773; engraved by J. Neagle in 1813. (BM: Girdlestone 1913, frontispiece)

163. Moreau: John Paul Jones. Engraving, 1789. (Courtesy of the Bostonian Society, Old State House)

164. P. Ozanne: The French fleet blocking the British fleet before New York Harbour. Watercolour, 1778. (LC: Geog. & Map Div. Mahan 1913, pp. 67–8)

165. F. Sablet: Charles Henri, Comte d'Estaing. Before 1790. (JCBL. Dictionnaire Historique 1822, X:64–6)

166. Great Encouragement for SEAMEN. Poster 1777. (Essex Institute, Salem. Morison 1959, pp. 138–55)

167. R. Paton: The Memorable Engagement of the Serapis with the Bon Homme Richard. Engraving by Lerpinière and Fittler, 1780. (BM. Sherburne 1825, pp. 116–17, 126–7; Album American Battle Art 1947, pp. 37–9)

168. Capt. Paul Jones shooting a Sailor who had attempted to strike his Colours in an Engagement. Mezzotint, 1780. (BM: P & D 5566. Fanning 1806, pp. 40–1)

169. Seix (?): British preventive action before the invasion of Rhode Island by General Sullivan. 1778. (Alnwick Castle, Percy Coll.)

170. P. Ozanne: The French and British fleets at Newport, Rhode Island. Watercolour, 1778. (LC: Geog. & Map Div. Duncan 1902, I:161; Mahan 1913, pp. 72–5)

171. P. Ozanne: The Languedoc demasted; attacked by the Renown. Watercolour, 1778. (LC: Geog. & Map Div. Note by Clara Egli LeGear in LC Map Room; Mahan 1913, p. 76)

172. The Siege of Rhode Island. Engraving, 1779. (BMC. Gentleman's Magazine 1779, p. 100)

173. J. Watson: Richard Viscount Howe. Mezzotint, 1778. (BM. American Printmaking 1969, No. 58; Gruber 1972, passim)

174. Diderot: Drill and Manoeuvre (detail). 1763. (BM: *Diderot 1763, I: Art Militaire, Exercice, Pl. III*)
175. Brunton(?): A Prospective View of old Newgate, Connecticut's State Prison. Engraving, 1799. (*Connecticut State Library, Hartford. Crary 1973, p. 216*)
176. Anburey: American dollars, 1776. Engraving, 1789. (BM. *Anburey 1789, opp. p. 400*)
177. J. Hills: A Plan of the Surprise of Stoney Point. Map of 1784. (BM)
178. T. Colley: Count de Rochambeau. French General of the Land Forces in America Reviewing the French Troops. Cartoon of 1780. (BM. *George 1935, V:422, No. 5706*)
179. Cypher letter from Arnold to André, 12 July 1780. (WLCL, *Clinton Papers*)
180. Stedman: King's Ferry at Stony Point (detail). Map of 1794. (BM: *Stedman 1794, II*)
181. T. W. Freeman: The Taking of Major André by the Incorruptible Paulding, Williams and Vanvert. Mezzotint, 1812. (BMC. '*Joshua King to_____, June 9, 1817*', Historical Magazine, *1:294–5*)
182. E. Savage: General Anthony Wayne. (NYHS. DAB *1932, XIX:563–5*)
183. B. West: Colonel Guy Johnson and Joseph Brant. 1775. (*National Gallery of Art, Washington, DC, Mellon Coll.*)
184. André: Self-portrait. Pen and ink, 1 October 1780. (LC)
185. The Allies–Par nobile Fratrum! Cartoon of 1780. (BM. *George 1935, V:371, No. 5631*)
186. L. Evans: Middle British Colonies in America. Map of 1755. (BM. *Gipson 1939; Klinefelter 1971*)
187. Collot: A log cabin. 1796. (BM: *Collot 1826, Vol. 3, Pl. 7*)
188. Anburey: Block-house. Engraving, 1789. (BM: *Anburey 1789, I. 138*)
189. Hutchins: A Plan of the several Villages in the Illinois Country. Map of 1778. (BM: *Hutchins 1778. Brown 1959, pp. 113ff*)
190. P. Campbell: An American New Cleared Farm. Engraving by McIntyre, 1793. (LC. *Campbell, 1793, ed. Langton and Ganong 1937*)
191. General John Sullivan. 1780. (BM: *Murray 1780, II:241.* DAB *1932, XVIII:192–3*)
192. Reynolds: Lieutenant-Colonel Banastre Tarleton. *c. 1782*. (*National Gallery, London*)
193. View of Tiby Lighthouse at the Entrance of Savannah River. 1764. (BM)
194. A View of Cockspur Fort at the Entrance of Savannah River. 1764. (BM)
195. Hubley: A Sketch of the Encampment of Wyoming. 1779. (HSP: *Hubley's journal*)
196. The route of Sullivan's expedition against the Indians of the Six Nations in Western New York. *c.* 1779. (LC)
197. General John Sullivan's Order of March upon leaving Wyoming. 1779. (BM. *Cook, ed. Journals 1887, p. 66*)
198. T. Jefferys: Guerrilla warfare. See plate 119.
199. Sullivan's route: the expedition in Western New York (detail of plate 196)
200. G. Gauld: 'Bay and Harbour of Pensacola'. 1780. (BM: Atlantic Neptune. *Hamer 1930–1, pp. 351–66*)
201. Serres: A North View of Pensacola, on the Island of Santa Rosa. Watercolour, *c.* 1776. (BM: *K. Top. CXXII. 97. Caughey 1934*, passim)
202. The Georgia–South Carolina Coast and Siege of Savannah. Map, *c.* 1780. (*National Maritime Museum, London:* Atlantic Neptune)
203. Ozanne: 'Vue de la Ville de Savannah'. 1799. (LC)
204. Ozanne: Siege of Savannah. (LC)
205. Stedman: Plan of the Siege of Savannah. Engraving, 1794. (BM. *Stedman 1794, II: opp. p. 132. Brun 1959, No. 637*)
206. Kitchin: Georgia and South Carolina. 1780. (BM: London Magazine, *May 1780, opp. p. 224*)
207. The Harbour of Charlestown in South Carolina. (BM)
208. G. Sproule: A Sketch of the Environs of Charlestown in South Carolina. 1780. (*National Maritime Museum, London:* Atlantic Neptune. *Uhlendorf, ed. 1938, pp. 182–3; Thomson 1966, pp. 105, 139;* LC, *Faden Coll. No. 48*)
209. The Investiture of Charlestown by the English Army in 1780 with the position of each corps. (LC, *Faden Coll., No. 49*)
210. H. Mouzon: Map of North and South Carolina. 1775. (BM)

211. T. Coram: Mulberry House and Grounds. Oils on paper, after 1775. (*Carolina Art Association. Bilodeau 1970, p. 73*)
212. Lieutenant-General Sir Henry Clinton. Engraving after portrait by J. Stuart. (*Radio Times Hulton Picture Library, London. Clinton, ed. Willcox, 1954, p. 284*)
213. Plan of the Battle Fought near Camden. Engraving by William Faden, 1787. (BM: *Tarleton 1787, opp. p. 108*)
214. A New and Accurate Map of North Carolina, and Part of South Carolina (detail). Engraving by John Lodge, 1780. (BM: *Political Magazine I, 1780, 731*)
215. Graham: King's Mountain, 7 October 1780. Engraving, 1853. (BM: *Ramsey 1853, opp. p. 238. Draper opp. p. 546; Schenck 1889, pp. 166, 174*)
216. Nelson: Cornwallis retreats from Charlotte. 1780. (*Cornell University Library, Sparks Coll. Davidson 1951, pp. 71–90; Rankin 1971, pp. 249–51;* State Rec. No. Car, *13.899; 16. 622ff*)
217. A real representation of the Dress of An American Rifleman. Engraving,
218. A. Dupré: The Battle of Cowpens. Crayon, *c.* 1781. (*Musée de la Coopération Franco-Américaine, Blérancourt. Young 1843, pp. 87–8*)
219. Trumbull: Brigadier-General Daniel Morgan. Oils, 1792. (*Yale University Art Gallery. Letter Morgan to Gates, 24 June 1780, Gates Papers,* NYHS, *quoted in Higginbotham 1971, p. 102*)
220. Tarleton: The Marches of Lord Cornwallis in the Southern Provinces (detail). 1787. (BM: *Tarleton 1787, frontispiece*)
221–3. General Greene turns George III's face to the wall. 1781. (*Henderson 1912, pp. 67–103; reproduced from 1912 photograph of originals owned by Mr A. G. Andrews, Jr., Raleigh, NC. Greene 1890, 3:159; Rankin 1971, pp. 277–8*)
224. Battle of Guilford. Engraving, *c.* 1810. (BMC. *Rankin 1971, pp. 299–313*)
225. Battle of Guildford. Engraving, 1787. (BM: *Tarleton 1787, opp. p. 276. Tarleton 1787, pp. 274–5*)
226. Vallancey: Sketch of the battle of Hobkirk's Hill, near Camden. Engraving, 1794. (BM: *Stedman 1794, 1: Pl. 10. Rankin 1971, p. 327*)
227. G. Stuart: Francis Rawdon Hastings, Earl of Moira. Engraving by J. Collyer, from original owned by Dr Hayes. (JCBL. *Hastings 1930–47, III: 155, 180, 192*)
228. Allen: Skirmish at Richmond. *c.* 1781. (BM: *194. a. 18, opp. p. 212. Simcoe 1787, pp. 110–12*)
229. L. le Paon: 'Le Marquis de la Fayette. Conclusion de la Campagne de 1781 en Virginie'. Engraving by N. le Mire, *c.* 1781. (BM. *Lafayette 1837, p. 449*)
230. March of the army under Cornwallis from the junction of Petersburg till their arrival at Portsmouth. 1781. (BM: *Add. MS. 57715/11*)
231. I. Jones: Earl Cornwallis. 1793. (JCBL. *Cornwallis, ed. Ross 1859, I:87*)
232. 'Carte de la Partie de la Virginie ou l'armée combinée de France & des Etats-unis de l'Amérique a fait prisonnière l'armée Anglaise.' Engraving, *c.* 1781. (LC)
233. Coudert: Washington and Rochambeau give final orders for the attack on Yorktown. Engraving, *c.* 1787. (*Radio Times Hulton Picture Library. Trumbull 1876, pp. 334–5*)
234. Peter Francisco's Gallant Action, 1781. 1814. (BMC. *Howe 1845, p. 118; Porter 1929*, passim, American Battle Art *1947, pp. 42–5*)
235. Van Blarenberghe: The Siege of Yorktown, with the arrival of French troops, 14 September 1781. 1784. (*Musée National de Versailles; Photo: Giraudon. Dict. Historique 1822, 3.450–2; Encyc. World Art, 1959–68, 10:186*)
236. Van Blarenberghe: The Surrender at Yorktown, 18 October 1781 (detail). 1784. (*Musée National de Versailles; Photo: La Photothèque, Paris, Thacher 1827, pp. 288–9*)
237. Benjamin West: The American Peace Commissioners. *c.* 1783 (*Winterthur: Photo: Radio Times Hulton Picture Library. Adams 1850–6, III. 344*)
238. Americaner Soldat. *c.* 1775. (BMC)
239. John Mitchell: 'Amérique Septentrionale'. Engraving by Le Rouge, 1777. (*Archivo Historico National, Madrid: Estado, Legajo 6609, Expediente 2362; ibid., Legajo 3885, Expediente 1*)
240. South Prospect of the City of New York. 1756–61. (NYHS)

Index

Numbers in italic refer to illustrations

351